# ACTION RESEARCH IN THE EDUCATIONAL WORKPLACE

EDITED BY

MARGARET FARREN

JACK WHITEHEAD, BRANKO BOGNAR

ACADEMICA PRESS

BETHESDA - DUBLIN - PALO ALTO

Library of Congress Cataloguing-in-Publication Data

Action research in the educational workplace / Margaret Farren, [editor].
   p. cm.
Includes bibliographical references and index.
   ISBN 978-1-936320-05-9
1. Action research in education.  I. Farren, Margaret.
   LB1028.24.A287 2010
   370.72--dc22

                              2010033900

Academica Press, LLC
Box 60728
Cambridge Station
Palo Alto, CA. 94306

Website: www.academicapress.com

to order: 650-329-0685

# TABLE OF CONTENTS

ACKNOWLEDGMENT ................................................................ vivii

EDITORS.................................................................................ixx

CONTRIBUTORS....................................................................xi

INTRODUCTION. Margaret Farren, Jack Whitehead, Branko Bognar ...............xv

USING A LIVING THEORY METHODOLOGY IN IMPROVING PRACTICE
AND GENERATING EDUCATIONAL KNOWLEDGE IN LIVING
THEORIES. Jack Whitehead...............................................................1

CO-CREATING AN EDUCATIONAL SPACE. Margaret Farren .....................33

PUPILS AS ACTION RESEARCHERS: IMPROVING SOMETHING
IMPORTANT IN OUR LIVES. Branko Bognar, Marica Zovko.........................55

IN PURSUIT OF COUNTERPOINT: AN EDUCATIONAL JOURNEY. Moira
Laidlaw .................................................................................115

A NARRATIVE OF MY ONTOLOGICAL TRANSFORMATION AS I
DEVELOP, PILOT, AND EVALUATE A CURRICULUM FOR THE
HEALING AND REFLECTIVE NURSE IN A JAPANESE FACULTY OF
NURSING. Je Kan Adler Collins....................................................165

LOVE AND CRITIQUE IN GUIDING STUDENT TEACHERS. Sigrid
Gjøtterud ..............................................................................203

CREATING SPACE:  ACCOUNTING FOR WHERE I STAND. Jane Spiro...241

HOW CAN I ENCOURAGE MY PUPILS TO THINK CRITICALLY
THROUGH COLLABORATIVE ONLINE-LEARNING?. Donal O'Mahony..285

HOW CAN I ENCOURAGE MULTI-STAKEHOLDER NARRATIVE AND
REFLECTION ON THE USE OF ICT IN TEACHER PROFESSIONAL
DEVELOPMENT PROGRAMMES IN RWANDA?. Mary Hooker ...............311

HOW CAN I HELP MY STUDENTS PROMOTE LEARNER-AUTONOMY IN ENGLISH LANGUAGE LEARNING?. Li Yahong............................................367

INDEX..............................................................................................415

# ACKNOWLEDGMENT

Working on this book has been a truly collaborative process involving people from a range of workplace contexts and across different continents. We wish to thank and acknowledge the following people for their part in helping to review the papers published in this book; Professor Yves Bertrand, Canada; Professor Chet Bowers, USA; Dr. Pip Bruce Ferguson, New Zealand; Catherine Dean, Kenya; Dr. Jackie Delong, Canada; Ian Hughes, Australia; Professor Jean McNiff, UK; Dr. Shankar Sankaran, Australia; Dr. Jacqueline Scholes Rhodes, UK; Dr. Ram Singh-Punia, India and Tian Fengjun, China.

# EDITORS

**Margaret Farren**, Ph.D. is a Lecturer at Dublin City University, Ireland. She coordinates the Masters in Education and Training Management programme. Participants come from all levels of the education system, as well as from corporate industry, nursing, government agencies and NGOs. Margaret's research area is in the development of methodologies in the human sciences and in the field of e-learning. She is interested in the human capability to create, share and contribute to new knowledge and lifelong learning through the use of information and communication technology. Margaret supports doctoral research students as they seek to create knowledge of the educational uses of digital technologies in their various workplace contexts (http://webpages.dcu.ie/~farrenm/).

**Jack Whitehead**, Ph.D. is an Adjunct Professor at Liverpool Hope University, UK, a Visiting Professor at Ningxia Teachers University in China and a Visiting Fellow at the University of Bath where he worked in the Education Department for 36 years. In the last 14 years he has supervised 26 doctoral students to successful completion. Jack supports doctoral students in pursuing research inquiries of the kind, 'How do I improve what I am doing?' They are encouraged to engage in a process of developing themselves as knowledge creators in ways that directly improve and enhance their professional practice and to extend and understand the educational influence they have in their own learning, in the learning of others, and in the learning of the wider social contexts in which they live and work (http://www.actionresearch.net). This approach enables doctoral students to make a significant contribution to the development of a knowledge base that includes values and relationships as central to the education process.

**Branko Bognar,** Ph.D. worked as a pedagogue in a primary school 'Vladimir Nazor' in Slavonski Brod for 12 years (1993-2005). In the role of a pedagogue he has tried to assist teachers in introducing changes with the intention of breaking away from the boundaries of traditional teaching. In 2005 he became an assistant professor at the Department of Pedagogy at the Philosophical Faculty at the University of Josip Juraj Strossmayer in Osijek. At the Philosophical Faculty of the University of Zagreb, Croatia, he gained an M.A. degree in May 2003. His dissertation was entitled 'Critical-emancipatory approach to a professional development of primary school teachers.' The main aim of his research was to help a group of primary school teachers to become action researchers. It was the first attempt to help teachers to become action researchers in a Croatian school context. In December 2008 he successfully defended his Ph.D. dissertation entitled, 'The possibility of becoming a teacher-action-researcher through e-learning.'

# CONTRIBUTORS

**Je Kan Adler-Collins,** Ph.D. entered the British Military at the age of 18 where he trained as a Registered Nurse in the Royal army Medical Corps. After being medically discharged in 1990 he developed an interest in Complementary and Alternative Medicine (CAM) and how they could relate to nursing practice and education. In 1995 he became ordained as a Japanese Buddhist priest of Shingon Shu (Koyasan). In 2007 he moved to the Associate professor position of a health promotion centre at Fukuoka Prefectural University, Japan with a focus on developing community training and courses in health care and CAM. This resulted in the opening of the first 'End Of Life Care Centre' run by community therapists for their own community.

**Sigrid Gjotterud** started working as a nurse in 1979 but soon changed to teaching healthcare in vocational training in high-school. Since 1997 she has been a lecturer in postgraduate teacher education, first in Akershus University College, Norway, and since 2000 in the Norwegian University of Life Sciences. She is currently undertaking her Ph.D. research. The focus of her research is, 'How can I, and we as a group, improve my/our practice in guiding student teachers towards their professional competency?' As a teacher educator she aims to be a role-model inspiring student teachers to inquire into their own teaching practice, developing their own living theories.

**Mary Hooker,** M.Sc. is an education specialist with over 30 years experience working in the educational sector in Ireland and Africa. Since 2007 Mary has been working with the Global e-Schools and Communities Initiative (GeSCI) as the Education Specialist assigned to their Office in Dublin, Ireland, and subsequently as the Research Manager for Global Programmes. Mary worked for ten years as a technical advisor to the Ministry of Education in Mozambique, engaging with Teacher Education institutions on pilot projects for teacher support, linking pre and in-service provision to the challenges encountered by teachers in real classroom contexts.

**Moira Laidlaw,** Ph.D. has been a teacher since 1978 never having wanted to do anything else. She taught English, German and Psychology in two English secondary schools, spent a few years teaching education in University of Bath and gained her doctorate in 1996 with Jack Whitehead as her supervisor. In 2001 she went to China as a volunteer with Voluntary Services Overseas (VSO) until the beginning of 2007, and in 2004 her university department opened an International Centre for Educational Action Research in Foreign Languages Teaching. For details see: http://www.actionresearch.net/moira.shtml. Moira is currently based on the East Coast of England and teaches students registered with the Open University.

**Donal O' Mahony,** M.Sc. is a secondary-school teacher of History and Religious Education. He has almost thirty year's teaching and administrative experience, both in Ireland and Japan. He is currently an Assistant Principal in Portmarnock Community School, Ireland. In 2005 he completed his Master's studies on collaborative online learning. He is currently engaged in Ph.D. research in Dublin City University, Ireland, on improving teaching and learning through the use of the communicative, creative and collaborative nature of social-software. His enthusiastic introduction of varied online and digital resources to enhance teaching and learning in Portmarnock Community School has resulted in an active community of practice, amongst teachers and students, which has generated much interest from educationalists beyond his own school.

**Jane Spiro,** Ph.D. is Learning and Teaching Development Leader at Oxford Brookes Institute of Education, UK, teaching literature, language, teacher development, action research and creative writing on undergraduate and M.A. programmes. Her experience includes: Head of Applied Linguistics at Oxford Brookes University, UK; Director of the English language centre at Nottingham University, UK; Course Director of the Cambridge ESOL DELTA programme in Switzerland; developing an in-service teaching award for University teachers in Baja California, Mexico; English Language testwriting and workbook writing for Cornelsen Verlag; co-editor of the journal Reading in a Foreign Language; judge for the first Poetry in a Foreign Language competition.

**Li Yahong** was born in a village of Shaanxi, a northwest province of China. She went to college in 1994, studying English-language education, and became an English-language teacher in a high school four years later. In 2003, she furthered her study on Curriculum and Teaching in Shaanxi Normal University and obtained a Master's degree in 2006. During her Master's degree she learnt much about the new ideas of China's New Curriculum and the West's education system. Since 2006 Li Yahong has been working as an English-language teacher in Shangluo University which lies in the south of Shaanxi.

**Marica Zovko** graduated from secondary nursing-school and then enrolled in the Teachers Academy in Zagreb, Croatia. After finishing at the faculty in 1985 she was not able to find a full-time job so she worked in several small rural schools around Požega. Because of the bad economic situation at the beginning of the nineties she had to spend several years in Germany working as a nurse in a hospital. When she got a full time job in Croatia in 1997 she decided to return and continue her private and professional life in the village where she owned a family house. From that time she was finally able to devote herself to teaching.

# INTRODUCTION

**Margaret Farren, Ireland**

**Jack Whitehead, UK**

**Branko Bognar, Croatia**

Contributions in the book are focused on living theories generated by individuals as they seek to enhance the quality of their productive lives. There is often a firm boundary established between the personal and the professional in writings about professional practice. We believe that living a productive life involves living as fully as possible the values that give meaning and purpose to our lives. This requires bringing these values into our professional practice and research to enhance the educational influences of our practice.

Our vision of education is that it is a means of humanising society and of facilitating the flourishing of humanity. As editors and contributors to this book, we believe that the expression of this commitment and responsibility involves generating and sharing our own living educational theories as we explore the implications of asking, researching and answering questions of the kind, 'How do I improve what I am doing?' Contributors offer their evidence-based stories of how they are learning to live their values of humanity as fully as they can within their workplaces and communities. They are willing to account for their own lives and learning to themselves and others in terms of these values and understandings.

A significant feature of the collection of papers in this book is that it provides evidence of the influence of living educational theories in contributing to both improving practice and generating knowledge. A separation between theory and practice often exists between 'academic' and 'professional' writings, between what is seen as 'academic' and what is seen as 'vocational'. Living educational theories, as contributions to an educational knowledge base, are generated by a form of research which can be understood as both academic and professional. A living theory methodology also embraces the vocational nature of practitioner-research as the researcher seeks to live their ontological values as fully as they can in their practice. These values can be understood as ontological as they are values that give meaning and purpose to a person's life. They can also be understood as vocational in the sense that they are the reasons why individuals do what they do.

All of the papers published in this book were published in the web-based Educational Journal of Living Theories (EJOLTS - http://ejolts.net/). It is distinguished from other Journals because of its commitment to publishing multi-media living theory accounts of practitioner-researchers from a wide range of global, social, cultural and professional contexts. Living theories are the explanations that individuals produce for their educational influences in their own learning, in the learning of others and in the learning of social formations. EJOLTS focuses on personal journeys and collaborative pathways and explanations of educational influences in learning, that connect a flow of life-affirming and life-enhancing energy with living values that carry hope for the future of humanity, such as love, freedom, justice, compassion, courage, care and democratic evaluation.

We are aware that print-based media has limitations as a means of communicating the energy-flowing values we express in our educational practice and in our explanations of our educational influences in learning. However, we see the book as a complement to the web-based journal, EJOLTS (http://ejolts.net), and hope it can help to spread those values to a wider audience.

The papers have emerged from a range of social and cultural contexts including Croatia, Ireland, UK, Japan, China, Norway and Rwanda. Each individual generates their living educational theory in relation to improving their practice and making a contribution to educational knowledge. Each individual engages critically with the most advanced and established social and educational theories of the day. What we mean by a critical engagement is that insights from these established theories are used with good reason in the generation of living theory. The purpose of critical engagement is not to make a contribution to the particular discipline from which the established theory emerged but to enhance the contribution to educational knowledge. This is done through including insights from these theories in the generation of the individual's living educational theory within the process of improving practice.

In establishing EJOLTS for this purpose we have embodied our democratic values in the review process and use the most advanced digital technology of the day to enhance our communications.

Within EJOLTS we have created space for communications across national and international boundaries by using the open source technology Moodle. This has shown that to realize valuable projects, money is not the decisive factor. The decisive factor is a commitment of people to live their values in their practice and everyday life.

We embody our democratic values in the open review process. This means that communications between reviewers and authors are transparent and creative and our readers are also able to participate in the whole process.

You may be interested in publishing your living theory accounts that explain your educational influences in your own learning, in the learning of others and in the learning of social formations. If you are then you can submit your contributions to the open peer-review process. You could also participate in the open review process as an EJOLTS reader. As we help others to deepen and extend their own living theories in the process of improving practice and generating knowledge in the workplace we help improve our own learning. In that way you won't be just an ordinary reader of the book, but you will become an active participant in cooperating with this ongoing project.

Here are some reflections on the contributions made to this book:

The focus of the contributions to this book is each author's own practice. In a self-study approach each researcher focuses on what they do so that they can help others to develop their capacity and potential as learners. Throughout the book the authors provide evidence of how they have engaged with others as part of the learning journey. The core message from all of the research accounts is the need to understand our own ethical values and the importance of clarifying our embodied values and knowledge in the course of their emergence in practice. The authors show how embodied values manifest themselves as living standards of judgment (Laidlaw, 1996). These living standards of judgment are formed within complex ecologies of diverse social and cultural contexts and have as their purpose the enhancement of educational opportunities and experience of the learner.

The authors exercise their own creative, social imagination through the research process. The range of accounts in the book shows the development of innovative forms of teaching, learning and research supervision, new approaches to curriculum and assessment, use of new media to promote sustainable learning, more person-centred approaches to education, and engagement with policy makers.

In chapter 1, '*Using a living theory methodology in improving practice and generating educational knowledge in living theories*' Jack Whitehead in the UK asks 'How do I improve what I am doing?' This question forms the conceptual framework of the book. He explores the distinction between traditional education theory and educational living theory that places the educator at the centre of the research. He offers a definition of living theory as an explanation produced by an individual for their educational influence in their own learning, in the learning of others and in the learning of the particular social formation in which they live and work. He highlights the importance of including narrative wreckage in the story of a well-lived life.

In chapter 2, '*Co-creating an educational space*' Margaret Farren in the Republic of Ireland provides evidence of how she has opened up an educational space for a community of postgraduate researchers to improve their practice and develop their capacity as learners and researchers. In the research account she explains her educational influence through explanatory principles, which embrace Celtic spirituality and the educational opportunities for learning opened up by digital technology.

In chapter 3, '*Pupils as action researchers: Improving something important in our lives*' Branko Bognar and Marica Zovko in Croatia recognise that although an increasing number of teachers are carrying out action research inquiries in their educational practice, the role of learners is still not sufficiently explored. The authors show how ten-year-old learners engage in the action research process. Their account is grounded in their shared sense of freedom as the most important value.

In chapter 4, 'In *pursuit of counterpoint: an educational journey*' Moira Laidlaw develops the idea of 'counterpoint' as a way of describing and explaining the management of educational values in her practice and as a way of theorising. She shows how in her work in China she has developed action research approaches with Chinese characteristics and how this has led her to understand more about her own educational development whilst enhancing it as well as helping to improve learning for teachers and students, both in higher education and in schools.

In chapter 5, '*A narrative of my ontological transformation as I develop, pilot, and evaluate a curriculum for the healing and reflective nurse in a Japanese faculty of nursing*' Je Kan Adler-Collins reflects on how he has developed a healing curriculum for the healing nurse. In the process he has had to resolve the Western and Eastern ways of being in the context of a nursing curriculum. The Buddhist Four Noble Truths are a basic framework to help him make sense of his world.

In chapter 6, '*Love and critique in guiding student teachers*' Sigrid Gjøtterud in Norway explores how love and critique are an important source in the guiding process of initial teacher-education, both with her student teachers and colleagues. Through learning how to critique and how to relate to her own experiences of being critiqued, she comes to an understanding with her colleagues and students of how to develop a more person-centred guiding process.

In chapter 7, '*Creating space: accounting for where I stand*' Jane Spiro in the UK explores the nature of her own creativity as a teacher/educator, team leader and writer, and how her creativity impacts on her practice and her professional community. She believes that the creative process involves the discovery of deep knowledge and the changing of this knowledge into something specific, shaped and new that she can communicate to others. In coming to terms with some of the contradictions in her work she learns how to enhance the dualities and to transform them into something new.

In chapter 8, 'How *can I use Moodle, a collaborative online-learning environment to improve my practice as a History teacher as I encourage my pupils to think critically?*' Donal O'Mahony in the Republic of Ireland begins with an awareness that although he values critical thinking his didactic teaching approach would sometimes negate this. In order to resolve this contradiction he examines different ways of using technology, reflecting on his own learning and on the learning of others.

In chapter 9, '*How can I encourage multi-stakeholder narrative and reflection on the use of ICT in Teacher Professional Development programmes in Rwanda?*' Mary Hooker demonstrates how she encourages reflection on ICT in professional development in Rwanda. She shows how she endeavours to improve her own practice as she assists the various stakeholders in developing their own solutions to the challenges of ICT integration in their education system.

In chapter 10, '*How can I help my students promote learner-autonomy in English language learning?*' Li Yahong reports on how she helps her students as an English language teacher to develop learner-autonomy in English language learning. She shows how she values learners' capacity in critical thinking, learning potential, attitude, confidence and interest. She observes that these factors had been absent from China's school education.

The editors are excited about the original contributions made to this book. The contributions show evidence of how practitioner have lived more faithfully their educational values in practice and how their particular values act as living standards of judgment that have enabled them to theorise from the grounds of their practice and influence social formations. We believe that these contributions can support other practitioner-researchers in developing their capacity to be living educational theorists in the process of improving their practice and making their own contributions to educational knowlege.

We invite the reader to access the media clips and photographs of practice that complement the written word. Some urls of multi-media sources are included in the text and in the reference-lists at the end of each chapter.

# USING A LIVING THEORY METHODOLOGY IN IMPROVING PRACTICE AND GENERATING EDUCATIONAL KNOWLEDGE IN LIVING THEORIES

## Jack Whitehead, UK

## WHAT IS A LIVING THEORY?

A living theory is an explanation produced by an individual for their educational influence in their own learning, in the learning of others and in the learning of the social formation in which they live and work.

### Why did I feel the need for a living theory?

In 1967, in my special study on my initial teacher education programme, on *A Way To Professionalism In Education* I wrote about the importance of a professional knowledge-base for education. In my later studies of educational theory between 1968-72 I began to see that the dominant view of educational theory, known as *the disciplines approach*, was mistaken. It was known as the disciplines approach because it was constituted by the disciplines of philosophy, psychology, sociology and history of education.

The mistake was in thinking that disciplines of education could explain the educational influences of individuals in their own and in each other's learning. The error was not grounded in mistakes in the disciplines of education. The mistake was in the disciplines approach to educational theory. The mistake was in thinking that the disciplines of education, individually or in any combination, could explain adequately an individual's educational influence in their own learning and in the learning of others.

My recognition of this mistake between 1971-1972 came midway through my studies for a Masters degree (Whitehead, 1972) in the psychology of education. As I was conducting a controlled experiment design for my dissertation on the way adolescents acquired scientific understanding, I began to feel a tension between an explanation that assumed individual learners could be validly represented in dependent and independent variables and an explanation I constructed for my educational influence that was grounded in my conscious lived experience. I also began to see that my explanations for my educational influences in the learning of my pupils could not be subsumed within any conceptual framework in the psychology of education or any existing discipline of education. This recognition re-focused my vocation. It moved from being a school teacher, teaching pupils science in secondary schools, to becoming a university academic and educational researcher, researching the creation and academic legitimation of valid forms of educational theory. Such theories could explain the educational influences of individuals in their own learning and in the learning of others. I believed then and still believe now that the profession of education requires such a professional knowledge-base.

My move to the University of Bath in 1973 was motivated by this desire to contribute to the creation and legitimation of educational theory. I continue to identify with the Mission of the University of Bath, which includes having a distinct academic approach to the education of professional practitioners.

The damage inflicted on the teaching profession by the disciplines approach to educational theory may be judged from the fact that Paul Hirst, a main proponent, acknowledged a mistake in the following two quotations from 1983 where he says that much understanding of educational theory will be developed:

> ...in the context of immediate practical experience and will be co-terminous with everyday understanding. In particular, many of its operational principles, both explicit and implicit, will be of their nature generalisations from practical experience and have as their justification the results of individual activities and practices. (Hirst, 1983, p.18)

The damage can be appreciated through Hirst's understanding that the practical principles you and I use to explain our educational influences in our own learning and in the learning of others *would be replaced* by principles with more theoretical justification:

> In many characterisations of educational theory, my own included, principles justified in this way have until recently been regarded as at best pragmatic maxims having a first crude and superficial justification in practice that in any rationally developed theory would be replaced by principles with more fundamental, theoretical justification. That now seems to me to be a mistake. Rationally defensible practical principles, I suggest, must of their nature stand up to such practical tests and without that are necessarily inadequate. (Hirst, 1983)

The hegemony of the disciplines of education continues to dominate what counts as educational research. As J. Allender and D. S. Allender point out:

> The belief that educational research trumps practice, historically and still is one of the major obstacles. The results of scholarly inquiry have managed to become the top of a top-down world. The not-so-subtle message is that there is a better known way to teach and teachers ought to change their practices accordingly. And, teachers have a way of willingly participating in this system when they persist in searching for the new trick to quickly and magically make their teaching easier. Progress depends on giving up the hegemony of scholarly inquiry. Knowledge has many sources, and they are best honoured when they are used as part of a lively dialectic. The obvious shift is for teachers to give themselves credit for

having an expertise that is uniquely valuable to themselves, and others. (J. Allender and D. S. Allender, 2008, pp. 127-128)

J. Allender and D. S. Allender (2008) also believe that 'somewhere in history, the status of the teaching profession lost ground – setting up teachers to be viewed as incompetent. They believe that this view handicaps every teacher, and that there is a dire need to escape this undeserved status' (p. 128).

It may be, that by clearly distinguishing what counts as education research from educational research, in terms of new living standards of judgment, then valid forms of educational knowledge and educational theory could be legitimated in the Academy.

## Making a clear distinction between education research and educational research

I am suggesting that education research is research carried out from the perspectives of disciplines and fields of education such as the philosophy, sociology, history, psychology, management, economics, policy and leadership of education. In my view, educatio*nal* research is distinguished as the creation and legitimation of valid forms of educational theory and knowledge that can explain the educational influences of individuals in their own learning, in the learning of others and in the learning of the social formations in which we live and work.

This focus on the epistemological significance of what counts as educational knowledge has been highlighted by Bruce Ferguson (2008) where she notes that the increase in diverse perspectives and presentation styles in research are indicative of an epistemological transformation in what counts as educational knowledge (p. 24).

Stimulated to respond to Bruce Ferguson's point I claim that this epistemological transformation will require new forms of representation and educational standards of judgment in Journals of Educational Research (Whitehead, 2008a). In this contribution to EJOLTS I am directing attention to how the evidence, showing the nature of these forms of representation and living standards of judgment, can be accessed by those with the technology to do so. The evidence includes multi-media representations of flows of energy and values in the embodied knowledges of educators and their students. I recognize that the development of such representations costs money. Access to the most advanced technology of the day, with the use of communicative power of the internet, has economic implications.

My own research programme has benefited from access to this technology. I also acknowledge the influence of the economic context on my research programme in that I have held a tenured contract at the University of Bath with secure employment from 1973 to the end of the contract in 2009. I do not want to underestimate the importance of this economic security in my capacity to keep open a creative space at the University to develop my research programme.

In making a clear distinction between education and educational research and acknowledging the importance of technology and economics I also want it to be understood that I value the integration of insights from the theories from education researchers into my own living theories. For example, the historical and cultural contexts of my workplace are western and mainly white. These contexts are changing with multi-cultural and postcolonial influences (Charles, 2007; Murray, 2007) questioning the power relations that sustain unjust privileges and the dominant logic and languages that sustain what counts as knowledge in the Western Academies.

In my early work between 1967-73 I followed this dominant logic and language. By this I mean that I used a positivist and propositional view of knowledge derived from the influence of my first degree in physical science. In my positivist phase I believed that controlled experimental designs gave access to the highest form of knowledge and that the theories generated from this approach should be presented within propositional statements about sets of variables that excluded contradictions. During the middle period of my research between

1977-1999 I extended my epistemological understandings to include dialectics (Ilyenkov, 1977) with its nucleus of contradiction. Since 2003 I have been exploring the implications of an epistemology of inclusionality (Rayner, 2004), which has much in common with African, Eastern and other indigenous ways of knowing (Bruce Ferguson, 2008). I want to stress again that this is not to imply a rejection of all my insights from propositional and dialectical theories. I continue to value insights from these theories as I deepen and extend my understandings of living educational theories and a living theory methodology with the evolution of the implications of asking, researching and answering 'How do I improve what I am doing?'

I will examine below the significance of these epistemological understandings of propositions, dialectics and inclusionality when I consider the use of a living theory methodology in the processes of improving practice and in the generation of educational knowledge. In this process I follow Ryle's insight, *'[e]fficient practice precedes the theory of it; methodologies presuppose the application of the methods, of the critical investigation of which they are the products'* (Ryle, 1973, p. 31).

## WHAT IS A LIVING THEORY METHODOLOGY?

### Using action-reflection cycles as a method

My understanding of action-reflection cycles emerged from my practical question, 'How do I improve what I am doing?' The method emerged before my awareness of its significance as a research question. I asked this question on my first day in 1967 as a science teacher in Langdon Park School, a London Comprehensive School[1]. I felt a passion to help my students to improve their

---

[1]     Editors' note: The term 'comprehensive' in conjunction with the term 'school' designates it as a secondary institution offered by the state in England and Wales. It is the most common form of secondary education in these countries.

scientific understandings. In my first lessons I could see that my pupils were not comprehending much of what I was saying and doing. However, I did not feel my concern to be grounded in a 'deficit' model of myself. I felt a confidence that while what was going on was not as good as it could be I would be able to contribute to improvements. My imagination worked to offer possibilities about improving what I was doing. I chose a possibility to act on, acted and evaluated the effectiveness of what I was doing in terms of my communications with my pupils. This disciplined process of problem-forming and solving is what I call an action-reflection method.

## Developing an understanding of a living theory methodology

A methodology is not only a collection of the methods used in the research. It is distinguished by a philosophical understanding of the principles that organize the 'how' of the inquiry. A living theory methodology explains how the inquiry was carried out in the generation of a living theory.

For example, my awareness of the importance of improving practice is grounded in my passion to see values of freedom, justice, compassion, respect for persons, love and democracy lived as fully as possible. Hence, in my living theory methodology, you should expect to see the meanings of these values emerge in the course of my practice. Because the expression of energy in the meanings of these values cannot be communicated using only words on pages of text, I will use video-data in a visual narrative to help with the public communication of these meanings.

One of the distinguishing characteristics of action research from action learning is that the researcher must make public the story of their research in a way that is open to others to evaluate its validity. A living theory methodology includes the processes of validation.

I work with Michael Polanyi's (1958) decision about personal knowledge. This is a decision to understand the world from my own point of view as an individual claiming originality and exercising judgment responsibly with universal intent. I know that the local identity of my 'I' is influenced by the non-local flows of space and energy through the cosmos. Yet I do work with a sense of responsibility for the educational influences I have in my own learning. I also recognise myself as a unique human being with this responsibility and I do exercise a sense of personal responsibility in validating for myself my claims for what I believe to be true. In doing this I take account of responses from a process of social validation I have developed from the ideas of MacDonald and Habermas.

Since 1976 I have used a process of democratic evaluation, described by MacDonald (1976), together with the four criteria of social validity proposed by Habermas (1976), to strengthen the personal and social validity of living theories (Whitehead, 1989). By this I mean that I submit my explanations of educational influence to a validation group of peers with a request that they help me to strengthen the comprehensibility, truthfulness, rightness and authenticity of the explanation. Within comprehensibility I include the logic of the explanation as a mode of thought that is appropriate for comprehending the real as rational (Marcuse, 1964, p. 105). Within truthfulness I include the evidence for justifying the assertions I make in my claims to knowledge. Within rightness I include an awareness of the normative assumptions I am making in the values that inform my claims to knowledge. Within authenticity I include the evidence of interaction over time that I am truly committed to living the values I explicitly espouse.

The social sciences have influenced what counts as educational research. Some researchers believe that educational research is distinguishable as a social science. I do not share this belief. My reasons are related to my meanings of educational and social where my meanings of educational cannot be subsumed within my meanings of social. Here are my meanings of social and educational to explain my understandings of some differences.

My meanings of 'social' in social validity, social action, social behaviour and social formations are influenced by the ideas of Habermas (1976) as described above, Schutz (1967) and Bourdieu (1990). I am most influenced in my meanings of social, social action and social behaviour by the work of Alfred Schutz in his Phenomenology of the Social World:

> Following the logic of our own terminology, we prefer to take as our starting point, not social action or social behavior, but *intentional conscious experiences directed toward the other self.* However, we include here only these intentional experiences which are related to the other *as other*, that is, as a conscious living being. We are leaving out of account intentional Acts directed only to the other person's body as a physical object rather than as a field of expression for his subjective experiences. Conscious experiences intentionally related to another self which emerge in the form of spontaneous activity we shall speak of as social *behavior.* If such experiences have the character of being previously projected, we shall speak of them as *social action.* (Schutz, 1967, p. 144)

What I take from this is that a social action can be distinguished from social behaviour by the spontaneous activity in behaviour and the previous projection in an action.

In using the idea of social formations in such phrases as the 'educational influences in the learning of social formations' I want to distinguish educational influences in one's own learning and in the learning of others from the educational influences in the learning of a social formation, such as a university. Because of cultural and historical influences in the social contexts in which we live and learn I want to acknowledge the importance of having an educational influence in the learning of such social formations. I know that the nature of meaning is complex, but I think we can work with the idea of educational influences in the learning of social formations as being highly significant. For example, when the University of Bath changed the regulations governing its social formation in 2004 to allow the submission of e-media I refer to this as an educational influence in the learning of a social formation. I think of it as an educational influence because it has extended the cognitive range and concerns of the forms of representation that can be used in the public communication of living educational theories.

I take the form of something to be fundamental in making sense of it. I need form to make sense. If something doesn't have a form I find that I cannot comprehend it. I use social formation in the sense used by Bourdieu in his point about the analysis of social formations in relation to the habitus:

> The objective adjustment between dispositions and structures ensures a conformity to objective demands and urgencies which has nothing to do with rules and conscious compliance with rules, and gives an appearance of finality which in no way implies conscious positing of the ends objectively attained. Thus, paradoxically, social science makes greatest use of the language of rules precisely in the cases where it is most totally inadequate, that is, in analysing social formations in which, because of the constancy of the objective conditions over time, rules have a particularly small part to play in the determination of practices, which is largely entrusted to the automatisms of the habitus. (Bourdieu, 1990, p. 145)

I want to be clear that I do not subsume the experience and expression of the life-affirming energy in my explanations of educational influences in learning to meanings of 'social'. My educational relationships are social in the sense that they can be distinguished as *intentional conscious experiences directed toward the other self* (Schutz, 1967, p. 144). However my explanations for my educational influences include the non-social flows of life-affirming energy that distinguish my social relations as educational.

Whilst expressing this life-affirming energy in my social relations I want to emphasise that I bring energy that flows from outside the social through the cosmos into my educational relationships. I use the expression of this energy in my accounts to distinguish what is educational from social relations. Hence I do not subsume my understanding of what is educational to a concept of 'social' in the improvement of practice and in the generation of knowledge. At the same time I recognise the importance of social relations in influencing my educational relationships.

## IMPROVING PRACTICE WITH A LIVING THEORY METHODOLOGY

### The importance of forming good questions

I like the point made by Collingwood about the relationship between propositions and questions:

> Whether a given proposition is true or false, significant or meaningless, depends on what question it was meant to answer; and any one who wishes to know whether a given proposition is true or false, significant or meaningless, must first find out what question it was meant to answer. (Collingwood, 1991, p. 39)

The questions we ask about our practice can be influential in what we do. For me, a good question for improving practice is, 'How do I improve what I am doing?' I found myself asking this question in the first lesson I taught in 1967. During this lesson I found myself feeling that I was not helping the pupils to improve their learning as well as I could. The question flowed with a life-affirming energy to do better. It flowed with the values and understandings of scientific inquiry and knowledge I brought into my work as a teacher of science.

Some 41 years after asking this question and asking, researching and answering it continuously in my research programme, I am still finding it a good question. It is at the heart of my focus on seeing what I can do to understand better how to enable the responses of educators to their pupils and students to be included in explanations of educational influence in learning. I am thinking of an educational influence that supports individuals to create their own living educational theories of their lives and learning as they seek to improve their practice.

### Using action-reflection cycles in improving practice

From the ground of a good question such as, 'How do I improve what I am doing?' I found my imagination worked spontaneously in generating ideas about how I might improve my practice. I consciously chose one possibility to act on and formed an action plan. I acted and evaluated the effectiveness of my actions. In 1967 I followed this action-reflection cycle intuitively as I began my work in education and only made it explicit later (Whitehead, 1976).

Making it explicit helped me to see the importance of strengthening the data I collected to make a judgment on the effectiveness of my actions and understandings. Making it explicit also helped me to understand just how important it is, for the creation of valid explanations of educational influences in learning, to submit one's own interpretations to a validation group to receive the benefit of the mutual, rational controls of the 'inter-subjective criticism' of others (Popper, 1975, p. 44).

**Using action-reflection cycles in clarifying and evolving the energy-flowing and values-laden explanatory principles in generating knowledge about improving educational influences in learning**

In the process of expressing concerns when values are not being lived as fully as they could be, imagining possible improvements, choosing a possibility to act on, acting and gathering data and evaluating the influence of actions, the energy flowing values used to distinguish what counts as an improvement are clarified and evolved. Clarifying these values is a necessary condition for judging whether improvements in learning are occurring. For example, at one time in my classrooms I felt that I was imposing too much structure on the lessons so that there was insufficient freedom to enable my pupils to engage in any inquiry learning that involved them forming their own questions. It was only by clarifying my understanding of inquiry learning and showing the development from a highly structured classroom to one that included the possibility of inquiry learning that I could clearly communicate what I meant by an improvement in learning (Whitehead, 1976).

**Using responses from validation groups to enhance the imagined possibilities for improving educational influences in learning, and for improving the gathering of data to make a judgment on the effectiveness of the actions**

One of the best illustrations of this use of a validation group is in Martin Forrest's (1984) MA dissertation. As a tutor working in the continuing professional development of teachers Forrest supported teachers to help their pupils to improve their learning. Forrest researched his educational influence with a teacher in helping some primary aged children to think historically with objects from a Museum service. Another teacher working with similar-age pupils from a different school did not believe this thinking to be possible. For his first validation meeting Forrest made claims to have influenced the practice of the first teacher but with insufficient evidence to convince the validation group of the validity of his claims. The validation group explained that they would need to see more conclusive evidence of his influence in the learning of a teacher and the pupils, than he provided in his initial narrative.

At a validation group some months later, Forrest produced video evidence in his explanation of his influence showing that the second teacher, on being shown a video-tape of what the first teacher was doing with her pupils, had tried the work with the historical artefacts. She found to her surprise that the pupils could think historically about the objects in a way that she initially had not thought to be possible. Forrest had documented his work with the second teacher. He had video-evidence from the classroom showing the pupils working with the artefacts and developing their historical thinking. His analysis with the video-data convinced the group of the validity of his claims to know his educational influences in the learning of the teacher and pupils. Forrest shows how the primacy of practice and of improving practice is not separated from the generation of knowledge. Here is how a living theory methodology can assist in the generation of knowledge.

## GENERATING KNOWLEDGE WITH A LIVING THEORY
## METHODOLOGY

### The importance of forming good questions

As with improving practice, generating knowledge relies on asking, researching and answering good questions. At the present time there is much work to be done on establishing the appropriate epistemology for evaluating the quality of claims to educational knowledge from within a living theory perspective. So, I think good questions in the present can be focused on the expression, clarification, evolution and legitimation of living standards of judgment (Laidlaw, 1996).

### Using action-reflection cycles in the generation of educational knowledge

The generation of educational knowledge includes knowledge of a living theory methodology. In the story of the growth of my educational knowledge my most recent contributions have focused on the explication of a living theory methodology for improving practice and generating knowledge (Whitehead, 2009). In my analysis of an individual's educational development (Whitehead, 1985) I suggest that educational researchers adopt an action-reflection form in generating a living form of theory:

> The approach to educational theory I am suggesting we adopt, rests on a number of assumptions concerning both the idea of a 'living form of theory' and the personal and social criteria, which can be used to criticize the theory. I use the term a 'living form of theory' to distinguish the suggested approach from the 'linguistic form' in which traditional theories are presented for criticism. In a living approach to educational theory I am suggesting that teacher action-researchers present their claims to know how and why they are attempting to overcome practical educational problems in this form:
> I experience a problem when some of my educational values are negated in my practice;
> I imagine a solution to my problem;

I act in the direction of my solution;
I evaluate the outcomes of my actions;
I modify my problems, ideas and actions in the light of my evaluations. (p. 98)

In a living theory methodology the individual includes the unique constellation of values that are used to give meaning and purpose to their existence. In the course of the inquiry these values are expressed, clarified and evolved as explanatory principles in explanations of educational influences in learning. The values flow with a life-affirming energy and are expressed in the relational dynamics of educational relationships.

One of the tasks, for those interested in spreading the educational influence and academic legitimation of living educational theories and a living theory methodology, is to find appropriate ways of representing the flows of life-affirming energy with values as explanatory principles in narratives of educational influences in learning. It is to find appropriate ways of engaging in the boundaries of the power relations that are both resistant and supportive of the legitimation of living theories and living theory methodology.

I have outlined above the tensions I experienced in my early studies of educational theory. The tensions arose because my practical principles were seen by adherents to the disciplines approach to educational theory as pragmatic maxims that had at best a crude and superficial justification in practice and which would be replaced in any rationally justified theory. Similar tensions continue because the majority of renowned and internationally recognized Journals of Educational Research continue to be text-based rather than web-based and eliminate multi-media representations from their contents. Hence my tension in seeing that visual representations of flows of life-affirming energy with values are being eliminated from Journals of Educational Research.

**Using multi-media representations to clarify and share meanings of the flows of energy in embodied values and their expressions in explanations of educational influence in learning**

I am suggesting that we are all living with the capacity to express and develop a relationally dynamic awareness of space and boundaries with life-affirming energy and value. However, I am also claiming that the dominating forms of representation used in Universities for explaining educational practices and influences in learning, remove valid expressions of this energy with values from the explanations. I am claiming that the forms of representation that dominate printed text-based media cannot express adequately, in the standards of judgment and explanatory principles of academic texts, the embodied values we use to give meaning and purpose to our lives in education.

I believe that the reason for this removal lies in the continuing tendency of academic theories to replace the practical principles used by individuals to explain their lives, by principles with justifications in abstract rationality. What I am saying we should be creating are educational theories from a perspective of inclusionality developed by Rayner and Lumley:

> At the heart of inclusionality... is a simple shift in the way we frame reality, from absolutely fixed to relationally dynamic. This shift arises from perceiving space and boundaries as connective, reflective and co-creative, rather than severing, in their vital role of producing heterogeneous form and local identity...
> To make this shift does not depend on new scientific knowledge or conjecture about supernatural forces, extraterrestrial life or whatever. All it requires is awareness and assimilation into understanding of the spatial possibility that permeates within, around and through natural features from sub-atomic to Universal in scale. We can then see through the illusion of 'solidity' that has made us prone to regard 'matter' as 'everything' and 'space' as 'nothing', and hence get caught in the conceptual addiction and affliction of 'either/or' 'dualism'. An addiction that so powerfully and insidiously restricts our philosophical horizons and undermines our compassionate human spirit and creativity. (Rayner, 2004)
> I want to highlight the importance of understanding that, from a

perspective of inclusionality, we are all included in the dynamics of a common living-space that flows with life-affirming energy. As Ted Lumley, one of the originators of the idea of inclusionality, points out about the importance of recognizing a 'pooling-of-consciousness'.

> ...an inspiring pooling-of-consciousness that seems to include and connect all within all in unifying dynamical communion.... The concreteness of 'local object being'... allows us to understand the dynamics of the common living-space in which we are all ineluctably included participants. (Lumley, 2008, p. 3)

Working with such a relationally dynamic awareness of space and boundaries does not mean that everything is to be included in an undifferentiated mush. The living boundaries of cultures in resistance sometimes include the need for protection against damaging influences, especially those involving a lack of recognition (Whitehead, 2008c, 2008d).

In learning how to combine our voices as practitioner-researchers in the generation and testing of living educational theories I am aware of the importance of including narrative wreckage in the story of a life well-lived. I am thinking of the kind of narrative wreckage that involves a lack of recognition. A smooth story of self might initially feel comfortable to a listener, but without the acknowledgment of what has been involved in persisting in the face of pressure, a story can lack authenticity (Whitehead & Delong, 2008).

In my experience most lives involve some form of narrative-wreckage in which difficulties have been encountered that require some effort in re-channelling destructive emotions into a flow of life affirming energy. I am thinking particularly of re-channelling destructive responses to a lack of appropriate recognition. I am thinking of the development of protective boundaries, in the face of such violations, that can continue to be open to the flow of life-affirming energy and values that carry hope for the future of humanity:

> Human beings seek recognition of their own worth, or of the people, things, or principles that they invest with worth. The desire for recognition, and the accompanying emotions of anger, shame and pride, are parts of the human personality critical to political life. According to Hegel, they are what drives the whole historical process. (Fukuyama, 1992, p. xvii)

In overcoming and circumventing obstacles to the flows of energy with values of humanity I feel that two affirmations have been most significant in my practitioner-research:

The first affirmation is the experience of an energy that I feel is flowing through the cosmos. This energy is life-affirming for me and I associate this energy with the state of '*being affirmed by the power of being itself*'. When I read these words in Paul Tillich's work in *The Courage To Be* (1962, p. 168), I understood that this affirmation referred to a theistic experience in a relationship with God. Having no theistic desires myself I use the words 'state of being affirmed by the power of being itself' to communicate my experience of a flow of life-affirming energy that when combined with my values provides me with explanatory principles to explain why I do what I do. I believe that a similar energy is informing an Ubuntu way of being as this is expressed by Nelson Mandela and brought into the Academy by Eden Charles (2007) as a living standard of judgment in his doctoral thesis. I also identify this energy with Joan Walton's living standard of judgment in her doctoral thesis of 'spiritual resilience gained through connection with a loving dynamic energy' (Walton, 2008, Abstract).

The second affirmation is in relationships with others when mutual recognition evokes a flow of life-affirming energy. One event in which I experienced this affirmation was on the evening of Jacqueline Delong's graduation day on 18 December 2002, when Peter Mellett led a celebration for Jacqueline in the Department of Education of the University of Bath. I believe that you will feel this affirmation 32 seconds into the video-clip when the laughter bursts out (Whitehead, 2006a).

To communicate my meanings of the importance of a life-affirming energy and values such as academic freedom, pleasure, humour, love and justice in explanations of educational influence I shall use two multi-media representations. The first is a video of a keynote to the International Conference of Teacher Research in New York in March 2008 on *Combining Voices In Living Educational Theories That Are Freely Given In Teacher Research* (Whitehead, 2008b, 2008c). In presenting the keynote I felt that I was loving what I was doing. Such keynotes offer the opportunity to communicate ideas from my research programme that are directly related to what it has meant to me to live a loving a productive life in education. The following video-clip (Whitehead, 2008e) shows me using multi-media to explain the importance of visual representations to communicate flows of life-affirming energy and loving recognition in explanations of educational influences in learning.

I am using the video-clip (Whitehead, 2008f) from the keynote to show a form of spiritual resilience gained through connection with a loving dynamic energy (Walton, 2008). The video shows me, to myself, responding to the living memories of most difficult experiences of my working life. In these responses I am hopeful that you experience the flow of loving energy with pleasure, humour and a passion for knowledge-creation that I feel distinguish my educational relationships and explanations of educational influence.

As I watch this video-clip I see myself expressing a loving energy, pleasure, humour and understanding as I describe judgments from the University that generated the most difficult experiences of my working life. My purpose in including them in my accounts of my educational journey and knowledge-creation is to avoid presenting a smooth story of self that contains no narrative wreckage. In my experience of listening to many life-histories, everyone has encountered difficulties that have required spiritual resilience and a connection with a loving energy to move beyond the difficulties. Jacqueline Scholes-Rhodes (2002) has expressed her experience of spiritual belonging as a sense of 'exquisite connectivity'. She creates an 'intricate patterning of personal stories and dialogical inquiry process in forming a sense of coherence from the juxtaposition of emotional images with the clarity of a reflective and cognitive dialogue' (Scholes-Rhodes, 2002). The coherence I am seeking is one which includes emotional difficulties as 'exquisite connectivity' is broken, denied and re-established.

With the exception of the experience of 2006 described below I have documented most of the difficulties experienced over the 30 years between 1976-2006 in previous publications (Whitehead, 1993, 2004). They include a 1976 judgment by the University that I had exhibited forms of behaviour that had harmed the good order and morale of the School of Education. They include the 1980 and 1982 judgments that I could not question the judgments of examiners of my two doctoral submissions under any circumstances. They include the 1987 judgment that my activities and writings were a challenge to the present and proper order of the university and not consistent with the duties the University wished me to pursue.

In 1990, based on this judgment about my activities and writings, as evidence of a prima facie breach of my academic freedom, Senate established a working party on a matter of academic freedom. They reported in 1991: 'The working party did not find that... his academic freedom had actually been breached. This was however, because of Mr. Whitehead's persistence in the face of pressure; a less determined individual might well have been discouraged and therefore constrained.'

In the video *Responding to matters of power and academic freedom* (Whitehead, 2006b) is my re-enactment of a meeting with the working party where I had been invited to respond to a draft report in which the conclusion was that my academic freedom had not been breached; a conclusion I agreed with. What I did not agree with was that there was no recognition of the pressure to which I had been subjected to while sustaining my academic freedom. In the clip I think you may feel a disturbing shock in the recognition of the power of my anger in the expression of energy and my passion for academic freedom and academic responsibility. Following my meeting with the working party the report that went to Senate acknowledged that the reason my academic freedom had not been breached was because of my persistence in the face of pressure. This phrase, 'persistence in the face of pressure' is a phrase I continue to use in comprehending my meaning of Joan Walton's standard of judgment of spiritual resilience gained through connection with a loving dynamic energy (Walton, 2008).

I have included this video-clip (Whitehead, 2006b) on the grounds of authenticity. To understand the educational significance of the video of my keynote of March 2008, in my explanations of educational influence, requires an understanding of the significance of the rechanneling of the energy in the anger in the above video. I expressed this rechanneling in the keynote. This rechanneling was related to a persistence in the face of pressure. This persistence was possible through remaining open to the flows of loving dynamic energy in the passion for improving practice and contributing to educational knowledge.

Whilst much valuable learning can take place in response to difficulties I do want to emphasise the importance of the affirmations of those I have worked with in generating their own living educational theories, in sustaining my own passion for education. These affirmations, expressed most delightfully by Spiro in the story-epilogue of her thesis *Learning and teacher as fellow travellers: a story tribute to Jack Whitehead* (Spiro, 2008, p. xv). This flows with a loving recognition, respectful connectedness and educational responsibility (Huxtable, 2008). These help to sustain my own loving relations and productive life in education.

One of the greatest difficulties I have experienced in remaining open to a flow of loving energy for education is in responding to a lack of recognition of my contributions to educational knowledge. This lack of recognition has been sustained over the 30 years 1976-2006 in judgments made about these contributions in the University. The latest judgment was in 2006 with the rejection of my application for a Readership on the grounds that I needed to develop my case further by focusing on producing articles which can be disseminated via established and renowned international refereed journals. Bruce Ferguson (2008), Whitehead (2008a, 2010), Laidlaw (2008), Adler-Collins (2008) and Huxtable (2009) have all made a case in the British Educational Research Association Publication, *Research Intelligence*, to explain why the forms of representation in established and renowned international refereed journals need extending to include the new forms of educational knowledge being communicated through EJOLTS. EJOLTS is being established because the existing established and renowned international refereed journals are not providing appropriate forms of representation for the communication of living educational theories. Laidlaw's (2008) contribution is particularly significant in communicating meanings of living standards of judgment because she includes live urls, in the e-version of *Research Intelligence*. These take readers directly to the work of Branko Bognar (2008a; 2008b) with teachers and pupils in classrooms in Croatia, as well as to educational relationships with Moira Laidlaw's students in China.

We can all help each other, whatever age, to create our own living educational theories in which we account to ourselves for living our values and understandings as fully as we can.

You can see at http://www.actionresearch.net/writings/mastermod.shtml and at http://www.actionresearch.net//living.shtml the living theories of master and doctor educators that have been freely given for sharing through the internet, in the hope that they will contribute ideas that may be of value in the generation of your living theories as we combine our voices in enhancing our educational influences in improving our local and global contexts.

As I write I am feeling the pleasure of anticipation of seeing this contribution to EJOLTS appearing in print and so being made accessible to those without technology. I am sharing these ideas with you in the hope that you will find something of value for yourself that resonates with your own life-affirming energy, values and understandings.

In conclusion I want to briefly focus attention on the importance of acting locally and publishing our ideas globally in ways that can support national and international collaborations.

**Developing national and international collaborations for improving practice and generating educational knowledge**

My experiences of action researchers from different countries include action research workshops and presentations in China, Japan, Australia, Malaysia, The Republic of Ireland, South Africa, UK, USA and Canada. The workshops and presentations have helped me to recognise the importance of understanding the normative backgrounds of different cultures (Whitehead, 2008c, 2008f, 2008g, 2008h, 2008i). I recognise that the emphasis placed on collective identities in China and Japan is different to the emphasis placed on individual identity in Australia, Ireland, UK, USA and Canada. Western views of democracy, which influence my own identity, have been questioned by Islamic scholars:

> There exists in Islam a mechanism for consulting the believers, the Shura, which is an integral part of Islam. However, the system in Western democracy whereby the majority decides what is lawful and what is not, can never be acceptable in Islam, where the laws and framework of society are revealed by Allah and are unchangeable. (Abdul-Rahman, 1982, p. 35)

Whatever our socio-cultural history I believe that educators around the world have a responsibility to enhance the flow of values and understandings that carry hope for the future of humanity. This involves sharing our different understandings of what constitutes a good social formation and which values and understandings carry hope for the future of humanity.

For example, Jane Spiro (2008) in her research into knowledge-transformation engages with her own creativity as a creative writer, educator, manager and educational researcher. She holds herself to account in her thesis and research programme in relation to the values and understandings that she believes carry hope for the future of humanity. By making public her thesis with these values and understandings, in the flow of communications through web-space, Spiro is fulfilling one of the fundamental responsibilities of an educational researcher. I am thinking of the responsibility to engage in systematic inquiry that is made public. In her thesis, produced locally through her research at Oxford Brookes University, (UK) Spiro explains how the embodied knowledge of a writer, educator, manager and researcher can be made public, in a distinct academic approach that includes the exercise of creativity and narrative inquiry in the generation of a living educational theory. This thesis is now available through the international communication channels of the internet (http://www.actionresearch.net/janespirophd.shtml). It is my belief that the insights in this thesis, about how to make public the embodied knowledge of a practitioner-researcher, will travel across cultural boundaries to captivate the imaginations and practices of others.

You can see how this kind of communication has already moved across cultural and national boundaries in the work of Dean Tian Fengjun and Professor Moira Laidlaw (Tian & Laidlaw, 2006, Laidlaw, 2006) with their Colleagues, in China's Experimental Centre for Educational Action Research in Foreign Languages Teaching, at Ningxia Teacher's University. The action researchers at Ningxia Teachers University are developing a collaborative approach to living theory action research with Chinese characteristics. You can access the living theories of teachers and students about their learning and implementation of the New Curriculum at Ningxia Teachers University from http://people.bath.ac.uk/edsajw/moira.shtml. You can also access some of my suggestions for international collaborations in the development of collaborative living educational theory action research in China from http://www.jackwhitehead.com/jack/jwkeynotechina8june08.pdf.

Dr. Margaret Farren and her colleague Yvonne Crotty at Dublin City University are evolving a living theory action research approach for improving practice and generating knowledge with information and communications technology. Dr. Farren is a lecturer in e-learning at Dublin City University who is working to support international collaboration with the *Action Research Collaboratory* and the *e-Life Connecting People Project* (Farren, 2008).

Professor Jean McNiff has been most influential through books, workshops and conference presentations in spreading the influence of a living theory action research approach (McNiff & Whitehead, 2006, Whitehead & McNiff, 2006). This influence can be seen particularly through her work in South Africa (Wood, Morar & Mostert, 2007), in Ireland, Iceland, Canada and in the UK.

I want to end with references to two photographs from graduation ceremonies in 2008 from Limerick University and the University of Bath to symbolize the spreading global influence of the living theories of individuals produced in their local contexts.

In a picture taken in January 2008 (University of Limerick, 2008) Jean McNiff is in her doctoral robes from the University of Bath celebrating the success of Margaret Cahill and Mary Roche on their graduations with their living theories doctorates[2] from the University of Limerick. The symbolism of the robes in relation to ideas travelling through national boundaries is that ideas generated by Jean McNiff in her doctoral research programme at the University of Bath have been integrated in the living theory doctorates of Cahill and Roche at the University of Limerick.

Jean McNiff has supervised three other living theory doctorates (Glenn, 2006; Sullivan, 2006; McDonagh, 2007), to successful completion at the University of Limerick with graduations in 2006 and 2007 and more are on the way. The explicit embrace of enhancing the expression of the values of social

---

[2]     Margaret Cahill's (2007) thesis is on *My living educational theory of inclusional practice*, and Mary Roche's (2007) thesis is on *Towards a living theory of caring pedagogy: Interrogating my practice to nurture a critical, emancipatory and just community of inquiry.*

justice and holistic educational practice, in the theses, provide evidence of an educational engagement with issues of power and privilege in society.

**Figure 1.**    Jack Whitehead, with Jane Spiro and Je Kan Adler Collins on Graduation Day

Figure 1 shows myself on the left, with Jane Spiro (2008) and Je Kan Adler-Collins (2007) on their graduation with their doctorates on the 25 June 2008. We three are alumni of the University of Bath. Ideas from my research programme have been integrated within the theses of Spiro and Adler-Collins as they generated their own original living educational theories. Adler-Collins' research programme involved the development, implementation and evaluation of a curriculum for the healing nurse in a Japanese University. Spiro's research programme includes family history from Poland where in Chapter 4 of her thesis on *Writing as finding a voice: From Finchley to Lithuania.* She writes: 'This chapter explores my novel-writing process, the struggle to understand the actual life stories/histories of those I grew up with, and to honour this specificity, at the same time as transforming it symbolically into a larger, and 'universal' story' (Spiro 2008, p. 82).

The image brings back the memory of the expression of life-affirming energy, pleasure, hope and friendship between us. The supervision relationship has now changed to one of doctoral colleagues in our three universities who are supporting each other in our post-doctoral research. The process of researching our actions locally and publishing our research globally continues with the extending interconnecting and branching channels of our communications. I do hope that you will feel moved to contribute your own living educational theory to our educational journeys in our shared living space, whatever your professional practice and accredited or non-accredited enquiry.

## REFERENCES

Abdul-Rahman S. A. (1982). *Educational theory: A Qur'anic outlook.* Makkah, Saudi Arabia: Umm Al-Qura University.

Adler-Collins, J. (2008). Creating new forms of living educational theories through collaborative educational research from Eastern and Western contexts: A response to Jack Whitehead. *Research Intelligence, 104,* 17-18.

Adler-Collins, J. (2007). *Developing an inclusional pedagogy of the unique: How do I clarify, live and explain my educational influences in my learning as I pedagogise my healing nurse curriculum in a Japanese university?* (Doctoral disertation, University of Bath, UK). Retrieved January 28, 2008, from http://people.bath.ac.uk/edsajw/jekan.shtml

Allender, J. & Allender, D. S. (2008). *The humanistic teacher: First the child, then curriculum.* Boulder: Paradigm Publishers.

Bourdieu, P. (1990). *The logic of practice.* Stanford, CA: Stanford University Press.

Bognar, B. (2008q). Pupil - action researchers [Video file]. Retrieved August 28, 2010 from http://www.vimeo.com/1230806

Bognar, B. (2008b). Validation of pupil's action research report [Video file]. Retrieved August 28 , 2010, from http://www.vimeo.com/1415387

Bruce Ferguson, P. (2008). Increasing inclusion in educational research: Reflections from New Zealand. *Research Intelligence, 102,* 24-25.

Charles, E. (2007). *How can I bring Ubuntu as a living standard of judgment into the academy? Moving beyond decolonisation through societal re-identification and guiltless recognition.* (Doctoral dissertation, University of Bath, UK). Retrieved September 10, 2008, from http://www.actionresearch.net/edenphd.shtml

Collingwood, R. G. (1991). *An autobiography.* Oxford: Oxford University Press.

Farren, M. (2008). *The e-life connecting people project.* Retrieved September 29, 2008, from http://www.jackwhitehead.com/farren/eLife.htm

Fukuyama, F. (1992). *The end of history and the last man.* London: Penguin.

Forrest, M. (1984). *The teacher as researcher.* (Master's thesis, University of Bath, UK).

Glenn, M. (2006). *Working with collaborative projects: My living theory* (Doctoral dissertation, University of Limerick, Ireland). Retrieved September 29, 2008, from http://www.jeanmcniff.com/glennabstract.html

Habermas, J. (1976). *Communication and the evolution of society.* London: Heinemann.

Hirst, P. (Ed.). (1983). *Educational theory and its foundation disciplines.* London: RKP.

Huxtable, M. (2008, September). *How do I improve my educational practice as I support educators who are developing inclusive and inclusional theory and practice of gifts and talents whilst responding to national developments?* Paper presented at the British Educational Research Association Annual Conference, Edinburgh, Scotland.

Huxtable, M. (2009). How do we contribute to an educational knowledge base? A response to Whitehead and a challenge to BERJ. *Research Intelligence, 107*, 25-26. Retrieved January 11, 2010, from http://www.actionresearch.net/writings/huxtable/mh2009beraRI107.pdf

Ilyenkov, E. (1977). *Dialectical logic.* Moscow: Progress Publishers.

Laidlaw, M. (2008). Increasing inclusion in educational research: A response to Pip Bruce Ferguson and Jack Whitehead. *Research Intelligence, 104*, 16-17.

Laidlaw, M. (2006). *How might we enhance the educational value of our research-base at the New University in Guyuan? Researching stories for the social good* (Inaugural Professorial Lecture). Retrieved September 22, 2008, from http://www.jackwhitehead.com/china/mlinaugural.htm

Laidlaw, M. (1996). *How can I create my own living educational theory as I account for my educational development?* (Doctoral dissertation, University of Bath, UK). Retrieved September 10, 2008, from http://www.actionresearch.net/moira2.shtml

Lumley, T. (2008). *A fluid-dynamical world view.* Victoria, British Columbia: Printorium Bookworks, Inc.

McDonagh, C. (2007). *My living theory How do I enable primary school children with specific learning disability (dyslexia) and myself as their teacher to realise our learning potentials?* (Doctoral dissertation, University of Limerick, Ireland). Retrieved September 29, 2008, from http://www.jeanmcniff.com/mcdonaghabstract.html

MacDonald, B. (1976). Evaluation and control of education. In D. A. Tawney (Ed.), *Curriculum evaluation today: Trends and implications* (pp. 125-136). London: Macmillan Education.

Marcuse, H. (1964). *One dimensional man.* London: Routledge and Kegan Paul.

McNiff, J. & Whitehead, J. (2006). *All you need to know about action research.* London: Sage.

McNiff, J. & Whitehead, J. (2008). *Evaluating quality in doing and writing action research in schools, neighbourhoods and communities: AERA professional development training and extended courses proposal.* Retrieved March 3, 2008, from http://www.jackwhitehead.com/aeraictr08/jmjwaeraprofdev08.htm

Murray, Y. P. (2007). *How I develop a cosmopolitan academic practice in moving through narcissistic injury with educational responsibility: A contribution to an epistemology and methodology of educational knowledge* (Doctoral submission, University of Bath, UK).

Polanyi, M. (1958). *Personal knowledge: Towards a post-critical philosophy.* London: Routledge and Kegan Paul.

Popper, K. (1975). *The logic of scientific discovery.* London: Hutchinson & Co.

Rayner, A. (2004). *Inclusionality: The science, art and spirituality of place, space and evolution.* Retrieved July 6, 2008, from http://people.bath.ac.uk/bssadmr/inclusionality/placespaceevolution.html

Ryle, G. (1973). *The concept of mind.* Harmondsworth: Penguin.

Schutz, A. (1972). *The phenomenology of the social world.* London: Heinemann.

Scholes-Rhodes, J. (2002). *From the inside out: Learning to presence my aesthetic and spiritual being through the emergent form of a creative art of inquiry.* (Doctoral dissertation, University of Bath, UK). Retrieved September 10, 2008, from http://www.actionresearch.net/rhodes.shtml

Spiro, J. (2008). *How I have arrived at a notion of knowledge transformation, through understanding the story of myself as creative writer, creative educator, creative manager, and educational researcher.* (Doctoral dissertation, University of Bath, UK). Retrieved August 28, 2010, from http://www.actionresearch.net/living/janespirophd.shtml

Sullivan, B. (2006). *A living theory of a practice of social justice: Realising the right of Traveller children to educational equality.* (Doctoral dissertation, University of Limerick, Ireland). Retrieved August 28, 2010, from http://www.jeanmcniff.com/bernieabstract.html

Tian, F. & Laidlaw, M. (2006). *Action research and the foreign languages teaching.* Xi'an, P.R. China: Shaanxi Tourism Publishing House.

Tillich, P. (1962). *The courage to be.* London: Fontana.

University of Limerick. (2008). *University of Limerick Winter Conferrings 2008.* Retrieved September 9, 2008, from http://www2.ul.ie/web/WWW/Services/News?did=721750371&pageUrl=/WWW/Services/News

Walton, J. (2008). *Ways of knowing: Can I find a way of knowing that satisfies my search for meaning?* (Doctoral dissertation, University of Bath, UK). Retrieved September 10, 2008, from http://www.actionresearch.net/walton.shtml

Whitehead, J. (1972). *A way to professionalism in education.* (Master's thesis, University of London, UK).

Whitehead, J. (1976). *Improving learning for 11 – 14 year olds in mixed ability science groups.* Swindon: Wiltshire Curriculum Development Centre.

Whitehead, J. (1985). An analysis of an individual's educational development - the basis for personally orientated action research. In M. Shipman (Ed.), *Educational research: Principles, policies and practice* (pp. 97-108). London: Falmer.

Whitehead, J. (1989). Creating a living educational theory from questions of the kind, 'How do I improve my practice?' *Cambridge Journal of Education, 19*(1), 41-52.

Whitehead, J. (1993). *The growth of educational knowledge: Creating your own living educational theories.* Bournemouth: Hyde.

Whitehead, J. (2004). Do action researchers' expeditions carry hope for the future of humanity? How do we know? *Action Research Expeditions*, October 2004. Retrieved August 28, 2010, from http://www.actionresearch.net/writings/jack/jwareoct04.pdf

Whitehead, J. (2006a, December 5). Peter Mellett celebrating on Jacqueline Delong's Doctoral graduation [Video File]. Retrieved August 28, 2010, from http://www.youtube.com/watch?v=HxqRF2tVLB4

Whitehead, J. (2006b, December 30). Responding to matters of power and academic freedom [Video File]. Retrieved August 28, 2010, from http://www.youtube.com/watch?v=MBTLfyjkFh0

Whitehead, J. (2008a). Increasing inclusion in educational research: A response to Pip Bruce Ferguson. *Research Intelligence, 103*, 16-17.

Whitehead, J. (2008b, March). *Combining voices in living educational theories that are freely given in teacher research.* Keynote presentation for the International Conference of Teacher Research on Combining Voices in Teacher Research, New York, USA. Retrieved August 28, 2010, from http://www.jackwhitehead.com/aerictr08/jwictr08key.htm

Whitehead, J. (2008c). Keynote presentation for the International Conference of Teacher Research on Combining Voices in Teacher Research, New York [Video File]. Posted to mms://wms.bath.ac.uk/live/education/JackWhitehead_030408/jackkeynote ictr280308large.wmv

Whitehead, J. (2008d, March). *How are living educational theories being produced and legitimated in the boundaries of cultures in resistance?* Paper presented at the Cultures in Resistance Conference of the Discourse, Power, Resistance Series, Manchester UK. Retrieved August 28, 2010, from http://www.actionresearch.net/writings/jack/jwmanchester250207.htm

Whitehead, J. (2008e, August 27). Jack Whitehead's keynote ICTR 08 clip 1 [Video File]. Retrieved August 28, 2010 from http://www.youtube.com/watch?v=gWabP2acxfk

Whitehead, J. (2008f, August 27). Jack Whitehead's keynote ICTR 08 clip 2 [Video File]. Retrieved August 28, 2010 from http://www.youtube.com/watch?v=KXLqGAAK-D0

Whitehead, J. (2008g, March). *How can S-STEP research contribute to the enhancement of civic responsibility in schools, neighborhoods, and communities?* Paper presented in the session: Becoming Innovative Through Self-Study Research, at the Annual Conference of the American Educational Research Association, New York, USA. Retrieved March 3, 2008, from http://www.actionresearch.net/writings/jack/jwaera08sstep.htm

Whitehead, J. (2008h, March). *How can I~we create living educational theories from research into professional learning?* Paper presented in the Symposium convened by Jean McNiff on Communicating and testing the validity of claims to transformational systemic influence for civic responsibility, at AERA, New York, USA. Retrieved September 20, 2010, from http://www.actionresearch.net/writings/jack/jwaera08jmsem.htm

Whitehead, J. (2008i, June). *Collaborative living educational theory action research in China.* Keynote presented at a conference of China's Experimental Centre for Educational Action Research in Foreign Languages Teacher, Ningxia, China. Retrieved September 20, 2010, from http://www.actionresearch.net/writings/jack/jwkeynotechina8june08.pdf

Whitehead, J. (2009). How do I influence the generation of living educational theories for personal and social accountability in improving practice? In Tidwell, D., Heston, M., & Fitzgerald, L. (Eds.). *Research methods for the self-study of practice* (pp. 173-194). New York: Springer.

Whitehead, J. (2010). The role of educational theory in generating an epistemological transformation in what counts as educational knowledge with educational responsibility: Responses to Huxtable and Rayner, and Biesta, Allan and Edwards. *Research Intelligence*, 110, 25-26. Retrieved May 8, 2010, from http://www.actionresearch.net/writings/jack/jwri110p2526opt.pdf

Whitehead, J. & Delong, J. (2008, March). *Persisting in the face of pressures: How have we contributed to the generation of cultures of inquiry?* Paper presented at the International Conference of Teacher Research (ICTR) 2008 with the Theme: Combining Voices: Building a Teacher Research Community. New York, USA. Retrieved September 20, 2010, from http://www.leeds.ac.uk/educol/documents/172701.htm

Whitehead, J. & McNiff, J. (2006). *Action research living theory*. London: Sage.

Wood, L. A., Morar, R. & Mostert, L. (2007). From rhetoric to reality: The role of living theory action research. *Education as Change*, *11*(2), 67-80.

# CO-CREATING AN EDUCATIONAL SPACE

**Margaret Farren, Ireland**

*What lies behind us*
*And what lies before*
*Are tiny matters*
*Compared to what*
*Lies within us*
(Ralph Waldo Emerson)

## PROLOGUE

As I sit at my office desk in the university's Education Department preparing for my next lecture, sounds of laughter come from the playground of a nearby primary school. On opening my office window, the excited sound of children at play floods the room. Thankful for the break, I watch their interaction: one child passes the ball to another who takes the ball, and, balancing it on his left foot for a few seconds – an act that takes his school mates by surprise – he skilfully slides it under his left foot to another child. She continues the ball-play. I wonder what it is about ball-play that can hold our attention and interest? Is it the possibilities that a game opens up? Is it the sense of excitement, of uncertainty, of not knowing how it will all end? Is it that each person is called on actively to participate? Is it that once play starts each person is dependent on the other and yet needs to act independently as well, when she runs with the ball? Is it that even when you're not playing the ball you have to continue actively to read the game?

As I watch, the children are totally engaged in the game: each child with their part to play, as they pass the ball from one to the other. I reflect that as an adult I can enter the world of the children in a curious and imaginative way, feeling that I am an active participant, promoting in my thoughts and occasionally by word and gesture the flow of the game with them.

I reflect that life, like the game, can be full of uncertainties. Each of us can be a learner who strives to develop their knowledge and skills to make sense of the world around us. This view emphasises the importance of interaction with people and the world (Bertrand, 2003). Our values of caring and sharing need to be developed if we are to construct the world in a positive way. Who knows what will come from these small beginnings? How can I develop social formations (Whitehead, 2005) that can lead to active, inquiring and creative learning in a variety of contexts? How can we help develop a love of learning from an early age? In our current Higher Education – where talk is of knowledge-transfer rather than pedagogy – are the learner's needs being overlooked? Are students recipients of a curriculum instead of largely choosing and/or making it themselves (Barnett, 2000, p. 163)? Should we not consider the 'why' of education rather than just the 'how' (Webb, 1996; Walker, 1999; Rowland, 2000)? Wouldn't it be interesting to step into the shoes of the learner at the other end of our classroom and experience what it is like to be looking in from the other side?

Were we mentally and habitually to exchange places with our pupils or students, as teachers we would have to rely more on our imaginations. We would have to deal with uncertainty and ambiguity and treat them as part of the learning process. We would not be able to plan everything in advance but would probably allow knowledge to emerge and grow in and through the practice. We would listen to our learners more carefully; indeed we would have their voices in our heads and respond to their individual needs. Shor and Freire's *A Pedagogy for Liberation* (1987) emphasises the importance of dialogue in our learning; 'we each stimulate the other to think, and to re-think the former's thoughts' (p. 3). Freire regrets that teachers are told that they have nothing to do with the production of knowledge: 'If I spend three hours with a group of students discussing, and if I think that this is not researching, then I do not understand anything' (Shor and Freire, 1987, p. 8). Perhaps we need to learn from musicians, artists, designers and children who play games, even those who hold the ball in both hands and run! As Schön points out:

> It is rare that the designer has the design all in her head in advance, and then merely translates it. Most of the time, she is in a kind of progressive relationship: as she goes along, she is making judgments. Sometimes, the designer's judgments have the intimacy of a conversational relationship. Where she is getting some response back from the medium, she is seeing what is happening – what it is that she has created – and she is making judgments about it at that level. (Schön, as cited in Winograd, 1996, p. 176)

In my own learning and educational development, I rely on my previous knowledge, experience, attitudes and skills, and of course the greatest faculty of all, the imagination, as I live and learn in relation to others. Learning is essentially a human, creative and dynamic exploration.

Is it not important for me as a higher education educator to strive to articulate and live my educational values and to give form and shape to them in my practice (Whitehead, 1989a, 2004)? Is it not important that in professional development programmes, we, as co-practitioners should become actively engaged in learning to share our understandings, articulate our values, design and construct artefacts that reflect them and learn from one another? With such a stance, would we not, as 'professional learners' learn to take ownership and responsibility for our own learning, as we go on our educational journey? According to Rowland, 'improving teaching involves critique, personal inquiry and openness to change' (Rowland, 2004, p. 99).

For today's teachers, new technologies allow for new ways of doing things. Information and Communications Technologies (ICTs) hold out much promise in this area. With developments in bandwidth, learners can communicate different forms of representation in the form of multimedia. There is also the opportunity to move beyond the walls of the classroom and opportunities for collaboration with others. ICT is constantly shifting and developing and we can feel we are moving and exploring unknown terrains: 'With the advent of new technology-rich teaching on a large scale there are many opportunities for creative and innovative teaching and new relationships both with students and the shifting world of knowledge' (Skilbeck, 2001, p. 89). New technologies allow for new forms of representation and impact on how we disseminate our knowledge, research and teaching.

Early computers laboured over tasks that are now done in nanoseconds. Speed makes the computer a friend that can whisk us along rather than leaving us in frustration. But we need to be attentive to the journey rather than become too fascinated by the technology. We need to connect with our own values and grow with the larger community in an inter-related and dynamic way. In the learning-game, each of us has to use our gifts to create opportunities, open a path that can lead to new understandings, new and wonderful sights and sounds!

## CONTEXT

My research programme for the past 12 years (1998-2010) at Dublin City University has focused on the human capability to create, share and contribute to educational knowledge and lifelong learning through creating explanations of educational influences in one's own learning, in the learning of others and in the learning of social formations.

By referring to the education of social formations, I raise the question of how organisations learn to live more fully the values that can carry hope for the future of humanity (Kilpatrick, 1951). I have supported practitioner-researchers from a variety of workplace backgrounds in their generation of knowledge from their research into improving educational practice.

Dublin City University (DCU) was created as the National Institute for Higher Education in Dublin in 1975. It enrolled its first students in 1980 and was elevated to university-status (with the University of Limerick) in 1989.

> Twenty years ago in 1988 NIHE Dublin had 2,500 students and consisted essentially of the Albert College and Henry Grattan buildings. We didn't have mobile phones, the internet or email, and unemployment stood at 17%! Twenty years on, DCU has nearly outgrown its current campus with over 10,000 students practically all of whom have mobile phones and we are effectively at full employment. What changes will another twenty years bring and what plans do we need to put in place to ensure DCU's success? (DCU Foresight Report, 2008)

The report highlights the need to look at different approaches to learning – face-to-face, online, group (p. 14) – and new models of communication – e-based versus face-to-face communication and interaction, and their application across different areas of life (p. 16). DCU is a young University and has grown over the past twenty five years to become recognised, nationally and internationally, as a centre of academic excellence.

I joined the staff of DCU in November 1997 as a Research Officer at the Centre for Teaching Computing, in the School of Computer Applications, when I began to research my own professional practice in Higher Education. In February 1999, I joined the lecturing staff in the School of Computer Applications and I began teaching on the M.Sc. (Master of Science) Computer Applications in Education programme. I have worked and researched in two different contexts in DCU, first in the School of Computer Applications on the Masters programme in Computer Applications in Education from 1999-2002 and secondly, since September 2002, I have been working in the School of Education Studies. Soon after I joined the School of Education Studies I established an e-Learning Strand on the existing Masters in Education and Training Management Programme. I now coordinate the Masters in Science (M.Sc.) Education and Training Management Programme.

As a teacher in a Sixth Form college in London in the late 1980's I made extensive use of co-operative group-work and group discussion and found it to be an effective way of teaching and learning. My research into the unique educational features of interactive technology began during my Master of Education (M.Ed.) degree at the University of Bath in the early 90s. I explored the use of an interactive video programme for my Masters dissertation. I believed that learners needed to become more involved in shaping their own learning. The research was published as *Interactive video and group learning: two action inquiry based evaluations* (Cloke, Farren and Barrington, 1996). After I had completed my Masters degree I taught in The British School in Brussels for five years. I taught 'Computer Studies and ICT' to GCSE (General Certificate in Secondary Education) level (Year 10 and 11); 'Computer Studies' to A (Advanced) level (Years 12 and 13); and 'Communications and Marketing' on BTEC (British Technical Education Council) courses. I believed that the principal strength of the new syllabus in Information Technology was its open-ended nature. In other words, it wasn't prescriptive. The syllabus valued the process of inquiry as well as the product. It provided learners with the opportunity to explore and experiment with ICT and to carry out project work in areas of interest and relevance to them. It provided me with some scope for applying my interactive approach to Information Technology (IT) teaching in the classroom.

The next stage of my teaching and learning journey took me to Dublin. In 1997 I was appointed Research Officer at the Centre for Teaching Computing, in the School of Computer Applications at Dublin City University. The Centre for Teaching Computing provided me with the opportunity to continue my interest in the educational uses of interactive technologies. Whilst working with the Centre for Teaching Computing in 1998 and 1999, I developed links with international academics through participation in several online learning professional development courses with Sheffield University, The University of Greenwich, UK, and Southern Cross University in Australia. I found that even though there was extensive literature on student use of the internet, little reference was made to teachers communicating with each other via the internet and the way collaborative work could lead to improvements in teaching practice. I believed that these should have been areas of priority in research. I became involved in researching how educators could use an online learning environment to develop their practice.

In February 1999 I joined the lecturing staff in the School of Computer Applications. I began teaching on the M.Sc. in Computer Applications in Education programme – a two-year part-time programme which had been established in the department in 1996. This new role provided me with the opportunity to begin to fill some of the gaps in the available literature in the practical application of interactive and collaborative learning environments. A paper *Using Information and Communications Technology (ICT) to support Action Research and Distance Learning* (Farren, 2000) explores the educational applications of desktop videoconferencing.

I taught in the School of Computer Applications from February 1999 to August 2002. The programme was geared towards technical understanding of ICT rather than about ICT as applied to education. It had been envisaged that teachers would already have sufficient knowledge of pedagogy and would require mainly technical understanding and skills that would enable them to make use of ICT in their teaching. It is clear now that this technical approach to ICT was important but it underestimated the need of teachers to examine possible pedagogical uses of ICT in day-to-day teaching and learning.

## LIVING EDUCATIONAL THEORY APPROACH

In 1993, the Self-Study research group of the American Educational Research Association (AERA) was established by a group of international Higher Education educators. The importance of the Self-Study group is in its contribution to the development of a new epistemology for teaching and learning. *The International Handbook of Self-Study of Teaching Practice* (Loughran, Hamilton, LaBoskey, & Russell, 2004) provides evidence of how self-study research is influencing teacher education. The research-based practice approach to learning that I have developed at DCU ensures that participants – working educators on a postgraduate programme – provide evidence of how they are improving educational practice and at the same time contributing to new knowledge in their disciplines.

My continuing commitment to supporting practitioner-researchers to develop their living educational theories is a consequence of the importance I attach to providing space for practitioner-researchers to ask, research and answer the question, 'how do I improve my practice?' Barnett (2000) has referred to the need for a 'higher education', that is, where action, self and knowledge are given equal weight in the learning process. The research programme that I have developed and sustained at DCU is concerned with supporting practitioner researchers to develop their practice and improve their capacity to account for their practice and contribute to new knowledge.

Participants in the Masters programme use an action research approach to reflect systematically on their practice in order to bring about improvement and contribute to new knowledge. In its focus on practice, action research is rooted in the concerns of practitioners in real-world settings and in disciplined self-evaluation and reflection. In action research, the researchers do research on themselves and define the areas for improving learning, developing action plans, acting on the plans, gathering data, assessing their own learning, and redefining the areas for improvement. There is now a body of researchers, who are convinced that research in the human sciences should take account of the potentiality for creative action of all relevant participants and relate to broader social environments (Bognar & Zovko, 2008). Jack Whitehead has been working at the University of Bath for over thirty years and he has developed the action research approach he has called 'living educational theory' (Whitehead, 1989b). He believes that by asking questions of the kind, 'how do I improve what I am doing?' practitioners can create their own living educational theories by embodying their educational values in explanations of their practice (Whitehead, 2004). Whitehead (McNiff & Whitehead, 2006) believes that an educational theory must explain our educational influence in our own learning, in the learning of others, and in the education of social formations.

## CO-CREATING AN EDUCATIONAL SPACE FOR PRACTITIONER-RESEARCH

In this paper, I am showing, with the help of video clips what I do in my educational practice as I facilitate a community of practitioner-researchers to account for their own educational development. The live links to the video clips can be accessed in the Reference section of this paper. I relate to Bruce Ferguson's (2008) call to, 'validate forms of research that can convey knowledge not easily encapsulated just within pages of written text and work to overcome those whose knowledge and skills have been, in the past, inappropriately excluded' (p. 25).

I hope I can communicate with the help of video how I am explaining my educational influence through explanatory principles, which embrace Celtic Spirituality. The Celtic spiritual tradition is among the most ancient in Europe and its origins can be traced over 3000 years. The feature of Celtic Spirituality that I regard as most relevant to my work is the opening up to connections and relationships and an awareness and commitment to understanding the other. There is also an awareness of the inward and outward journey and how this is central to the development of our living of human values such as love, care and courage. As in the photograph which I had the pleasure of experiencing one early Spring morning Celtic Spirituality recognises the connectedness of all things (http://ejolts.net/files/images/sunrise.jpg). In his book *Divine Beauty: The*

*Invisible Embrace* the Irish theologian and philosopher, John O' Donohue uses the term web of betweenness to refer to the interconnectedness of all things, 'as in the rainforest, a dazzling diversity of life-forms complement and sustain each other. There is secret oxygen with which we unknowingly sustain one another' (O'Donohue, 2003, pp. 132-133). O'Donohue's idea of community extends beyond the social to the idea of a community of spirit in which the individual emerges and grows: 'The human self is not a finished thing, it is constantly unfolding' (p. 142).

In my view spirituality is an essential part of being human. The meaning of Celtic Spirituality as expressed in my teaching and learning situations is the value I place on dialogue, teamwork and co-operation. I try to create an educational space in which the participants and I can develop our own human capacity as we learn with each other. I approach validation meetings with the intention to facilitate each individual practitioner-researcher to make the inward journey that prompts the articulation of the values that give meaning and purpose to their work. The inward journey also connects us with the ancient Greek aphorism 'Know Thyself'.[3] In addition to this individual personal reflection, the sharing of our individual narratives with each other creates trust between each individual and in this way a sense of community is formed:

> [A] true community is not produced. It is invoked and awakened. True community is an ideal where the full identities of awakened and realized individuals challenge and complement each other. In this sense individuality and originality enrich self and others. (O'Donohue, 2003, p. 133)

The first four video clips (Farren, 2008d, 2008e, 2008f, 2008g) in this paper were taken during a validation meeting that was organised as part of the Masters degree research process. The purpose of a validation meeting is to provide practitioner-researchers with the opportunity to present their research to others. Validation also enables participants to gain new insights into the research

---

[3]     The attribution of this exhortation is often attributed to Socrates, but this is contested ("Know Thyself," 2008).

process. With the permission of all, I video-recorded this meeting. The four teachers in the video clips were carrying out a self-study of their own educational practice. Two of the teachers were studying for the Masters degree in Computer Applications in Education in the School of Computer Applications and two of the teachers were studying for the Masters degree in Education and Training Management in the School of Education Studies.

The importance of video technology is that it allows one to video-record the validation meetings and to share the cooperative learning with a wider audience. The participants at the validation meeting can review the video and learn from their own reflections and the interactions between the group members. The video clips also allow me to provide evidence of how I am facilitating a cooperative learning process based on dialogue and participation. Eisner (1988, 1993, 1997, 2005) advocates the need to extend the forms of representation in our understandings of educational research to include multi-media forms of representation.

At the time of this study, Fionnuala Flanagan was teaching Maths and Science in a post-primary school, Chris Garvey was teaching Science in a post-primary school, Bernie Tobin was Assistant Principal in a primary school and Mairéad Ryan was also a teacher in a primary school.

The video clips show the importance of 'storying' experience (Clandinin and Connelly, 2004). The storying process is central to encouraging reflection. We can create stories of the reflective journey with the use of digital video. I hope you can see the creativity, inquiring mind and critical judgment of each practitioner-researcher as they inquire into their own learning and articulate the values that give meaning to their work.

Bernie Tobin (Farren, 2008d) explains the step-by-step approach that she and her colleagues used in order to introduce the new writing approach to pupils in primary school. Bernie expresses her own educational values as she explains the process of her learning and her influence in pupil learning (Tobin, 2002).

Fionnuala Flanagan (Farren, 2008f) discusses how she introduced concept mapping to help students at post-primary level to problem solve in mathematics classes. She explains how concept-mapping allowed the students to think more clearly about how they were solving a problem and how they were then able to transfer their solution to animation more easily (Flanagan, 2002).

Mairéad Ryan (Farren, 2008e) emphasises the value she places on pupils being actively involved in explaining their own mathematical thinking. An educational space is created in which each individual is present and attentive to Mairéad's inquiry (see Ryan, 2002). There is a relational dynamic in our various contributions to the discussion, and an engaged response from each of us to Mairéad's inquiry. Rayner refers to this as 'relationally dynamic':

> At the heart of inclusionality, then, is a simple shift in the way we frame reality, from absolutely fixed to relationally dynamic. This shift arises from perceiving space and boundaries as connective, reflective and co-creative, rather than severing, in their vital role of producing heterogeneous form and local identity within a featured rather than featureless, dynamic rather than static, Universe. (Rayner, 2004)

At the end of the validation meeting Chris Garvey asked for clarification on the action research cycles (Farren, 2008g). The presence of the other participants helped Chris to see how his learning could relate to the action research cycles (see Garvey, 2002). In a later email Chris pointed to the:

> ...significance of the peer validation meetings and how they were worthwhile and meaningful and extremely useful. They brought home to me the necessity to engage constantly in critical reflection and dialogue, not only in educational research itself but also within all areas of my educational practice. (C. Garvey, personal communication, July 14, 2004)

The validation meeting challenged the participants to consider the data they needed in order to present evidence that they had improved student learning. The meeting represented part of my endeavour to live my own values of collaboration and dialogue in the learning process.

*Pedagogy of the unique* is a standard of judgment that recognises the importance of singularity; that is, each individual has a particular and different constellation of values that motivates their inquiries and each operates in a different context from within which their inquiries develop. The web of betweenness is a standard that recognises the relational dynamic (Rayner, 2004) of human existence. My commitment to the fostering of a web of betweenness reflects my belief that learning is a social interactive process involving members of a group of sharing participants who can develop new understandings through dialogue (Laidlaw, 1994; Shor and Freire, 1987). The communications-rich characteristics of Information and Communications Technology (ICT) can support this process.

Since September 2002, I have been working in DCU's School of Education Studies. A Master of Science degree with a focus on leadership was established in the School of Education Studies in 1995. When the MSc. in Computer Applications in Education closed in 2002 I started to develop a new ICT/e-Learning programme and this was established as an e-Learning strand on the existing MSc. Education and Training Management programme in the School of Education Studies. The student body has diversified from the M.Sc. in Computer Applications in Education programme and participants are now drawn from across the primary, post-primary, further, higher, and adult education sectors, as well as from corporate training in industry and nursing and from government and non-government departments and other state agencies (http://webpages.dcu.ie/~farrenm).

In addition to the core modules of Research Design, Education and Training Management and Management Thought, participants in the e-Learning strand take specialist e-Learning modules that include e-Learning Policies and Strategies, Visions for Emerging Technology, Educational Applications of Multimedia (part 1 and 2), Emerging Pedagogies and Collaborative Online Learning Environments. In my research programme at DCU I have generated and sustained a creative educational space in the classroom and online that has supported practitioner-researchers from a wide range of workplace-contexts in the creation and testing of their living educational theories. The innovative approaches to the use of technology that students have experienced have encouraged them to seek out new ways of harnessing digital technologies in their work context. The article E-Learning and Action Research as Transformative Practice (Farren, 2008a) shows how I have integrated online discussions into the programme to help participants to examine their own educational values and practices in a peer group setting.

The e-Learning strand started in 2003 with 10 students. Since September 2005 there are over 40 students in year 1 and 2 of the programme. An example of how I try to promote dialogue and teamwork, in face to face sessions, can be seen in the video (Farren, 2008h). This video was taken during the first class session in year one of semester (term) two, 2005. At the start of the class-session I asked students to work in groups and relate the module goals to their own needs and interests. Hattie and Timperley (2007) state that, 'teachers often assume that students share a commitment to academic goals, whereas the reality is that developing this shared commitment needs to be nurtured and built' (p. 89). In the video, Rachel Hobson – an educator from an e-Learning company – reports on behalf of her group on their particular areas of interest. She also emphasises the usefulness of the learning journals and how the group would like to continue to use journals throughout the programme.

In 2005 I introduced a practicum element as an option for the dissertation element in order to encourage participants to develop multimedia narratives for explaining educational influences in learning (Farren, 2005; Farren & Whitehead, 2006). This provided participants with the opportunity to design and develop a multimedia learning artefact with 10,000 words of supporting text rather than the traditional 20,000-word dissertation. Participants have the opportunity to present their artefacts and provide an analysis as part of a presentation forum, for evaluation by their tutors and peers. In her Masters research inquiry Yvonne Crotty (Crotty, 2005) developed a visual narrative of learning to express her educational values. Yvonne now coordinates the e-Learning strand of the programme and has redesigned the multimedia elements of the programme and related them more fully to the overall programme modules. With Yvonne's influence a number of participants are now exploring visual forms of representation (Crotty, 2010).

Building new international networks and communities of research interest has enabled us to further develop our expertise in the learning opportunities opened up by digital technology. The e-Life Connecting People Research Project (Farren & Crotty, 2007), supported by DCU's Learning Innovation Unit, makes use of e-media accounts of learning to demonstrate how practitioner-researchers, in a variety of workplace-settings, are improving practice and generating knowledge through their action research inquiries. In order to provide the educational opportunities that digital technologies are opening up we are also networking with colleagues across the University as we explore the infrastructure required to provide teachers and students in higher education with enhanced learning opportunities to access digital video and TV recordings. This will strengthen and support the current use of online and flexible learning resources by providing access to visual educational resources.

The innovative learning approaches in the e-Learning strand support practitioners, from a variety of workplace settings in bringing their own embodied knowledge into the public domain (Snow, 2001; Hiebert, Gallimore, & Stigler, 2002) as they create new ways of using digital technology in their workplaces. The following two video clips (Farren, 2008b, 2008c) were taken in May 2007. The students were invited to present their research work before the final submission of practicum and dissertation research in June 2007. The session was attended by Dr. Jack Whitehead, University of Bath, UK.

You can watch the video of Yvonne Mulligan, (Farren, 2008b), a nurse tutor, discuss how she designed, developed, implemented and evaluated an e-Learning tutorial. Taking a living educational theory approach, Yvonne places herself at the centre of the research inquiry as she asks, how can I improve my practice? In the video, she explains her aim in developing an e-learning artefact and in providing an environment that supports and facilitates learning.

Donal O'Mahony (Farren, 2008c) discusses how he introduced web-based technologies into his History class in order to encourage his pupils to think critically. Donal discusses how he engages with the philosophy underpinning the Masters programme as he tried to work in a collaborative, dialogical way with his students.

The presentations helped the students to reflect on their own learning in the research inquiry. It also helped them to consider the data they had collected and determine whether they could show evidence of improvement in student learning.

## DEVELOPING A POSTDOCTORAL RESEARCH PROGRAMME

I have endeavoured to engage students at undergraduate and postgraduate levels in 'critical inquiry' (Skilbeck, 2001, p. 94) as they apply their learning to innovative educational research. In the case of developing research at undergraduate level this involved the establishing of the Setanta Project, between the School of Computer Applications and St. Aidan's Secondary School. It was intended that the students and teachers in St. Aiden's would learn useful ICT skills and learn from technology. At the same time, undergraduate students would develop their technical skills and skills of collaboration, as they worked with real users to complete project work for their B.Sc. in Computer Applications. A paper entitled *Setanta: A University-School Collaboration Project* (Farren, Mooney & Pentony, 2001), traces the development of appropriate courseware in response to the specific needs of Secondary pupils studying Art at Leaving Certificate level.

The impact of new technologies for the dissemination of knowledge is now acknowledged by the Higher Education Authority (HEA), Ireland. 'The intellectual effectiveness and progress of the widespread research community may be continually enhanced where the community has access and recourse to as wide a range of shared knowledge and findings as possible.' In the same way, Shulman points out that if pedagogy is going to be an important part of scholarship there must be evidence of it, 'becom[ing] visible through artefacts that capture its richness and complexity' (Shulman, 2004, p. 142).

In order to meet the needs of individuals in a variety of workplace-settings and support them in their lifelong learning, my research programme focuses on the educational opportunities for learning opened up by digital technologies. I am currently supporting doctoral research students as they seek to live their values more fully in their practice as they create knowledge of the educational uses of digital technologies in their various workplace contexts. It is my intention that my post-doctoral research programme will benefit the Higher Education research community and the wider society.


**CONCLUSION**

In this paper, I hope that my influence is seen in the opportunities I provide for practitioner-researchers to reflect critically on their learning through peer validation meetings. I am conscious of the need for each individual to have the educational space to develop their own voice. I have endeavoured to create an educational space for practitioner-researchers to articulate the values that give meaning and purpose to their life and work. The constellation of values I use to explain my educational influence emphasises the flow of energy and meaning in Celtic Spirituality and the educational opportunities for learning opened up by digital technology. I hope that I have shown how my embodied educational values can now be seen to be communicable standards of judgment.

My research programme has been founded on the belief that digital technologies can provide genuine life-long learning opportunities within Higher Education and the wider society. The applied learning approach of a living educational theory can support knowledge creation and contribute to an 'epistemology of practice' (Schön, 1995).

**REFERENCES**

Barnett, R. (2000). *Realizing the university in an age of supercomplexity.* Bucks: Open University Press.

Bertrand, Y. (2003). *Contemporary theories and practice in education* (2nd ed.). Madison, Wisconsin: Atwood Publishing.

Bognar, B. & Zovko, M. (2008). Pupils as action researchers: Improving something important in our lives. *Educational Journal of Living Theories, 1*(1), 1-49. Retrieved August 28, 2010, from http://ejolts.net/node/82

Bruce Ferguson, P. (2008). Increasing inclusion in educational research. *Research Intelligence, 102,* 24-25.

Cloke, C., Farren, M. & Barrington, J. (2006). Interactive video and group learning: Two action inquiry based evaluations. *British Journal of Educational Technology, 27*(2), 84-91.

Clandinin, J. & Connelly, M. (2004). *Narrative inquiry: Experience and story in qualitative research.* San Francisco: Jossey Bass.

Crotty, Y. (2005). *How do I create a visual narrative and contribute to the learning of others?* (Unpublished master's thesis). Dublin City University, Ireland.

Crotty, Y. (2010). Should We Judge a Book by its Cover? Addressing Visual Literacy and Creativity in Higher Education. *Diverse International Conference, Portland, Maine, USA*

DCU Foresight Report. (2008). *Managing our destiny in uncertain times.* Retrieved September 18, 2008, from http://www.ryanacademy.ie/themes/foresight/index.shtml

Eisner, E. (2005). *Re-imagining schools: The selected works of Elliot W. Eisner.* Oxford & New York: Routledge.

Eisner, E. (1997). The promise and perils of alternative forms of data representation. *Educational Researcher, 26*(6), 4-10.

Eisner, E. (1993). Forms of understanding and the future of educational research. *Educational Researcher, 22*(7), 5-11.

Eisner, E. (1988). The primacy of experience and the politics of method. *Educational Researcher, 17*(5), 15-20.

Farren, M. (2000). *Using information and communications technology to support action research and distance learning.* Retrieved August 28, 2010, from http://webpages.dcu.ie/~farrenm/esai.html

Farren, M. (2006). *How am I creating a pedagogy of the unique through a web of betweenness?* (Doctoral dissertation, University of Bath, UK). Retrieved August 28, 2010, from http://www.actionresearch.net/farren.shtml

Farren, M. (2008a). E-learning and action research as transformative practice. *Innovate, 5*(1). Retrieved October, 1, 2008, from http://www.innovateonline.info/index.php?view=article&id=543

Farren, M. (2008b, March 17). E-learning and nurse education [Video file].
      Retrieved      August      28,      2010,      from
      http://www.youtube.com/watch?v=JvlY6tlHhFk

Farren, M. (2008c, March 17). Critical thinking and online learning [Video file].
      Retrieved      August      28,      2010,      from
      http://www.youtube.com/watch?v=PcTrDrsQGY0

Farren, M. (2008d, August 23). Introducing a new writing approach [Video file].
      Retrieved      August      28,      2010,      from
      http://www.youtube.com/watch?v=UvYPuenLeLM

Farren, M. (2008e, August 23). Explaining mathematical thinking [Video file].
      Retrieved      August      28,      2010,      from
      http://www.youtube.com/watch?v=BMJPifbM-Ok

Farren, M. (2008f, August 27). Concept-mapping and problem solving [Video
      file].      Retrieved      August      28,      2010,      from
      http://www.youtube.com/watch?v=IETMk7C6Es0

Farren, M. (2008g, August 27). Action research cycles [Video file]. Retrieved 28
      August 2010 from to http://www.youtube.com/watch?v=mG1KK8VElZk

Farren, M. (2008h, September 18). Co-creating an educational space [Video file].
      Retrieved      August      28,      2010,      from
      http://www.youtube.com/watch?v=P8CYIZN6nI8

Farren, M. & Crotty, Y. (2007). *E-life connecting people project.* Retrieved
      September 1, 2007, from http://www.jackwhitehead.com/farren/eLife.htm

Farren, M. & Whitehead, J. (2005). *Educational influences in learning with visual
      narratives.* Paper and video-conference presentation at the 5th DIVERSE
      International Conference on Video and Videoconferencing in Education,
      Glasgow,      UK.      Retrieved      August      28,      2010,      from
      http://www.actionresearch.net/writings/monday/mfjwwebped2.htm

Farren, M., with Mooney, M. & Pentony, D. (2001). *Setanta: A university-school
      collaboration      project.*      Retrieved      September      30,      2008,      from
      http://odtl.dcu.ie/wp/2001/odtl-2001-01.html

Flanagan, F. (2002). *An educational inquiry into the use of concept-mapping and
      multimedia in the understanding of maths.* (Masters dissertation, Dublin
      City University, Ireland). Summary retrieved August 28, 2010, from
      http://webpages.dcu.ie/%7Efarrenm/fionntech.PDF

Garvey, C. (2002). *An educational inquiry into the potential use of a course
      management tool to support learning in an all-girls science class.* Dublin:
      Dublin City University. Summary retrieved August 28, 2010, from
      http://webpages.dcu.ie/%7Efarrenm/christech.PDF

Hattie, J. & Timperley, H. (2007). The power of feedback. *Educational Research*,
      *77*(1), 81-112.

Hiebert, J., Gallimore R., & Stigler, J. (2002). A knowledge base for the teaching profession: What would it look like and how can we get one? *Review of Educational Research*, *31*(5), 3–15. Retrieved September 30, 2008, from http://www.aera.net/uploadedFiles/Journals_and_Publications/Journals/Ed ucational_Researcher/3105/3105_Hiebert.pdf

Higher Education Authority of Ireland. (2008). *Higher education authority policy relating to: The open access repository of published research.* Retrieved September          30,          2008,          from http://www.hea.ie/files/files/file/Open%20Access%20pdf_.pdf

Kilpatrick, W. H. (1951). Crucial issues in current educational theory. *Educational Theory*, *1*(1), 1-8.

Know thyself. (2008, October 5). In *Wikipedia, The Free Encyclopedia*. Retrieved October          13,          2008,          from http://en.wikipedia.org/w/index.php?title=Know_thyself&oldid=243255207

Laidlaw, M., (1994). The educational potential of dialogical focus in an action research inquiry. *Action Research Journal, 2*(1), 224-241.

Loughran, J., Hamilton, M.L., LaBoskey, V.K. & Russell, T.L. (Eds.). (2004). *The international handbook of self-study of teaching and teacher education practices.* Dordrecht: Kluwer Academic Publishers.

McNiff, J. & Whitehead, J. (2006). *All you want to know about action research.* London: Sage Publications.

O'Donohue, J. (2003). *Divine beauty: The invisible embrace.* London: Transworld Publishers.

Rayner, A. (2004). *Inclusionality: The science, art and spirituality of place, space and       evolution.*       Retrieved       August       24,       2008,       from http://people.bath.ac.uk/bssadmr/inclusionality

Rowland, S. (2000). *The enquiring university teacher.* Buckingham: The Society for Research into Higher Education and Open University Press.

Ryan, M. (2002). *An educational inquiry into the potential use of games in a junior primary school: Enabling mathematical thinking and understanding* (Master's thesis, Dublin City University, Ireland). Retrieved       August       28,       2010,       from http://webpages.dcu.ie/~farrenm/mairead.pdf

Schön, D. (1995). Knowing-in-action: The new scholarship requires a new epistemology. *Change, 27*(6), 27-34.

Shor, I. & Freire, P. (1987). *A pedagogy for liberation: Dialogues on transforming education.* Mass: Bergin and Garvey Publishers, Inc..

Skilbeck, M. (2001). *The university challenged: A review of international trends and issues with particular reference to Ireland.* Retrieved August 10, 2008,                                                                        from http://www.iua.ie/publications/documents/publications/2001/Report_11.pdf

Snow, C. (2001). Knowing what we know: Children, teachers, researchers. *Educational Researcher, 30*(7), 3-9.

Tobin, B. (2002). *An educational inquiry into the implementation of the approach to writing outlined in the English Language curriculum.* (Master's thesis, Dublin City University, Ireland). Retrieved August 28, 2010, from http://webpages.dcu.ie/%7Efarrenm/bernie.pdf

Walker, M. (1999, September). *Doing criticality: Mapping a HE project.* Paper presented at the British Educational Research Association (BERA) Annual Conference, Brighton, UK.

Webb, G. (1996). *Understanding staff development.* Buckingham: Society for Research into Higher Education (SHRE)/Open University Press.

Whitehead, J. (1989a). How do we improve research-based professionalism in education? A question which includes action research, educational theory and the politics of educational knowledge. *The British Educational Research Journal, 15*(1), 3-17.

Whitehead, J. (1989b). Creating a living educational theory from questions of the kind, 'How do I improve my practice?' *Cambridge Journal of Education, 19*(1), 41-52.

Whitehead, J. (2004). What counts as evidence in self-studies of teacher-education practices? In J. Loughran, M.L. Hamilton, V.K. LaBoskey & T.L. Russell (Eds.). *The international handbook of self-study of teaching and teacher education practices* (pp. 871-904). Dordrecht: Kluwer Academic Publishers.

Whitehead, J. (2005). *How can we improve the educational influences of our teacher-researcher quests?* Keynote Presentation to the 12th International Conference of Teacher Research at McGill University, Montreal, Canada. Retrieved August 5, 2008, from http://www.jackwhitehead.com/ictr05/jwictr05key.htm

Winograd, T. (1996). *Bringing Design to Software.* New York: ACM Press.

# PUPILS AS ACTION RESEARCHERS: IMPROVING SOMETHING IMPORTANT IN OUR LIVES

Branko Bognar, Croatia

Marica Zovko, Croatia

## PHILOSOPHICAL BACKGROUND

When more than 60 years ago Kurt Lewin and John Collier promoted the idea of action research, they were not just concerned with methodology. Their central interest was far deeper. They realised that science, stripped of its sophisticated methodologies, could serve evil as well as good:

> Unfortunately there is nothing in social laws and social research which will force the practitioner toward the good. Science gives more freedom and power to both the doctor and the murderer, to democracy and Fascism. The social scientist should recognize his responsibility also in respect to this. (Lewin, 1946, p. 213)

By putting a clear emphasis on values Lewin and Collier stressed the importance of the philosophical and creative aspects of science. As Collier (1949) wrote:

> The whole man is the productive social researcher: to wit, that the feeling-out, the tracing, and the persuasively and courageous statement of the

implications of research findings is the way that the findings are brought into world meaning, the way that values generically emerge from scientific findings, and one of the ways that social science delivers its weight to the world. (As cited in Cooke, 2004, p. 27)

Although this approach was not immediately acceptable to a wider academic audience (Hodgkinson, 1957) and even to Lewin's closest co-workers (Lippitt, 1949, as cited in Cooke, 2002; and Lippitt, 1950), contemporary approaches increasingly acknowledged the importance of values in an action research inquiry (Foshay & Wann, 1954; Kemmis & McTaggart, 2005; McNiff & Whitehead, 2006; Reason & Bradbury, 2006; Stringer, 1996; Whitehead, 1989). This approach was seen as very different to the positivistic approach in which researchers are supposed to refrain from expressing personal values so they can gain an 'objective' understanding of social phenomena. However, by repressing the integration of their values into their research, scientists merely realise someone else's aims, bringing into question fundamental presuppositions about professionalism and autonomy (Stenhouse, 1975, p. 144). Indeed, the value-neutral approach is itself value-driven, but in this case it is the values of the person or organisational body that buys the skills of the scientific research that prevail, and these are mostly representative of ruling structures, or sometimes powerful or rich people who are able to engage experts to forge their own desired ends. Social scientists support hidden value-systems, often based on authoritarianism, with an orientation towards profit. Independent professionals can observe problems and then try actively to contribute to their resolution.

Claiming particular values does not necessarily represent an effort to achieve personal advantage: on the contrary it can be an expression of professional freedom as well as a sense of responsibility for creating the world we live in. The main precondition of any responsible contribution to a better world presumes that we are concerned about freedom for everyone. Hegel (1900) claimed that freedom is not just a quality of Spirit but a fundamental pre-requisite: 'All the qualities of Spirit exist only through Freedom; that all are but a means for attaining Freedom; that all seek and produce this and this alone' (p. 17). As opposed to matter, Spirit has a self-contained existence, grounded in freedom:

> For if I am dependent, my being is referred to something else which I am not; I cannot exist independently of something external. I am free, on the contrary, when my existence depends upon myself. This self-contained existence of Spirit is none other than self-consciousness—consciousness of one's own being. Two things must be distinguished in consciousness; first, the fact that I know; secondly, what I know. In self consciousness these are merged in one; for Spirit knows itself. It involves an appreciation of its own nature, as also an energy enabling it to realize itself; to make itself actually that which it is potentially. (Hegel, 1900, p. 17)

This leads us to another important question: What is the essence, nature or truth of a self-aware and free subject? This does not refer to what already is, that is to say Being and knowledge about it, but that it is true in that sense in which it exists as a potential. Whatever has potential is not simply a matter of scientific knowing but creativity; and only that is able to bring an idea into being. On the other hand social science inquiries try to put emphasis on what is, not on what ought to be:

> Social philosophers liberally mixed their observations of what happened around them, their speculations about why, and their ideas about how things ought to be. Although modern social scientists may do the same from time to time, it is important to realize that social science has to do with how things are and why. (Babbie, 1992, p. 28)

If this pre-condition were applied to the situation in Auschwitz during the Second World War, it would mean the social scientist was not expected to change a particular situation, but only to make an effort to detect the precise situation and then find a related cause. Everything else would be beyond their immediate responsibility. However, determining any *social truth* in Auschwitz at an epistemological level would be meaningless, because any such inquiry would deny human potential. The results of such research would be factual but meaningless in relation to a better world. We believe it is the duty of every human being to try to change such *untruthful* situations, and not merely to enquire about them *scientifically* (Bognar, 2001a, p. 75).

Through creativity, freedom is not just a possibility but a fully-realised
humanity – our culture. However, from ancient times the most important problem
of scientific thought has been the separation of two important aspects of the
human mind. Aristotle divided the mind between the theoretical and practical:

> Whereas in the theoretical mind, the observation of thinking or reason,
> which is not interested in action - it is inactive since it deals with that
> which is unchangeable, that could not be different, i.e. with that which is
> inevitable. Whereas the practical mind, or moral will, deals with what
> could be different, since it is not inevitable but on the contrary possible.
> Aristotle also recognized that for the theoretical mind, i.e. observing
> thinking or scientific reason, good and evil are not anything else other than
> simply truth and untruth. Truth is goodness and untruth is evil. Therefore,
> in the theoretical mind the separation of knowledge from values does not
> exist, they are interlaced. But the theoretical mind per se is meant as
> inactive, contemplative, pure observing. It is not involved in the existence
> of its matter (which is what it is by itself, and which does not depend of
> observing subject). (Polić[4], 2006, p. 15)

It is only the modern concept of practice, that in fact means creativity
(Kangrga, 1984, p. 23) that can prevail over such a separation of theory and
practice: only in the act of creativity is there no separation of artistry, theory,
action, and epistemology. *Creativity seeks for truth, but its truth is not something
that already exists; on the contrary its truth is that it does not exist yet, but that it
should be produced, created.* Truth for a composer is the music they want to
create; truth for a teacher is the educational environment they want to attain. And
this truth cannot be actualised through scientific research whose aim is making a
perfect description of an imperfect situation, but only by our personal engagement
in the processes of creativity grounded in our values – and their main precondition
- freedom.

Each practice possesses its own medium of expression: for music it is
sounds, for poetry it is words, and for education it is the relationships between the
people learning together. If a composer wants to make their music available to
other people as some kind of cultural deed they can express it in a symbolic form,

---

[4]     Trans. Bognar.

e.g. in the form of an orchestral score, or as music recorded on a compact disc. In the same way we need to make available our educational experiences, but not merely as theories that represent abstract experiences, but as living forms (Whitehead & McNiff, 2006) which reveal the interlinking of our theorising and actions. Representation of our creativity, or methodology, should also be creative. Therefore a methodology should not restrict practice, but serve as a medium of its own representation, understanding and dissemination.

Action research represents one such possibility of considerate, deliberate and creative action that finds its challenges in various social situations but does not intend to give final answers to all the problems practitioners face. The problems themselves serve as motivation for devising solutions that are historically and contextually fulfilling. The solutions practitioners create should respond to the requirements of specific contexts and the times in which they have emerged.

Thus the eternal quest for an oracle to offer universal solutions for all specific problems practitioners can face in their everyday practice ceases to be appropriate. Each genuinely creative solution is deeply connected to the particular context in which the creators are taking action. If somebody tries to replicate something out of a particular historical context, then it is merely a copy that through replication becomes dimmer, finally becoming a caricature of its former creativity. This can easily be discerned in art, but it is visible in other creative fields including education. We are not saying that a creative deed is valuable only in an ephemeral historical context, after which its significance ceases to exist. In fact a genuinely creative deed possesses universal value since it indicates what is left behind – and this is the creative human being. In a creative process everything already made (culture in the widest sense) serves as a means or inspiration for new creation.

Therefore, the final meaning and purpose of creativity are not revealed from within a single deed or in a theoretical explanation of the process, but in the essential energies that gave rise to the deed. By creating something a human being produces their own world and also their own creative impetus. It means that the end-purpose of creativity is the human being who has produced their own humanity – their innate culture.

Following this logic, the purposes of science therefore cannot be reduced to the excavation of more and more theoretical explanations of current situations based on a ritual application of statistical or qualitative procedures. Instead it can become part of a creative process oriented to life with the awareness, thoughts and inclination that it should be enabled differently (Kangrga, 1989, p. 35). In a creative approach to science, theory does not exist only in relation to what already exists as a mere epistemological function, but represents the genuine birth of the creative process, referring to that which is not yet realised, but which could be.

In that sense, *we believe the central point of an action research inquiry is not merely acquiring knowledge, but developing our creative potentials and it is only from them that we are able to create new realities, and thereby new knowledge.* The focus of such an approach to action research is therefore in our own practice, not other people's. At the centre of an action research process are active and autonomous people who:

> ...speak on their own behalf and encourage others to do the same... In living theory approaches researchers focus on themselves and their own learning. They recognise that they are always in company with others, so reflecting on one's practice with others means investigating how one can ensure that the practice is educational, that is, mutually beneficial and life-affirming to all parties. In undertaking action research a researcher is investigating how they can improve their own learning so that they are better placed to help others. (McNiff with Whitehead, 2002, p. 89)

We began our research from the assumption that action research denotes a process of systematic and productive actions. These presume a philosophical consideration of values, creatively and in visionary ways – devising new challenges, actively participating in the realisation of productive ideas, gathering data about the process of creation, (self)critical reflections, monitoring of the whole process, publishing the results of our efforts (theorising, (co)creating, reflecting and learning) and the generalization of the living theories that have emerged from the process of (co)creation. *Generalizations in this case can only be obtained actively - through new processes of (co)creation so that our living theories could become part of our local culture and perhaps contribute to culture at an international level.*

This paper is a short story of life-long endeavour for creative approaches to action research that have been grounded in our shared sense of freedom as the most important value. The philosophy fuelling this effort has allowed us to be aware of what we wanted to do and what constituted the essence of our educational activities. This is not mere armchair-philosophy committed to abstract academic discussion, but a philosophy which remains a part of our creative lives. This is a living form of philosophy.


## PERSONAL AND PROFESSIONAL CONTEXTS

### Marica's personal and professional contexts

I teach in a small, rural school in a village called Mihaljevci. This is the same village I was born in and where I met my husband with whom I now have two grown-up children. I grew up in a traditional worker's family that did not nurture my freedom and independence. I graduated from secondary nursing-school and my parents wanted me to study medicine. Nevertheless I enrolled in the Teachers Academy in Zagreb at my husband's suggestion. When I had finished at the teacher's faculty in 1985 I was not able to find a full-time job and because of the bad economic situation at the beginning of the nineties I had to spend several years abroad working as a nurse in a hospital. Although it was not what I wanted I gained useful experiences from the German school-system as my children attended school in Frankfurt where we then lived. Finally, when my husband and I got a full time job in Croatia in 1997 we decided to return and continue our private and professional lives in our homeland.

I was lucky to be hired in the school in the village where I was born and owned a family house. I was finally able to devote myself to the job that was becoming a vocation. In the beginning we – the teachers in the school – organised parents to help us in the arrangement of the school environment. I also embarked on my own professional development, which became more intensive when I met Branko Bognar who was organising a learning-community with the aim of helping teachers improving their practice.

My school, where there are three other teachers, was built 30 years ago and was recently refurbished. Apart from the children from Mihaljevci, pupils from two neighbouring villages also attend this school. At the time of our research we only had two classrooms with old furniture, a hall and an improvised teachers' room.

Teaching in the school is organised into two shifts and between those shifts there is a programme of pre-school education for children who are going to carry on with their schooling the following year. Teaching for the morning shift starts at 8 o'clock and lasts until 12.15. Afternoon school begins at 13.30 and finishes at 17.35. The lunch hour, as in other Croatian schools, lasts 45 minutes and there is a break between each lesson of five minutes. There is also a long break that lasts for twenty minutes after the second lesson. Because there is no bell in the school, teachers decide for themselves how long the various activities last. This means that some classes are longer or shorter than the designated times. Teachers don't have this kind of autonomy in the bigger schools where lessons are determined by the school bell. Teaching is organised in a framework of six subjects, which are not connected but systemised through their orientation towards propositional knowledge.

I started my collaboration with Branko in 2000 after he informed me about his new project on teachers' professional development and action research. Although I derived theoretical knowledge and information about action research within the context of the learning-community led by Branko, I lacked sufficient confidence to take the initiative to go it alone. At this stage I was a reflective practitioner, but had not made the leap to being a fully-fledged action researcher. I was exchanging emails with Branko on a daily basis – a dialogical form of learning through e-correspondence. This process seemed to offer me the learning-opportunities I needed at this stage in my professional development. I tended towards this style of learning rather than a more community-based one. However, participation in the learning-community encouraged me to start with changes in my teaching (Bognar, 2008e).

During this period I started to consider my own practice more deeply, and for the first time realised it was important to recognise the individuality of my pupils. I also recognised how much this viewpoint deviated from a more traditional view of teaching. During the three years of co-operation and action research inquiries I facilitated them in free play (Isenberg & Jalongo, 1997, p. 41). I also tried to help them with their socialisation and in their critical thinking skills. These aspects comprised my action research cycles.

### Branko's professional context

I was employed as a teacher at the end of the eighties and after six years spent in the classroom I completed a study of Pedagogy and started to work in another school, named after the poet Vladimir Nazor, in Slavonski Brod, which is 50 km away from Marica's school. The role of a pedagogue in Croatian schools isn't fully specified but is generally dependent on the expectations of the head-teacher. Unfortunately in most schools a pedagogue's job is reduced to various administrative, organisational and technical activities. I found such practices to be unsatisfactory. In the first year of my pedagogical practice I was disappointed because as a teacher I'd been able to utilise my creativity more effectively. My technological knowledge enabled me to complete administrative tasks very quickly. So, I taught other school administrators and the head-teacher how to use a computer and in that way I freed up my time for more meaningful tasks: for example, teachers' professional education, or working with pupils. I was able to inaugurate and head-up schools' projects. In a short time those kinds of tasks were to become perhaps my most significant endeavours.

At the end of the nineties I enrolled in a postgraduate study of Pedagogy at the Philosophy Faculty in Zagreb. Then, for the first time, I discovered action research and decided to achieve my MA research in that discipline and to help other educators to become action researchers as well. I also tried to popularise action research in a Croatian educational context in general (Bognar, 2001b, 2004b, 2006a, 2006b) and in my school in particular.

Marica and I started our intensive professional cooperation in 2000 in the project: 'A critical emancipatory approach to the professional development of primary school teachers,' which I had begun as my postgraduate research. The aims of the project were to facilitate reflective practice and action research processes - to help teachers to undertake new roles in our Croatian context as reflective practitioners and action researchers. Overall my intentions were to move from a technocratic to a more creative view of teaching and learning.

Most participants of this project were teachers from my school and some of them were from other schools in the area, like Marica. Because the place she lived and worked in was 50 km away, she had to drive to my school every second Wednesday evening of the month to attend workshops/meetings of the learning communities. In addition to meetings, participants visited each others' lessons, which were videotaped, and there were occasions for me to visit the project-participants' classrooms, some of which were also video-taped.

After the end of the whole project three teachers, including Marica, decided to carry on working with me. We wanted to start a new project with the aim of working on several quality action research inquiries and publications, initially as a book, and then later, when opportunities arose, to publish papers abroad. To ensure our continuing co-operation we decided to organise regular meetings on Saturdays and to communicate by using a forum at the internet (http://mzu.sbnet.hr/).


## OUR EDUCATIONAL VALUES

### Marica's values

For the first time I clearly began to understand my values when I joined in the project: *A critical emancipatory approach to the professional development of primary school teachers*. Within the learning-community we talked about the meaning of autonomously-developed values and tried to work out the difference between espoused theories and theories-in-use (Argyris & Schön, 1975). This helped me in a thorough consideration of my educational practice and accelerated the processes of change. I wrote about the process of taking over the responsibility for defining and living out my values at the Moodle site that Branko had established for the learning and cooperation of action researchers in his Ph.D. project:

> I became acquainted with the concept of personal educational values several years ago when I took part in Branko Bognar's projects. I have to confess that working in a traditional school only required me to fulfil the official curriculum based on some general social values and aims. At that time I did not consider my personal values to have any special meaning. I often call this phase of my practice, 'teacher-craftswoman' as it was not really important to reflect on my job, but only to follow guidelines from my superiors. Today such a relationship with my job is past history, but more about this process another time. (M. Zovko, personal communication, October 8, 2005)

After active participation in the project-team and constructive discussions with Branko as well as other participants, I then considered freedom to be the main value I was endeavouring to fulfil in my life. However, for a long time freedom had been a neglected value in my life. It seemed to me that it would never have been achievable in my current circumstances until then. I always tried to find a justification for the limitations of the system, and in my wish to satisfy official expectations I was not able to live out my professional as well as personal freedoms as I was afraid of the responsibility that freedom demands. When other people made the decisions about everything, I did not have to take the responsibility for the results of my activities. When my values developed and I started to live out my value of freedom, I started to respect the freedom of my pupils as well. Alongside freedom, cooperation began to have a significant place in my value system, and I started to become more aware of other people's values.

I became aware of my living contradiction (Whitehead & McNiff, 2006) when I watched my teaching on the video that Branko had organised. I recognised my domination of the classroom and the lack of my students' freedom to express their ideas and creative abilities. However, even at that time (which I call the period of being a teacher-technician) I was still able to allow students their own creativity but only as an addition to my lesson and not as its central part. Namely, at the end of teaching my student Anica informed me that she had prepared a play with puppets, and so I allowed her to perform it for us (Bognar, 2008d).

### Branko's values

I was aware from early adolescence that freedom was the most important value I wanted to live out. I considered freedom something that anyone could aspire to through their own creativity. A deep appreciation of freedom and creativity as my driving values were the main reason I decided to take on action research as the creative approach in my own practice and in a wider educational context.

During the nineties in Croatian society and in wider regions, despite an ostensible acceptance of democracy, the opposite processes were actually taking place (Čular, 2000; Lalović, 2000). This was particularly apparent in the school system under the strong control of the state-legislatures. Every liberal idea and initiative was under suspicion and instead of opening towards the needs of children, schools came under the influence of contemporary political interests. It meant that everything significant was decided outside of the schools themselves[5].

In such circumstances it was not easy to live out the value of freedom or to avoid a clash with the authorities. In spite of that both of us (independently of each other) tried to live out our values, striving to put an emphasis on the methodologies of active learning, education for human rights, peace studies (Branko) and critical thinking (Marica). It is important to emphasise that this inquiry started at the time when, in our wider social context, real democratic changes had begun, without which we could not have made significant improvements in our practice.

After three years of trying to match her teaching to the needs of her pupils Marica seemed to lack ideas on how to continue with the improvement of her teaching in accordance with her educational values. At a meeting of the learning-community organised at the end of 2003 I suggested she try to help her pupils in their independent action research inquiries. She accepted this suggestion with enthusiasm. Therefore, we started this process of action research with the following question: *How can we help the ten-year old pupils to become autonomous action researchers?*

---

[5]     At present in Croatia the curriculum is strongly subject-oriented, with an emphasis on the cognitive capacity of students. The central authority (The Ministry, in co-operation with national expert bodies) is responsible for: the process of curriculum-design on different administrative levels; the collection and dissemination of curriculum-related information; understanding the needs of societal development, and reflecting these in the education system; defining basic and new skills (particularly language learning, computer-use, communication skills, problem solving capacity, teamwork, project orientation etc.).
The process of curriculum-design takes no account of either the issue of decentralisation or the relationship between central and local decision-making. The legislative, regulatory and financial framework does not leave room for qualified local actors being involved in the design or flexible adaptation of curricula to new social needs and labour market-requirements. The university and teacher-training institutions, the teachers associations, NGOs, the social partners – including the very active Chambers of Craft and Commerce – are now seen as outsiders rather than legitimate stakeholders in the system which should play a role in curriculum-design and articulation. (OECD, 2001, p. 12)

## ACTION RESEARCH PLAN

### What we knew about pupils as action researchers

John Dewey was one of the first advocates of the notion of students' inquiries. He considered that thinking represented a basic method of intelligent learning and that thinking was, in essence, a process of inquiry:

> To say that thinking occurs with reference to situations which are still going on, and incomplete, is to say that thinking occurs when things are uncertain or doubtful or problematic. Only what is finished, completed, is wholly assured. Where there is reflection there is suspense. The object of thinking is to help reach a conclusion, to project a possible termination on the basis of what is already given. Certain other facts about thinking accompany this feature. Since the situation in which thinking occurs is a doubtful one, thinking is a process of inquiry, of looking into things, of investigating. Acquiring is always secondary, and instrumental to the act of inquiring. It is seeking, a quest, for something that is not at hand. (Dewey, 1921, p. 173)

For Dewey (1921), thinking based on inquiry 'includes all of these steps, - the sense of a problem, the observation of conditions, the formation and rational elaboration of a suggested conclusion, and the active experimental testing' (p. 174).

It is important to mention, however, that Dewey considered experimental research in physics to be a model to which social sciences should also aspire (Dewey, 1929, p. 251). From that we can conclude that students' inquiries should be a kind of experimental research distinct from positivist and post-positivist scientific paradigms (Lincoln & Guba, 2000, p. 165; Heron & Reason, 1997). In terms of our intention to help pupils to become action researchers, Dewey's idea was not fully appropriate since action research and experimental inquiries belong to different research- paradigms. But we accepted Dewey's ideas of progressive and democratic education anyway, based as they were on active, experiential learning in which students autonomously determine and define their own problems; this represents the foundation of the project-method configured by William Heard Kilpatrick (1918). He emphasised the importance of purposeful acts in which the purpose was determined by students:

As the purposeful act is thus the typical unit of the worthy life in a democratic society, so also should it be made the typical unit of school-procedure? We of America have for years increasingly desired that education be considered as life itself and not as a mere preparation for later living. The conception before us promises a definite step toward the attainment of this end. If the purposeful act be in reality the typical unit of the worthy life, then it follows that to base education on purposeful acts is exactly to identify the process of education with worthy living itself. The two become then the same. All the arguments for placing education on a life basis seem, to me at any rate, to concur in support of this thesis. On this basis education has become life. And if the purposeful act thus makes of education life itself, could we reasoning in advance expect to find a better preparation for later life than practice in living now? (Kilpatrick, 1918)

We accepted Dewey and Kilpatrick's idea that the purpose of students' inquiries, and thereby students' action research inquiries, should not be education for a future life, but that education *is* life. In that sense, if students do not choose a concern for their action research by themselves, but it is done by adults, as, for example in the research of Atweh, Christensen and Dornan (1998), then it is questionable whether this should be considered full-blown students' action research. In that particular example of participatory action research, poor students in the final year of a Brisbane middle-school were invited to participate in a three-year project whose aim was 'increasing the participation in higher education of students from low socio-economic background schools' (p. 117).

Students had an active role in all phases of the project, except in the determination of the problems emerging from the value-orientation of 'four university researchers who shared a commitment to social justice and equity issues' (Atweh, Christensen & Dornan, 1998, p. 121).

The project consisted of three phases:

(a) attending training sessions at the university; (b) planning the study and gathering the data required to identify the need to increase student participation in higher education from their locality; (c) analysing the data and writing a report from this investigation with appropriate recommendations. (Atweh, Christensen & Dornan, 1998, p. 121)

Although most of the students did not seem to feel alienated from the aims of the project two of them expressed their sense of a lack of proprietorship:

For one student, the input from the university staff gave the students a sense of lack of ownership over the project. She felt that 'We were doing it all for them sort of thing'. To her the task was a job that you had to do to please the employer. Another student felt that the students were used as guinea pigs in an experiment to see how the methodology can be utilised. (Atweh, Christensen & Dornan, 1998, p. 128)

In our opinion those reactions were the result of students not feeling included in the very important part of an action research inquiry – the selection of the concern. However, this project allowed students to contribute to the main project-aim, thereby increasing the participation in Higher Education of students from schools in low socio-economic areas with their action research reports. Ten minutes of video-footage about the project were made with the aim of helping students from similar schools to engage in similar projects.

We also decided to videotape the presentations by the pupil action researchers and in that way make them available to students and teachers from other schools. As our pupils were ten-year-olds we were not sure whether they would be able to take control of the complex processes of action research. We were encouraged by the experiences of researchers from different parts of the world presented in Alderson's (2000) account, which showed that even pupils from the early years of primary schooling were able to conduct 'child-centred research'. Alderson noted several different levels of control-sharing and of children's involvement in the research process:

At the lowest levels is the pretence of shared work: manipulation, decoration and tokenism. The next levels involve actual participation: children being assigned to tasks although being informed and consulted and adults initiating but also sharing decisions with children. The top two levels concern projects more fully initiated and directed by children. (Alderson, 2000, p. 248)

We realised it was not sufficient for students merely to participate in action research initiated and conducted by teachers, they needed to take control over all the essential phases of the inquiry in order to become real action researchers. However, it became clear to us that a traditional school (in which pupils are just 'passive recipients of official truths' (Steinberg & Kincheloe, 1998,

p. 13) would not be an appropriate place for the realisation of pupils' own action research. We were aware that it would be possible only in a school where the pupils could become self-directed human beings:

> In our view the authority of the critical teacher is dialectical; as teachers relinquish the authority of truth-providers, they assume the mature authority of facilitators of student inquiry. In relation to such teacher authority students gain their freedom – they acquire the ability to become self-directed human agents. (Steinberg & Kincheloe, 1998, p. 17)

Despite our readiness to help pupils to take over the role of action researcher there was a lack of specific examples from other teachers who had experience in it. In the available literature we were not able to find practitioners' research suitable to our professional context – primarily for ten-year-old pupils. However, this did not discourage us since we had a confidence in the pupils' potentials being higher than expected from a traditional school.

**What we intended to do**

*Marica's plan*

Before starting my research I announced a plan at the virtual space of cooperation[6] which we were using to facilitate cooperation between a group of teacher action researchers. I decided first to familiarize pupils with the procedures for data-gathering. I presumed that ten-year-old pupils would be able to learn how to conduct an interview, compile questionnaires and rating-scales, and know how to keep a research-diary. To achieve those ends I made a time-specification of three weeks. After that period I planned to devote a week for the negotiation of choosing an area for improvement. It seemed to me that it would be appropriate for pupils to improve their relationships with others and present the results of their learning. Branko warned me that in the process of planning I should include the pupils, since action research is not research *on* but *with* people (Reason, 1994). I

---

[6] This forum was available only for members of the research team; therefore it represents a type of personal communication over the Internet.

accepted this suggestion and it meant that I did not develop a detailed plan after all but refined it instead with my pupils, all of us working together. In the process I respected the suggestions of my critical friends about my increasing understanding of the action research process. I worked out what might need to be done to help the pupils to achieve their own desired activities during the two-or-three-week period, and then I worked out how to obtain validation for their research. Several teachers positively commented on my ideas and plans to help pupils become action researchers themselves:

> Marica, I've read your new AR plan. It seems much clearer and achievable - if indeed I understand it properly - that your pupils are becoming action researchers. Very interesting. (L. B., personal communication, December 9, 2003)
> It would be interesting to follow up on you and your pupils. (J. Z., personal communication, December 9, 2003)
> After reading your new plan and experiences with young action-researchers, I have a better insight into your research, which I like and which is going in the right direction. It also illuminates a road for the rest of us. (V. Šimić, personal communication, January 1, 2004).
> Branko wrote the following reflective record at a later time about my plan

and research:

> Marica started with this activity although she did not elaborate her plan in detail. However, her excitement about the research was more significant. Anyway, is it possible for us to plan everything in advance if action research truly is a cooperative process in which emphasis is placed on respecting other participants, especially if they are also action researchers as is the case with Marica's pupils!? (B. Bognar, personal communication, 2005)

### *Branko's plan*

My interest was connected with the teachers' action research so that meant my plan was somewhat different from Marica's. I planned the following:

a.  To help Marica and other teachers in the realisation of their action research. I intended to place a particular emphasis on familiarizing participants with examples of teachers' research conducted abroad as such examples were not numerous in Croatia. In addition I planned to teach teachers about how to gather data from their activities and infer meanings from the results.

b. I decided to provide support to teachers using the Internet and at regular meetings on a Saturday.

c. I also made an agreement with teachers about visiting their classrooms as a critical friend. Those visits had a dual purpose: giving feedback to teachers about their activities during their action research inquiries and helping them with data-gathering in particular, videotaping their classroom activities. However I was not able to predict something that later became very important for this inquiry:

> What I hadn't planned, and which has emerged as a possibility, is the cooperation with action researchers from abroad, that is becoming very important and makes an important contribution to the achievement of the wider aim – the popularisation of action research in our region. (B. Bognar, personal communication, March 14, 2004)

**Data-gathering and criteria for judgment**

Since most communication was in written form via the forum at the Internet, it became an important source of data. We also made an agreement to keep our research diaries on the Internet forum[7]:

> This forum provides us with the possibility to write down concisely what we have done, what we are thinking, what problems we've noticed and what we intend to do about them. For everything we write down we can get feedback from other members of the team very quickly and we do not need to inform them about our postings since we all regularly read and write our postings at the forum (which I am especially pleased about). I suggest that at least twice a week each of us write down what s/he has achieved in their research even if it seems unimportant. (B. Bognar, personal communication, November 16, 2003)

---

[7] The research-diary represents an important data-source in action research (McNiff, Lomax & Whitehead, 1996; Mills, 2000; Altrichter, Posch & Somekh, 1993) but it was also mentioned as a possibility in action research literacy recently (e.g. McNiff & Whitehead, 2006). Our personal communication was realized mostly through the internet forum (http://mzu.sbnet.hr/).

We intended to use video and audio records and photographs as important sources of data. Although film and particularly photographs have had a long tradition in ethnographic research[8] they are relatively rarely used in action research inquiries in spite of their great potential. But fortunately there have been changes, especially in action research at the University of Bath in England with Jack Whitehead and his colleagues (e.g. Whitehead, 2003, 2005a; Farren & Whitehead, 2005). Videos have been used for archiving as well as for qualitative and quantitative analyses of teaching activities, and for encouraging teachers' reflective thinking (G. Spindler & L. Spindler, 1987). So the use of video was becoming increasingly important because it enabled action researchers to see what they were actually doing in their classrooms and what their actions looked like from another perspective. In addition we thought it would produce very important evidence to help teachers in the generation of their reports; we thought the reports ought not to depend entirely on written words or questionable feedback, as they would not be able to depict a living situation in the teacher's practice. We agree with McNiff & Whitehead (2006) in their statement that 'the development of multimedia narratives is an exciting and important innovation in the field' (p. 144), and we would add that videos can contribute to the quality of action research as well as the learning of teachers, especially at an international level[9].

---

[8]    Anthropologists Margaret Mead and Gregory Bateson were pioneers in the use of film for ethnographic research. They first used cameras—both still and motion picture—in their work in Bali in 1936-1938. They used film to record 'the types of non-verbal behaviour for which there existed neither vocabulary nor conceptualized methods of observation' (deBrigard, 1995 as cited in Ulewicz & Beatty, 2001, p. 5).

[9]    Ulewicz & Beatty (2001) point out that video technology has become a powerful methodological tool in comparative educational research and teachers' learning:

> International video studies generate data that may create audiovisual glossaries of teaching strategies and skills that expand the repertoire of possible teaching approaches. This audiovisual glossary provides a reference point for teaching practices that are difficult to describe in words, particularly when foreign languages and cultural contexts create barriers to interpretation and communication. Carefully-selected videotapes can introduce teachers to a variety of practices, to help them rethink what they might otherwise take for granted; to consider the pros and cons of different approaches, and, in general, to become more reflective practitioners. (p. 1)

In our case, we intended to use videos as evidence of the success of planned improvements. Since the main aim of this project was the pupils' independent action research inquiries, it was important to determine whether they really were able to perform and understand all the important phases of action research in order to gauge their progress. For example, did their research show:

- the choice of a concern on the basis of educational values;
- planning;
- the realisation of a plan;
- data-gathering and data-analyses;
- working with a critical friend within a defined relationship;
- writing;
- a presentation;

and finally

- the validation of an action research report?

With the aim of determining Marica's pupils' understanding, we conducted a group-interview with them. The validation was planned to take place in Marica's and another teacher's classroom. The possibility of presenting the results of this research at an international level via video emerged afterwards.

Since both of us were emphasising the significance of freedom as a shared value we considered it to be very important to allow pupils to decide freely whether they wished to engage in action research or not. Therefore, the engagement in an action research inquiry was not an imposed activity. This was, ipso facto, a criterion for the success of the project.

## THE REALISATION OF THE PLAN

### How I helped my pupils to become action researchers – Marica's story

Although I tried to achieve an environment that was conducive to learning for children by taking into account their distinctiveness and by developing their independence, I still considered this could be improved upon. In previous attempts I had endeavoured to develop my pupils' competences, to empower them in the important aspects of school life, and help them in the recognition and development of their own potentials. Some of these improvements I managed in the form of action research. I was also concerned whether pupils could do it all by themselves.

At the beginning I planned to familiarize pupils with some of the processes of data-gathering: questionnaires, interviews, rating-scales and a research-diary. I tried to achieve these aims through play and by engaging in interesting activities with them. Rating scales appeared to me easy and useful procedures but pupils seemed to have a problem in using them. They could not hypothesise or construct rating-scales. We managed to practice interviews, which the pupils coped with fairly easily:

> Yesterday pupils played at being journalists and interviewing. It was good: they liked interviewing. They devised interesting questions. We searched for the questions which have only one answer (closed questions) and those which allow us to say more (open questions)...This was a good preparation for the use of an interview in their action research inquiries. (M. Zovko, personal communication, December 18, 2003)

After familiarizing themselves with the procedures of data-gathering, pupils individually defined their values, and we then determined our shared values.

> I carried out an activity with the pupils that we called 'The flowering of our values'. The children were first divided into groups of four. They wrote down their individual values on the petals and in the centre of the flower they put their shared values. On the petals we wrote down values of particular groups and then in the middle we mentioned the shared values of the whole class. For example, on some flowers, pupils mentioned freedom, play, love, learning, friendship, peace, parents, family togetherness. Pavle wrote that the only important thing for him was for his mother, who had found out she had cancer three years ago, stayed alive. If I had not been there I don't believe the pupils would have come up with all the ideas they ended up writing in the petals by themselves. At the end, in the middle of the class's flower, they wrote the following values: FRIENDSHIP in the classroom; and FUN AND ENTERTAINMENT,

FAMILY – health, understanding, trust, support. (M. Zovko, personal communication, January 19, 2004)

We discussed how they might do something to improve some of their values. I left them enough time to think about it and the next day several pupils presented their ideas:

> Ana: I'll make all my friends happy. We'll play together and have fun and all of us will be cheerful and satisfied. In school we need more play and fun since children don't have enough fun at home[10].
>
> Anica: I'll try to understand my family: my sister needs a bit of peace, mum needs help when she can't find time to do the dishes; I'll be there for dad to do some jobs, help grandmother and aunt with the cleaning, listen to my little sister etc. To check the efficiency I'll use questionnaires, interviews and certificates[11] of action[12]. (M. Zovko, personal communication)

When pupils first read the plans of their actions, I explained to them the concept of an action research inquiry. I told them that in action research they would be able to improve something important according to the values they wrote down on the class's flower. They could make a plan about how to achieve their aims; they could gather data, discuss everything with other people and at the end present what they had done. We did not bother too much with an explanation of concepts since for the children it was more important to *do*, than know what it was called. In spite of that they accepted the concept of 'action research' very quickly as a means to their own ends.

---

[10]   Ana suggested a general plan without too many concrete details. Later I noticed that she improvised activities in the classroom every day or she devised them a day beforehand and then conducted them successfully. Although she revised her plan later, she was as satisfied as the other children. She planned amusing activities according to her interests and carried them out with other children. She later cooperated with Lucija.

[11]   The Certificate represents parents' or somebody else's signature when some activity was successfully completed.

[12]   Anica outlined an activity to show her understanding to each member of the family. She devised clear activities on how to improve understandings within the family. She regularly kept a diary and acted according to the plan. In the classroom she conducted critical analyses of her work. She finished her action research inquiry and wrote a report. She concluded that such work took her a lot of time, but she was satisfied with her self-improvement. In the second cycle she tried to organise activities in which pupils could discuss their problems.

Despite mostly positive attitudes, some pupils did not make plans. This situation reminded me very strongly of us when we started our action research inquiries. We also found it much easier to talk about ideas and about what we could do rather than write something about it. After a week I explained to the pupils that they did not have to carry on if they did not want to. I think some pupils were hesitant to say openly they were not enjoying it or that they did not know how to participate. Only a few of them decided not to participate in action research. At the end of the first week most pupils wrote down their individual plans.

These children were very interested and individually they came out with more and more ideas about what to do. They were full of questions and they seemed happy as their new ideas emerged during our discussions. I wrote in my research-diary that previously-developed social competences and trusting relationships appeared to be important in that phase of my action research. Branko noted that in action research such activities could exceed the limits of traditional classrooms in which children were largely passive. In order for pupils to be able to engage fully with an action research inquiry, it was necessary to free up their sense of independence, critical thinking and creativity.

In the beginning I helped the pupils with their inquiries by myself, and later this was done by the more involved pupils. My role appeared to be most important in communication with pupils who had lost confidence in their abilities or had some sort of crisis.

> Today the first crisis occurred. Everybody had something planned and some of them started to put their plans into practice. In the process Ana and Lucija were particularly active in making up amusing plays which were part of their action plan. Ana coped in an excellent manner with the role of organiser of amusing plays in the classroom. Other children enjoyed what they were doing and tried to contribute to their plans. However, some pupils were less confident and they decided to stop participating. When they read out their plans I asked them what the problem was and they did not know. I think that the crisis emerged since it seemed to them that they wouldn't realise their research as well as Ana

and Lucija who conducted their plans with confidence and in doing so they were enjoying themselves as much as the other children.

Probably many pupils pass through a phase of worry in which it appears their situation is impossible to change and improve. Stoll and Fink (2000) also write about such a problem with teachers. I concluded earlier that a similar process occurs in action research with adults as well as action research with children. (M. Zovko, personal communication, January 23, 2004)

Our day started with a conversation about action research. Each pupil who had something to share with us was allowed to say something. Other pupils, even those who did not complete their action research, listened to them with interest and respect. I respected the choice of those pupils who gave up doing action research, although some of them claimed they had been doing action research right up to the end of the research-period. They had not actually done this, but I did not contradict them. After the morning meeting we arranged further activities and tried to find the best solutions for implementing the pupils' suggestions and my duties. I tried to avoid burdening myself with my routine schedules, but I couldn't completely neglect the official curriculum and my regular obligations.

There was a lack of time but the children were tireless. When we had finished the part connected with action research (usually during the first two lunch hours), pupils had many ideas about what we could do 'from the lessons' as they used to say. They often stayed in the school after lessons were finished and sometimes I had actually to send them home since another teaching-shift had to start.

Pupils sometimes arrived full of ideas about their actions and about gathering data. They talked about interviews with members of their families, or with their classmates. The more active pupils kept research diaries. Through their action research they tried to improve the following aspects of their lives: *play and fun, family relationships, solving a conflict* and *friendship*. It is interesting that no one chose to improve their own learning of subjects. Valentina K. who decided to improve relationships in her family made a plan and kept notes in her research-diary:

I chose my family. Why did I do this? I did this because I wanted my parents, sister and brother to notice that I'd changed myself.

Plan: I'll help with the house work. I'll always be supportive of learning and other things. I'll be full of understanding. When they're ill, I'll nurse them. I'll start from tomorrow.

Research-diary: I did the dishes, wiped the dust, swept the floor, and encouraged my sister before she went to driving-school. Mum complained and I understood why: she was tired and she has a big job.

I arranged the crockery in one of our cabinets, swept the floor, and washed up the plates, tidied up the dishes and in the process broke a glass; mum did not shout. I prepared the tea.

Questions for mum:

Valentina: Did you notice that I changed because I did the cleaning?

Mum: Yes, it really happened!

Valentina: How did you feel?

Mum: Surprised.

Valentina: Were you pleased?

Mum: Certainly.

Valentina: Would you like it to stay like this forever?

Mum: Yes. (M. Zovko, personal communication, January 31, 2004)

In this action research project I needed the support of critical friends almost as much as I did at the beginning. 'I didn't expect to because I'd already completed my action research. And it indicates something important about this process and the necessity for a critical friend regardless of experience' (M. Zovko, personal communication, January 22, 2004). Branko and Vesna Šimić (a teacher in Branko's school) sent me their comments. Their opinions and support were very important to me:

> Marica, your action research is in full flow. I have the impression that in your classroom everything buzzes about like bees in a hive and this is without any doubt good. (B. Bognar, personal communication, January 24, 2004)
>
> Marica, your actions are increasingly clear to me. Bravo! I especially like the way you and your pupils recognise how you're 'forging ahead and making progress' in the work. (V. Šimić, personal communication, January 24, 2004)

In spite of previous experiences in action research, I felt uncertain. Probably part of my uncertainty emerged from the feeling that I still did not know enough about action research, and also because of the fact that the processes of our intensive inquiries were increasingly dissimilar to regular lessons.

> I feel a chronic lack of time, because what the students are dealing with requires time; I also have to fulfil the official curriculum. I personally consider these activities to be very important, and probably more so for pupils' development than expressive reading, but I'm worried because of the continuous improvisation. It's only the thought that other teacher-action-researchers face the same worries that consoles me. I still have to write in one way, and do something else. Very often I act on two different levels, like dealing with two jobs. Perhaps this will continue to happen until action research becomes part of the official curriculum. Maybe it's one of the reasons why teachers hardly ever work with action research, as doing anything additional is not officially recognised and therefore not important despite their own personal beliefs and experiences. (M. Zovko, personal communication, February 3, 2004)

I wonder why we as teachers so often devote detailed planning to what we think should be done, when children seem actually much more interested in planning by themselves. However, just as I needed the support of critical friends so did my pupils. Children who were active from the beginning became critical friends to their classmates. They suggested to each other how to improve their activities. Several pupils visited the homes of pupils carrying out their research with their families.

> Today, Valentina K. informed us about the processes of her action research. She was visited by her critical friend Tena. Tena wrote her opinion about Valentina's work. Valentina was not satisfied, however, because Tena was shy and she didn't talk with members of her family about the improvements Valentina was trying to make. Tena noticed that Valentina regularly kept a diary and that her plan and records matched each other and she commended her for this. Valentina, as a researcher, thought that Tena should also notice more about how she acted and not only how she kept a diary. Valentina K. is generally very active and she was enjoying her action research. (M. Zovko, personal communication, February 4, 2004)

After two weeks pupils doing action research decided to perform critical analyses of the completed work. I did not have to explain to them how to organise it since Anica – who became a real expert in action research – did it for me. We made an agreement that at the end of each school day we would each analyse one or two pieces of research. Tena's was first. She presented her action research and Valentina K. commented that from Tena's records it wasn't completely clear what she had intended to achieve. Tena agreed with her and added she had noticed that earlier too! I observed that she did not achieve her planned activities over the three days stipulated and I told her so. Children very soon realised what it meant to be a critical friend and they tolerated praise as well as criticism. It was lovely to see them feeling empowered. My presence and comments were very significant in this situation:

> I always point out important things, always praise them, because there is always something to be praised and I soften any negative comments. In this phase it is very important that children feel empowered and positive after any discussion about their inquiries. It is very important to reveal one's own thoughts and experiences to others, but it is equally important to hear what they think about them. In the first phase, when children are learning to be action researchers, criteria tend to be lenient. Even if the children didn't complete their own action research, the process they participated in was still extremely valuable, since there seemed no better way for developing self-confidence other than from this kind of process of action research. (M. Zovko, personal communication, February 4, 2004)

After critical analyses some pupils were satisfied with their action research and improvements, and some planned what to do next within their elected research-fields. It was at this stage that I acquainted pupils with reports and helped them in how to make them for themselves. The children wrote down everything about their action research and presented it to classmates on the big paper (Bognar, 2008b).

I helped pupils to validate their action research without too much explanation of the term. I utilized (in a slightly adjusted way) Jack Whitehead's (1989, p. 6) approach by raising the following questions:

- Was the inquiry carried out in a systematic way?
- Did the pupils try to fulfil their own values?
- Is their explanation understandable to others?
- Do they have evidence for their actions?
- Why are their improvements significant?

After three months of doing action research we all felt tired. It was a sign for us to finish our project, but that did not mean the children stopped their activities.

> Yesterday pupils who were active from the beginning told me they were very tired and that they couldn't achieve anything further, so they didn't want to continue with action research, but they wanted to carry out parts of their plans. It is not difficult for them to carry on, but it is a problem to monitor everything and to gather evidence. I remember such a feeling too. I also feel less of a burden now as I'm not engaged with the pupils' action research on an everyday basis. (M. Zovko, personal communication, February 27, 2004)

When pupils had had enough experience in action research I asked them to write down what they first thought of when I told them that we were going to do action research. Pupils initially thought they might gather data about ancient Egypt; they might inquire about forest plants and animals, make experiments in the laboratory; that perhaps it was some new game, something done for a final grade; that somebody might question them. Three pupils thought it would be stupid, difficult and boring. Almost all the students expressed positive attitudes towards action research since they had achieved self-improvement, as well as helping and understanding families and friends.

What pupils considered positive in their action research I found out by using a questionnaire:

- I like helping others, improving myself, and keeping a research-diary;
- The family gave me more time during the research. I liked it when they praised me and noticed I was working;
- This is good because we have fun, improve and even learn through action research;
- That I can improve relationships in my family, friendship and play;
- I liked working to improve something;
- I liked helping my family;
- I consider it is very good. I liked being very active, helping my family, and I wanted to do this because it suits me;
- To prove that in life something can always be improved;
- I liked it when we did things and wrote about changes;

- Each human being should do action research. In that way s(he) will get acquainted with herself/himself and found out that s(he) can be better. (M. Zovko, personal communication)

What did child learn from their action research?

- That people can be different, that they can understand the family better. I've experienced lovely moments as well as bad ones;
- I brought a lot of happiness into the family because it made me happy when mum kissed me with a smile on her face; I learned that it is beautiful to improve something in the family;
- I learned that I could be closer to friends;
- That is possible to improve a lot when you want to;
- I learned many things - that friendship is good and that what seems boring can be interesting;
- I thought that I helped mum too much with housework, but when I was cooking  lunch with mum during my action research, I realised that mum worked very hard. Since then whenever I can, I help mum, and much more than before;
- How to live better. (M. Zovko, personal communication)

**How I helped Marica in her effort to help pupils to become fully-fledged action researchers – Branko's story**

In September 2003 I invited four teachers – participants of the previous project – to continue our cooperation in order to manage several action research inquiries and publish them in a shared book. We made an agreement to communicate through the virtual space of cooperation[13] as well as through meetings on Saturdays. Participants individually defined the fields in which they wanted to continue with their action research, and I tried to help them. At the beginning Marica was not easily able to determine her concern, because during the three-years of our cooperation she had already succeeded in making improvements to her practice and she did not know what else to improve.

---

[13]     The system for virtual cooperation consists of forums, archives, content-management tools and photo-albums. We received this system as a donation from a computer programmer who, over time, also became a member of our team.

However, it seemed to her that she could focus on the development of pupils' critical thinking:

> In accordance with my values and the circumstances in which I work, it seemed to me a logical solution to choosing a field of critical thinking and I discussed that with Branko Bognar. Several years ago I participated in the project 'Reading and Writing for Critical Thinking.' I had some knowledge about critical thinking as a complex and multidimensional process and I had practised some teaching-techniques to contribute to pupils' development. My pupils have participated in such activities from the first grade and particular improvements became clear: they became much more confident when they presented their own opinions and showed their readiness to respect other people's opinions. I considered this could still be improved on through an action research inquiry. (M. Zovko, personal communication)

After two months of skirting about the topic of critical thinking - which did not present a fundamental change as she had already developed it with pupils since the first grade – Marica presented her concern at a meeting of the action research group. After that I came up with the idea that the children would surely cope with the research by themselves as her plan had included everything she wanted to achieve: freedom, self-determined activities, self-confidence, critical thinking and the pupils' cooperation. Marica wrote about my idea in the following way:

> After yesterday's meeting I feel much better and more confident. Thanks Branko for another step in the development of action researchers in our team! Probably this is generalisable in action research: if you do not know where and how to go forward, talk with critical friends. That is how I've felt recently: I've had crises and I've not been sure what to do with this critical thinking thing at all. I wrote as the title of my action research: 'How can I improve the critical thinking of my pupils?' and I thought it really would be possible to do what I was already doing. Such a perception hadn't satisfied me and I've not known how to do the research at all. Therefore the help of a critical friend is important. (M. Zovko, personal communication, December 7, 2003)
> I responded to her immediately:
> Marica, I am glad that you like my idea about action research with students. This is a step forward but at the same time corresponds with your current educational practice. Namely, everything you've managed with your pupils can be integrated into your pupils' action research projects. Anyway, consider how to enable students in their data-gathering and

action research inquiries as a whole. Most important to note is that we can learn action research only by doing. I am looking forward to seeing what will happen. (B. Bognar, personal communication, December 7, 2003)

With the aim of helping pupils take over the role of action researchers Marica started with activities, which they could learn how to construct and apply to various processes of data- gathering. She tried to achieve that through play. She also realised it was important to ask pupils whether they actually wanted to participate in action research:

Today it occurred to me that I should ask pupils whether they wanted to do action research. I didn't want just to be the only one giving suggestions; I wanted to allow those who wanted to, to lead the others. Anyway, I will respect the decisions of those pupils who choose not participate. What gives me the right to assume that everybody wants to do action research just because I suggest it!? (M. Zovko, personal communication, January 13, 2004)

I encouraged her in both intentions: 'It is excellent that you start from play and that you want to give the possibility of choice to the students,' (B. Bognar, personal communication, January 14, 2004). In spite of my sympathy with Marica's way of introducing pupils to action research, it seemed to me that she was placing too much emphasis on data-gathering and somewhat neglecting the development of pupils' understanding of the action research process as a whole process. I read her revised plan and wrote some suggestions:

Marica: Students will conduct their action research in small groups. They are likely to want to deal with improvements in their relationships. As I am learning to gather data, my pupils will learn to do it. Their questions and their concerns should be corroborated by data.

Branko: The processes of action research can be completed only if we know how. Therefore, pupils also need to learn something. You started with data-gathering, but it is also advisable that pupils learn the following about action research:

- [It] is about improving some field of our lives and this usually starts with question 'How can we improve...?'
- That in action research we start from particular values that can serve as the criteria for the assessment of the success of our actions;
- That a process of action research consists of planning, acting, data-gathering, critical consideration, revised planning etc.;
- That in the realisation of our plan other people can help with their own suggestions and criticisms – we call such people critical friends;

- Gathered data needs to be distilled, sorted out, and finally analysed with the aim of making conclusions about the realisation of a particular plan;
- It is advisable to present the results of our action research publicly in the form of posters, reports, video-presentations, computer-presentations, photo-presentations, comic strips…
- Then we can invite other people (parents, pupils from other classes or schools…) to assess the comprehensibility, truth, candour and appropriateness of our presentations.

Maybe this could be the basic plan of your action research. How does it seem to you? Data-gathering is just one aspect of what pupils need to learn about action research. I am not sure at the moment whether it is necessary to explain it in advance or whether you should introduce pupils to action research step-by-step. What do you think?

Marica: I'm going to plan the process of my action research inquiry and at the same time I'll teach and help the pupils in the planning of their action research.

Branko: It is important that they determine what data they should gather. The same applies to you.

Marica: I changed my plan so that I won't start with research for the first week. Pupils will learn through play to decrease their anxiety.

Branko: Afterwards the pupils could write stories, fables, or fairy-tales about three of their most important values. To describe their values they could draw or act out something. Pupils could be divided into groups according to their chosen values. The next step could be planning improvements of some part of their lives (inside or outside school) with the aim of fulfilling the highlighted values. Pupils need to choose what they want to do and to change. It is advisable to warn them to start small. (M. Zovko & B. Bognar , personal communication, January 14, 2004)

During that time, other than the communication through the forum at the Internet, we often talked on the telephone. During those conversations I tried to explain to Marica that the essence of action research is improving something in our everyday lives. Marica was beginning to realise that from the example of her pupils' initiative in deciding independently to establish a class library:

After my conversation with Branko again the light dawned. I told Branko that several pupils in my classroom were trying to establish a class library. They planned everything. They even knew why they were doing it and had ideas about possible improvements. Branko told me that it could be a small classroom action research project. When I discussed this with the pupils, I noticed that their work already contained elements of an action research inquiry. If Branko had not mentioned action research, I would

never have recognised it in the activity of my pupils. Thanks to Branko for another idea! (M. Zovko, personal communication, January 15, 2004)
Pupils who had the initiative for establishing a class library easily accepted

action research as a natural part of their lives. As a mentor Marica wrote:

> I feel a bit awkward as a mentor to the pupil action researchers. I do not like theorising with them, but really I want to help them in their work. I have to confess that the children's approach to the research work is simpler and more spontaneous than ours (adults). To them everything is pretty straightforward.
>
> My pupils Anica, Valentina and Tena and I discussed their attempts to establish a library today and we arranged for them to write down their ideas and plans by the next day. On questioning them about their reasons to do things in particular ways, they had clear answers: they knew what they wanted to improve. They had a plan of how to achieve everything. They even had an idea about how to get feedback from other pupils about working on the class library. They had a plan about how to motivate pupils to read. Like us they could make contacts in school, over the 'phone and through visits even though they are from different villages. They have assistants: parents and a teacher. My problem: This is pupils' action research but how can it become my action research when I don't do anything? I am proud of my work up to now and of my class, but my current role is minimal. How can this be my action research? Even the idea of improving something is not mine, but the pupils.' (M. Zovko, personal communication, January 15, 2004)

I responded to Marica:

> Marica, you asked how this can be your action research inquiry when you are doing nothing. Everything you mentioned about your pupils' project has elements of action research, but the missing link is the critical friend. What you say about critical friends and their role being necessary when someone gets stuck are details that aren't very visible. It's true that critical friends cannot take any lead in someone else's action research, but only in their own. Apart from may be that we actually do the most when our role is hardly perceptible at all. In a traditional school we're taught to take on the dominant role, although it's most effective when it's imperceptible. (B. Bognar, personal communication, January 16, 2004)

In spite of the feeling that she was surplus to requirements she came to

realise that her role was very important. Her leadership and the activities she

suggested were decisive for the development of the pupils' action research. Pupils

were able to isolate their individual and shared values through activities called

'The flowering of our values'. After that the pupils talked about ways to fulfil the highlighted values in their lives:

> Pupils quickly listed ideas and we made an agreement that for a day we would consider everything and try to find ways of making improvements in accordance with their values. One pupil asked me after some reflection what would happen if she made a plan and acted in accordance with it, but there were no improvements or others didn't recognise them. It seems she must have read Jean McNiff and Jack Whitehead's (2002) text which Branko translated for us: 'Making sense of what happens when things do not go according to plan is just as much part of an action inquiry as when they do. The research is in education, whether the action goes as we hope or not. The learning is in the practice' (p. 71). I told pupils that I would help them in devising and achieving their plans as well as in monitoring and data-gathering. (M. Zovko, personal communication, January 19, 2004)

I noticed with pleasure a significant change in Marica's actions which were in accordance with her intention to help pupils fulfil their action research:

> Marica, this is excellent. I feel you go in the heart of the thing – the realisation of your own action research. After this period of reflection, reconnaissance and reading I feel that things have settled down and now the most important phase of action research begins – the action. There will be ups and downs, planned achievements, unplanned surprises, but in that all lies the beauty of action research inquiries – their openness to a life that is rich and unbounded.
>
> Your action research is not the result of just a current plan, but a reflection of the results of your overall educational endeavour. Nothing of what you experience now as so thrilling would have happened if you hadn't managed particular aspects. All of this could help you in making a new plan, whose aim is introducing action research to the pupils' real worlds.
>
> My sincere congratulations to you and to your young action researchers. I am happy in your enthusiasm, openness and readiness for action research. (B. Bognar, personal communication, January 19, 2004)

As well as me, Teacher Vesna Šimić noticed changes in Marica's research:

> Marica, I looked at the virtual space of cooperation which connects and links us again ...I am glad that your pupils have an opportunity and the freedom to express their values worked through with their experiences and needs. If we succeed in promoting the highlighted values with our pupils, we will surely achieve some small improvements in our practice. (V. Šimić, personal communication, January 19, 2004)

Despite the pupils' initial enthusiasm Marica noticed that the majority of them did not complete their action research plans. This fact did not disappoint or even surprise her. She was aware that it was a new field for children and it seemed that some pupils might see it as a form of homework:

> Altogether I am not disappointed, since this was anticipated from the beginning. For the children this is a new field, and I believe that some pupils perceive it as a sort of voluntary homework so they didn't do it.
> It was good that I knew this beforehand because I was able to react appropriately and to plan subsequent activities. I didn't show any negative feelings to the children because I didn't feel them. Through this it becomes clear that the dynamic relationships we've developed, together with my suggestions that must have enthused them, are very important. Today I've also noticed the importance of the mutual trust we have developed. (M. Zovko, personal communication, January 20, 2004)

I encouraged Marica in her detailed, regular and public diary-writing so it was easy to discern what had happened in her classroom:

> Marica, I like this way of keeping a diary because it's sufficiently detailed to enable us to discern important processes occurring in our research and since it is public everybody can learn something, and at the same time write their own comments. (B. Bognar, personal communication, January 21, 2004)

To me it was particularly important because I then had a complete and up-to-date insight into the significant processes for carrying out her action research inquiry. Problems emerging in relation to the pupils' action research plans once more made me emphasise to her that:

> ...without doubt it would not be good for pupils to view action research as some kind of homework; on the contrary it should be an expression of their own wish to participate in action research and they should be empowered to do it. (B. Bognar, personal communication, January 21, 2004)

Marica told me my words of support were important to her and she continued to keep a diary about events in her class:

> Cooperative relationships prevail among the children; all the time they are making arrangements and proposing things. My regular or orthodox teaching plan was achieved only after their action research activities. Regular lessons according to the official schedule were not fully completed, but the children were not worried. They had practical solutions about how to compensate for the lost subject-matter.

This class is accustomed to planning, making proposals and being independent. I already noticed in previous years that children become more active and satisfied if they are able to deal with activities that transcend the teaching curriculum and which enable the development of particular competences. For me the problem always emerges when I have to square academic subjects in the official curriculum with what I actually do, since at the end of the school-year the completion of my curriculum has to be at the same level as the other teachers', although my pupils were enriched by other possibilities.

After this sort of work I feel exhausted. I have tried listening to each child and helping them with their action research planning. Children felt important and cheerful after my constructive comments and suggestions, as we feel in our action research with Branko as our critical friend. (M. Zovko, personal communication, January 21, 2004)

I shared Marica's and her pupils' vitality and commitment to their action research inquiries, but I noticed that she was worried because of her inability to complete the official curriculum. I wrote to her with the following suggestion:

I am aware that you can hardly harmonise an old system in a new way. It's happening to Vesna too at the moment. I mean that new ideas cannot be fitted into an old mould, but it isn't actually necessary. As you mentioned, your children won't know any less than the other children, but they will be enriched by an experience other pupils will probably not get during their entire schooling. (B. Bognar, personal communication, January 22, 2004)

Apart from my comments Marica needed:

...additional stimulating literature. I went through my theoretical understanding from the literature again, particularly those relating to the context of my actions. My notes from books make me more confident. It seems to me that I am actually more confused than I am happy telling you about. On the one hand I have to deal with an external framework in which there no place for the work we do, and on the other hand there is my system of values grounded in previous work and education – it all confuses me, and makes me unconfident. I need theoretical confirmation for my current actions although I've often introduced innovations in the past. I feel better if I have the support of literature for my practice, and this time it was particularly noticeable. Maybe I would like to reassure myself since I know that this way of working is not official school practice. I am aware that these are normal feelings in the context of a traditional school. (M. Zovko, personal communication, January 22, 2004)

Despite the fact that she did not have any special support other than mine, Marica continued to help her pupils in the realisation of their action research inquiries. I conducted group-interviews with pupils trying to check if they truly understood the process of action research (Bognar, 2008a).

> Branko: Would it be possible if you needed to explain to, let's say Teacher Vesna's students, what action research is, how would you, in the most simple way, explain this to them? So, would you like to tell us?
>
> Tomislav: Well it is research in which you want to, I don't know, research or improve something, something in your life, it doesn't have to be in your life, you just want to find out something about it.
>
> Branko: Good. Go ahead. How would you explain it?
>
> Anica: It is improving something important in your life.
>
> Branko: Good. And how, if they were to ask, how are you going about this research now?
>
> Anica: I make a plan and decide that according to the plan I will try to improve it.
>
> Branko: And how do you know if you have improved something?
>
> Valentina B.: Well somebody can confirm it through an interview. To question somebody whether it has improved. Or record it on tape.
>
> Branko: Good.
>
> Tina: Simply find a critical friend, develop a questionnaire or an interview… I mean, have him watch.
>
> Branko: You just said a critical friend. What do you mean by a critical friend?
>
> Valentina: I already said that he tells you what you haven't done too well, what you can do better, not just praise you: 'Oh that's great, oh that's wonderful'.
>
> Branko: Good. Go ahead. Did you want to say something?
>
> Ana: A critical friend is always with you and he will always give you [ideas], tell you what is missing or what not to do and what to do, he always says…
>
> Tomislav: It's a friend who gives you advice about the things you didn't do right in your plan and the things that you did and what you could improve.
>
> Branko: Good. Thank you. Did somebody else want to say something?
>
> Branko: Well, tell me are you, when somebody tells you… for instance someone tells you that something is not good, that you didn't do something right, gives you some kind of remark, criticism, how do you feel? Are you angry with your critical friend or are you glad that he said that to you?
>
> Ana: No, because if there was something missing, he was supposed to tell me because I chose him to tell me such things.
>
> Branko: Go ahead. Did you want to say something?
>
> Marsel: Well, I am glad that he tells me that because we have to know something about ourselves as well, to gather some information.

Branko: Good. Did you want to say something?
Marijana: Well, I don't get angry if he tells me something's wrong. I don't get angry about that.
Branko: Is there anybody who didn't feel too comfortable?
Valentina: Me. I mean, to me, when they say it, I feel sort of regretful, but I still take it because I know that sometimes I have to face consequences in life.
Branko: Good. And tell me, when you finish with a certain part of your performance, your activities and when you complete your own plan, what do you do after that?
Anica: Start with new plans.
Branko: How do you start with a new plan?
Anica: Well, the same way we did with the first one. I'll make a plan and start researching again.
Branko: Will it be related to what you have previously done or will it be something completely different?
Anica: It can be completely different or it can be something similar.
Branko: If it is related to your previous work, how will you previous work helps you?
Anica: Well it'll help with the plan. The way I did it, the way my family reacted, that way I'll be able to see how I will develop my plan, how I can act. (Bognar, 2004a)

On the basis of conversation with pupils as well as from Marica's detailed research-diary I realised that pupils understood that action research included the following aspects:

- Improving something important in their lives;

- Processes consisting of planning, carrying out, data-gathering and critical analyses,

- Cooperation with critical friends whose critical suggestions help in carrying out the research.

However, at that time the pupils were not accustomed to doing an action research report and going through the processes of validation. I suggested that Marica pay particular attention to this aspect of action research:

From the conversation it seems that the children understand action research very well up to the parts relating to reporting and validation. It would be good if you read the section in my MA dissertation devoted to writing a report and the processes of validation again. If you want we can

talk about it. Afterwards it would be good to consider how to bring [these processes] closer to children.
You could fit the writing of reports into lessons about the Croatian language, e.g. written exercises. As regards validation, maybe Vesna's or Daniela's pupils could be the validation group and help you in the assessment of the success of your action researchers' work. (B. Bognar, personal communication, February 10, 2004)
Several pupils succeeded in writing reports and I made an agreement with Vesna Šimić to have the validation process in her classroom. Marica took four students in her car to Vesna's school in Klakar where they presented their action research inquiries. Vesna's pupils listened to Marica's pupils attentively, asked questions and then rewarded them with spontaneous applause. As shown in video *Validation of a pupil's action research report* (Bognar, 2008d) it's possible to see that Marica's pupils had prepared written reports in the form of posters on big sheets of paper and with my support they fulfilled the validation aspects of their action research. Later Marica repeated this procedure in her classroom and helped pupils to gain control over the whole process of action research.

During the process of our research I started working with action researchers at an international level. Cooperation was enabled through an e-mail list, established and led by JeKan Adler-Collins, Associate Professor of Nursing at Fukuoka Prefectural University in Japan, and Jack Whitehead, Lecturer in Education at the University of Bath in UK. I sent the transcript of my conversation with pupil action researchers to this list. Several participants on the list replied very quickly and asked me to publish a video of this conversation. Because of technical problems (slow Internet connection, lack of the space at the Internet) I was not able to do it at that time. But one year later I published videos from our research with subtitles in English during the BERA Practitioners-Research SIG e-seminar. Moira Laidlaw, at that time a volunteer with Voluntary Services Overseas (VSO) was particularly impressed by the videos and wrote a detailed review about the video with my conversation with pupil action researchers. She particularly pointed out the pupils' freedom to choose whether or not they participated in action research:

And here's the essence for me. A moment of genius. You are 'walking the talk'. In other words you are not only genuinely allowing the students to opt out, but you are enabling them to understand the educational significance of that action, in fact commending their choice because it comes as a conscious, responsible one. This relates so strongly to that moment before in terms of what I was saying about the dialectic between responsibility and freedom. And by describing it so respectfully, I sense no worry on the part of the pupils themselves at being different from those who chose to do AR. They account for their reasons as confidently, it seems to me, as those like Anica, who's done such sterling AR work! I think if pupils can tell the truth to power (sorry, can't remember the reference) then there's something so powerful going on here. So often in society (I'm talking about mine here in the UK and not yours, because I don't know) power is more significant and holds greater sway than truth. I am thinking of a national curriculum, which divides knowledge into segments and then sets the values around it like a constellation. And this, is the implied meaning, is truth! Mm. I don't think so! Your classroom, Teacher Marica's classroom, stands as a beacon of hope in enlightenment, empowerment, change and challenge, as well as respect, love, delight, intellectual stimulation, and emotional kindness... (Laidlaw, 2005)

## INTERPRETATION

Despite the fact that action research is becoming a growing trend in teachers' practices, at the beginning of our project we were faced with a lack of literature about pupils' action research. From the accounts available to us we were able to conclude that pupils could become action researchers, but we lacked any accounts by teachers who had also tried to help younger pupils to become action researchers. This is a problem because the literature about action research for adult researchers is not adequate for teachers intending to help pupils to become action fully-fledged researchers themselves. In our case the pupils were introduced to data-gathering through a form of play and with various stimulating activities. On the other hand, O'Brien and Moules (2007) organised, 'training in interview skills carried out through the use of role-play' (p. 393). Other than that, pupil action researchers gathered data during the fun-day when all the researchers were dressed in fancy dress:

Throughout this day, which included face painting, t-shirt, bag-design and art work, the young researchers gathered data from children and young people via the use of interviews, questionnaires and various creative methods such as a graffiti wall, comments box and a diary room. (O'Brien & Moules, 2007, p. 394)

In organizing appropriate activities for novice pupil action researchers, the creativity of teachers as well as children was able to emerge. Daily teaching practices – stimulating pupils' independence, confidence, creativity, critical thinking, and social competences as well as giving them enough space for play, and experimentation with various freely-elected activities – were able to contribute to put down fertile roots from which young action researchers could learn. We also think it a necessary precondition that a teacher, before deciding to help pupils to become full-blown action researchers, should undertake several teacher action research projects themselves. In that way, a teacher and the pupils will become acquainted with the processes of action research that could later make it easier for the pupils to become fully-fledged action researchers themselves.

**Figure 1.**     Approaching a school-based, child-oriented classroom with Marica

**Table 1.**  Our understanding of differences between the traditional and the
child-centred school

| The traditional school | The child-centred School |
|---|---|
| The purpose of a traditional school lies in the training of pupils to fit into traditional social patterns, power relationships and as a preparation for their participation in economic production, in which the main aim is an increase in material wealth. In such a school teachers undertake the fulfilment of those values defined and determined by external forces, and not instigated by the participants of the teaching processes themselves. | The purpose of a child-centred school is the development of the creative/ productive potentials that revitalise the culture of previous generations as well as promoting development. The main aim of such a school is the self-production of, 'the wealthy man and the plenitude of human need. The wealthy man is at the same time one who needs a complex of human manifestations of life, and whose own self-realization exists as an inner necessity, a need' (Marx, 1961, p. 137). Education is grounded on values that are autonomously chosen by its participants – students, teachers, parents etc. |
| Teaching is organised on the basis of official curricula that are always planned in advance and in detail by teachers whose main task is the transmission of the knowledge of different academic subjects to their students. | Teachers respect the needs and individual abilities of pupils who are also deemed sufficiently capable and responsible to participate in curriculum-planning. The teaching process starts from a democratically-agreed premise, which is perceptible to all the participants of the educational processes. |
| To fulfil the official curricula the most responsible and significant person is the teacher. The teacher devises teaching-activities with the aim of informing pupils about official truths and to develop some officially-desired skills. | Pupils as well as teachers are responsible for the achievement of planned activities. The main aim of learning is the ability to learn in self-directed ways that can take control of any essential changes. |
| The evaluation of learning is carried out by teachers and external official bodies, that determine the criteria and methods of assessment and grading. | Pupils and teachers participate equally in self-evaluation in which the intention is to gauge the achievement of self-chosen concerns and the results of learning. |

However, the most important precondition for pupils' active participation in child-centred action research has to be the child-centred school (Figure 1, p. 96). In traditional schools where the most important prerequisite is the implementation of official curricula, pupils' action research isn't going to find its own place (Table 1, p. 97). We consider our previous efforts in creating a school-environment oriented to children (Bognar, 2008f), which were themselves a part of our own action research projects, were decisive for the success of pupils as action researchers.

Marica considered it important to start from the point of enabling pupils to gather data. This is without doubt an important precondition for any research, let alone pupils' action research. This form of research must not be reduced merely to data-gathering because it represents much more than that (Kemmis & McTaggart, 2005, p. 568). As Anica expressed it beautifully, action research is first of all about 'improving something important in your life.' Therefore, we sought ways to help pupils become fully-fledged action researchers, not only research-advisers, data-gatherers and co-interpreters of data as was the case in the ethnographic research conducted by Leitch et al. (2007, p. 463).

It is interesting that in their own research the pupils did not decide to improve learning within any of their school subjects. This gives us a clear message about how important such learning was for them. Other than that, in the research conducted by Ros Frost (2007) seven and eight year-old pupils asked research questions that had an epistemological slant:

> The children chose to undertake research into why a shed they enjoyed playing around had been taken away, why people appeared to care more about football than saving trees from being cut down, how God was made, why humans were cruel to animals and why people smoke. (Frost, 2007, p. 447)

The purpose of those questions was not to improve or change some important aspect of the children's everyday lives, but instead an expression of the pupils' natural curiosity and in some measure their critical thinking. On the other hand, our pupils – the participants in our action research programme – raised obvious questions as an attempt to change something. This revealed them to be in accordance with their own autonomously-determined values. We consider that such a difference occurred because of the influence of the adults whose understanding of action research processes had an effect on the pupils' selection of research-questions. Although Frost expressed her concern that she 'was manipulating pupils into yet another adult agenda albeit one that had the express intention of empowering them in the future' (Frost, 2007, p. 446), it could not save her from the influence she had on pupils. On the other hand we weren't concerned about our influence, but we were aware of the responsibility this influence could signify. While we were helping pupils to carry out their action research inquiries we made efforts to respect their freedom and to support their creativity within the model of action research we personally believed in. This could clearly be interpreted as manipulation, but we are more inclined to call this, 'realness', 'genuineness' or 'congruence' in the facilitator of learning:

> When the facilitator is a real person, being what he or she is, entering into relationships with the learners without presenting a front or a façade, the facilitator is much more likely to be effective. This means that the feelings that the facilitator is experiencing are available to his or her awareness, that he or she is able to live these feelings, to be them, and able to communicate them if appropriate. It means that the facilitator comes into a direct, personal encounter with the learners, meeting each of them on a person-to-person basis. It means that the facilitator is being, not denying himself of herself. The facilitator is present to the students. (Rogers, 1980, p. 271)

In terms of our action research being conducted in a school in which the main task was pupils' learning, it is important to explain what connection exists between action research and learning. Our explanation is pretty simple: since action research represents a process of learning (McNiff & Whitehead, 2006, p. 7; Kemmis & McTaggart, 2005, p. 563; Winter & Munn-Giddings, 2001, p. 21) we consider its place in a school to be central to all the educational processes regardless of the pupils' age. As far as our own value-orientation is concerned, our approach was grounded on humanistic theories of learning, the sort that were elaborated by Carl Rogers (1969):

*1)*      *'Human beings have a natural potential for learning' (Rogers, 1969, p. 157).*

Although the processes of action research are not simple and require a lot of effort, pupils accept them as an integral part of their lives. The pupils were delighted and engaged happily in their own action research inquiries in such ways that might suggest their action research had been achieved without any support from teachers, but this is far from true. Action research is a process of learning in which pupils go beyond their current abilities. In this process a teacher's role is crucial since the cultural development of higher functions, particularly scientific thought, can only be realised within educational processes in which important interactions take place between pupils and a teacher. For an understanding of such processes of learning, an important role is what Vygotsky called 'the zone of proximal development', that describes the influence of adults on the learning of children. The difference between the learning achieved alone and the learning only achievable with the help of adults represents the zone of proximal development (Vygotsky, 1993, p. 53). It means that learning and development do not completely correlate. Learning is more successful when it exceeds the actual level of development. In that way a series of functions is enabled that cannot be developed on their own. Vygotsky (1993, p. 57) emphasized that learning can occur only in activities that have specific cultural meaning and only when a child interacts with people in their own environment – in cooperation with their peers. In order to help pupils to develop their creative potentials: 'the best stimulus ... is to organize their life and environment so that it leads to the need and ability to create' (Vygotsky, 2004, p. 66).

Therefore, Marica presented her pupils with a challenge that went beyond their abilities at that time, and in that way action research became a real educational opportunity for pupils. Because of the eagerness with which pupils responded to this challenge it sometimes seemed to Marica that her role was superfluous, but that was just an illusion. The teacher's role is the most influential when it is imperceptible, when it does not hamper pupils' enthusiasm and creativity (Montessori, 1949, p. 404). That Marica's role was decisive is shown by the fact that none of the pupils continued to undertake action research inquiries when they passed on to higher educational levels. Action research, therefore, represents the pupils' potential when the learning does not only take place by itself but with the benefit of teachers well qualified to enable its success, and who recognise and appreciate its educational importance.

> 2)    'Significant learning takes place when the subject matter is
>        perceived by the student as having relevance for his own purposes'
>        (Rogers, 1969, p. 158).

We consider this characteristic as particularly important for the processes of learning that occurred during the pupils' action research. That is to say in their inquiries pupils did not deal with other people's problems but their own, problems that emerged from their self-chosen values. Without the pupils' independent determination of their own problems, or better still, challenges (which presume an improvement of some important living situation) we wouldn't really be talking about pupils' action research so much as progressive and democratic education (John Dewey, 1921). By using the following questions, Dewey clearly differentiated between formal problems that pupils solved in order to achieve high marks and those problems that are connected to their own interests:

> (a) Is there anything but a problem? Does the question naturally suggest itself within some situation of personal experience? Or is it an aloof thing, a problem only for the purposes of conveying instruction in some school topic? Is it the sort of trying that would arouse observation and engage experimentation outside of school? (b) Is it the pupil's own problem, or is it the teacher's or textbook's problem, made a problem for the pupil only because he cannot get the required mark or be promoted or win the teacher's approval, unless he deals with it? (Dewey, 1921, p. 182)

> 3)    'Learning which involves a change in self-organization – in the
>        perception of oneself – is threatening and tends to be resisted'
>        (Rogers, 1969, p. 159).

This feature was very important for the processes of learning by the adult participants in this project – particularly Marica who was painfully aware that pupils' action research represented a fundamental deviation from the prevailing practices of other teachers. This fear was certainly not baseless, since accepting child-centredness as a value at the same time meant rejecting some of the values of traditional schools. The decision to start this action research inquiry required a certain level of courage, as we were aware that our professional positions and development depended on people of higher professional rank who were not required to look kindly on our efforts. Unfortunately, such fears turned out to be well-founded since Marica's request for professional promotion recently was turned down despite her clear educational achievements.

4)      *'Those learnings which are threatening to the self are more easily perceived and assimilated when external threats are at a minimum'*
        *(Rogers, 1969, p. 159).*

Marica tried to promote a safe atmosphere within which pupils could overcome problems and insecurities during the realisation of their action research inquiries, by constantly praising them and emphasising successful results, and by curtailing any of the students' negative comments. As well as that, Branko's support and the support of other teacher action researchers with whom we co-operated, helped Marica to overcome her doubts and fears. Branko received support from people who live abroad (e.g. Moira Laidlaw in China and Jack Whitehead in the UK). Connecting with people who were dealing with similar issues created a community to whom our efforts were visible. We minimised external threats chiefly by ignoring them and by persistently acting in the public domain, where we gained the sympathy of some of the people employed in the Agency for the Education of the Croatian Republic. Their support was important since it thwarted any threats that would be dangerous in a local context. Therefore, the diminishing of external threats is possible through the creation of public networks that:

> ...generate communicative power; that is, the positions and viewpoints developed through discussion will command the respect of participants not by virtue of obligation but rather by the power of mutual understanding and consensus. Thus, communication in public spheres creates legitimacy in the strongest sense, that is, the shared belief among participants that they freely and authentically consent to the decisions they reach. (Kemmis & McTaggart, 2005, p. 589)

This communicative power (Habermas, 1998) made our learning and the adult-participants' exchange of experiences available, and at the same time provided necessary support during the processes of making essential changes.

5)      *'When threat to the self is low, experience can be perceived in different fashion and learning can proceed' (Rogers, 1969, p. 161).*

Despite our efforts to reduce external threats we were aware that the pupils' action research was not part of the official curriculum and this made Marica feel guilty. However, this feeling quickly evaporated when she became conscious that pupils weren't losing anything in an educational sense by engaging with action research but instead were gaining an opportunity to participate in education of the highest quality. Moira Laidlaw confirmed this when she wrote:

> I watched your colleague's classroom, with the children accounting for their action research (Validation), and as I watched I knew again how education, especially education of that highest quality, is the answer to the world's ills. I and other people I work with round the world have been saying that for years, and in your videos, I saw the antidote... The great thing is... that your form of educational life can give hope not only to you and your colleagues and students and country, but also to the world, because the values you embody with your colleagues and students are those, I am convinced, that can change the world. (Laidlaw, 2005)

We may conclude that the most important precondition for the successful realisation of this project was our readiness to face our own fears, which might have been more exaggerated than any real threats. Although we did not have any particular support during the project, there were no particular threats endangering its success. When we realised that, we directed our creative energies towards supporting pupils who were also facing their own feelings of insecurity in their abilities, particularly when they compared themselves with other, more successful, class-mates (see Marica's record from p. 78). It is interesting to note that children as well as adults faced similar feelings, although the causes were different. However, pupils' successful overcoming of these problems greatly depended upon their teacher's ability to cope with doubts and crises, all of which were unavoidable in the processes of learning and therefore during the realisation of action research as well. Because of that the care for pupils' action research above all else meant a care for teachers as well, because it is their support which is decisive for pupils' success in any significant learning.

> *6)     'Much significant learning is acquired through doing. Placing the student in direct experiential confrontation with practical problems, social problems, ethical and philosophical problems, personal issues, and research problems, is one of the most effective modes of promoting learning' (Rogers, 1969, p. 162).*

Instead of a theoretical explanation of action research principles and methodologies, to the pupils it was far more important that they did it. But at the same time, from video *Pupil action researchers* (Bognar, 2008a) and video *Validation of a pupil's action research report* (Bognar, 2008d) it is obvious that they fully understood all the important ingredients of action research. Therefore, the main message from our research for teachers intending to do something similar would be to reduce any theorising about action research as much possible; it seems advisable to allow pupils to learn by doing. Pupils will soon realise the meaning of particular terms, for example by doing, and they will probably surprise us with their original and appropriate definitions. Pupils' complete understanding of action research helped us in our own projects subsequently when it became necessary to explain in a simple way to teachers and students of the teachers' faculty the essential features of action research. In that way pupil action researchers contributed to the popularization of action research in Croatia, and we believe, abroad too, since their videos were available at the Internet and they were published in several international publications (e.g. Whitehead, 2005b; Whitehead & McNiff, 2006).

7)      *'Learning is facilitated when the student participates responsibly*
        *in the learning process, when he chooses his own directions, helps*
        *to discover his own learning resources, formulates his own*
        *problems, decides his own course of action, lives with the*
        *consequences of each of these choices, then significant learning is*
        *maximized' (Rogers, 1969, p. 162).*

We consider that action research represents an excellent opportunity for pupils to show their responsibility in learning how to make their own lives and the lives of other people more meaningful. *We are wondering, is this not perhaps the purpose of learning, not only in school but throughout our lives?*

One of the problems we faced while attempting to help pupils to become action researchers was appropriately-detailed planning. Namely, it was difficult to envisage everything in advance, especially if we wanted to respect pupils' freedom and creativity. We consider that a teacher's detailed planning of the action research process could bring into question pupils' freedom and responsibility for the processes of their learning. Because of this we tried to talk things over all the time. In that way we aimed to avoid any teacher's research becoming a controlling process. Our intention was for the whole project to become a genuinely democratic process in which all participants were equal, regardless of prior knowledge and age. It was the only way that all of us genuinely could become learners.

8)      *'Self-initiated learning which involves the whole person of the*
        *learner's feelings as well as intellect is the most lasting and*
        *pervasive' (Rogers, 1969, p. 162).*

That it was not merely about learning, 'which takes place only from the neck up' (Rogers, 1969, p. 163) but about holistic learning was affirmed by Moira Laidlaw:

The children in this classroom seem connected to themselves and their motives, their feelings and their delights, their minds and their hearts all at

once. In China there is a New Curriculum, which specifies that learning in
the classroom should be about the whole child. I sense that if
curriculum-planners were to see your work, Teacher Marica's work, the
pupils' work, then they would see what it means to teach a child
holistically. There is a sense of organic growth in this classroom at this
moment. I see rapt attention. I see enthusiasm. I see purpose. I see
understanding. I see logic, and thinking. I see delight. I see life itself!
(Laidlaw, 2005)

We consider that pupils' action research represents an excellent
opportunity for holistic learning by which pupils set out to obtain essential
changes in their lives. Everything they learned by doing was according to their
own values and was deeply connected to their real needs. They learned how to be
better friends, how to improve relationships in their families, how to be active,
how to help others to be happy too, how to live better. This learning was not
realised in a theoretical fashion, but through the pupils fulfilling their own values
actively. These processes provoked much excitement from them and from other
people who participated in the process.

9)      *'Independence, creativity, and self-reliance are all facilitated when
self-criticism and self-evaluation are basic and evaluation by
others is of secondary importance' (Rogers, 1969, p. 163).*

Freedom and creativity were the two most important values we had
intended to realise not only in this project, but in other living situations too. That
the pupils truly did have complete freedom in each phase of the research, as well
as in their choice *not* to choose to do action research at all, was affirmed by the
video *Pupil action researchers* (Bognar, 2008a) (from 3.22 to 4.30 minutes). In
addition, this aspect was highlighted independently by Moira Laidlaw in the
comments we mentioned earlier. Our research demonstrated that children as well
as adults are capable of showing the full range of creative potentiality in an
atmosphere of freedom. However, freedom and creativity were not just a
reflection of pre-existing social conditions, but instead depended on each
participant being wholehearted in the pursuit of such life-affirming values. To be
free means to be ready to dedicate one's own time and creative potential to the

creation of truth that cannot only be realised through our own creative and responsible actions. Pupils who decided to engage in action research inquiries showed a readiness and an ability to accept comments from the critical friends they chose, because they truly wanted to find out something about themselves and about what they were doing. Therefore, an evaluation of their research was not conducted by Marica, although she helped them all the time, but they did it primarily with the help of critical friends – their class mates. In that way they substituted traditional assessment schemes of knowledge with self-evaluation through self-directed learning.

> 10)     'The most socially useful learning in the modern world is the learning of the process of learning, a continuing openness to experience and incorporation into oneself of the process of change' (Rogers, 1969, p. 163).

Action research represents the systematic and responsible implementation of changes in different living situations, and these actually constitute learning. Additionally, action research means learning about the processes of learning and this occurs through the creation of a report and submitting it for validation. Several pupils who became fully-fledged action researchers wrote their action research reports in the form of a big poster that was presented to the pupils from another school (Bognar, 2008d). By doing this they were able to understand more of the significance of action research. Their reports were not just a written exercise but a template by which an exchange of experiences with other pupils became possible. And these pupils listened, wrapt, to the presentations of their peer-group action researchers. Questions they raised helped pupil action researchers to understand completely the significance of improving what was important in their lives.

From the description of the project (in the previous section) and the resulting evidence it is possible to conclude that some pupils were able to take control over all the important aspects of action research. At the same time it is important to mention that only five of twenty two pupils managed this, therefore only a minority of pupils became fully-fledged action researchers. However, almost all the pupils, to a greater or lesser extent, engaged in action research inquiries and felt themselves to be equal participants. We consider that the whole process of action research inquiring had an educational benefit for all pupils, despite the fact that only a minority of them became full-blown action researchers. Therefore, we cannot draw the conclusion that action research is an appropriate activity only for gifted children, but rather that it is important to help all pupils become action researchers regardless of the final results. We consider the establishment of an exclusive action research group of pupils could produce negative feelings like distrust and hostility from the pupils who are excluded. The joy of participation in the creative process, and the sense of inclusionality of all pupils, were reasons enough for such a conclusion.

It is important to note as well that all the pupils who became fully-fledged action researchers took leading roles in helping other pupils complete their inquiries. Branko noticed a similar occurrence with the students at the teacher's faculty whom he has been facilitating to become action researchers in the course called 'Research about Education'. Those who quickly understood and accepted the processes of action research with delight, later helped other students with their action research inquiries, especially in writing up their reports. It is also true to say, however, that such pro-active and creative students may sometimes hinder the creativity of other students. Namely, those students who imitated their more advanced colleagues sometimes lost their own originality. Generally-speaking though, examples from the more advanced students had a positive effect on their class-mates. For that reason Branko regularly invites students from previous classes and teacher action researchers to present their own successful projects in order to stimulate novice action researchers. Moreover, when explaining the main terms about action research he utilizes the videos of the ten-year-old action researchers (Bognar, 2008d, 2008a). In addition, pupils expressed their ideas about action research in concise, simple and telling ways that are available to us as ideals and models for our own personal learning.

Although we plead for action research as an educational strategy, in our opinion it would be improper to establish action research as the set teaching activity that pupils have to engage in, in order to get a grade or for any other formal reason. For pupils, action research can only be meaningful if it is dealt with on the basis of their own needs, interests and self-chosen values. Any process that inhibits the pupils' freedom will only compromise the benefits of action research and its educational value.

Having said that, we are not really advocating action research to improve learning about traditional bodies of knowledge either, since we want to appeal to the learning of the whole person (Rogers, 1969, p. 5, 1980, p. 264) or their significant learning (Rogers, 1995, p. 281). The bearers of such learning are real pupils, with their lived experiences, needs and creative potentials who participate in making the world into one they believe in and the one they would like to live in. *Action research is not a preparation for life; it is life itself.* Therefore, it can hardly be expected that the traditional school would become a place where pupils only engage in action research. Things are further complicated by the fact that action research represents a threat to schools:

> ...in which students are thought to surrender themselves to the system and become passive recipients of official truths. The idea of students as researchers who explore their own lives and connect academic information with their own lived experience is alien to many schools. (Steinberg & Kincheloe, 1998, p. 13)

Although traditional schooling still has deep roots all over the world, we agree with Steinberg and Kincheloe (1998, p. 19) that teachers who understand the value of action research and child-centred learning should become public-relations experts, able to popularise a new approach through their own action research. It is illusory to expect that it could be done by someone not experienced in the beauty of education, in which the development of the whole person's potential is what enables us to make our own lives meaningful and worth living.

Communication between adult participants in this project was made possible through modern communication-technology based on a freeware web-system. Our communication through the web-forum appeared to be an excellent opportunity for discussion about all the important aspects of our action research inquiries as well as for documenting the whole process. That is to say, instead of research diaries we kept our records at the forum, which allowed us to send prompt responses. In that way we created a community of practice (Wenger & Snyder, 2000; Wenger, White, Smith & Rowe, 2005) in which the support was important for maintaining shared efforts. The meaning of such support became particularly important when we connected with people at an international level, who pointed out to us the importance of that we were doing and of whose significance we had not been really aware beforehand. We realised that our action research work was important not only at a local level, but that our experiences could also be encouraging for other educators and their pupils if they intended engaging in similar projects. Stimulated by such feedback, we continued using modern communicational technologies in our subsequent projects, of which the establishment of the journal EJOLTS is now a significant example. We are convinced that pupils will easily be able to use these web-based technologies for communication, data-gathering, publishing and validating of the accounts as well. We are going to explore this in our future action research projects.

Finally, it would be interesting to find out how pupil action researchers understood the whole process they actively participated in. In order to get to know how they explained their own experience of conducting action research, we invited Anica and Valentina (pupils) on 5th August 2005 who, when they had finished 5th grade, were no longer being taught by Marica. Our conversation was video-taped and Branko made a transcript and a translation (15 minutes) of this talk (Bognar, 2008c).

## REFERENCES

Alderson, P. (2000). Children as researchers: The effect of participation-rights on research methodology. In P. Christensen & A. James (Eds.), *Research with children: Perspectives and practices* (pp. 241- 257). London & New York: Falmer Press.

Altrichter, H., Posch, P., & Somekh, B. (1993). *Teachers investigate their work: An introduction to the methods of action research*. London & New York: Routledge.

Argyris, C. & Schön, D. (1975). *Theory in practice: Increasing professional effectiveness*. San Francisco, Washington & London: Jossey-Bass Publishers.

Atweh, B., Christensen, C. & Dornan, L. (1998). Students as action researchers: partnerships for social justice. In B. Atweh, S. Kemmis, & P. Weeks (Eds.), *Action research in practice: Partnership for social justice in education* (pp. 114-138). London & New York: Routledge.

Babbie, E. (1992). *The practice of social research*. Belmont: Wadsworth.

Bognar, B. (2001a). Pedagogy: Science and creativity. *Metodički ogledi, 8*(2), 69-77.

Bognar, B. (2001b). Critical-emancipatory approach to action research. *Život i škola, 47*(6), 45-60.

Bognar, B. (2004a). *Student interview transcript based on a video recording recorded on 3 February, 2004*. Retrieved October 6, 2008, from http://ejolts.net/files/Transcript_of_conversation_about_AR[1].pdf

Bognar, B. (2004b). The stimulation of creativity in a school context. *Napredak, 145*(3), pp. 269-283.

Bognar, B. (2006a). Action research in school. *Educational sciences, 8*(1), pp. 209-227.

Bognar, B. (2006b). How to assess the quality of action research. *Metodički ogledi, 13*(1), 49-68.

Bognar, B. (2008a, June 25). Pupils action researchers [Video file]. Video Posted to http://www.vimeo.com/1230806

Bognar, B. (2008b, July 27). Validation of a pupil's action research report [Video file]. Video Posted to http://www.vimeo.com/1415387

Bognar, B. (2008c, July 28). Conversation with pupils action researchers [Video file]. Video Posted to http://www.vimeo.com/1421265

Bognar, B. (2008d, October 4). Initial video of Marica Zovko's teaching [Video file]. Video Posted to http://www.youtube.com/watch?v=UiDmLxYqh1M

Bognar, B. (2008e, October 6). The meaning of a learning-community for my practice [Video file]. Video Posted to http://www.youtube.com/watch?v=DBPBgJz3Zy8

Bognar, B. (2008f, October 6). Approaching a school-based, child-oriented classroom with Marica [Video file]. Video Posted to http://www.youtube.com/watch?v=923FwXtNX4I

Cooke, B. (2002). A foundation correspondence on action research: Ronald Lippitt and John Collier [Working paper]. Retrieved June 18, 2007, from School of Environment and Development, Manchester University: http://www.sed.manchester.ac.uk/idpm/research/publications/wp/mid/docu ments/mid_wp06.pdf

Dewey, J. (1921). *Democracy and education: An introduction to the philosophy of education.* New York: Macmillan.

Dewey, J. (1929). *The quest for certainty: A study of the relation of knowledge and action.* New York: Minton, Balch & Company.

Čular, G. (2000). Political development in Croatia 1990-2000: Fast transition - postponed consolidation. *Politička misao: Croatian political science review, 37*(5), 30-46.

Farren, M. & Whitehead, J. (2005). *Educational influences in learning with visual narratives.* A paper and video-conference presentation at the Diverse Conference 2005. Retrieved July 23, 2008, from http://people.bath.ac.uk/edsajw/monday/mfjwwebped2.htm

Foshay, A.W. & Wann, K. D. (1954). *Children's social values: An action research study.* New York: Teachers College, Columbia University.

Frost, R. (2007). Developing the skills of seven and eight-year-old researchers: A whole class approach. *Educational Action Research, 15*(3), 441–458.

Habermas, J. (1996). *Between facts and norms: Contributions to a discourse theory of law and democracy.* Cambridge & Massachusetts: The MIT Press.

Hegel, G. W. (1900). *The philosophy of history* (J. Sibree, Trans.). New York: Colonial Press.

Heron, J. & Reason, P. (1997). A participatory inquiry paradigm. *Qualitative Inquiry, 3*(3), 274-294.

Hodgkinson, H. L. (1957). Action research - a critique. *Journal of Educational Sociology, 31*(4), pp. 137-153.

Isenberg, J. P. & Jalongo, M. R. (1997). *Creative expression and play in early childhood.* New Jersey: Prentice-Hall.

Kangrga, M. (1984). *Practice – time – world.* Beograd: Nolit.

Kangrga, M. (1989). *Thought and reality.* Zagreb: 'Naprijed'.

Kemmis, S. & McTaggart, R. (2005). Participatory action research: communicative action and the public sphere. In N. K. Denzin & Y. Lincoln (Eds.), *Handbook of qualitative research* (3rd ed.) (pp. 559-604). Thousand Oaks, London and New Delhi: Sage.

Kilpatrick, T. H. (1918). The project method. *Teachers College Record, 19*, 319–334. Retrieved July 23, 2008, from http://historymatters.gmu.edu/d/4954/

Laidlaw, M. (2005). *Response to Branko Bognar.* Retrieved July 23, 2008, from http://www.jackwhitehead.com/monday/mlonbb.htm

Lalović, D. (2000). Crisis of the Croatian Second Republic (1990-1999): Transition to totalitarianism or to democracy? *Politička misao: Croatian political science review, 37*(5), 47-60.

Leitch, R. et al. (2007). *Educational action research, 15*(3), 459–478.

Lewin, K. (1946). Action research and minority problems. In Lewin, G. W. (Ed.), *Resolving social conflicts: Selected papers on group dynamics* (pp. 201-216). New York: Harper & Brothers.

Lincoln, Y. & Guba, E. (2000). Paradigmatic controversies, contradictions, and emerging confluences. In N. K. Denzin, & Y. Lincoln (Eds.), *Handbook of qualitative research* (2nd ed.) (pp. 163-213). Thousand Oaks, London & New Delhi: Sage.

Lippitt, R. (1950). Action-research and the values of the social scientist. *Journal of Social Issues, 6*(4), 50-55.

Marx, K. (1961). Economic and philosophical manuscripts (T. B. Bottomore, Trans.). In E. Fromm (Author), *Marx's concept of man* (pp. 93-196). New York: Frederick Ungar Publishing Company.

McNiff, J., Lomax, P. & Whitehead, J. (1996). *You and your action research project.* London: Routledge.

McNiff, J. with Whitehead, J. (2002). *Action research: Principles and practice.* London & New York: Routledge/Falmer.

McNiff, J. & Whitehead, J. (2006). *All you need to know about action research.* London, Thousand Oaks & New Delhi: SAGE Publication.

Mills, G. E. (2000). *Action research: A guide for the teacher researcher.* Upper Saddle River, New Jersey: Prentice-Hall Incorporated.

Montessori, M. (1946). *The absorbent mind.* Adyar; Madras: The theosophical publishing house.

O'Brien, N. & Moules, T. (2007). So round the spiral again: A reflective participatory research project with children and young people. *Educational Action Research, 15*(3), 385-402.

OECD. (2001). *Thematic review of national policies for education – Croatia.* Retrieved July 23, 2008, from http://www.see-educoop.net/education_in/pdf/oecd-review-cro-enl-t05.pdf

Polić, M. (2006). *Facts and values.* Zagreb: Croatian Philosophical Association.

Reason, P. (Ed.). (1994). *Participation in human inquiry.* London: SAGE Publications.

Reason, P. & Bradbury, H. (Eds.). (2006). *Handbook of action research.* London, Thousand Oaks & New Delhi: SAGE Publications.

Rogers, C. (1969). *Freedom to learn.* Columbus, Ohio: Bell & Howell.

Rogers, C. (1980). *A way of being.* Boston: Houghton Mifflin Company.

Rogers, C. (1995). *On becoming a person: A therapist's view of psychotherapy.* New York: Houghton Mifflin Company.

Spindler, G. & Spindler, L. (1987). *Interpretive ethnography of education: At home and abroad.* Hillsdale: Lawrence Erlbaum Associates.

Steinberg, S. & Kincheloe, J. L. (1998). *Students as researchers: Creating classrooms that matter.* London & Bristol PA: Falmer Press.

Stenhouse, L. (1975). *An introduction to curriculum research and development.* London: Heineman.

Stoll, L. & Fink, D. (2000). *Changing our schools: Linking school effectiveness and school improvement.* Zagreb: Educa.

Stringer, E. T. (1996). *Action research: A handbook for practitioners.* Thousand Oaks: SAGE Publications.

Ulewicz, M. & Beatty, A. (Eds). (2001). *The power of video technology in international comparative research in education.* Washington: National Academy Press.

Vygotsky, L. (1993). Extracts from Thought and Language and Mind in Society. In B. Stierer & J. Maybin (Eds.), *Language, literacy, and learning in educational practice: A reader* (pp. 45-58). Clevedon: Multilingual Matters Ltd.

Vygotsky, L. (2004). Imagination and creativity in childhood. *Journal of Russian & East European Psychology, 42*(1), 7-97.

Wenger, E. & Snyder, W. (2000). Communities of practice: The organizational frontier. *Harvard Business Review, 78*(1), 139-145.

Wenger, E., White, N., Smith, J. & Rowe, K. (2005). *Technology for communities.* Retrieved Jun 19, 2007, from http://technologyforcommunities.com/CEFRIO_Book_Chapter_v_5.2.pdf

Whitehead, J. (1989). Creating a living educational theory from questions of the kind, 'How do I improve my practice?' *Cambridge Journal of Education, 19*(1), 41-52.

Whitehead, J. (2003). Creating our living educational theories in teaching and learning to care: Using multi-media to communicate the meanings and influence of our embodied educational values. *Teaching Today for Tomorrow, 19,* 17-20.

Whitehead, J. (2005a). Living educational theories and multimedia forms of representation. In F. Bodone (Ed.), *What difference does research make and for whom?* (pp. 77- 91). New York, Berlin, Brussels, Vienna, Oxford: Peter Lang.

Whitehead, J. (2005b). Living inclusional values in educational standards of practice and judgment. *Ontario Action Researcher, 8*(2). Retrieved October 6, 2008, from http://www.nipissingu.ca/oar/PDFS/V821E.pdf

Whitehead, J. & McNiff, J. (2006). *Action research: Living theory.* London, Thousand Oaks & New Delhi: SAGE.

Winter, R. & Munn-Giddings, C. (2001). *A handbook for action research in health and social care.* London: Routledge.

# IN PURSUIT OF COUNTERPOINT: AN EDUCATIONAL JOURNEY

Moira Laidlaw, UK

## RATIONALE

In the story of my educational journey I will try to present the living standards of judgment and logic as I ask myself the question, 'How can I live the most worthwhile form of life?' In contributing to this first issue of EJOLTS I want to offer readers an original contribution to the conversation started by Donald Schön (1995) about the need for a new epistemology.

In my doctoral thesis (Laidlaw, 1996) I originated the idea of living and developmental standards of judgment in the generation of living theories. As my research evolved in China (2001–2006) I came to understand that action research with Chinese characteristics involved the kind of receptive and responsive standards of judgment used by Rayner to distinguish his work on inclusionality (Rayner 2004 – see later). In explaining my educational influences as my living educational theory I am also aware of needing a *living* logic – i.e. one that can develop as my insights develop – to distinguish the sense I am making of my existence. I am thinking of living logic in the way I developed in a paper I wrote

(Laidlaw, 2004a) for the Bath Action Research Group which met at the University of Bath  In short I describe and explain my logic as stemming from a belief that:

> My life has a purpose. It's for something. I chose education as the principle articulation of my life's focus a long time ago... I see myself as acting in the name of education and being in the loving service of humanity...The distillation of the above in language is fairness and in the form of my sense-making in mind and thought is logic and in motivation and actions is love. (p. 3)

I go on to say that this living logic develops through experience with others over time in my practice. It is not static and isn't used as a theory from which I extrapolate my practice. It is living in the sense that my practice develops my theory, which develops my practice and so on. My logic is developing through my melding of theory and practice into praxis.

In this paper for EJOLTS I wish to account for my own educational development which is a description and explanation of how I have tried to live my values more fully in my educational practice. If, in our rubric at EJOLTS we say: 'We are particularly interested in publishing explanations that connect a flow of life-affirming energy with living values such as love, freedom, justice, compassion, courage, care and democratic evaluation', then it is important that we show how we are accounting for these values in our actions.

When I agreed to work in EJOLTS[14] I did so because I felt this could be a journal in which people could share their desire to learn, one in which we could enable better processes for learning as well as facilitate democratic processes, values of freedom, love and equality together. I wanted to help build a learning community.

## COUNTERPOINT AND RELATED TERMS USED IN THIS PAPER

I need to start by explaining the term 'counterpoint' and related expressions used in this paper. 'Counterpoint' is a musical term denoting the

---

[14]     Editor's note: Moira Laidlaw was the first Chair of the Editorial Board at EJOLTS.

fusion of different voices into a harmonious whole. 'Voice' is the 'technical' term given to single strands of melody in a composition, in which no voice is subsumed within the whole, but each one is necessary to the whole and the whole is necessary to the individual voice. Counterpoint is the musical equivalent of holding the one and the many together as Socrates said in his exposition about what constitutes the art of a dialectician. In order to help explain what I mean, if you are reading this on the internet I would invite you to click on the url after the following few paragraphs. If you don't have the internet, please have a look at the footnote below, which I hope offers some explanation of what I want to say[15].

In the extract, the counterpoint begins at 2 minutes 50 seconds. On the screen you will see the voices represented as coloured bars and you can see how they interweave. There is a symmetry and sense of challenge and resolution. Although the whole integrates, no one voice is lost in the developing of the arguments, yet the resolutions are beautiful. Watch and listen particularly at just after three minutes, when the first voice is heard again and then a new development is forged. You can see on the screen as well as hear how there is argument or exposition, counter-argument, resolution, voices listening to voices, or persistence when a voice needs to influence other voices. Look at the dialogue at four minutes 26. It is a true dialogue in the way in which neither suppresses the other, but in which both have their say and add to the overall impetus, yet retaining at the same time their individuality.

I believe all of this has been framed by Bach with a sense of purpose, and that purpose manifests itself in his determination to evolve the highest forms that those voices can evolve separately and together, and for those voices to speak with authority and confidence and for those voices to do it beautifully! In

---

[15]     The youtube presentation plays Bach's Toccata and Fugue, which is a piece of music for organ. The notes are visually represented in colour-coding for the individual voices, and intervals between notes are depicted bars of colour on the screen going up or down. As the music develops you watch its development and interplay of voices in a visual form, and see the weavings of the various voices. It is a visual as well as aural counterpoint.

educational terms this music represents to me a principled expression of beneficial purposes in the world, of collaboration, of the expectation that voices can work together towards goals which matter, and harmonise eventually into something even better than there was before. It is something that relies on the creativity of individuals and groups. I perceive a link between counterpoint and educational processes.

In the way I am using it in this paper, an educational counterpoint is a space in which people are learning something worthwhile and to their greatest potential. Learning how to create, facilitate and hold this space becomes the counterpoint of my practice.

So, after all this preamble, have a look and listen to Bach's Toccata and Fugue (http://www.youtube.com/watch?v=ipzR9bhei_o).

## THE RELATIONSHIP BETWEEN COUNTERPOINT AND MY EDUCATIONAL VALUES

In my thesis (Laidlaw, 1996) I maintained that all the values in my practice were not separable in meaningful ways: that the whole and the parts were one and they were continuously developing dialectically. This sense of the living and evolving values became my original contribution to knowledge. I now believe the notion of counterpoint offers me a way of expressing these ideas more completely. The degree of counterpoint in my practice also indicates my own learning.

### Democratic practices

I am aware that I cannot write about values as if they are static. Values become apparent through our actions. From the beginning of my professional practice I have consciously sought to embed democratic principles within educational processes and have rated the success of a particular series of lessons or teacher-observations to the degree to which democratic principles are being encouraged (Laidlaw, 1996). I accept this notion of democracy: 'Democracy [is] not majority rule: democracy [is] diffusion of power, representation of interests, recognition of minorities' (Calhoun, as cited in Roper 1989, p. 63).

Working out to what degree I was enabling this space and how I could improve it has usually been the stuff of my educational theorising from the beginning of my career – as far as I could say I did any theorising at the beginning of my career. And in this paper (Laidlaw, 2008) I think you will see the degree to which my understanding of democratic practices has developed and become a significant voice in the counterpoint of my professional development. I am claiming that within any counterpoint of my educational life, the inquiry into how I can improve the value of democracy is always a recurring theme. I place the idea of it here in the paper so that you can bear it in mind in subsequent parts. Within my particular developing value of democracy comes an increasing understanding and integration of what I and others perceive as fairness as well (Laidlaw 1997, 1998, 2000, 2001a).

### Freedom

I also want to draw your attention to my value of freedom. It is my belief that I try to act in ways that will enhance individuals' and groups' freedom. By freedom I don't mean licence. With freedom come responsibilities, because what we do impinges on others. I believe that individuals and groups have the right to self-determination if this does not infringe the freedoms of others. I also believe responsible freedom encourages creativity and through creativity we fulfil and challenge ourselves.

**Equality**

Linked to the above values is my notion of the equality of all human life. All people – regardless of religion, faith, ethnicity, race, history, geography, language, gender, age, physical or mental abilities – are equal. That this notion is not universally recognised has meant that I have sometimes had to strive for it overtly in my practice. This is not only to enable worthwhile learning about something like English or Psychology, but more importantly to draw attention to the necessity of raising equality as an issue. If I do not treat all my students, colleagues and pupils as equal, then I am violating one of my core values, and the counterpoint is distorted. Experiencing a sense of being respected as an individual is, I believe, a human right. The degree to which I succeed or fail as I embed this value within my practice is a degree to which I am maintaining a counterpoint of practice.

**A desire for wholeness**

In addition I see a desire for wholeness as an important value in my work. I perceive wholeness (which had an original connotation of holiness) to be likened to integrity. I am referring to the healthy unfolding of something/someone towards a goal, which is not necessarily fully understood or planned for, but gains creative momentum as aspects begin to fit together in harmony. In my own educational development and in influencing the educational development of others, I have sought wholeness rather than pieces or fragments. I have sought a degree of symmetry. Integrity also suggests honesty or adhering to certain ethical principles. I believe that developing my values of democracy, love, freedom and equality has integrity because I can show how such integrity has led to improvements in learning something of value. My desire for wholeness is about wanting to cohere particular values within my educational processes. I detail more about my understanding of wholeness and fragmentation later on in the paper.

**Love**

In his doctoral thesis Finnegan (2000, as cited in Civille 1981, p. 300), states that 'love enables justice to see rightly'. This is a telling phrase for me. Love is what essentially motivates me to do what I do and guides me towards actions which are conducive to living out the above values more fully. In a review of a previous draft of this paper, Lewis Husain (2008) asked me why I care. I care because I see no other way of creating for myself a worthwhile life. I chose a long time ago to see life as meaningful as opposed to meaningless. As Scott Peck (1978) wrote, love is not so much a feeling as an orientation. It is hard work. It requires dedication and a belief and hope in oneself and the other. Love is what motivates me and keeps me going when it's tough. Love, for example, has helped me in the creation of this paper, which has been one of the most difficult in my life to write. I do it because I hope it will speak to you and that you may find some inspiration in it. If I choose not to see what I do as meaningful, then I will never create anything worthwhile. In the end I believe that we create ourselves in our own images and I don't want to be ugly on the inside. If, on the other hand, I believe my life is meaningful, then it requires dedication to see it through. It is love which provides sustenance as well as motivation for the journey.

The pursuit of counterpoint in my educational life requires a balance of the degree of emphasis given to any particular value at any particular time. In educational terms counterpoint is about balancing all the values and beliefs and experiences and insights at any given moment for the benefit of the learners.

## CREATING STANDARDS OF JUDGMENT FROM VALUES

The values I am highlighting of love, democracy, freedom, equality and wholeness for the purposes of any evaluation become my standards of judgment. These standards of judgment help me to frame my educational practice and theorising. I hope that these values can be seen to be emerging clearly in this paper. I believe you will see them manifesting themselves as the standards of judgment you can apply when I:

1. facilitate individual and collective voices into becoming a meaningful whole, in which individuals voices are neither subordinated to the whole, nor important only in relation to it;

2. (help to) improve practice and theorising; and

3. help teachers to develop greater understanding of their social and epistemological contexts in order to fulfil both personal and social values.

I will try to show my students and colleagues speaking for themselves as part of the explanation of my educational influences in my own learning, in the learning of others and in the learning of the social contexts in which the actions take place. (Again, the notion of students speaking for themselves is a democratic one in which I have been aided by reading the work of Dewey (1997[16]), Neill (1960), Rogers (1983) and Foucault (1980).) Now I want to show you where it all began.

## SOME PERSONAL HISTORY

I have been engaged in education all my life. I grew up in a middle-class family, went to several 'academically-inclined' schools, and then to university to study English and German. I gained a Postgraduate Certificate in Education (PGCE), and in 1978 I went into my first job at a comprehensive (state) school in Shropshire, which, in 1976 had been extolled by the HMI (Her Majesty's Inspectorate) as one of 'Ten Good Schools' (HMI, 1977) in England and Wales. Its reputation was founded on the headteacher's and senior staff's open style of leadership, in which they facilitated democratic forms of policy and curricular processes with staff. The headteacher, Mr. Richards, always seemed to bear in mind the axioms that teaching is for learning and that we were there for the

---

[16]     Of course Dewey originally wrote his epic book *Democracy and Education* in 1916.

children and not just for the sake of earning money. At my interview I made the distinction that it was my belief I would be teaching children not English. I believe it is indicative of my educational development that I would now say I learn with others, rather than teach anyone anything. It was the former sentiment that got me the job, however.

In this school of over 800 children, Mr. Richards seemed to know every child: I saw him over ten years address countless children by name. He appeared to be acquainted with many of their parents and their circumstances. His management style was easy-going but astute. He took great pains to find out what was happening in his school: a kind of leadership by walking around, I suppose. In my experience over ten years he used his knowledge to enable and not to control. I believe it was stemming from his leadership that teachers would eagerly collaborate to find ways of improving innovations and continuity without systemic distortion or pressure. We loved the children and we loved Mr. Richards. To me he was a genius. If he had been a composer, he'd have written counterpoint, I'm sure of that! I was lucky to have him as a role model for the first ten years of my career.

I also want to pay tribute to Brenda Pogson, the senior mistress, for the first few years of my stay in Much Wenlock. Her professionalism and many personal kindnesses to me were inspiring. From both of these role models I began to learn about keeping my eye on the whole picture as well as the moment. I look back now and see Mr. Richards holding the one and the many together, weaving counterpoint in his school between himself, students, teachers, governors, the community, and the local educational authority. From him I had my instincts confirmed about the importance of respecting individuals as a way of harmonising educational relationships on a wider scale.

After ten years I came to Bath on secondment to do a Master's degree in Education. Afterwards I stayed in Bath as a part-time tutor in the University's education department. I started a Ph.D. with Jack Whitehead, graduating in 1996.

During this former period at the university, I worked with 28 PGCE students on action research cycles on teaching practice who wrote finally up their findings. Many case-studies showed a concern with how they might enable their own students to improve their practice, which tended to encompass ideas around freedom of speech, and learning how to take responsibility for their own learning. This mirroring of tutor's and students' and *their* students' own inquiries focused me on the importance of mutuality in an inquiry. I came to understand that my students' and *their* students' liberation and my own were linked at profound levels, and that any account of my educational development would necessarily focus on those aspects of mutuality (Laidlaw, 1996).

## FRAGMENTATION AND WHOLENESS

In this section I am focusing on strands of my educational development that emerged in later years as significant catalysts of change. The categorisations of 'wholeness', or 'fragmentation', (values I referred to earlier) are tools I'm using to help you access important aspects of my educational development. Here I need to devise linguistic tools to approximate to what I mean although I don't find always find language very helpful when it comes to explaining my experiences.

Its limitations are helping me to understand more about the value of multimedia presentations in living theorising. Have a look at videos Jack Whitehead (2008c, 2008d) made of a lecture he gave recently. This shows, more powerfully than any description I could render in words, the flow of energy, the enthusiasm, the effort, that Jack makes to live his values more fully in his practice. Margaret Farren's (2008) current work shows this energy-flow as she improves her practice in facilitating learning through the creation of a dialectical relationship between the use of multimedia technology and Celtic Spirituality. You can read her paper as well as part of our first issue of EJOLTS.

In 1994 I administered the 'Third World Congress on Action Learning, Action Research and Process Management' in Bath (see Laidlaw, Lomax & Whitehead, 1994). The theme of the congress was 'Accounting for Ourselves.' In 1995 I became an English teacher in a local girls' comprehensive school where I was able to work on my doctoral and postdoctoral research, increasingly beginning to focus on equalising opportunities. This came more and more to mean nurturing people to speak in their own voices about issues which concerned them (Foucault, 1980).

I believe responsibility for learning and accounting for oneself are cornerstones of good learning (Laidlaw, 1994a). I believe, if responsible, self-expression is an aim of my teaching its processes are necessarily democratic and should highlight the significance of individual voices and group-harmony. By group-harmony I am alluding to counterpoint again, which enables dissonances in opinion rather than conformity, and in educational terms this can be related to MacIntyre's (1991) idea of 'constrained disagreement'. A tautness can exist between different voices (as in the YouTube presentation at the beginning), but this should be characterised by critical thinking and tolerance, as well as a sense of responsibility for knowing where one stands and why. Those realisations in practice are some of what I aspire to.

These ideas are related to Rayner's idea of inclusionality (Rayner, 2004) in which all things are organically related, yet have their own individual characteristics; a free flow between them in an osmotic way suggests health in a process, just as mental health may depend on having secure, yet reactive boundaries (Redfield-Jamieson, 1997). In reading Bohm's work as part of my revision-work for the resubmission of this paper I find myself saying immediately: *Yes, this is what I believe!* And this tacit belief in the unity of being, and a fear of fragmentation, is, I am claiming, a central force in my work. Bohm writes:

> The notion that all these fragments is separately existent is evidently an illusion, and this illusion cannot do other than lead to endless conflict and

confusion. Indeed, the attempt to live according to the notion that the
fragments are really separate is, in essence, what has led to the growing
series of extremely urgent crises that is confronting us today. (Bohm,
1998, pp. 1-2)

With a far-reaching voice of warning, Bowers (2008), in a response to an

earlier draft of my paper, writes:

> ...the individual is separated from traditions (that is, culture), community
> is separated from the other participants in the local ecologies, the
> environment is reduced to what can be exploited, and organic processes
> are interpreted as having component parts which can be re-engineered to
> improve profits and external sources of control.

I wish I'd written both of those above extracts, because they perfectly

express a concern I share about the importance of trying to heal what can

sometimes be over-systematised, and de-humanised educational processes. The

notion of counterpoint sets me free from such restraints and puts me in touch with

something more powerfully human. It gives me a way of expressing my

ontological truths, whilst at the same time developing structures that can be made

porous enough to support creative, dialectical and democratic processes of

education.

Perceiving fragmentation disturbs me on profound levels and it always

has: from broken relationships in childhood, to social deprivations in the world

that appal me in adulthood. It disturbs me in educational relationships when

communication has broken down. It disturbs me in Art if I perceive form and

meanings at odds, even warring with each other, or bellowing hatred, destruction

and dissolution in classical forms that seem to promise cohesion. It disturbs me in

moods and atmospheres, which suddenly become splintered and fractured and

unable to achieve wholeness again. It disturbs me in aims and objectives,

brokenly conceived and imposed on others, and then the processes vaporising into

disappointment and resentment on both sides. It disturbs me when I perceive the

larger societies with their factions and groups so angry at each other, building up

resentments and justifications and polarisations in their fury. Processes *leading* to

that frame of mind, as well as that frame of mind itself, strike me as insidious, divisive, and essentially self-defeating. I believe them to be dangerous to the well-being of individuals within their social contexts.

When voices cannot harmonise with their societies and are prevented from doing so, or indeed, prevented from helping those societies to become more redolent of the values already discussed in this paper (and claimed for later on), then those societies are unhealthy in my opinion. When voices and societies are harmonised in a creative dialectic that enables individual potential to be realised for the common good, and generatively acknowledges and nurtures those individuals for themselves and the groups they are harmonising with – then these, in my opinion, are healthy societies. I believe there is a sense of integrity, or wholeness within such potentials that leads to creativity and desires it.

Bognar and Zovko (2008), in another of the papers published in EJOLTS[17], express it well in my opinion when they say:

> Therefore, the final meaning and purpose of creative actions are not merely revealed in a deed or in a theoretical explanation of a process, but in the essential strengths that gave rise to the deed. By creating something a human being produces their own world, themselves, and also their own creative power. It means that the end-purpose of creativity is the human being who has produced their own human nature – their culture. (p. 4)

Fromm (2003) also writes about the significance of creativity: 'In the act of creation man transcends himself as creature, raises himself beyond the passivity and accidentalness of his existence into the realm of purposefulenss and freedom' (p. 35).

In my doctoral thesis I put forward the idea through the leit-motif[18] of the *Ancient Mariner* in which his act of shooting the albatross – a creature sent by God and a part of the wholeness of being – fragmented the harmony of the mariners' lives. The Mariner was punished because he destroyed the inherent harmony and wholeness of the cosmos and thus fragmented reality. I cite this

---

[17] Editors' Note: See earlier paper in this volume.
[18] A leit-motif refers to a repeated theme in a piece of music.

example because it's a significant stop-over on my educational journey that has me led here (and from where I am still travelling).


## AN EXPERIENCE OF WHOLENESS

I want to include now something that has tremendous resonance and numinosity for me. I know that not everything can be expressed in words, because some experiences and insights reach beyond language and into spirit and what I would call soul. I want you to know I hesitated about including this description because it isn't simply an anecdote that describes a precious experience I once had. In fact, I believe the experience expresses me, and I believe it is wholly germane to this paper because it shows in stark relief what it is I seek in my educational life.

My sense as a child of the oneness of the universe was begun in my seventh year when I experienced something I can only describe as a living hallucination. I heard Bach consciously for the first time. Standing in the school-hall after Assembly[19] the children filed out to a record playing Bach's Brandenburg's        first        concerto,        the        slow        movement (http://www.youtube.com/watch?v=LCnJ1Rk93_g) I stood impaled with light and felt and saw and sensed all around me a living oneness. The desk I stood beside became living wood again, rather than a shaped block, inert and unfeeling. The voices I heard in the playground outside were woven into the music's counterpoint. I looked at my hands, turning them over and over and seeing that they were not simply parts of my body, for there were no parts; they were joined to me, but they were joined to everything around me as well. All of me was. There was a daffodil in a cracked vase on the teacher's desk across the room and I felt

---

[19]     Assembly refers to the then compulsory period of religious worship during a school day (usually first thing in the morning) that all schools performed daily by law at that time (early 1960s).

my heart expand with love for the flower and it too, I realised, was part of me and I of it. I understood its petals and why it was yellow and what being yellow felt like. There was absolutely nothing frightening about this experience; on the contrary I felt awash with harmony, peace and love. It was the most beautiful experience of my life because, in the language of this paper, it felt as if I were in a state of counterpoint with the universe.

Then a larger sense entered my understanding. Not only was it this classroom and these children outside on the playground that were connected to me and me to them, but beyond that to the way home, to London (the city nearby) to other countries, then outwards to the stars, which had always fascinated me. As C. S. Lewis says: 'Something must drive us out of the nursery to the world of others' (Lewis, 1964, p. 41).

Lewis' solution is suffering. Mine, however, is joy. I experienced the reality of others as well as the connections and responsibilities we all have to each other, the world we live in and the cosmos. The music infused me with understanding of a type I have never forgotten. It is this kind of understanding I seek in my work, not as an aim, but as a value, as a living personal truth and one which, I believe, connects me to all creation. Everything became a voice in the counterpoint. The whole, more than the sum of its parts was, I now believe, God. The living logic of this recognises my limitations in ever articulating what I perceive as true. However, I believe that the multimedia descriptions and explanations for practice, such as the ones we are developing at EJOLTS, may help us to get closer to a sense of fusion, coherence, and wholeness. It is one of the reasons I am excited about the Educational Journal of Living Theories: it may narrow the gaps between what we do, what we say and what we are.

Descriptions of such mystical experiences are hardly unique! Maslow called them peak experiences in a process of actualisation (Maslow, 1970, p. 161). This seems to me a European way of seeing people and their relationships to their contexts – i.e. as divisible in clear-cut ways, the power of analysis over synthesis.

I realise I have opened a huge box here, which this paper is not designed to answer. In China where I spent nearly six years I found that some cultural ways of seeing are unlike European ones, and the highly influential *Dao de Jing* (*The Way*) (道德经) of Lao-zi (老子) does not isolate the individual from experiences of oneness. Instead of writing about individual enlightenment, this series of poems concentrates on what underlies every process of human experience:

(道可道、非常道。名可名、非常名無名天地之始有名萬物之母。故常無欲以觀其妙、常有欲以觀其徼。此兩者同出而異名。同謂之玄。玄之又玄、衆妙之門)

I - The Flow of Life -

*The Flow of the universe is not one you can explain*
*And its true name is not one you can speak.*

*For the universe began without words*
*And then we gave names to all things.*
*In the world of non-being, we embrace its mysteries*
*And in the world of being, we interact with it.*

*These two flow into one another*
*And are separated only by name.*

*Together they form a mystery.*
*Enigma in enigma —*
*Gateway to all wonders.*
(老子; Lao-zi)

I think there are links here between these Daoist ideas and Rayner's (2003) ideas about inclusionality. In addition have a look at Whitehead's (2008a) and Farren's papers already alluded to, as they also write about the energy-flow in human experiences that can be enhanced for the good of us all.

I realise my experience as a child is not unique but it was formative for me and I believe it has influenced my life ever since. The legacy of this experience has been to give me clues whereby I can recognise the 'Yes, that's it!' moments. In other words, my mystical experiences have helped me to gauge situations in my educational life. This does not mean I am goal-oriented, so much as having a facility sometimes to work with groups of children – and sometimes adults – in such a way to help us cohere as a community of learners, as well as helping individuals find their own voices and their own particular creative abilities.

That early experience has also infused me with huge energy and drive to do what I can in trying to make the world a better place. In those precious minutes as a child I experienced awe for the cosmos, for myself, the beauty of my own body, and of the world around me and the biggest insight of all, that when seen in this way, everything made sense. Simply that. It made sense and I was at peace with all of it and it was at peace with me because we were all one. There was no fragmentation because there is no fragmentation.

I will always reject processes leading to fragmentation – well, such is my self-belief. For me such splintering leads towards the dark and I want to experience the light and help others to do so. This is my tacit knowledge, which I do not believe can be gainsaid by you as you read this paper. What you *can* gainsay, and what I hope you will contradict if you find my logic flawed, is what I have chosen *to do* with this knowledge, and it is about this that my paper revolves. In actual fact it is around this that all my papers (http://www.actionresearch.net/writings/moira.shtml) revolve, whether overtly or not. My understanding and my actions in the world aspire to achieve this creative dialectic, this counterpoint – voices merging, fusing, diverging, learning and celebrating. My knowledge, values and theorising understandings of my professional practice have developed, in the sense I can both articulate them, and evoke their power in helping me improve what I am doing. My educational life is a living process of becoming. I was never quite able to articulate or explain all this in my thesis to my satisfaction, because I still didn't understand it all as a process of pursuing counterpoint. Once this metaphor took root in me, as once the legend of *The Ancient Mariner* (Coleridge, 1798) did in my thesis, I began to understand more about how my living educational theorising works.

I also want to say that I slip in and out of this understanding of the interrelation between my knowledge and values. I am a part of the chaos and beauty around me and inside me, and so there are times when I am not as wise at all as I experienced in those profound moments of insight at the age of seven. If I were all the time so close to the meanings I glimpsed then, my educational development would always have held the one and the many together, always woven the voices into the living fabric of our canvases more educationally; it would always have cohered into counterpoint. Such hasn't always been the case.

Let's now look at the beginnings of this weaving of voices and values, and the evidence for my educational development and significant learning emerging out of the processes.

## WHAT HAVE I DONE?

### My first ten years of professional practice

My first ten years of professional practice are scant on evidence of any educational influence on my students. Coincidentally, in the writing up of this paper in preparation for our first issue at EJOLTS, I received this letter through the web-based friendship network, 'Friends Reunited' from a student I taught in the sixth-form back in the 80s. She wrote:

> I don't know whether you'll remember me! (I do!) School was so long ago now and some of the most vivid and best memories I have are times spent in English with you at the helm! I still have the copy of *Jude the Obscure* you gave me and funny but every time I see it I think of you!!

And then nearly at the same time, this from another former student:

> I was in your tutor group in my 1st year (1980); you also took me for some lessons. I have spoken about you so many times over the years as you are always the teacher that I remember the most, I always felt that you believed in me. Hope you are O.K.

And this one from a former student (an 11 year old then) I taught in my first year (1978): 'I remember English, sitting in the library classroom with

Charlie & Jinks, taking it in turn to read passages from books (*Animal Farm*?). [You were] one teacher who made school pleasurable...'

This latter student participated in an Assembly (a coming together of a whole school under one roof once a day for some religious purpose (this was the law back in 1978)) in which his whole class and I created a short series of sketches about the poem by William Blake, Tyger Tyger (http://en.wikipedia.org/wiki/Image:Tyger.jpg). One of his classmates coincidentally wrote to me recently out of the blue, offering me an mp3 rendition (http://ejolts.net/drupal/files/webfm/audio/Tyger_Tyger.MP3) of the cassette-recording made of the Assembly.

I think these unsolicited comments and the motivation to send me this recording show that I connected meaningfully with these particular students, but it shows little about how, or whether we were able to learn from our experiences, or whether I influenced their learning or they influenced mine; or indeed whether we evolved any kind of useful theories from our work. There were, however, times I would claim when we truly approached counterpoint – in the sense of collaborating on that assembly, each student busily working on their own ideas towards a common goal, yet one that didn't in any way subsume individuals within the whole. There was enjoyment, creativity, worthwhile learning and so on. I claim this, but I have no compelling evidence.

One anecdote can give you the flavour of those early teaching days, however, when I was consciously learning how to democratise the learning processes with my students. I had early-on recognised the need for such goals in my teaching and it has been a leit-motif in all my educational development (see Laidlaw, 1994a, 1994b, 2008) because I understood that democratic processes value each voice in harmony and balance with the community: the two are held in a creative dialectic as issues of power and knowledge are debated and resolved. I wanted that space for my students, so here is a short story about its beginnings.

For the assembly already mentioned, all the children assigned themselves tasks after we'd discussed what we might choose as our material. As the class' English teacher, I wanted us to discuss what we might do to contribute to the Assembly in our lessons rather than telling each child what to do. Over three weeks the work evolved, some choosing to paint scenery, others to be in charge of props, some writing short stories or poems of their own or organising short plays and so on. All of them had a choice about what to do, but at the end of each week each child had to account to us all for what s/he had achieved.

One day Joanne (one of the writers above) looked at me wandering around the classroom from desk to desk, to see what was happening, and said to me: 'Why aren't you doing anything?' I have to admit, it hadn't occurred to me before that I should. I asked for suggestions. 'Set the poem to music,' Joanne said authoritatively: 'It needs some music. Right!' I said.

And so, at the instigation of a pupil and with the assent of the class, I wrote the music and that's what I accounted for at the end of that week! To me that says something about the values I was working with thirty years ago. I was trying to respect individuals and developing with them a space in which each voice counted. I was also showing myself willing to change what I was doing at pupils' instigation when I felt it was educational.

However, it was to take me until my time at Bath to begin to realise the importance of becoming more accountable for my work in terms of any serious claims to have influenced the learning of anyone. During my time in Shropshire, given the personal and professional freedom to develop through that whole school system with Mr. Richards, I put my heart and soul into the school. I left it in 1988 with a great sense of hope that I would be able to continue with something of value in Bath.

**Tutoring at a university**

From 1990-1993, I tutored part-time at Bath University's School of Education. In 1991 I decided to do a Ph.D. engaging in action research processes with Jack Whitehead. I had a passion for teaching and felt completely alive in the classroom. I wrote a *Guide to Action Research for Student-Teachers* in 1992, which was the first time I wrote anything substantial in my educational writing, because I had recognised the importance of building on the learning I had done with my students. Have a look at *The Pre-Service Guide to Action Research* (http://www.actionresearch.net/writings/preserve.shtml) in which some of my students were able to account for themselves as they worked on action research inquiries into the question: *How can I improve my practice?*

I wanted my students to have a chance to be the best they could be. I helped my tutorial students to formulate their own standards of judgment by which they would want their own voices to be heard and judged. Those standards still had to work inside the social and systemic standards expected of students in the schooling and university-systems, of course.

As I mentioned before, in 1994 I administered the third World Congress in Action Research, Action Learning and Process Management at University of Bath. It was a watershed for me. I began to learn more about the importance of treating others as individuals, regardless of whether I could see them face to face or not. Before that all my work had been concentrated on children in my classrooms. I had always found working at a distance with people less rewarding, less real somehow. I found it more difficult to recognise the simple truth that someone writing to me from New Zealand, say, or South America, or from South Africa was as fully real to them in their life as I was to me in mine. Just because I hadn't met them didn't lessen their reality! It is an embarrassing truth, but I didn't begin to grasp it consciously until that year. I struggle with it still when I hear news of the joys and calamities of people living in countries I may never visit. This narrowness of vision is something I consciously try to fight against as it is in direct contradiction to that sense of oneness I had as a child and still have sometimes in listening to music or reading poetry, and often with children, students or colleagues in classrooms.

My paper for the World Congress dealt with issues of responsibility, empathy and respect for others (Laidlaw, 1994b). The idea of accounting for myself (see Laidlaw, Lomax & Whitehead, 1994) became important to me then. It is something to do with taking responsibility for my actions and that's worthwhile because it shows respect to others implicated in the work, and also because it enables democratic challenges, such as the ones I hope we're developing here at EJOLTS.

## Two living contradictions

In 1995, just before finishing my doctorate I got a job in a Bath comprehensive (state school) for girls. I wanted to work in an all-girls' environment for several reasons, one of which I believe is pertinent to this paper: I felt that girls might gain more from their learning by themselves than if they were in a mixed environment, where it was my experience that girls could be marginalised in classrooms. For me it was an equal opportunities issue (see also Spender, 2001). I had perceived during my time at Much Wenlock that not only were the boys the most vocal in class, but that they also received more of a teacher's time and more of my time as well. I once recorded myself on cassette-tape (now lost) – at the instigation of Sarah, one of my 14-year-old students – to register how much of my time was being given to boys and how much to girls in a series of our German lessons. I was shocked at the time – it was about 60/40 in favour of boys and this was when I was trying! Sarah had challenged me, saying that we teachers regularly gave boys more time than girls. When I look back on it now I'm pleased to think that Sarah felt she could challenge me. I have always attempted to accept challenges to my authority (the institution endows me with power) as opportunities for learning. It could be quite painful at times, but I grew to accept that these challenges were indications of the freedom to learn in self-chosen ways I had influenced. In other words, the fairer the processes of education, the more challenges I was likely to experience. Such opportunities for learning have struck me always as constituting fairness.

Since my China days, however – see later – I have come to see single-gendered schooling less enthusiastically. I can now see that because we are a mixed-gendered society, inequities in teaching boys and girls together because of their different needs may need to be dealt with from within a mixed-gendered system. I now believe that it becomes incumbent on teachers, administrators and leaders to find ways to create equal opportunities for learning despite the apparently different learning styles of girls and boys (Matthews, 2005).

I began to realise that my value of democracy was growing into something that also required explicit structures to support fairness and equal opportunities. Such values were assuming greater significance in my development of democratic practices than it had before.

I now believe that fairness is what equalising opportunities is about, and since about 1997 that has been my conscious aim in all my professional practice (http://www.actionresearch.net/writings/moira.shtml, scroll down below the Guyuan work). Some of my deepest learning occurred when my students told me I was contradicting my espoused values and I then researched the situation (see papers in above website).

In 1997 and 1998 I worked with a mixed-attainment class of fifteen year olds on some poetry. The following conversation marks the beginning of a huge learning curve for me because I wasn't balanced in the way in which I was trying to live out my values in practice. One student, Sally, remained behind after class one day. This is the conversation we had (from field-notes directly after the lesson):

> Sally: I'm fed up with this school! I hate this …school!
> Moira: Why is that, Sally? Come on, sit down over here and let's talk about it.

Sally: (crying, sitting down) I've had it up to here with white Geography, white History, white bloody everything. (Looking at me accusingly) And even white bloody English! When I was in London we learnt about Black culture. The teachers, a lot of them were Black too. I hate this bloody school! I hate it. I hate all the teachers. I just hate everything.

Moira: I remember what you wrote in your autobiography. Do you remember when you read it out to the class? 'And then they cast me out in a white desert.' Is that what it's like for you?

Sally: Too bloody right. Oh Miss, I want to go home.

Moira: Where? To London?

Sally: Yeah.

Moira: Well for the moment that isn't possible, is it? What can I do to help you in English here, Sally? What would make you feel you were learning something worthwhile for you? You know that Black Anthology I gave you, how are you getting on with it? We'll be studying it next term.

Sally: It's great, Miss. I love Maya Angelou. I've started reading 'I know why the Caged Bird Sings'.

Moira: Oh, I love that. Could you lend me it after you've finished with it? I haven't read it for ages and my copy's gone walkabout.

Sally: (laughs) O.K., Miss. (May, 1997)

This was a turning point in my career. Sarah at the school in Much Wenlock had alerted me to perceived injustices in my practice – and now Sally was doing the same in Bath. Both challenges represent, I believe, an insight that I was acting unfairly and these constituted watersheds for me. I was suppressing Sally's voice rather than encouraging it. In counterpoint there is no one voice sapping another. All voices are wholesomely working towards resolution, or at least, as I said before, a healthy balance. The first dissonance with Sarah had revealed to me something about implicit gender dynamics in schooling, and now Sally was raising my consciousness as regards race. Because of Sally's intervention I found a way to install the poetry of Maya Angelou as part of our examination coursework. Sally helped me to continue learning how important it was critically to examine my own values and actions. Before Sarah's and Sally's challenges I had been sure that I was acting fairly.

The rhetoric of my educational development has always been that I want each child to feel herself being valued for being herself. Sally didn't as Sarah hadn't. I simply hadn't realised what it might feel like to be in their positions.

This necessary quality of empathy is something that Rawal (2008)[20] writes about dramatically in her doctoral thesis. Such insights and practices (because empathy has to be acted upon to be worth anything) are so vital to evolving educational relationships. Sally and Sarah helped me to see that without that quality, the educational and ontological value of what I was doing was simply not good enough! From these two examples of my own living contradictions I believe did some of the most profound learning in my career because those examples are always in my mind. I can't dispose of them because, I suppose, they still have work to do.

On the day she left the school (July, 1997) Sally came to see me, thrilled to bits about gaining a place at a Drama school in London.

> Sally: I feel I have come alive... Reading this poetry[21] is like coming home. Do you remember you asked me that question? About coming home?
> Moira: Oh yes, it isn't one I'm likely to forget. Why is it like coming home?
> Sally: I am doing what I want. I decide. I say. (Tears in eyes) It helps that you've helped me, but I make the decisions. (She clasps my hands in hers.)
> Moira: (tears in eyes too) Oh yes, absolutely. That's what it's all about, isn't it? Oh, Sally, I'm so happy for you.
> Sally: (big grin) So am I. See you, Miss (relinquishes my hands).
> Moira: See you, Sally.

There isn't room here to go into more details about the educative relationships I evolved within that class, but you can read the paper (http://www.actionresearch.net/living/MOIRAPHD/Kaylab.htm) in which I documented the processes of learning. Suffice it to say that I was learning about my own practice from my students as well as influencing them educationally. I was evolving the skills that Branko Bognar (2007), in reviewing this paper in an earlier draft highlighted: that it wasn't for me to become a good teacher so much as to become a good learner if I wanted to glean the most educational value from

---

[20]  See Chapter Eight (http://www.jackwhitehead.com/rawalpdf/Chapter8.pdf).
[21]  I put together an anthology of poetry written by Black authors. It included Maya Angelou, Alice Walker and Jackie Kay.

my professional life and influence others educationally. Sally, and to a lesser extent Sarah (because I wasn't ready to learn so much) taught me the value of questioning my own practice from the students' point of view; in addition they helped me to realise that I could not hope to encourage fair practices in others if I were myself acting unfairly. There are several other papers (http://www.actionresearch.net/writings/moira.shtml) I wrote during the years at the Bath school, all of which deal with my continuing desire to improve learning.

### Using a camcorder in the classroom

Towards the end of my time at the Bath school I taught a class of twelve-year olds English (Laidlaw, 2001). In one of our units of work on the poet William Blake[22] I asked the children to do a project about his poetry, covering ground we'd studied, but presenting it entirely in their own ways. I acted as a facilitator. The students chose to be with the girls they felt most comfortable to work with – usually in groups of about five. They also had to include self-developed standards of judgment whereby they and the other students and I could evaluate the work. I sought consciously not to interfere with the direction of their studies but I was always available for discussion.

In the following video clip, you will see me working with Hayley[23] (http://www.youtube.com/watch?v=tmM4QiXUtbU). The video represents Hayley talking about her two chosen poems from those we studied. I hope you

---

[22]   See pictures (http://www.oceansbridge.com/oil-paintings/section.php?xSec=940) by Blake on the two poems Hayley was studying (http://en.wikisource.org/wiki/Nurse%27s_Song_%28Blake%2C_1789%29. http://en.wikisource.org/wiki/Nurse%27s_Song_%28Blake%2C_1789%29).

[23]   In the video Hayley is talking about her reasons for presenting her work in the way she does. She is articulate and apparently keen to show me what she knows. She is capable of contradicting me and is clearly pleased with what she has accomplished. Her comments also reveal a clear sense of understanding about the poems she has studied. All the girls and their parents gave their permission for this and related clips to be uploaded onto the web.

can see her drawing her own conclusions from what she is learning with a sense
of what that learning means for her own development. Hayley said later:

> Working in this way was new. You didn't tell us what to do. You helped
> us see what the whole thing was like, but then we had to work out for
> ourselves how to present our learning to the class. It was really difficult.
> There were times when I just wanted you to tell me what to do, but you
> wouldn't. But now, when I look back, I feel so proud. (Pause) This is MY
> work, you see. I did it. It's mine.
> Moira: Yeah, that's right. And how does that feel?
> Hayley: …I feel fantastic! I never felt about my work like this! It was
> exciting and as the weeks went on I wanted to do it more and more. It was
> so good. So good. My dad used to tell me off in the evenings because I
> was spending time working all the time instead of going to bed and getting
> some sleep, but I wanted it to be perfect. For me. My work. My ideas. I
> don't want this time to end. (Hayley & M. Laidlaw, personal
> communication)

Visitors often came into our classroom because we welcomed them having
a look at what we were doing. Many remarked they could not tell this was a
mixed-attainment class (Laidlaw, data archives) and that the students were
enjoying a lot of freedom and saying what they thought. I believe that freedom
and speaking for oneself are not mixed-attainment issues at all, but the natural
potentials of all human-beings in any environment conducive for learning. I
realised in Shropshire that a school can stand for responsible dissension, critical
thinking and aspiration towards individuality and wholeness. Dissension is not a
negative response; indeed it can be wholly positive if it represents critical thinking
and the struggle for freedom from oppression. I think this is one of the reasons at
EJOLTS we chose to have an open reviewing system. It suits this kind of inquiry
and development of values. It encourages personal responses and hopefully over
time will stimulate vigorous debate, challenges and healthy growth.

Striving for freedom of expression constitutes the dynamics that would be
expected in counterpoint in which voices sometimes pull apart as well as pulling
together in order to realise wholeness. There is clearly a struggle for each voice to
be heard, and yet each voice is heard, and how wonderfully! The music only
reaches its full potential both as individual voices and counterpoint, when each

voice delights in its own strengths and potentials and relishes the whole. Anyway, as I illustrated with the youtube visual presentation of a Bach fugue, I think you can hear and see this happening: how at the end, one of the voices is played at half the speed, having found another way to be significant. Some say Bach was a great mathematician because of the symmetry of his designs. I say he was an amazing human being!

At this Bath school I tried to exercise my tacit belief in the potential of children to rise above what they are, into what they can become. I claim that Hayley's comments show a certain trust, a sense of well-being, and a decided opinion about the worthwhileness of the processes she has been through. I will return to this video again later, as I changed my view later on about the video as a whole.

### Going to China: In search of integrity

In 2001 I went to rural China as a volunteer with VSO. Originally the contract was to last for two years, but I stretched it to five in Ningxia Teachers University (originally a teachers college) because I loved it so much. My reasons for choosing to leave my comfortable job in Bath for a volunteer's life in rural China are detailed elsewhere (Laidlaw, 2001b). Suffice it here to say that I wanted a broader challenge and felt that I had more to offer than I was offering in England. I needed to extend my own creative life. It was, in a way, a search for wholeness. I felt I could do more. I felt by not doing more I was not being true to myself or living up to my potential. I did it because I could. For me there is a compelling logic in that statement, like a teacher who said to me once when I asked her why she was a teacher: 'I teach because I was taught.' I didn't understand the portent of that until I went to China, but her words had a sympathetic resonance to my own aspirations and so I've never forgotten them. They really make sense now.

Apart from a language barrier (admirably overcome by my colleagues and students by speaking English, rather than by any of my paltry attempts to speak Mandarin) there were cultural, historical, ethnic, systemic, philosophical and material differences to surmount in my new environment. Descriptions and explanations of my claims for educational development during these five years can be found under the heading *Moira Laidlaw's Papers and Writings* (http://www.actionresearch.net/writings/moira.shtml). These writings deal with the ways in which I attempted to facilitate students and colleagues' own voices within their contexts as they underwent varying processes to improve practice.

## Bringing in the social contexts of my work

I want to write something now about how important it was for me to learn about the significance of the social contexts in my work, because before I went to China there was a gap in my understanding about the links between my social context and the work I did. Mr. Richards brought it to my attention once in 1987. He exhorted me to look at the bigger picture and not simply concentrate on the classroom. I thought he was wrong (talk about youthful arrogance!) because I didn't understand the dialectic that exists between learning and the social context. I didn't realise that my classroom was not the world, although it often felt like that. I suppose at the time I was more involved with teaching than learning.

In December 2006, an educational colleague[24] wrote the following to me in response to a paper I was working on:

> ...Your living theory could carry an enhanced analytical quality by extending through the unquestionable authenticity of the first-person consciousness of your writing into a third-person discussion of the material and structural context in which the first-person consciousness is being mediated (and both will be, of course, in flux and transformation I suspect)... (Colleague, personal communication)

---

[24] This is from an email by a colleague, wishing to remain anonymous, who was involved in their own living educational theory research programme.

I didn't disagree but felt that I was doing more to bring my work into the public arena of accountability, and that I had taken on board the epistemological significance of so doing. I replied: 'Much of the validity of what I believe and do, rests on the results of collaborating with others over time on issues that concern us'.

But to be fair, I haven't rigorously contextualised my accounts through the economic and political factors that hegemonise the conditions directly affecting my work in China. There are several reasons for this:

a)  I was in a privileged but precarious position of trust. As a volunteer, I was a guest. Going public on specific human-rights issues would be metaphorical suicide. I would simply be thrown out of the country and nothing would improve. It's not an excuse, it's pragmatism.

b)  My understanding of China remains fairly limited. Five years in no way makes me an expert. I was a foreigner looking in and do not believe I would ever be able to become a full insider (Laidlaw, 2004b, 2006). My understanding of contexts is limited.

c)  I am slow to recognise historical, political and social influences. I naively regard the people I work with - child or adult, Chinese or English, Black or white - as having common characteristics beyond mere social, cultural, ethnic, geographical, religious, gender, and historical boundaries. These are to do with the desire to speak in their own voices about their own issues. I tend to concentrate on those. I accept that criticism of my writing. I am not sure how much this specific focus diminishes my practice. This is something I am hoping readers can help me with.

There is a living contradiction (Whitehead, 1989), however, as long as I am not addressing these aspects above in my practice, which includes what I am doing with my educational research-writing. I hope the rest of this writing meets some of the challenge of those limitations and resolves the discord.

In China my work with colleagues thrived more than working with my student-teachers on their teaching methodology. By 'thrived' I am meaning that the work became self-sustaining to a degree and generated worthwhile learning and lots of energy from those involved. Colleagues were eager to say my students were gaining more jobs after graduation because there were classes in 'Western' teaching methodology now. With my colleagues, working on our action research inquiries[25] breathed new life into stale processes, and enabled us to take more responsibility for our own learning and teaching, as well as empowering individuals and groups to speak in their own voices about the issues that concerned them. It is difficult to distinguish at times whose influences helped to create which outcomes. Educational processes aren't linear or directly causal. I have learnt that for something to be educational, processes cannot follow an entirely pre-determined route at all.

Educational action research is a dialectical process whereby individuals and groups can come to know their practice better in order to improve it and to transform the contexts in which they find themselves for the good of all involved. I see living educational theory approaches in action research inquiries as placing more emphasis on the ontological and epistemological development of processes and people, individually and together, as they devise ways uniquely suited to their needs. These must be in dialectical and developmental relationship to the contexts in which the practices are undergone. Living educational theories are ever-increasing cycles of understanding, action, reflection, development, evaluation and aspiration[26]. Thus, if I am to extrapolate my social influence in this deeper dimension of counterpoint in my educational practice in any meaningful way, I have first to say something of the contexts and the people with whom I was working.

---

[25] My five-year inquiry was entitled: 'How can I promote sustainable educational development at Guyuan?'

[26] See http://www.jeanmcniff.com for further explanations of the spiralling nature of action research inquiries and by extension, living theorising.

Until I went to China my work was centred on my own educational development, and I wrote about it as if it were possible to abstract the 'I' from the setting in which the 'I' locates its identity. In China, this was harder to do in relation to my professional life (see case-studies at http://www.actionresearch.net/writings/moira.shtml).

During my placement the head of my department Dean Tian and I, together with experienced colleagues Li Peidong and Liu Xia (2004), built up an action research group in the department. We started with five members in February 2002, and by July 2006, we had nearly forty. We also worked with a local Moslem school (see Ma, 2006). We built up a network of teachers improving their practice, and held several workshops about action research in the New Curriculum for the teaching of English in China. This curriculum has carried the weight of law since September 2005. The New Curriculum advocates critical thinking, peer and self-evaluation, teaching as learning, and building partnerships in the learning process. This is nothing like the traditional Confucian way, in which classrooms are run on lines of military-discipline. The New Curriculum and action research approaches share the view that knowledge can be dialectical and that there is a relationship between the growth of a human being and the growth of knowledge (VSO, 2004). It also extols the learning partnership between teacher and student, and opens spaces for self-evaluation as part of the assessment system. This curriculum is, in other words, democratic in design, and because of this our action research work developed into individual inquiries that would meet its demands (see papers from colleagues at the previous website).

In December 2003, Dean Tian with officials from Ningxia Province's Education Bureau, the College President, and Professor Jean McNiff from Great Britain, opened China's Experimental Centre for Educational Action Research in Foreign Languages Teaching (CECEARFLT)[27]. In 2005, the Centre was given

---

[27]    See    pictures    and    the    Centre's    mission    statement (http://www.actionresearch.net/living/moira/mlarcentre.htm).

official status from the Education Bureau in Beijing, a necessary step in the legitimation process in China. Our Centre is the first of its kind in the world. In China this is seen as a great coup (Perrement, 2005).

Our work became increasingly focused on how we might help schools and our own colleagues and students to embrace the values of the New Curriculum in practical ways. Tian Fengjun and I edited a book of case-studies (Tian & Laidlaw, 2006), which detailed how our work was enabling new and experienced teachers to teach in ways that encouraged critical thinking and interactive dynamics in classrooms in order to improve learning. This was commented on favourably at local and national levels in the media (Guyuan Daily – 固原报, 2004, October 1st; Ningxia Daily – 宁夏报, 2004, October 3rd; Perrement, 2005) In 2004 I was awarded the State Friendship Award. Given annually to a few dozen people, the award is a state acknowledgement of individual foreigners' work in education, business and social administration, finance, import-export, and medicine. For six months, Dean Tian gathered information about me from colleagues, the local constabulary, VSO, and students. He submitted his application on my behalf to Beijing, where there is a full-time committee working on this annual event. I wrote in an email to Jack Whitehead:

> I had always accounted the social context as being the classroom before, if I'm honest, rather than looking at the contexts - political, social and cultural - that help to sculpt the art of practice and the significance of outcomes and even values to an extent. (M. Laidlaw, personal communication, June 5, 2007)

The State Friendship Award was conferred as a social validation of the work that had been done collaboratively with me simply as a symbol of something new and hopeful in a poor and remote rural town in northwestern China[28]. I am not diminishing my creative and original contribution, but I know that without the

---

[28] Friendship Award picture: http://www.actionresearch.net/living/moira/mlawardphoto2.rtfd/Photo_03.jpg I am sitting in the front row in a long, blue dress. Premier Wen Jiabao is four people to my left.

inspirational leadership of Dean Tian[29] and warm collaboration with colleagues, as well as the co-operation of the Ningxia Education Board and our own president of the University, such an award could not have been orchestrated. The organisation for this event is an example of counterpoint, in which so many agencies worked together in order to find a way of celebrating collaboration and international harmony.

The college was immensely proud, not just of me, but of having orchestrated this particular event. Dean Tian, a politician as well as a close personal friend, saw the potential of our collaborative work. It was a mark of his professional respect for my work that inspired him but this award raised Guyuan's visibility to Beijing. It was a huge event. There was also a letter from the Vice Principal of Ningxia's government to the college extolling our work, as well as a documentary on television about my life and work there. Such visibility as Guyuan gained from our work was a spin-off I had not foreseen, but I believe Dean Tian was astute enough to maximise all possible opportunities. These events energised the hope in the college (Wang, 2004; Tian, 2005; Liu Hui, 2006; Sun, 2006).

An individual was highlighted but it was as much a conferment on the society and the groups within that society, as it was on me. An illustration of this was when I came back home to Guyuan from the ceremony in Beijing. People stopped me on the street and shook my hands, eyes gleaming with enthusiasm, because they had seen the televising of the ceremony and Wen Jiabao shaking my hand and his assistant saying I came from Guyuan in Ningxia. What was most significant was not me, but the mention of Guyuan. A school in Haiyuan, a town near Guyuan, also felt touched by this award. The school was purpose-built as an Islamic school in the town, the result of positive discrimination on the part of the Beijing government to further the freedoms of Islamic people in China. The Guyuan group went to Haiyuan on a regular basis to assist in the development of

---

[29]     See Dean Tian's details: http://ejolts.net/node/42 He is one of EJOLTS' peer reviewers.

action research inquiries. See how Ma Yangui helped his senior English students to improve their writing (http://www.actionresearch.net/writings/china/MaYanguiar.htm). A member of the action research group, on a tip-off from Dean Tian, recorded the Awards ceremony and showed it to staff and pupils because it implicated them. It was their business. My experience in China was that when three people got together, even strangers on the street, they became an instant community. I saw this happen time and time again. The individual people, their voices, all the processes, insights, values, conversations, events, the educational developments, all were woven together into this Award. When the process was going on, I wasn't able to pick out the individuals' voices and what it all meant. I felt the honour but I now understand more about the Award's marvellous community and political implications.

This process of counterpointing isn't a fully conscious or individual process, because in the account you have read so far it is not simply I who has engaged in the processes, or conducted them. Many others created their own parts, and their influences wove the themes that stand out. Collaboration is a vital theme and was developed by us[30] as a way of improving what we were doing (Li & Laidlaw, 2006). We were engaging in worthwhile pursuits in the name of education (Tian & Laidlaw, 2007). Dean Tian and I discussed this idea (Laidlaw, 2006) during one of our marvellous 'putting the world to rights' sessions in his office, drinking lovely green tea and smoking endless cigarettes. We were specifically discussing our logical differences:

Dean Tian: What I do is about helping the whole to become balanced.
Moira Laidlaw: What I do is often about enabling individuals to find their voices.
Dean Tian: I don't see this as a living contradiction!

---

[30] 'Us' here refers to myself, my colleagues in Guyuan and Haiyuan, the citizens of Guyuan and Haiyuan and anyone else who was moved by the broadcast of the Award, the politicians who made the choices for the ceremony, Wen Jiabao and his contribution to the process of making visible the work done in his country in the name of education.

Laughter
Dean Tian: You are focused on individuals. I am focused on the whole.
We can complement each other.

Dean Tian had the wisdom not to seek to elevate himself above what we were doing, but instead conducted his own action research inquiry into how he might help his colleagues to become more collaborative in order to promote sustainable development (Tian, 2006). This was a profound development in the work of the Centre, because politically, culturally and historically, deans are hierarchically above most of their colleagues and do not open their work to the criticism of staff. However, as one of our chief aims at the Centre was for sustainable educational development,[31] Dean Tian knew he had to take the unprecedented step – at least it's unprecedented as far as I know in China. For a dean to become a learner and be seen to be a learner seemed to signify huge steps towards a democratisation of our work, which, as I have already explained, I perceive as being in itself educational and a necessary dimension. This changed the nature of what we were able to do together. In contrapuntal terms, his voice became more sonorous as it took upon itself the underlying hues of freedom, democracy and an openness to learning; his decision influenced all the processes we were engaging in. For a man in his powerful position to say that he was a learner and not a teacher, if you like, enriched the soil in which we could all grow.

Dean Tian's ability to include himself within the body of the work as well as being in a facilitating role for the whole initiative, encapsulates much of the same logic by which I was also working. Adding his voice so strongly to mine on this issue changed the epistemology of our work. Democratising the processes of learning in China is not a widely-pursued aim. Doing this work in Guyuan, a small, rural 'backwater', presented us with a chance to change the way in which learning happens. There was an augmentation at this point of the significance of

---

[31]    I heard from Dean Tian (November, 2007) that the Centre had won an award from the University in terms of its research. I left in July 2006.

our work. The particular values we were living out, like the democratisation of learning processes, were becoming stronger.

Alongside these changes in epistemology I was undergoing a seismic shift in perspective – from one of a deep individualism to a greater openness to the importance of the collective. It used to be uncomfortable (Laidlaw, 2006) but it has become a spur to learning because it helped me to understand and use the significance of what happened to me when I was seven.

My work shows increasing understanding over this period about the importance of collaboration within a social context (Laidlaw, 2004a, 2006). It isn't that I now diminish the significance of the individual; the individual is still central to me. However, in China I learnt more about the counterpoint of human realities. I learnt more about balancing the one and the many. Existentially and educationally now, I stand within the paradoxes of being myself and being one of a crowd, of being responsible and being a recipient, of even the reality that I don't exist either at one point or another but both at the same time and all exigencies in between. I exist in a quantum reality (Zohar, 1998).

### Some specifics of our work together in Guyuan

I now turn to an examination of some of the thinking and actions surrounding our work at the Centre. Li Peidong and I wrote a joint article (Li & Laidlaw, 2006 – alluded to above) and had a conversation in October 2005 that highlighted some stark differences in assumptions made between Chinese and some Western educational philosophies:

> Li Peidong: You seem to be assuming [in individually-oriented action research] that if someone learns something better that is enough to make the research valid. We don't see it that way at all. To be valid the research has to show that it connected usefully to the society in which we live. What impact does the research have at a social level?
> Moira: I'm not sure it's a western philosophy, I think it is descriptive of my interpretation of some of western thinking. What accords to my own assumptions perhaps.

Li Peidong: Perhaps yes, but my reading of western philosophy does place
the insights of individuals at the centre, rather than the observances of a
whole society. You value the single voice. We value the group voice.
Moira: Then what we need, perhaps, in our AR work here at the Centre is
some kind of dialectic between those two stances. Maybe that's AR with
Chinese characteristics.

My conscious goal during those years was to promote sustainable
educational development, which my colleagues and I understood to mean
engaging in action research with Chinese characteristics[32]. At an action research
meeting (June, 2006) in a discussion of what action research with Chinese
characteristics might look like, we highlighted values to do with love of family
(Liu, 2004) patriotism (Ma, X., 2006) and a selfless working towards goals of
educational improvement for all people, (Tian, 2005), and close collaboration
between colleagues and institutions and with local and national government (Li
and Laidlaw, 2006). It should be mentioned, however, that not all colleagues in
the department chose to be action researchers, and therefore I have little evidence
of their thinking about what we were doing, or how it squared with their own
educational philosophies and epistemologies. One of the senior members of staff
said to me before I left, however: 'I think this AR work is good for the
department. It makes other people know we are doing something special. Our
reputation is better because of AR.'

Visibility was a key element in the motivations of many colleagues as you
can see in their papers. To be successful in the work that enhanced our teachers'
ability to handle the New Curriculum added kudos to the department in the eyes
of the local education authority (which sent a letter of congratulation to the
department for their work in December 2004); the provincial authority gave its
financial support for Jack Whitehead's visit and, I believe, Beijing was showing
its recognition of our hard work in offering me the State Friendship Award.

In another instance of our work's social impact, Matt Perrement, a writer
for *China Development Brief*, one of China's foremost independent journals

---

[32]     See papers for corroboration (http://www.actionresearch.net/writings/moira.shtml).

(which has unfortunately now ceased operations), came to Guyuan for a few days to find out what the Centre was doing (Perrement, 2005). *China Development Brief* was a bi-monthly journal with articles about issues of interest in China in terms of culture, education, society, politics and economics. Its headquarters were in Beijing. The article detailed the educational and social value of the project to the college and the area, and what the author saw as the potential for the project to be extended into other areas of China in the future. Perrement revealed the group-nature of the success of the project and the way in which action research had become a way of helping teachers to implement the New Curriculum through the advocacy of critical thinking and pro-active learning techniques. In conclusion he wrote:

> The appeal of action research in Guyuan is undeniable and will doubtless outlast the presence of any individual. As teacher Li said: 'Action research is beyond education. It is about human beings and social development.' I always felt that, when analysing the differences in educational approaches, but have never seen it in action so clearly. (p. 6)

In Guyuan we wanted to enable greater consistency between espoused and lived values in the classroom with students, who would become teachers. I spent time working with individual colleagues in the deepening of their action research inquiries (see website for details of classroom observations and follow-up ideas), which often meant examining our living contradictions (Whitehead, 1989). Dean Tian, Li Peidong and I encouraged colleagues to write up their findings as we wrote up ours and we held validation meetings to enhance the educational value of the texts. Ma Xiaoxia (2006) wrote this about her conclusions about the purposes and value of the work she was achieving in her own educational development:

> The New Curriculum in China, in making performance more important than competence, shows a respect for [a] dialectical form of knowledge, because it accords students as well as teachers the right to find different ways of understanding the world.... The most important dilemma... in matters of educational values is whether people are enlightened with, or entitled to, certain freedoms to think and behave. As for static knowledge and dynamic knowledge, they are actually not completely in contradiction

to each other, and thus can collaborate with each other. That is, students should be enlightened with manifold freedoms to develop their own thinking patterns, and given the right and the responsibility to speak and create opportunities for mutual collaboration. (pp. 15-16)

In 2005 Jack Whitehead from the University of Bath, UK came to Guyuan. When I worked there in the early nineties, the political, social and economic factors impinging on the future lives of my students didn't concern me much because their relative affluence gave them a high degree of choice and self-determination. I assumed they came from similar backgrounds and expectations to myself so I never questioned the contexts. In Guyuan the contrasts of poverty in my surroundings and the harsher circumstances of my students' lives from those I had learned about in the West, were amply demonstrated by their lifestyles, their continuing worries about money, their responsibilities to their families' futures, their dedication to studying in order to justify their families' faith in them, and the low level of medical care available to them and their families. Extended families often pooled their collective resources in order to send one child to college, eventually to provide support for the family financially and as security in old age. There is no welfare state in China. This borderline poverty and lack of choice in individual lives were vividly visible to me in ways I had not encountered before. I could no longer separate the work I was doing in the classroom with the lives my students were leading outside it.

During his visit, Jack Whitehead (2008b) took some footage of the ending of a lesson with a hundred Teaching Methodology students, in which I was saying goodbye to them and trying to draw out one of the students from the crowd to thank her for her outstanding contribution in the lesson. Jack saw a value in what was transpiring. The significance of these moments was discussed at length between us and then Jack wrote this: 'We are agreed that what we are seeing in the video-clip can be described as a loving flow-form of life-affirming energy in educational relationships' (email correspondence).

There seem to me to be two intimately-related and significant aspects here. First is the way in which the capturing of this moment enables insights to be derived that might not be possible without such technology; attendant on this are the possibilities for educational development because of this refinement of visibility. The second aspect is that Jack and I were able to discuss such a moment and agree on something together about its educational and ontological value, which can carry through to our subsequent practice and theorising. It's not a template or a model for anything, but rather moments that enable us to focus more clearly on the values we wish to bring more fully into the world through our educational work. When we say that we are working in the service of education, what we are really saying is that the values we both recognise in the video of my work with Miss Tian embody those we identify with and seek to distil through practice over time. That's what it means to be in the service of education as we are improving our practice.


## COUNTERPOINT BETWEEN INDIVIDUALS AND GROUPS

With Sarah, Sally and Hayley I had worked through issues to do with empowerment and democratic forms of educational processes. With Hayley it was through the inauguration of developmental educational standards of judgment *in the classroom* as the video and her own words in my journal bear witness. With Sally and Sarah it was through enabling them to have opportunities that could help them to find their own creative levels.

Whilst studying the video of my actions with Miss Tian in the classroom in China, I decided (18 months ago) to look at the video of Hayley but I was shocked at what I saw. I ask myself now what was educational for Sam (her companion) about a process that excluded her, simply because Hayley had something to say that added to my sense of the evolution of an educational process. Hindsight is a wonderful thing! I cannot claim on the one hand that my work with Hayley was wholly educational or that my espoused value of fairness had been a part of the process either, when my work with Sam was so distinctly lacking in that quality.

I show no empathy for Sam at all in that clip, and that appals me now. What is even more worrying is that Hayley was allowed to see me treating another student with less respect then I showed to her. I believe that my educational development is characterised by being able to hear disharmony, picking out the strands that are discordant and then to attempt to avoid such consequences in the future. It has taken six years for me to hear this discord, so neither Hayley nor Sam can benefit from these insights. It is to be hoped though, that I and other people can benefit. When I watch the video now, I cringe, despite owning that there are some aspects which have stood the test of time. My error was in not including Sam in the discussion or showing any concern for her obvious discomfort. I was too task-orientated. I was teaching English and not children! Moreover, I wasn't open to what Sam might have been able to help me to learn.

In the video clip with Miss Tian, I believe I show in microcosm what I am meaning in this paper by counterpoint. We exist all together within a particular space and at a particular moment within which no one person is more significant than another. We are existing in harmony with the institution in whose name the educational development is being carried out through relational ties of experience, a common purpose, memories and significance. Counterpoint in educational terms juxtaposes respect for individuals and the whole group with a particular focus in this instance on one student, whose own learning needs were such that I needed to single her out. I did not want to sever the relationship with each student; I could have simply called Miss Tian out, stayed at my desk and allowed the other students to drift away. It would have been quicker to do it that way. However, I wanted to praise Miss Tian and single her out to herself for her unusual courage at volunteering information in a class at the same time as showing respect and affection for all my students. I felt her actions that day in class were a turning point in her learning journey but I had a responsibility to the whole as well as the individuals that go to make up that whole.

Standing at the door welcoming and waving off students was part and parcel of founding good relationships with them, for me the foundation of worthwhile learning. As the students flowed round me, I established contact with Miss Tian without losing contact with the other students, and in this way could help her recognise her specialness without rejecting the other individuals in the class.

As the crowd of students diminished Miss Tian and I were gradually brought into dialogue. Her voice had so rarely been heard in class, so I felt if I could only capitalise on it by affirming her courage and initiative, she might be able to sustain that necessary step in her own educational development. It seems she subsequently did this by becoming more communicative in class (Laidlaw, data archives). On the last day she came up to me, a most unusual act for her, took my hand and said how much she loved my lessons and was looking forward to becoming a teacher. I felt if she could not believe in herself sufficiently to make her voice heard, she would not survive in the competitive world that China is becoming. She would not be able to act as a role model for students growing up into a more complex world than their parents and grandparents perhaps could have known about in their own youth (Consulate General for P.R. of China, 2004).

It is a weakness of this account that I have only verbal evidence and my own journal entries with Miss Tian. She was one of 102 students in the class, but that is still an excuse! Working on valid evidence about individuals' educational development would be an educational process in itself should I ever find myself in that situation again. I acknowledge weaknesses in my systems of data-collection at this level. Anyway, Miss Tian said she was exhilarated (and a little wary) at being singled out, but she felt pride and achievement: her friend remarked that Miss Tian often alluded to the meaningfulness of this lesson to her. It is significant that the young woman applied for, and was awarded, her first teaching-post shortly before the end of the college-course. She returned to her home-town as many graduates do, in order to offer support for rural development. In 2004 at the State Banquet on October 1st (Labour Day) to commemorate the 55th Anniversary of the founding of The People's Republic of China, Premier Wen called to the people to unite in China's development programme, and particularly singled out the role of rural China in the country's economic revival (Wen, 2004).

To weave a pattern through my educational development is to see me, at my best, doing what I have written about above in terms of the educative relationships with Dean Tian, for example; or working with students and colleagues on their teaching and learning; evolving patterns with colleagues, students, friends, associates and citizens; or even with politicians in what became the Friendship Award in China. Weaving these patterns means evolving a sensitivity to disharmony when it arises, keeping a wider vision, working say, with an individual within a group but not severing the links. I suppose it is a little like being a conductor, but I think my job as a teacher has been less didactic than that.

## CONCLUSION

It is my belief that over five years in China I helped to develop standards of judgment such as the enabling of individual and collective voices, improving practice and theorising, and helping teachers develop greater understanding of their social and epistemological contexts in order to fulfil both personal and social values. I believe I did this by paying close attention to the values of freedom, democracy, equality, a search for wholeness and love within my practice. Engaging in action research with Chinese characteristics opened up channels of inquiry which challenged the hitherto accepted norms of a Confucian hegemony, by facilitating individuals to speak in their own voices about what they were trying to do with their own classrooms.

Similarly, *action research with Chinese characteristics* was conceived of as more than a sop to pacify detractors; we aimed to promote it as a genuine desire to see how to find new ways that suited the particular social, economic, political, interpersonal and professional needs of the people we were working with.

Chinese characteristics in our action research inquiries would, we hoped, diminish the chance of western imperialist imposition on indigenous cultural norms and might enable the people themselves to develop something they wanted to satisfy their own perceived needs (see Li & Laidlaw, 2006).

In broad terms I am claiming my educational development is increasingly characterised by respect for groups, individuals and the contexts in which we are working as we seek to improve learning. In personal terms I feel more adept and comfortable in the free-flow of life-affirming energy which can generate between groups and individuals as we are engaged in worthwhile tasks together.

By understanding my educational development as the pursuit of counterpoint – a musical form in which all voices are equal in value and in interest, and in which the whole is gradually developed into something which satisfies each individual voice – I am able to perceive my educational journey more clearly and thus relay it to you. Through the insight that my early mystical experience can be compared to counterpoint, I gained a way of understanding them both better. In my opinion, *counterpoint represents the highest achievement of my educational development.*

T. S. Eliot (2008) wrote about the beginning and end being fused. I started this paper with the assertion that at EJOLTS we are interested in 'publishing explanations that connect a flow of life-affirming energy with living values such as love, freedom, justice, compassion, courage, care and democratic evaluation' (http://ejolts.net/). I hope we are able to fulfil this promise. My action research inquiry has now become: *How can I work within EJOLTS in such a way to promote love, freedom, justice, compassion, courage, care and democratic evaluation?*

My educational journey is not over by any means, but for the time being I am ending my account here. I am eager to find out what you think/feel about this paper. By sharing our ideas and collaborating, we can improve the quality of our educational discourse, practices and theorising. We can help to make the world a better place for all of us to live in.

# REFERENCES

Bognar, B. (2007, December 24). Re: In pursuit of counterpoint [Msg 1]. Message Posted to http://ejolts.net/moodle/mod/forum/discuss.php?d=9

Bognar, B., & Zovko, M. (2008). Pupils as action researchers: Improving something important in our lives. *Educational Journal of Educational Theories,* *1*(1), 1-49. Retrieved August 28, 2008, from http://ejolts.net/node/82

Bohm, D. (1998). *Wholeness and the implicate order.* London: Ark Paperbacks.

Bowers, C. (2008, September 3). Serendipity/convergence [Msg 1]. Message posted to http://ejolts.net/moodle/mod/forum/discuss.php?d=9

Civille, J. R. (1981). Responsibility for truth, fidelity, honor, and justice. In E. J. Gratsch (Ed.), *Principles of Catholic theology: A synthesis of dogma and morals* (pp. 291-311). New York: Alba House.

Coleridge, S. T. (1798). *The rime of the ancient mariner: The lyrical ballads.* Oxford & New York: Routledge

Dewey, J. (1997). *Democracy and education.* New York: Free Press.

T. S. Eliot. (2008, October 12). In *Wikipedia, The Free Encyclopedia.* Retrieved October 13, 2008, from http://en.wikipedia.org/w/index.php?title=T._S._Eliot&oldid=244869836

Farren, M. (2008). Co-creating an educational space. *Educational Journal of Living Theories,* *1*(1), 50-68. Retrieved August 28, 2010, from http://ejolts.net/node/78

Finnegan, J. (2000). *How do I create my own educational theory in my educative relations as an action researcher and as a teacher?* (Doctoral dissertation, University of Bath). Retrieved August 28, 2010, from http://www.actionresearch.net/living/fin.shtml

Foucault, M. (1980). *Power/knowledge: Selected interviews and other writings 1972-1977.* (Gordon, C., Ed.). London: Harvester.

Fromm, E. (2003). *The sane society.* London: Routledge.

General Consulate of the People's Republic of China. (2004). *Chinese society in an accelerated restructuring period.* Retrieved September 22, 2008, from http://houston.china-consulate.org/eng/nv/t93560.htm

Guyuan Daily. (2004, October 1). *Local foreign expert gains state friendship award.* [Newspaper]. Guyuan: Guyuan Daily Press.

HMI. (1977). *Ten good schools.* London: HMSO.

Husain, L. (2008, September 2). Lewis Husain's comments on second revision of ML paper. [Msg 1]. Message posted to http://ejolts.net/moodle/mod/forum/discuss.php?d=9

Laidlaw, M. (1994a). The democratising potential of dialogical focus in an action research inquiry. *Educational Action Research, 2*(3), 223-242.

Laidlaw, M. (1994b). Accountability as responsibility and point of view: Working as chief administrator for the third World Congress on Action Research, Action Learning, and Process Management. In M. Laidlaw, P. Lomax & J. Whitehead (Eds.), *Accounting for ourselves: Proceedings of the third World Congress in Action Research, Action Learning, and Process Management* (pp. 61-64). Bath: Bath University Press.

Laidlaw, M. (1996). *How can I create my own living educational theory as I account for my own educational development?* (Doctoral dissertation, University of Bath). Retrieved September 22, 2008, from http://www.actionresearch.net/moira.shtml

Laidlaw, M. (1997). *In loco parentis with Sally: A matter of fairness and love.* Retrieved September 22, 2008, from http://www.actionresearch.net/living/MOIRAPHD/Kaylab.htm

Laidlaw, M. (1998). *Accounting for an improvement in the quality of my provision for some equal opportunities in my teaching from 1997-1998.* Retrieved September 22, 2008, from http://www.actionresearch.net/MOIRAPHD/mleo1.DOC

Laidlaw, M. (2000). *How can I continue to improve the quality of my provision of some equal opportunities values in my teaching of English to a Year Eight Group?* Retrieved September 22, 2008, from http://www.actionresearch.net/values/writings/values/mleqop.doc

Laidlaw, M. (2001a). *In the last months of my employment at X School, how can I help 8X to enhance their sense of community, as I assist them in improving the quality of their learning about English?* Retrieved September 22, 2008, from http://www.actionresearch.net/writings/values/ml8s.doc

Laidlaw, M. (2001b). *What has the Holocaust got to do with education anyway? Accounting for my value of 'responsibility' as a developmental standard of judgment in the process of helping to improve the quality of my educational influence with students over thirteen years.* Retrieved September 22, 2008, from http://www.actionresearch.net/writings/values/mlfinal.doc

Laidlaw, M. (2004a). *A description of my logic.* Retrieved September 22, 2008, from http://www.actionresearch.net/living/moira/mllogic.htm

Laidlaw, M. (2004b). *How can I help to promote educational sustainability at our AR Centre and beyond?* Retrieved September 22, 2008, from http://www.actionresearch.net/living/moira/mlwinter2004.htm

Laidlaw, M. (2006). *How might we enhance the educational value of our research-base at the New University in Guyuan? Researching stories for the social good* (Inaugural Professorial Lecture). Retrieved September 22, 2008, from http://www.jackwhitehead.com/china/mlinaugural.htm

Laidlaw, M. (2008). *Living educational theorising: How I developed a more democratic educational practice.* Retrieved September 22, 2008, from http://www.jackwhitehead.com/china/mllet10908.htm

Laidlaw, M, Lomax P., & Whitehead, J. (Eds.). (1994). *Accounting for ourselves: Proceedings of the third World Congress in Action Research, Action Learning and Process Management*. Bath: Bath University Press.

Lao-zi. (n.d.). *Dao de Jing: The flow and the power of good* (S. Kisa, Trans.). Retrieved September 30, 2008, from http://www.kisa.ca/daodejing.html

Lewis, C. S. (1964). *Surprised by joy*. London: Fontana.

Li, P. & Laidlaw, M. (2006). Educational change in rural China. *Action Researcher, 7*(3), 333-350.

Liu, H. (2006). *How can I help my students become more active in class?*. Retrieved September 22, 2008, from http://www.actionresearch.net/living/moira/LiuHui.htm

Liu, X. (2004). *How can I help my students' self-confidence through encouragement and respect?* Retrieved September 22, 2008, from http://www.actionresearch.net/living/moira/LiuXia.htm

Ma, X. (2006). *How can I balance my methodologies in the class in order to promote the learners' autonomy?* Retrieved September 22, 2008, from http://www.jackwhitehead.com/china/maxiaoxia.htm

Ma, Y. (2006). *How can I improve my students' writing?* Retrieved September 22, 2008, from http://www.jackwhitehead.com/china/MaYanguiar.htm

MacIntyre, A. (1991). *Three rival versions of moral inquiry*. Paris: University of Notre Dame Press.

Maslow, A. H. (1970). Motivation and personality (2nd. ed.). New York: Harper & Row.

Matthews, B. (2005). *Engaging education: Developing emotional literacy, equity and co-education*. New York & Milton Keynes: McGraw-Hill International & Open University Press.

Neill, A. S. (1960). *Summerhill: A radical approach to child-rearing*. London: Hart Publishing Company.

Peck, M. S. (1978). *The road less travelled*. New York: Simon and Shuster.

Perrement, M. (2005). Action research revolutionalises the classroom. *China Development Brief, 9*(4), 3-6.

Rawal, S. (2008). *The role of drama in enhancing life skills in children with specific learning difficulties in a Mumbai sSchool: My reflective account*. (Doctoral dissertation, Coventry University in collaboration with the University of Worcester, UK). Retrieved September 22, 2008, from http://www.actionresearch.net/rawal.shtml

Rayner, A. (2004). Inclusionality and the role of place, space and dynamic boundaries in evolutionary processes. *Philosophica, 73,* 51-70.

Redfield-Jamieson, K. (1997). *An unquiet mind: A memoir of moods and madness*. London: Picador.

Roper, J. (1989). *Democracy and its critics: Anglo-American democratic thought in the nineteenth century*. London: Routledge.

Schön, D. (1995). Knowing-in-action: The new scholarship requires a new epistemology. *Change, 6,* 27–34.

Spender, D. (2001). *The education papers.* London: Routledge.

Sun, W. (2006). *How can I create a more relaxed atmosphere in my College English class in order to improve learning?* Retrieved September 22, 2008, from http://www.jackwhitehead.com/china/sunweimin.htm

Tian, F. (2006). How can I help my colleagues to become more collaborative and thus promote sustainable educational development?. In Whitehead, J. & McNiff, J. (Eds.), *Action research: Living theory* (pp. 127-133). California: Sage Publications.

Tian, F., & Laidlaw, M. (2006). *Action research and the New Curriculum in China: Case-studies and reports in the teaching of English.* Xi'an: Shanxi Tourism Press.

Voluntary Services Overseas (VSO). (2004). *What's new about the New Curriculum?* Beijing: VSO Beijing.

Wang, S. (2004). *How can I help the students to improve their speaking ability through the speaking and listening part in the class of integrated skills of English?* Retrieved September 22, 2008, from http://www.actionresearch.net/living/moira/wangshuqin.htm

Wen, J. (2004). *Speech to the People's Congress: 55th Anniversary of the founding of the People's Republic of China.* Beijing: Beijing People's Press.

Whitehead, J. (1989). Creating a living educational theory from questions of the kind: 'How do I improve my practice?'. *Cambridge Journal of Education, 19*(1), 41-52.

Whitehead, J. (2008a). Using a living theory methodology in improving practice and generating educational knowledge in living theories. *Educational Journal of Living Theories, 1*(1), 103-126. Retrieved September 22, 2008, from http://ejolts.net/node/80

Whitehead, J. (2008b, December 5). Moira Laidlaw's non-verbal communications in teaching in China. [Video File]. Video Posted to http://www.youtube.com/watch?v=Z1jEOhxDGno

Whitehead, J. (2008c, August 27). Jack Whitehead keynote ICTR 08 clip 1. [Video File]. Video Posted to http://www.youtube.com/watch?v=gWabP2acxfk

Whitehead, J. (2008d, August 27). Jack Whitehead keynote ICTR 08 clip 2. [Video File]. Video Posted to http://www.youtube.com/watch?v=KXLqGAAK-D0

Zohar, D. (1998). *The quantum self.* New York: Harper Perennial Publishers.

# A NARRATIVE OF MY ONTOLOGICAL TRANSFORMATION AS I DEVELOP, PILOT, AND EVALUATE A CURRICULUM FOR THE HEALING AND REFLECTIVE NURSE IN A JAPANESE FACULTY OF NURSING

Je Kan Adler-Collins, Japan

## PROLOGUE

Before I offer you an account of how I began to make explicit my standards of practice, I need to say a few words about my spiritual values. These values are at the core of my being and actions. I am a priest of the Japanese Shingon Mikkyo Buddhist Order with the given name Je Kan. My name, I am told, is actually female, Ji Bo Kannon, an archetypal nurturing healing Mother. This energy represents unconditional loving associated with motherhood and with the ability lovingly to heal all without judgments or conditions, through the transition of one's own understanding of one's own issues, and thus, the individual 'I', truly transcends to the collective 'We' of community. Whilst this is not the appropriate place to tell the story of my development from Warrior to Priest (Adler-Collins, 1998) the story does provide some insights into the nature of my commitment to the spiritual values of the archetypal nurturing, healing

Mother, two of whose qualities are said to be trust, and making safe all forms of communication. Both of these qualities were issues of extreme distress and anguish in the formative years I spent in council childcare homes from the age of three, and an early manhood spent in the British Military.

I recognise that I am a product of my own educational journey, one in which reflective practice and researching my own understanding of my Western formed 'I' are fundamental aspects of my own being. Yet, in the same context, I see my Eastern Buddhist understanding as the dissolving of the concept of my 'I' as equally important and fundamental. This paradoxical struggle is a constant and unresolved issue in my learning as I struggle with attempting to see the separate areas of me: the nurse, the teacher, the reflective practitioner, the researcher and the monk, as separate items or areas of my selfhood, a position that is often required of me as an academic. For me they are all part of my whole understanding, and existence, in fact they form my holistic self in the Rayner (2003) sense of everything being connected through dynamic boundaries in a sense of wholeness and holonic[33] concept of self in the Wilber (2000) understandings of everything being nested and connected through and in holes.

From this, I create a sense of neighbourhoods of my multiple selves, which is constantly evolving, flowing into, and out of, defined aspects of selfhood. I see my conscious life-force weaving a web of experiences as I touch lightly with full consciousness with a sense of what I call *transient certainty*. By this, I mean that I only have the certainty of the moment in which to frame my understandings, and such understandings are fluid states of consciousness being adjusted and reframed as my sense of knowing and certainty change. This act of mindfulness in conscious inquiry is rooted in a sense of connectedness. This is represented as my assumed 'I' with its assumed values and identity shapes my living educational theory. Such shaping can be problematic. For example, as old aspects of an

---

[33]    Holonic was a term coined by Arthur Koestler, and taken up later by Ken Wilber. It refers to something being simultaneously both whole and part-whole.

assumed self or consciousness release new understandings which have the disturbing habit of disrupting familiar thinking and patterns of action. Such disruptions often require choice to be made. On the one hand, there is the choice to move forward and live with the new understandings and embrace them openly as new epistemological insights and filters of judgment or on the other, to stay with what is assumed known and has a degree of comfort due to our fear of the new and the unknown.

Such choices are seldom made in a vacuum as much of our behaviour is socialised and influenced by those around us. It can often be the case that those who are familiar and comfortable with our old projections and values of selfhood become distressed and angry at the new. New contextual awareness' is formed in the Schön's (1983, 1995) sense of reflection in and on action. My understanding of this is that reflection in action is the actual moment where many differing aspects of my selfhood search my neighbourhoods of being, with their embodied knowing, to make sense of the new experienced situation. From this process, I act in accordance with what I know. Reflection on action suggests to me that I am now in an evaluation phase. Did my action work? Could I have done any better?

In my learning, my new understandings have evolved a new epistemology, one that is very different from my foundational one, grounded in my Eurocentric gaze of my whiteness. I consciously came to question many of the values that I had taken as a given fact as I actively deconstructed the filters of my being. Such a process continued to create a series of paradoxes in my life-worlds as I lived with my new understandings. For example, at times I found myself as a Western white male in an Eastern male-dominated society. I found myself as a nurse, which is considered a female occupation because of its domination by women. I hold Buddhist values of spirituality in an Eastern system of education that appears colonised by the West and Western values. At times the system of education appears *more* Western than the West in actions and thinking. This observation has been pivotal in shaping the direction my life's work. I made the conscious decision not to comply with Freire's (2000, 2004) sense of supporting '*a banking education*', or being a '*banking educator*'. The following words of Freire entered my consciousness as an educator, that 'those truly committed to liberation must reject the banking concept in its entirety, adopting instead a concept of women and men as conscious beings, and consciousness as consciousness intent upon the world' (Freire, 2000, p.79).

Holding such a position has been highly problematic in my life and there have been times when the easiest course of action would have been to abandon my commitment. Yet every time I feel the fear of conflict and power washing over me I am reminded of the words of Palmer (1998) where he said:

> [A]s good teachers weave the fabric that joins them with students and subjects, the heart is the loom on which the threads are tied, the tension is held, the shuttle flies, and the fabric is stretched tight. Small wonder then that teaching tugs at the heart, opens the heart or even breaks the heart, and the more one loves teaching, the more heartbreaking it can be. The courage to teach is the courage to keep one's heart open in those very moments when the heart is asked to hold more than it is able so that teacher and students and subject can be woven into the fabric of community that learning and living require. (Palmer, 1998, p.11)

Perhaps my innermost disquiet is that it could have been so easy just to comply to the concept of being a banking educator as described by Freire. For the seductive conditioning of my own journey of learning in formal teaching, education and educational study, started on my medical discharge from the military in 1989 and provided me with a framework of western thinking and educational philosophy, which I readily embraced (for example, see Talbot, 1992; Tarnas, 2000; and Van Doren, 1992). In my MA dissertation (Adler-Collins, 2000) I delineated my epistemology and explored my ontology concerning the issues of '*space creating*', and how such a space was opened, held and protected by my values of love, compassion and critical reflection in a healing space. Over the next eight years, I explored how creating healing spaces that were protected through my enactment of those values, provided the necessary conditions for the healing and teaching of others and me to occur. My praxis was to create, maintain and understand a safe healing-space and to construct a valid account of my professional practice in nursing and teaching (Adler-Collins, 2007). In the next section, I move into describing the process through which I passed on my journey of becoming a professional educator.

## SETTING THE SCENE.

Historically I developed, and refined my educational content and structures of my curriculum by using it as the basis of my research as I passed through the Higher Education system of the United Kingdom. I loved to read and I now include an excerpt from my writings called *Warrior to Priest* (Adler-Collins, 1996). I believe that this writing shows that my desire to learn was a driving force for good in me at an early age:

> Big mistake!...One of the things I learnt, at three and a half years old, was, don't speak your truth, for your truth may not be received by those you speak it to with anything like the innocence in which you speak it. When we transgressed, which we always seemed to be doing, we were punished. The girls would get something done to them but if we were naughty, we were locked up in the coalbunker and left there in darkness. A friend of mine, a girl called Joy, and I were locked in this coalbunker quite often. It was a huge place, one that you opened a big door to, and then the coal was put behind big slats of wood. Joy was hysterical, for she could not stand spiders and of course, the hole, as we called it, was full of spiders. I think one of my proudest moments was when I sneaked in a battery and a light, two pieces of wires, it was a light bulb actually, and I hid them inside the coalbunker for I knew that we would go back in there again. The next time that Joy and I were thrown in the coalbunker was really quite wonderful because we had the light. I have no wish to bore whoever reads this narrative but they were desperately unhappy days. They were grey days, dark days, we were always hungry, our shoes, well they weren't shoes they were boots, always hurt and pinched the feet. I never seemed warm and the violence was quite extraordinary. (Adler-Collins, 1996, p.19)

I always wanted to be a teacher. However my military career and my rank precluded any formal educational qualifications that would be recognised in civilian life. Therefore, on my medical discharge, I embarked on becoming a qualified teacher and I completed my Further Adult Education Teaching

Certificates stages 1 and 2 (FAETC). I soon started teaching at a local technical college in a City & Guilds Health and Hygiene Programme, and a Pre Nursing course. At the same time as teaching I was required to pass a Postgraduate Certificate of Education (Further Education: PGCEFE) which led to a Master of Arts (MA) in Education at the University of Bath. By then I was completely hooked on education, teaching, curriculum design and research related to nursing issues. My Ph.D. soon followed, also at the University of Bath. I just loved it. I was in love with learning and drunk on the drugs of knowledge! A heady combination fraught with power issues and ego! However, I grounded my theory and ideas in my practice of my own school of healing studies in Bath, UK in 2000. I found what worked in terms of the curriculum. I found what could be improved and modified the learning outcomes of my curriculum accordingly. Embedded in this process were my experiences of serving in a Governmental Steering Group on Standards in Complementary Alternative Medicine (CAM). Through this process my curriculum was conceptualized, piloted, assessed and modified. I submitted it at the request of a friend to the Japanese Ministry of Education Science and Culture in the Autumn of 2000, and then promptly forgot all about it, as the next stage of my learning was to be in Japan as a Shingon Monk. It was only then that I started to step outside my process of schooling and to look at its conditioning. I was both angry and afraid. Angry in the sense that I felt I had been manipulated by a system to conform. I was afraid that such knowledge would take away the very foundations on which I had built my ideas of selfhood and status. Such enlightenment was a gradual process of critical self-reflection sustained over time. In the next section, I give an account of that process and my context.

In 2002 the Japanese Ministry of Education, Science and Culture (Mon bu kagaku sho) notified me that my curriculum of the healing Nurse, which I had submitted to the Ministry in 2000, had been selected for inclusion in the new curriculum of a new University being built in Tagawa City in Fukuoka Prefecture, the southern island of Japan. The University start date was April 2003. The University appointed me as an Assistant Professor in Mental Health to teach Healing Theory and Complementary Medicine. I came to that position well-versed in the theory and practice of Complementary and Alternative Medicine (CAM). It was in this appointment that I would come to challenge my own 'ontological sense of being' to the extent that they ceased to be mere words but became dynamic filters through which I understood the life-affirming energy to which I had dedicated my life. This feeling of connection to a flow or source is a very eastern idea, rooted in the ancient Chinese teachings of the way or Tao, which defies being locked into a cage of words, but is felt instantly when one-steps into or out of the dynamics of the flow or Tao.

What I offer next is, in many senses, what Frank (2006) suggests as chaos-narrative. I cannot show truly what I mean in a textual format. My narrative is my textual expression of a process that has dynamic elements all working in and on each other. For example, the six stages of living action research inquiry, as presented by Whitehead (1989), offered me another, more secure, framework than Frank's chaos narrative; one which I could use as a springboard into my inner world. In this sense, the framework of living action research was the link between my inner and outer worlds. I feel that this is what Bernstein (2000, p. 33) is referring to as the discursive gap between what he describes as *thinkable* and *unthinkable* forms of knowing. The semi-formal structure of living action research, with the assumed 'I' at the centre of the inquiry, offered me safety and a point of return as I free-fell into my inner depths of mystery using Moustakas's (1990) heuristic inquiry. Rayner's (2003) ideas about the fluid dynamics of boundaries and space allowed me to form and reform my emerging ideas and values using the solvent of consciousness. All the above processes are going on at the same time at different levels of my consciousness. This is perhaps better described by Talbot (1992) as a '*holographic universe*', one where the brain sees as though it were a hologram and '*lights up*' when consciousness is applied to stored knowledge. I believe that understanding the above point is crucial to understanding how I am approaching my learning methodologically. I truly believe that as I bring the dynamic mindfulness of my conscious mind to a body of knowledge, it illuminates the knowledge, which then can be tested and scrutinized. At the same time I find the mystery of the process both daunting and addictive. I have produced a multimedia account of my thinking, which can be accessed as a streaming video at: http://www.screencast.com/t/SJ91yROl. I should caution the reader that it is a lengthy account, as I work with different ideas and methods of expression, using different software. I am however, confident that if you persevere, you will have insights that cannot be expressed in words on printed pages of text.

I am now going to provide a clarification of the embodied values and the knowledge from which I designed and pedagogised my curriculum for the healing and inquiring nurse (Adler-Collins, 2007). These are applied to my teaching and nursing praxis. I am mindful at this point that I need to make clear how I am using words and values in my life-world as the same words can easily have different connotations and values to someone else. This research is a complex process in a complex context. Language barriers and cultural differences influenced the research. Many opportunities for misunderstandings and conflict existed, yet at the same time I had an understanding of the fluid dynamics of space and non-space that presented an opportunity to embrace inclusional thinking (Rayner 2003). I am suggesting that my ontology is the framing of the window and creates the spaces in which the different panes of glass each offers a different aspect - spaces of my life.

My boundaries of understanding are important to communication because their forms are bounded by my transitional certainty. Ones that are distinct but not discrete are those of the panes of glass. The reader is not separated from me, in individual terms, but shares with me a fluid dynamics of perception. I offer these panes, set in the frame of my selfhood, as a means of avoiding the separation of one from the other, and in so doing my reader and I co-create a journey of understanding and exploration. In this sense I believe that I am being inclusional. In an e-mail exchange on his work on inclusionality, Rayner said, 'inclusionality is an awareness of the vital inclusion of space in the fluid dynamic geometry of nature' (A. Rayner, personal communication, March 15, 2006).

Rayner's (2003) understandings are the closest I have seen to the Buddhist state of mindfulness which asks of its practitioners to bring conscious reflection to the interconnectedness of everything and to seek out our values with a compassionate heart to clarify their meanings.

I actively attempt to live with my embodied fundamental values. I do this with varying degrees of success. The values include those of respect, sensitivity, openness, flexibility, love, non-judgmentalism, non-violence, the capacity to forgive and compassion. I view my everyday living through the aspects of the active filters I am using - in that moment of knowing - through doing. By this I mean that as I teach I am using the aspect of me that is the teacher, grounded in my practice and supported and informed both by my practice and the theory, which I attribute to be necessary for my role as a teacher. When I change roles to a palliative care nurse, I change aspects of myself and the dominant aspect becomes that which is associated with my nursing practice. At the same time that I am engaging with my practice I am moving into and out of this practice by adding to or modifying the data-base of my nursing knowledge. I would therefore argue that multiple elements of different aspects of this relativity could be functioning in the same moment in an inclusional space. It is inclusional from the stance that all the aspects of self inform the dominant aspect of self but are not necessarily acted on by the dominant aspect. The dominant aspect of self is situational and relative to events of the moment. In Buddhist terms of mindfulness, the situational self is connected to everything and there is no separation of the individual from the wholeness of the cosmos.

Through the praxis of *where we are,* my conscious understanding deepens these values and solidifies them into *transient certainty.* From this positional understanding of *transient certainty* I set about building my framework, within which I see and make sense of the world. Such a framework is my *living truth.* I use *living truth* in the sense that Burke (1992) described as differentiated from the spectator truth. Burke suggested that the *living* or *authentic* truth of a situation can be fully understood only from within the situation; though the picture that emerges will never be as clear-cut as that provided by spectator truth with its imposed rationalized framework. I see that it is this framework – of a *living truth* – that emerges with my epistemology as my ontology is deepened and modified as a continual process of my conscious existence. In Rayner's (2004) sense, my epistemology evolves and morphs[34] into new forms of knowing in, on and around the moment of conscious understanding. I claim originality through my own authority of being. It is this concept upon which I build my pedagogy of the unique. It is my spirituality my truth and the very cosmology that I live by, which directly influence my being and are a direct result of my own experience. Through this process, by critical reflection, I seek to identify key aspects and the areas of learning that have occurred. My living truth, I believe, is grounded in the practice of my nursing, my teaching and the daily living of my humanity in which theory has to be born out in practice on a daily basis by the very nature of my work. I subject my living truth to the critical evaluations of others in order to strengthen the validity of my understandings with the insights of others. Submitting my ideas to EJOLTS for the critical evaluations of readers is part of this process.

In my teaching, I attempt to bring the instruction and ideas of experience and practice and offer these for open debate and analysis in the hope that the students will engage with these values. In this case, I can provide evidence of process but not evidence that the learning has been for *Good.* I can even provide analysis of the power structures and relationships to knowing and knowledge but

---

[34]        Morphs means changes, evolves.

I cannot prove student understanding without evidence from the students of the growth in their understanding. The universal nature of the core human values of mindful living embedded in my curriculum, is decided by the students in their selection of the seed values and making them their own or not as the case may be.

As I set these values, I designed and piloted a curriculum as a goal. What I ended up doing and where my new goal ended up are examples of the transformation of embodied values. My analysis of that transformation shows how living action-research extends to the borders and pushes the borders of expressions to embrace and evolve new epistemologies. Eisner (1997), in his paper *The Promises and Perils of Alternative Forms of Data Representation,* gave me insights in the process of exploring new knowledge:

> We are, in a sense, looking for new stars. We are also looking for new seas. We are, as I said earlier, exploring the edges. There is, I think, no better place from which to see the stars and no better position from which to discover new seas than the view one gets from the edge. (p. 8)

Eisner finished his paper with a poem by Christopher Logue, an English poet (1926- ) a poem often incorrectly attributed to Guillaume Apollinaire (1880-1918):

> *'Come to the edge', he said.*
> *They said, 'We are afraid.'*
> *'Come to the edge', he said.*
> *They came. He pushed them.*
> *And they flew.*
> (Eisner, 1997, p. 9)

Where I differ from Logue's stance in his poem; is that I do not agree with pushing people into fear; rather, I choose a different way, that of asking them to jump freely. For I believe the empowering of free-will in someone's learning, frees the mind from reliance on a guru or a power-relationship. Perhaps it is my Buddhist mindfulness nagging away at my thinking. I have repeatedly read the poem and keep asking myself: *'what of the ones who fail to fly... do they fall?'* Even the possibility of hurting another is unacceptable to a Buddhist.

In keeping with the cyclical nature of heuristic and living action research, each time I visit my experiences I seek their teaching and learnings. However, I need an entry point to the cycles of reflection and actions. For this I use the Buddhist teachings of the four Noble Truths, see below, as my declared ontological framework and my entry-point. They enable me to feel a degree of transitional certainty that I can find my way back to. In the next section of this paper, I place the framework of the four Noble Truths on my window and offer each one as a new pane of glass through which I open a window in my world.

## THE CONCEPTS OF THE FOUR NOBLE TRUTHS IN STRUCTURING MY EMERGING EPISTEMOLOGY

The Buddhist four Noble Truths are a basic framework for me as I seek to make sense of my world. Through engaging with the concepts of the four Noble Truths as my basic epistemology and being willing to risk entering the abyss in the sense of a space-void of meaning, I create my own yoga of participation (Skolimowski, 1994). With new insights into myself and my values I can move to new positions of understanding. For example, my commitment to a loving and compassionate self emerged through the experience of humiliation and suffering. I transcended knowing and not knowing, not by a theory in words, but by knowing through praxis. In releasing myself from my craving for a particular kind of self-knowledge I engaged in a process of improvisatory self-realisation (Winter, 1998). I evolved my living educational theory through my experiential doing.

## The First Noble Truth - Humiliation and Suffering (Jp[35]: KU-TAI)

In the Buddha's teachings of the first Noble Truth, there is an inevitability about our own humiliation and suffering. We are all subject to decay, old age, death, loss, disappointment or disease. As Kandy (1968) reported, '[B]irth is suffering, decay is suffering, disease is suffering, death is suffering, sorrow, lamentation, pain, grief and despair are suffering, to be united with the unpleasant is suffering, not to get what one desires is suffering' (p.52).

From the grounding of my experience of humiliation and suffering documented in my writings (Adler-Collins, 2003) and from the experience of my 100 day fasts (Adler-Collins, 1996; 2000.) I reflected on the conceptual meanings of the first Noble Truth and asked myself: *How does self give itself value?* The truth I now try to embody came out of answering this question as I became conscious of the significance of loving and feeling compassionate towards others and myself. I have reached the understanding that the pain I feel is the pain I give myself. A part of me wants this pain, it is my friend and I have such familiarity with it from a path well trodden. My negative learning experiences and conditioning from the Catholic nuns of my childhood related to my '*original sin*'. This installed a mindset of guilt and a feeling that I had to suffer to have God forgive me for my birth. In transcending this guilt, by accepting who and what was the source, I freed myself. I now accept that I can live a life of Love and service and that I need no longer feel the pain, especially as that pain was installed through the belief-systems of another in a position of institutional and religious power. Deep meditation proved to be pivotal in identifying issues in my psyche and emotions that were placed there by external influence such as my class, culture, whiteness, and religion. Once identified it was a matter of seeking appropriate teaching and then moving on. Living a life of loving compassion towards all humanity is the praxis embedded within my new consciousness.

---

[35]     Jp refers to Japanese.

It is the sharing of this consciousness that I intended to bring to my curriculum, where the way we look at suffering and pain could be modified through compassion and love. A value that has been embedded within the curriculum is the human-rights of our patients to be treated and seen as human beings, with feelings, emotions, worries, and fears, as members of a community, and as part of a family with a life history of living. What they *cannot* be reduced to, is a disease or a set of symptoms. Basic respect and compassion is a value that I believe should be embodied by every nurse.

### The Second Noble Truth - Thirst and Craving (Jp: JIT-TAI)

The Buddha described the cause of suffering as the arising of dukkha (pervasive unsatisfactoriness) from which emerges two types of craving and thirst. The first is a craving for sense pleasures; the second is a craving for existence and non-existence. Perhaps in modern terms we can equate this with narcissistic craving, the thirst for a fixed image of self, either something or nothing. This would suggest that the Buddhist approach tells of a core existential insecurity that is beyond the content of any individual's story. We wish to know ourselves securely, to be sure of who and what we are, but we are frustrated from the beginning by one essential contradiction. We, as experiencing subject, can never know ourselves satisfactorily as object. We cannot experience ourselves indivisibly but must experience ourselves as either subject as a knower, or object (as a knower) or as that which is known.

The Buddhist method of resolving this dilemma is to encourage states of not knowing. This is somewhat of a contradiction. I have doubts about myself and my 'I', for being the centre of my own universe in terms of consciousness. I feel that it is essential to discover if the truths and realities of my universe are really mine, or if I am seeing through the illusion and acquired filters of others, i.e. parents, culture etc., as previously described. I feel it to be essential to go into doubt rather than away from it, almost purposefully disrupting existing structures rather than indulging them. This process was traumatic for me, as the experience of two hundred-day fasts that I completed, were intended to be. A question I asked myself, with some concern for my sense of identity, was, 'If I were to remove the acquired filters of self from my Buddhist beliefs, then what is left?' This question remains unanswered. The Buddha, we are told, had an opinion on this subject, when asked the question; 'What is the nature of self?' The Buddha replied; 'there is neither self nor non-self. The question itself is flawed for it is being asked from a place that has already assumed that self was an entity.'

This seems to be a paradox of whether the self is just arising from the mental causation, but has no identity other than illusions that we create from our attachment to sensory data. My reflection about my thirst and craving for self-knowledge still has to be resolved, as the second Noble Truth remains one that creates in me dis-ease, as I struggle with the nihilism of the concept.

### The Third Noble Truth - Release (Jp: MET-TAI)

Goldstein and Kornfield (1987) introduced me to a Buddhist idea of release through the translation of the Dhammapada, a poem of joy that the Buddha was said to have exclaimed on his realisation of enlightenment:

> I wander through the rounds of countless births seeking but not finding the builder of this house; sorrowful indeed is birth again and again. Oh house builder! You have now been seen. You shall build the house, no longer all your rafters have been broken, your ridgepole shattered. My mind has attained to unconditional freedom; achieved is the end of craving. (Goldstein & Kornfield, 1987, p.76)

Because of our cravings, the Buddha appears to be teaching that we want things to become understandable. We reduce, concretise or substantialise. I cannot accept the strand of Buddhism that stipulates that we are born into humanness through our Karma through the wheel of life. I choose to believe that I create my humanness through my love and service to others. I do however recognise that by exposing my cravings and needs and bringing them to my attention, I release myself from unquestioningly following their demands.

My thirst for knowledge and understanding can also constrict rather than release me. I want things, including myself, to be understandable, to explain myself to myself and others as a singularity in the way Maclure (1996) has characterised the narratives of becoming an action researcher. In the release from this craving for objective knowledge, which emerged from my entry into my Abyss of the two hundred-day fasts I completed, I no longer seek to be perfect and no longer measure myself against standards of perfection, assumed or implied in the external standards of judgments that can be used to test the validity of claims to knowledge.

In releasing myself from my craving for a particular kind of self-knowledge, I now see myself and my knowledge as part of a continuous process of tension and creation, as part of a process of improvisatory self-realisation (Winter, 1998). I create my own living theories in the sense that I am creating my descriptions and explanations for my own learning, as I seek to improve my understanding and learning of my spirituality, nursing and educational practices. I believe my self-knowledge to be created through my fictions, my mirages, my shadows and my dreams. I also believe that I am a vessel of love and compassion and in service to the learning and healing of others, where my 'I' can be transferred and transformed into the 'We' of loving collective community.

### The Fourth Noble Truth - The Path (Jp: DO-TAI)

The fourth Noble Truth dictates the pathway which one walks. Embedded in my curriculum and pedagogy are the eight elements of the fourth Noble Truth and it is here that I have to point out a possible clash of languages because the text is written in Sanskrit, the translation of which suggest the *right way*. I am very conscious that this *right way* is bounded by Asian Buddhist concepts and could cause others to argue that it is not *their* right way. It is for the readers to assess for themselves if the values declared speak to them and their individual praxis. These are the values I identified as important to me in my praxis as a nurse and teacher. I share them with the hope that others will concur.

1. *Right Views (Jp: SHO-KEN):* respecting the humanity, originality and authority of each life without judgment and in humble service. Protecting the sick and the weak in your care, aspire to the relief of suffering on all levels: Spiritual, Mental, Emotional, Physical.

2. *Right Aspirations (Jp: SHO-SHIYUKI):* to aspire to do your best in the discharge of your charge of care through service.

3. *Right Speech (Jp: SHO-GYO):* never to speak in anger or to speak in jealousy, fear or reprimand. To use words sparingly, wisely and with care, understanding that the spoken or written word is never the received word as the values and concepts of speaker and writer may differ.

4. *Right Actions (Jp: SHO-GO):* to act mindfully, protecting your patient and students and their rights. To be courteous in your dealings with other healthcare professionals but not subservient.

5. *Right Livlihood (Jp: SHO-MYO):* to live life respectably and honourably; doing your best; to be mindful of others and their wants and needs.

6. *Right Effort (Jp: SHO-SHOJIN):* to do all actions with the maximum of effort (GANBARU).

7. *Right Mindfulness (Jp: SHO-NEN):* to be aware of the needs of others, understanding your limitations and value; see your place in the interconnected wholeness of creation.

8. *Right Meditation (Jp: SHO-JO):* calmness of mind and heart gives rise to a softness of eyes and touch; tranquility is conveyed in your words.

In essence, the fourth Noble Truth is the construct of my living educational theory, my pedagogy - for in order to walk my path I must continually self-survey, self-correct and self-improve in the stories of my learning. The fundamental truth is that it is my journey and my truth. The answers lie within me. It is not a re-inventing of myself or making up of a form of myself. I believe it is a discovery of a selfhood which is already there. In the next section of this paper, I explore the meanings of pedagogy in relation to my emerging values and their implications for standards of inclusional practice.

## INCLUSION PEDAGOGY AND THE PRIMORDIAL GAP

The concept of pedagogy was germane to the development of my curriculum and this paper. I am using my understanding of my pedagogy as a natural extension of my ontology and epistemology. It, too, is inspired by Rayner's (2003) concept of inclusionality, which resonates with Shingon-Shu Buddhism. For that reason, I refer to my pedagogical approach, as Inclusional Pedagogy. I build on (Bernstein, 2000) ideas of pedagogy when he states:

> Pedagogy is a sustained process whereby somebody(s) acquires new forms or develops existing forms of conduct, knowledge, practice, and criteria from somebody(s) or something deemed to be an appropriate provider and evaluator - appropriate either from the point of view of the acquirer or by some other body(s) or both. (p.78)

In relation to the pedagogising of my healing nurse texts, the distributive rules suggested by Bernstein (2000) are significant because they distinguish between two different classes of knowledge. Bernstein believes that it is the very nature of language that makes these two classes of knowledge possible. He terms them the 'thinkable class, and the unthinkable class' (p.30). He believes that there is a potential discourse gap between these two classes. He stresses that it is not a dislocation of meaning, but it is a gap. I would like to focus on this gap, which I refer to as the *primordial gap*. Within the primordial gap created by the thinkable class and unthinkable class there lies the opportunity for originality of mind.

For example, according to science (thinkable class), spiritual healing is firmly in the unthinkable class, consequently all the forces and power available to the thinkable class in terms of voice, validity and distribution are brought to bear in order to negate, silence or control. The answer to this problem, as I understand it, is within the primordial gap.

Understanding this primordial gap is particularly important for attempts to pedagogise knowledge. This is because, as Bernstein (2000) explains, any distribution of power will always attempt to regulate the realisation of this potential discourse gap between the thinkable and unthinkable knowledge. Bernstein believes that part of the reason why the rules of the pedagogic device are stable is that this gap will always be regulated. He points out that any distribution of power will regulate the potential of this gap in its own interest, because the gap itself has the possibility of an alternative order, an alternative society and an alternative power relation (p.30), thus posing a threat to the power holders.

In developing my own ideas of the primordial gap, I am mindful of the issues of stability in relation to colonial forms of knowing understood as the thinkable class. In the move to reduce the damaging aspects of colonial thinking and seeing with a colourless gaze, according to Buddhist teaching, it is important to examine Bernstein's work for what is – in effect an excellent critique and analysis of colonial workings. This limits the use of his work in terms of his understandings grounded in western thinking, but offers a sound analytical framework for analysing the colonial system of knowing and its power-relationships.

The advent of self-studies theses emerging around the world shows that, when ready, living educational theories do influence social formations. The hold that any distribution of power has in controlling the primordial gap is directly influenced by context. However, for those of us on the edge, in Apollinaire's sense, we keenly feel the negations of our values. It is my belief that as we emerge from the primordial gap with new forms of knowing and understanding we can offer hope in the new social formations that are creating the future. Living educational theories spawned, born and nurtured in this *primordial gap,* a sort of black hole, are outside the control of the formal educative space. However, the fact remains that those different power-agencies, including myself, support different, and perhaps conflicting, pedagogies. I have found that after years of constant struggle, some satisfaction is achieved when you can identify your influence for good and positive growth and learning in others.

## REDEFINING MY PRACTICE, MAKING EXPLICIT MY POSITION: UNDERSTANDING MY LEARNING

My living educational theory is occurring within the context of another set of contradictions (Whitehead, 1989). Within educational circles this is known as the paradigm wars described by Gage (1989) as: '...a minefield of conflicting polarities' (p.43); and this same issue was described by Schön (1995) as: '...an epistemological battle' (p.32). The paradigm wars are very real. Donmoyer (1996) writes:

> [t]he fact [is] that ours is a field characterised by paradigm proliferation and consequently, the sort of field in which there is little consensus about what research and scholarship are and what research reporting and scholarly discourse should look like. (p.19)

The paradigm war within the Western Academy[36] is at least explicit. Another kind of conflict is also occurring that is not so explicit and much harder to detect here in Japan. I am suggesting that this is not limited only to Japan but could easily be a global issue. As well as paradigm-clashes and conflicts, there is a paradigm-colonization underway.

For example, the importation of the concepts of ethics and research, and the subsequent use of those concepts, shows that there has been a change in the way the ideas are understood by the Eastern Academy in comparison with the

---

[36]    Academy refers to universities, their traditions, and their body of knowledge, as well as the power they wield in defining what constitutes truth.

Western Academy, although the ideas originated in the West. This could be understood as fusion or syncretism[37].

If that is true of the Western Academy, it is even truer when the Eastern Academy is included. Therefore, it is *critical* that I seek clarification of my own embodied values and knowledge, as I design and pedagogise a curriculum for the healing and enquiring nurse. I need to understand my own values – right from the beginning when I started to live the paradigm fusion, I reflected on this issue, asking myself various questions of the nature:

- What is my practice?
- How Do I improve my practice?
- What is the students' experience of my course?

I sought to make sense of what was often incomprehensible to me. As my analysis of my teaching and methodology progressed, the nature of the questions changed reflecting, I claim, a more inclusional understanding of the context in which I-we taught and learned. Examples of these questions are: *What is our practice and what do our patients require from us?* and *How can we improve this course for future students?*

I have concerns, as I not only watch the paradigm war unfold here in Japan, I also live in it, embedded as a foreigner in culture that has a feudal system of education. By feudal I mean that the professors have total control over what low ranking teachers can and cannot do. Time served is more important than efficiency and productivity or even higher degree awards.

Being so deeply involved in this living process in a culture not of my birth, it is sometimes problematic to give time for reflection, as I am in the middle of the experience, trying to understand and make sense of it. However, as I reflect on my experiences I am struck by the need for praxis. From the stance of the University, the curriculum was a success. I can claim this from the grades the students

---

[37]     Syncretism refers to the attempt to reconcile contradictory forms of knowledge and to allow for an inclusive approach to religious faiths.

achieved and the quality of their engagement and their final evaluations. However the real test of its success for me came as I placed all the worry and problems encountered in the delivery into an inclusional perspective. This success was epitomized in the words of a patient in a Japanese psychiatric ward where my students became the first Japanese nurses to be officially recognised through accreditation for using healing touch in their outside clinical practice. The patient said after his healing touch massage: 'I have been here 30 years and it is the first time I have been touched by a nurse... It was so comfortable' (K.Y., personal communication, October 19, 2007).

Within the patient's words was a story, one that nurses should heed, as it is not an isolated case within psychiatric nursing in Japan. His words also confirmed the value and uniqueness of compassionate human touch and the desperate need for nurses to start reforming their practice.

There remained the questions of why my colleagues were so distant, unhelpful or outright hostile? The issues were complex, educational ones about knowledge, knowledge-outcomes, teaching-methodologies and strategies. These were further complicated by the nuances of differing cultures and change. In seeking to enhance my understanding I gathered information and in so doing made one of most serious errors I could possibly make in Japanese culture. I approached the problems by using Western logic and an educational rationale that had been taught to me and served me so well in the past. I expected to have shared understandings in education and educational practices. My Japanese colleagues listened, smiled, but I found myself marginalised even more, and experienced a very difficult time. Coping became a matter of survival as I sank deeper and deeper into despair. *There were no shared understandings*, and in my naivety, I had assumed that, as nurses, we had a common ground in our aims. I had made no allowance for the very different types of nursing-culture and power-issues that existed between Western training and professionalism, and Eastern training and professionalism. What I had done in my ignorance of Japanese culture was entirely to ignore what the Japanese call *Amaeru* (Doi, 2001). I had also placed my colleagues in a position that no Japanese feels comfortable with, and that is of confrontation or being asked directly for an opinion. *Amaeru* is, in typical Japanese fashion, a word that translates poorly into English and is of a highly complex social-order and understanding. 'The inference was that it was impossible that a word describing a phenomenon so universal that it was to be found not only in human beings but even among animals should exist in Japan but not in other languages' (Doi, 2001, p.15).

What was happening was not only the paradigm wars being acted out but deeper cultural differences clashing in terms of knowing and knowledge. For example, nurses in Japan have little or no self-autonomy and due to poor training and educational requirements have little voice or academic ground to stand on as a profession. Improving nurse-education and the status of nursing in Japan are the declared aims of most faculty personnel with whom I speak. Yet, there is this conflict between words and actions that needs exploring. Educational paradigms are bandied about within the social formation, depending on the theoretical and research orientation of the senior professor's education. A good example of this conflict is the qualitative-quantitative debate, which in Japanese nurse-education is highly polarised. Japanese scholars take advanced degrees and Ph.D.s in Western countries, where mentors often use paradigms heavily influenced by Western perspectives on culture and knowledge. These scholars return to Japan almost colonized, with a new form of the "correct way". What happens next is that those in power then decide what is the thinkable and the unthinkable form of knowing (Bernstein, 2000). In my curriculum design, I was deeply conscious of these issues but had no idea of the meaning or importance of *Amaeru*. My Japanese peers for their part, had very little experience of a male western educated teacher who was also an experienced clinical nurse. For those who had never heard of action research and mixed-methods approaches, I was a source of great tension.

Culturally it is unacceptable for a lesser-grade teacher to question a higher-ranking one. This is not related to the educational qualifications held by the 'junior'-ranking teacher. In my case, I have a Ph.D. in education. Many of my peers do not hold Ph.D.s or formal teaching-licences. The Western methodology of critical questioning, for example, asking:

- What did they mean by using the word 'Learning Outcomes'?
- Against what criterion were they written?

Alternatively:

- What is the educational audit-trail for this unit?
- How were they assessed, and evaluated in terms of levels of knowledge, reliability, repeatability, and function?

Such questions brought about strained silence and were viewed as attacking the status of seniors. Such academic frailty, I believe, is institutionalized; more often than not it is embedded in power rather than in academic learning.

I also feel that there is another issue here that cannot be clearly expressed in words. However, I will try to articulate it as clearly as I can. The Western model of education is steeped in the philosophies of the individuality of the self and the rights of the individual, as explicated by such as notables as Maslow, Bloom, Schön, and Dewey. Critical inquiry and thinking flow naturally from those theories. I feel a sense of dis-ease almost as though the hidden agenda or hidden-curriculum of the real Japan with its values of *Amaeru* are clashing with its declared educational agenda of critical inquiry. Coming from the challenging Western European environment, especially in the Bath Action Research Group which met at the University of Bath (where all knowledge claims were required to be defended rigorously) to an environment where the silence of respect was expected, and in some cases demanded, has probably been the biggest cause of my distress and dis-ease.

My tension was that my ontological position challenged the Western Academy and the medical profession. Some of my basic life-truths, relating to the concepts of disease, are grounded in Chinese medicine, Eastern philosophy and concepts of spirituality; concepts which are still very alien to the West, although they have been used for centuries in the East. Therefore these learned bodies relegate my form of knowing to the 'unthinkable' (Bernstein, 2000). They claim it is neither academic nor scholarly even though there is a small but growing recognition that the Western Medical forms of education are suffering from 'Rightness and Whiteness'. My educational praxis focused on student-centred, co-creating knowledge that serves the profession by grounding nursing-education in the practice of nursing. This approach challenged the Eastern academy's rigid "Lecture, Chalk and Talk community."

It should be clear by now that what I lacked was a shared understanding of my experience. I felt I had made a cultural mistake. I suspect it was one of many as I sought to understand how the Japanese managed change – with their behind-the-scenes building of consensus referred to as *watering the roots*. This term not only implies a 'careful tending to', it is also about the importance of tradition, connections, having paid ones dues, and relationships that go back a long way in time. Compare that scene to my relative newness in the culture in which I had no long-term relationships or connections. I practiced an open style of management through negotiation and consensus-building by including all levels and grades to receive feedback on my curriculum. I found myself asking the question: *How, then, do I recreate and hold my teaching/healing space within the constraints and academic-social issues outlined in order to bring about a more socially embedded curriculum?*

To answer this question I outline next the practical principles that I believe distinguish my pedagogy. They are based on my living theory action research, in which I have reflected about the paradigm wars, what they mean to me, and what I need to do to enact my values. My pedagogy reflects the knowledge I have gained about what it takes to 'create and hold a healing-teaching space' as well as the nature of the social structure within which I was striving to embed my curriculum.

The following ten points are focused on distinguishing the practical principles I use in creating and holding a self healing-teaching space. The ten practical principles are distinguished in terms of:

1. Creating my safe teaching/ healing space;
2. Maintaining and holding my safe/ healing/teaching space;
3. Understanding my healing/teaching space;
4. Creating a safe teaching/healing space with students;
5. Maintaining a safe teaching/healing space. Gathering data for an analysis of classroom video with students' responses and journals;
6. Students understanding a safe healing space;
7. Students expressing love in the healing process;
8. Students expressing compassion in the healing process;
9. Students expressing understanding in the healing process;
10. Enabling the other to understand their healing process.

In the following ten sections I want to be very clear that I am focusing on distinguishing ten of the practical principles I use in creating and maintaining a safe teaching/healing space. There is as yet no analysis of the data but I offer the images with some of my own reflections and the evaluative reflections of my students to point to the power of images to communicate my meanings in relation to my practical principles. I recognise that as my research progresses then each practical principle and visual representation below will need analytic commentary that shows how my living theory of the creation of a safe teaching/healing space is being created with my explanatory practical principles.

### Creating my safe teaching/healing space

My healing space is my classroom. The room is warm, well ventilated and welcoming with soft lights, pleasant smells of oils and incense and candles as a symbol of the light that we work with in the process of healing and learning. Classroom layout is informal and tables and chairs are laid out to facilitate small groups.

The photograph[38] at http://living-action-research.org/Albums/Chapter_5_Photo/Image0.png is typical of the university lecture-setting, being highly formal, and the body-language of the students shows the power-issues of the sensei[39]/banking educator at work. This is an example of Hall's (1969) fixed-feature space.

The next photograph at http://living-action-research.org/Albums/Chapter_5_Photo/Image1.png presents a different image of my classroom-setting in which the space had been negotiated with the students. Group-learning is taking place in an atmosphere of co-operation. A comparison between the two pictures shows a marked difference in body-language. The first picture was of a formal environment controlled by the power of the establishment and the teaching style. The second picture suggests, through the body-language, a more relaxed approach to space and power-relationships. For example, the positioning of the two students on the left shows them to be comfortable with each other as they are leaning towards each other, combined with open body gestures. The gap between the two students in the middle of the picture suggests that they are not yet fully comfortable with each other. Group members were selected at random deliberately to show the students that they have to be flexible as nurses. This is important, as a nurse may well find that he or she is moved from

---

[38]   Consent to use these images and academic papers for research were given by all the members of this group. This is the case for all images in this paper. All photographs in this paper are copyrighted to Adler-Collins.

[39]   Sensei refers to the title in Japanese given to teachers and other professionals.

their team or ward as staffing and circumstances dictate in the work-environment. The ability to form effective team-relationships and exercise flexibility is, I believe, another basic nursing skill. The students are smiling in this picture and there is a look of engagement and fun on the students' faces, suggesting that they are relaxed with each other, the environment and the task at hand. The portfolio that can be seen in this group shows the dynamic use of colour and space as they debate the topic. What the picture does not show is what the students are smiling about or if they are engaged with the subject-material. They could be talking about anything and this is where the importance of establishing trustworthiness, as previously mentioned, becomes critical to the introduction and use of images as evidence. The photo showing the classroom lay out and student activity after we had negotiated our learning contract and expectations can be seen at http://living-action-research.org/Albums/Chapter_5_Photo/Image1.png.

### Maintaining and holding my safe/healing/teaching space

I took responsibility for my students whilst they were in my care and in the healing-space. I worked at maintaining the safe space and this required that my own mental and spiritual disciplines were in place. I worked at ensuring that I focused in the moment. This was achieved by the discipline of meditation and prayer. The students visited issues of pain and antagonistic issues in their lives, as it was these issues that were a source of their dis-ease. Healing and counselling were made available.

I valued my insights, which permitted me to see these issues without being invasive or abusive but at the same time strong enough to allow the process to take place. This often meant that I was exposed to antagonistic energies, which were released from the student in the form of emotional responses or even antagonistic thoughts and actions. My issues from my autobiography (Adler-Collins, 1996) were often reflected back to me during a course of teaching a healing curriculum, and I worked at responding to these in a way, which was helpful to the learning of the student, whilst reducing or avoiding projections on my part, from my autobiography, onto my students.

**Understanding my healing/teaching space**

I now want to take a *risk* in Winter's (1989) sense that the action researcher reveals himself or herself in a vulnerable way. In what follows I simply want to communicate that I understand my healing/teaching-space in terms of positive and negative energies, prayer, love and compassion. This is a process I have evolved. I work at transcending the antagonistic energy and making it "safe." I do this through the process of prayer, expressing love, compassion and understanding and listening without judgment. I also use incense and essential oils that evoke a sense of the sacred. My practice is based on a combination of my training and my intuitive recognition of these energies. This "decontamination" process, if you will, creates a feeling of safety for the students. I present an analysis of classroom video-clips showing the interaction of the students, which I believe could not have occurred in an environment of fear or control. The six-minute clip (see http://www.youtube.com/watch?gl=JP&hl=ja&v=va20gD95KM0) of a group of freshman-students[40] on the healing-theory course presenting back their work, ideas and feelings about the course and what they have learned. The spoken language is Japanese; I hope that that does not detract from the sense of fun and excitement I felt from this group in the youthful energy of their recital. Their words and voice for the most part are confident and they move around the space and text of the portfolio with ownership. The colours and use of Art-text is very Japanese in approach as are the drawings with their sense of embodied cultural youthfulness. The subject matter reflected a far deeper connection and engagement with the learning outcomes than I had expected or been led to expect.

---

[40]     Freshman, an American term, refers to *first-year* college students.

A valuable lesson for me in that I understood that given the freedom to explore their meanings of the subject matter, the students would have more connection to its relevance for them and for their patients.

In the next part of this paper, I wish to point out that the English has not been corrected from the journals and work of my students. I have left the text as it is to allow the reader to view the data without any editing. In this manner, my understanding can be placed in context with the text and images. In terms of the validity of this process, I draw on the data from the use of different instruments of data-collection to see to what extent I evidenced and communicated the following standards of practice.

### Creating a safe teaching/healing space with students

An individual students' reflections on portfolio building:

- I was able to tackle new things in a friendly atmosphere;[41]
- I think that a group or activity was completed happily. I think that relations were able to become very good by doing one thing into a group;
- It was very good that it was able to discuss writing many things all together;
- I thought that what is necessary was just to be able to carry out group activity many more after this;
- For me This lesson was really pleasant;
- It discussed with the member of a group and the portfolio was created.

    (Students, personal communication)

The students' portfolios are available at the link http://www.living-action-research.org/student%20portfolios%202003/Student%20portfolios%202003.htm. They show the process the students are going through as they create and show evidence of their own educational theories through their experiences of learning. By using this system of portfolio development, I believe that the knowledge

---

[41]     I would like to remind you here that the students' words have not been altered, for the sake of authenticity.

generated is culturally rooted in its Japanese context and avoids any form of colonisation on my part as a white, male teacher.

The video clip is available called *Having fun with portfolio evidence* (Adler-Collins, 2008). I believe that this video clip contains the evidence to support the claims listed above. The dynamics, fun and background-activity all indicate an engaged group of students. The students talking and presenting their portfolio are doing a very good job of showing their thinking and their written project work. The album available at: http://living-action-research.org/album.htm contains additional pictures of my classroom.

**Students understanding a safe healing space**

The student's own reflective journals extend the range of data available for analysis. For example:

> There was the healing theory and it was difficult for me. Since especially the talk about inside feelings. I was able to do very happily at the time of portfolio creation. I considered healing together with the friend and our group showed it with the picture as much as possible the time of a portfolio was very pleasant and I was healed. I did not consider and remember a disagreeable thing, but feeling became very easy. I entered in the inner part of the healing theory much more, and thought that I wanted many to know about healing. (Student A, personal communication, October 16, 2003.)
> Although we have received education from a school, a home, and society, need to question. I enjoyed myself with the others and thought it important an instruction and to learn. Finally, it is about a portfolio. The portfolio writes having learned or having thought [of us] collectively. Moreover, I thought that what I was can be communication with a teacher through a portfolio. (Student B, personal communication, October 21, 2003.)
> Here are some students' comments on the question of 'what is healing?'

that enable me to understand their perceptions:

- Healing exists?
- Healing theory having many kinds of another country admitting by scholarship;
- Music healing, massage healing, action healing, makes good effect with patients;

- But, healing effect cannot prove causality;
- Cannot prove by scientific methods yet;
- Also physically, man may be influenced by believing language and imagination.

**Students expressing love in the healing process**

The communication of expressions or love for what one is doing in one's practice in a research account is not easy. I believe that we need multi-media forms of representation for such communications and I have made a start in relation to love and healing touch in the pictures in the web-journal together with the students' evaluative reflections. The figure available at http://living-action-research.org/Albums/Chapter_5_Photo/Image8.png, I believe encapsulates the values that cannot be placed into words. The concentration and focus on touch displayed by these students allows an elderly volunteer to sleep in a public space. At the end of the session the volunteer said, 'I was so comfortable!' This I believe constitutes nurse-evidence.

Students expressed the following evaluative reflections about healing practice on:

- Healing given to the person met for the first time;
- Healing for the patient;
- It has actually practiced to a volunteer old person's man it is still far - I want to practice more;
- It is that it turns out that the model's complexion became good extremely although it does not understand whether to be using mind;
- Healing was truly made as a therapist (this is a great thing) with an external man. The person who did was glad and returned;
- Tsubo points interest me;
- The patient actually came and I gave healing, enjoyed;
- Although the partner of healing which I performed until now was a student, since I performed healing with ordinary persons for the first time, I became tense this time.

## IN SUMMARY

Inclusionality, in the sense of compassion and flexible dynamic boundaries, is in my stated ontology. Consciousness and reflection are in my epistemology and the Four-fold-path is in my praxis. My pedagogy of the healing-nurse curriculum embodies all of the above. It does so in the following way:

The assumptions of healing are grounded in inclusionality and inclusional practice. Expansion of my enquiring consciousness and reflection are the means by which I enter or become more aware of 'My' I-we-the others space/boundaries (I-We-you-us). I think this needs a sentence or two to clarify meanings of 'My' I-we-the others space/boundaries (I-We-you-us).

My intention is guided by the Four-fold path, and the praxis is my ability to engage in a transformative space-boundary adventure with another – a balancing act; it is a process whereby my intention sparks the others to recreate their matrix of wholeness and health. Inclusionality then becomes the living space within which healing, teaching and learning occur, and healing becomes the space of inclusionality. My meanings of inclusionality and healing then become my living standards of judgment (Laidlaw, 1996).

My emerging epistemology has been modified through this process of research in and on my actions, context, personal values and teaching skills. I am sensitive to the critical issues of race within education and the power relationships involved with the generation of knowledge and its control. I clarify my own limitations and frustrations as an educator and I make a lifelong commitment to improve them. I believe that the classroom can and should be a safe place for learning, where the students and the teachers co-create knowledge that is not only the given curriculum; and they also develop citizenship and life skills. I have questioned my values of love and compassion that are grounded in my Buddhist faith. While my understanding has deepened with the process of critical inquiry, my ontology has also been strengthened.

Nursing education in Japan has entered into university-settings with the stated objective to improve the competence of the nursing workforce. Such an objective is problematic for several reasons.

## CHALLENGES THAT REMAIN

1. As the new curriculum is now replete with non-Japanese academic theories, curriculum-design should reflect in its theory Japanese thinking and cultural sensitivities.

2. The actual practice of nursing education – in terms of hands-on training, the touching of patients, and learning the basic skills of their nursing craft – is dangerously limited.

3. Drawing experienced clinical nurses into nursing academia is not happening. This is problematic due to a shortage of suitably-qualified individuals. This problem is compounded by the increased commissioning of new faculties of nursing as Japan expands its number of university-level nursing schools. The current practice of not requiring nursing educators to stay current in their nursing practice also weakens the quality of nursing education. Nursing is an applied science and faculty without the grounding in current clinical practice are unable to consider practice relevant questions for research or teaching.

4. Japan has the lowest birth-rate in the world. Its nursing professional is predominantly female. With changes in social structuring in Japan, under the influence of Western thinking, women are expanding their choices of employment. Thus attracting top-level academic students to nursing will be a problem. The more famous and socially-elite universities will continue to select on academic criteria. The rural, prefectural universities

are likely to have to accept students of lower academic achievement just to fill places. This in turn will place pressure on the teachers in the system who will have to contend with having academically-challenged students coping with what is now a very challenging, theory-driven, academic curriculum. I believe Japan is correct in looking towards scholarship as a means to improve the professional ability of nursing in Japan. The challenge remains, however, in the balancing of theory and practice and finding suitable inclusional models of representing nursing-knowledge. Japanese scholars, in cooperation with their students and with the voices of their patients, need to be mindful of creating an educational programme that embraces Japanese values alongside those of the West. The curriculum of the healing and reflecting nurse is an important next step in that direction.

5.  A declared outcome of the Japanese education system is the development of English-speaking skills. Compared to the level of achievement of China, Korea, Taiwan and Indonesia, Japan is spectacular in its constant failure to achieve its objective. Japanese scholars and students of nursing are limited in their understanding of research-material because of their lack of language-skills in English. They have to rely on the few limited texts that are translated into Japanese.

6.  Japan has enjoyed nearly a century of economic leadership in Asia. She is being chased hard now and cannot afford any complacency in the use of English as the language of globalisation.

My final thoughts can be summarised by the words of my Ph.D. critical reader, Professor Emeritus of Nursing, Sarah Porter Ph.D., of Oregon Health & Sciences University.

> The most amazing and original thing about your project, I think, is that you developed a healing curriculum – in another country-culture far different from your own, received the highest level of official approval, gained access to implement the curriculum within a fairly traditional school of nursing, including commitment of resources and it has and is

being successful. Your reflections of your experience and why it happened for you that way and how you coped with it and what you learned and how you have changed – it seems to me to be the source of the unique. (S. Porter, personal communication, 2005)

What started out as a healing curriculum grounded in the concept of 'I' has been engaged with, modified and re-formed into the Japanese curriculum of a collective 'We'. Where this understanding will go is difficult to assess. However, the first steps have been taken and the theory has so far withstood critical tests in practice. What is needed to move these local findings into national and international contexts is the vision and courage to pick up the challenges highlighted in this paper and bring them into consciousness and practice in other contexts. This will require an openness of praxis through enhancing the fluidity and permeability of the boundaries that are presently constraining the development of Japanese Nursing scholars and practice-nurses. This is likely to include some political lobbying and socio-cultural 'educating' as a planned strategy of increasing the level of professionalism in Japanese Nursing. It will also require a shift of balancing theory and traditional values of nursing away from its dependence on the medical model for its authority of knowing. This is my dream. The words of John Lennon[42], '*maybe I am a dreamer, but I am not the only one*', sustain me in hope for the future.

---

[42]     John Lennon was a singer and songwriter with "The Beatles" Pop Group in England.

## REFERENCES

Adler-Collins, J. (1996). *My journey of transition from "warrior to priest".* Retrieved September 28, 2010, from http://www.living-action-research.org/writings/pdf/warrior_to_priest.pdf

Adler-Collins. J. (1998). Warrior to priest, a journey of transition: The day that changed my life (Television Programme, G. Pomeroy, Dir.). London: BBC Community Networks.

Adler-Collins, J. (2000). *How can I account to you for my educative journey through the exploration, meanings and values created in questioning my living 'I', through the process of making explicit and validating my claims to know?* (MA dissertation, University of Bath, UK). Retrieved September 20, 2010, from http://www.jackwhitehead.com/jekanma.pdf

Adler-Collins, J. (2003). Research or not research? The tensions around the use of action research methodology to add to the database of nursing knowledge by the use of self narrative studies: Voices in the silence. *FPU Journal of Nursing Research, 1*(1), 47-54.

Adler-Collins, J. (2007). Developing an inclusional pedagogy of the unique: How do I clarify, live and explain my educational influences in my learning as I pedagogise my healing nurse curriculum in a Japanese University? (Doctoral dissertation, University of Bath, UK). Retrieved March 3, 2009, from http://www.actionresearch.net/jekan.shtml

Adler-Collins, J. (2008). Having fun with portfolio evidence [Video file]. Retrieved August 28, 2010, from http://jp.youtube.com/watch?v=va20gD95KM0

Bernstein, B. (2000). *Pedagogy, symbolic control and identity* (Revised ed.). Maryland: Rowman & Littlefield Publishers Inc.

Burke, A. (1992). Teaching: retrospect and prospect. *OIDEAS, 39,* 5-254.

Doi, T. (2001). *The key analysis of Japanese behaviour: The anatomy of dependence.* Tokyo: Kodansha International Ltd.

Donmoyer, R. (1996). Educational research in an era of paradigm proliferation: What's a journal editor to do?. *Educational Researcher, 25*(2), 19-25.

Eisner, E. (1997). The promise and the perils of alternative forms of data representation. *Educational researcher, 26*(6), 8-9.

Frank, A. (2006). *The wounded story teller.* Retrieved October 30, 2006, from http://endeavor.med.nyu.edu/lit-med/lit-med-db/webdocs/webdescrips/frank759-des-.html

Freire, P. (2000). *Pedagogy of the oppressed.* New York: Continuum International.

Freire, P. (2004). *Pedagogy of hope.* New York: Continuum International.

Gage, N. (1989). The paradigm wars and their aftermath: A 'historical' sketch of research on teaching since 1989. *Educational Researcher, 18*(7), 4-10.

Goldstein, J., & Kornfield, J. (1987). *Seeking the heart of wisdom: The path of insight meditation.* Boston: Shambahala.

Kandy (1968). The world of Buddha? *Buddhist Publications Society, 14,* 52-53.

Laidlaw, M. (1996). How can I create my own living educational theory as I offer you an account of my own educational development? (Doctoral dissertation, University of Bath, UK). Retrieved September 20, 2010, from http://www.actionresearch.net/moira2.shtml

Maclure, M. (1996). Telling transitions: Boundary work in narratives of becoming an action researcher. *British Educational Research Journal, 22*(3), 273-286.

Moustakas, C. (1990). *Heuristic research: Design, methodology, and applications.* New York: Sage.

Palmer, P. (1998). *The courage to teach.* San Francisco: Jossey-Bass.

Rayner, A. (2003). Inclusionality - an immersive philosphy of environmental relationships. In A. Winnett, A. Warhurst (Eds.), *Towards an environment research agenda: A second collection of papers* (pp. 5-19). Palgrave: Macmillan.

Rayner, A. (2004). *Inclusionality.* Retrieved August 28, 2010, from http://people.bath.ac.uk/bssadmr/inclusionality/

Schön, D. (1983). *How professionals think in action.* London: Temple Smith.

Schön, D. (1995). Knowing in action, the new scholarship requires a new epistemology. *Change, 27*(6), 27-34.

Skolimowski, H. (1993). *A sacred place to dwell.* Brisbane: Element.

Skolimowski, H. (1994). *The participatory mind: A new theory of knowledge and of the universe.* London: Penguin.

Talbot, M. (1992). *The holographic universe.* New York: Harper-Collins.

Tarnas, R. (2000). *The passion of the Western mind* (Vol. 1). Reading: Pimlico.

Van Doren, C. (1992). *A history of knowledge.* New York: Ballantine Books.

Whitehead, J. (1989). Creating a living educational theory from questions of the kind , 'How do I improve my practice?'. *Cambridge Journal of Education, 19*(1), 41-52.

Wilber, K. (2000). *A theory of every thing.* Boston: Shambahala Publications Inc.

Winter, R. (1998). Managers, spectators and citizens: Where does 'theory' come from in action research? *Educational Action Research, 6*(3), 361-376.

# LOVE AND CRITIQUE IN GUIDING STUDENT TEACHERS

**Sigrid Gjøtterud, Norway**

## LOVE AND CRITIQUE

First I will try to clarify what I mean by love in student-guiding and explain why I have coupled the notion of love with the notion of critique. Peck (1998) defines love as 'the will to extend one's self for the purpose of nurturing one's own or another's spiritual growth' (p. 81). When our group of teacher educators started to focus on our guiding practice, by devoting full-day meetings to the purpose of sharing and discussing our practices, we became aware that we shared a common basis for our work that mainly coincides with Peck's definition. In various ways we all expressed that we strive to guide the students in ways that may nurture their growth as whole persons. Colleague Erling Krogh puts it this way: 'The aim is to support and challenge each student teacher to reach her or his potential as a teacher'. Buber (in Atterton, Calarco, & Friedman, 2004, p.15) explains 'spirit' as 'the totality which comprises and integrates all man's capacities, powers, qualities and urges'. He further states that human wholeness does not exist apart from a real relationship to others. It is this development of wholeness that is the vision of our guiding-practice. I choose to use the notion of personal growth, with the content of Buber's understanding of spirit, when I use Peck's definition of love as a basis from which to define love in education, as 'the will to extend one's self for the purpose of nurturing one's own or another's professional and personal growth'.

Buber (2004) phrases it beautifully when he separates love from feelings and says that 'feelings dwell in man; but man dwells in love'(p. 19). He says further that:

> ... in the eyes of him who takes his stand in love, and gazes out of it, men are cut free from their entanglement in bustling activity.[43] Good people and evil, wise and foolish, beautiful and ugly, become successively real to him; that is, set free they step forth in their singleness, and confront him as Thou. (Buber, 2004)

I believe that love enables us to see the other as Buber expresses here. In 'I and Thou' Buber establishes the notions of what he calls two primary words: I-it and I-Thou, and he says that the primary word of I-Thou establishes the world of relation, whereas the world as experience belongs to the primary word I-it. So when I use the notion of I-Thou it means that I want my relationship with 'the other' to have the relational quality I understand Buber (2007) to describe in the primary word I-Thou. I do not want to reduce the other to my experience of her or him. The ideal aim is to see the other from a 'stand in love', and thus see the other more fully as he or she really is. This is our responsibility as humans. Responsibility towards the 'otherness' of the other is what Levinas claims is the very essence of our being (Levinas, 1991; Moran, 2000). According to Levinas responsibility is a form of recognition. 'This recognition is not a cognitive act, that is, an identifying, re-presenting, re-cognizing act. It is effected in expressive acts by which one expresses oneself, expresses one's being, exposes oneself to the other' (Levinas, 1991, xix).

---

[43] I find the Norwegian translation captures a different sense of this statement when it says that 'men are cut free from their infiltration in the bustling life'. (Buber & Simonsen, 2003, p.16)

How does it manifest itself then when we see each other and recognize each other? And with what actions do we support each others' growth? I consider affirmation and support to be important actions. But with an increasing awareness of the truth of the statement that it is in the 'process of meeting and solving problems that life has its meaning' (Peck, 2008, p. 16), my understanding of the value of constructive critique has changed. I used to fear that my critique would hurt the student and cause pain, and thus tried to avoid any kind of direct critique. Through the process of self-inquiry for my doctorate I have learned to see opportunities for growth where earlier I only saw problems. I believe this shift in my own attitude makes a difference in the way I deliver the critique, as I no longer feel sorry for the student, but rather grateful that areas of possible growth have emerged and caught our attention. So I see critique as one aspect of love that is necessary in order to be able to nurture the growth of another. Constructive critique is included in love as love seeks to see the other and influence the other's learning and development.

By critique, I mean examination and evaluation, for instance of a text written by the student, that holds the potential to be received and become nourishment for development and improvement. Biesta (2006) discusses how learning might be looked upon as response rather than acquisition of knowledge. By responding to what is different, challenging or irritating, he argues that we show who we are and what we stand for. In this sense I believe that constructive critique may contain a challenging value that holds the potential of growth and development, as it may form the basis for responding.

One aim of our guiding practice may then be expressed with Biesta (2006) when he says that:

> education is not just about the transmission of knowledge, skills and values, but is concerned with the individuality, subjectivity, or personhood of the student, with their 'coming to the world' as unique, singular beings'. (p. 27)[44]

---

[44]    I.e., coming to the world as unique, singular beings.

I have experienced myself that having the values of love consciously present, represented in the notions of love and critique, helps me develop my practice in a desired direction. It is therefore the notions of love and critique I consider to be tools, not love itself. And in choosing the expression *tool* it is with the idea that tools have the potential to extend humans' ability for action. The tool may become an extension of body or mind. Polanyi (1983) claims that we start to inhabit the tool, just as we inhabit our clothes and our body. The notions of love and critique have extended my awareness of guiding situations in ways that I think have improved my guiding practice.

Love at work has been elaborated by authors such as Church (2004), Lohr (2006), Tian and Bognar (in Whitehead & McNiff, 2006). Their work has been highly inspirational in my own continuing search for ways of inquiring into my practice from a vantage point of love.[45]

Laidlaw (2004) writes: 'I see myself as acting in the name of education and being in the loving service of humanity' (p. 3). I find this statement beautiful. It expresses how I too wish to live and think about my life. I say this in the humble knowledge of often living in contradiction with the values embedded in the statement.

Lohr (2006) has accounted for how she wants love actively to influence the way she works with others, and how she wants to be an instrument of love at work. In this article I will try to show how our group of colleagues, through lived experience, has come to understand acts of love in guiding student teachers, or rather how love is being expressed through our practice. And I will explore how I can be an instrument of love when guiding student teachers. Does it show that I want to see the students as they really are? I will start this exploration by telling a story of an encounter with my supervisor Edvin Østergaard, after a concert in which his music was played.

---

[45]     I am grateful to Whitehead and Laidlaw for directing me to their work.

## BEING SUPERVISED – A RESERVOIR FOR INQUIRY

The guiding relationship between me and my Ph.D. supervisor has become an important source of inquiry and improvement. During the first year of our inquiry we had a disturbing encounter regarding my work. I felt he was not supporting me when he questioned the quality of the project with all our colleagues present. That was how I interpreted his statement. I decided to address the problem in a guiding session, as the sense of being undermined started to have a negative effect on our relationship. After the guiding session I made the following entry in my journal:

> When he questions whether we are doing research or not, it is an expression of his critical eye. And it is meant to be constructive. To me it is frustrating, but I realize that it is a driving force for the process... It feels like we have come closer during the session. (S. Gjøtterud, personal communication, March 15, 2007)

This experience made us both realize that reflecting on our guiding relationship was closely related to analysing guidance-competency in regard to the students. The two roles of being a supervisor and being supervised came together. The guiding relationship had developed into a relation of mutual learning. Next I will invite you into a situation in which the roles were switched; I was in a criticizing position and my supervisor on the receiving end.

### 'The seventh corner of the earth'

My supervisor Edvin, is not only a pedagogic researcher, he is also a composer of contemporary music. Edvin has won awards for his music, and I regard him highly as a person and as my supervisor. I attended a concert where his music was played: 'The seventh corner of the earth'. Despite the awards, this kind of modern music is not my 'thing'. I don't understand it, and listening to it does me no good – this I knew. Why, then, did I choose to attend the concert? One reason was I still felt it was a way of showing my respect for his work. I admire his dedication and creativeness, I realize he is so much more than the person I usually see at work and I wanted to get to know him better.

The concert was set in a church. I was curious – what would I hear? I was completely unprepared for the impact this one hour of music would have on my body. It was so strong, it was actually painful. I include 6 sound-tracks from the concert[46].

My realisation of my ignorance and failing ability to understand this kind of art is evident. Therefore I did not think I was in a position to give an informed evaluation at all, but I wanted to be able to praise his work. I was not able to do that and only greeted Edvin after the concert by asking if he was happy with the performance. I decided to talk with him later, and ask about his thoughts and motivations.

Then what happened? Over lunch a few days later a colleague, Linda, asked me: 'How did you like the concert?' I remembered my promise to myself not to speak of it before I had talked to Edvin, but despite this, all of a sudden I found myself telling of the painful impact the music had made on my body. Edvin entered the room and I started all over again. The impact on me had been strong and the words that I used were strong too. I did not intend to criticise his work (as I did not think of myself as being in a position to do that). He had not asked for my reaction, the others had. Still I offered a straightforward and honest description of how my reactions to the music had been – quite raw really. My intentions of having an inquiring and humble encounter were forgotten. I became aware that he might not appreciate my story although I could not read any discomfort in his attitude.

---

[46]     Die 7 Himmelrichtung (mms://elven.umb.no/sll/Die7Himmelsrichtung.wma);
         Meditation I (mms://elven.umb.no/sll/MeditasjonI.wma);
         Meditation II (mms://elven.umb.no/sll/MeditasjonII.wma);
         Meditation III (mms://elven.umb.no/sll/MeditasjonIII.wma);
         Meditation IV (mms://elven.umb.no/sll/MeditasjonIV.wma);
         Meditation V (mms://elven.umb.no/sll/MeditasjonV.wma).

**Living and contradictory values**

Afterwards a lot of questions came to mind. I wondered if I had encountered my colleague and supervisor with love and respect. In Levinas' terms, had I been responsible towards his 'otherness'? Edvin had rendered himself vulnerable, into his being, through the music. Did I make myself vulnerable in my response to him? Was I meeting him in Buber's terms of the ground-word 'I-Thou' – a relationship that is open, present, direct and mutual? Was I engaged in a genuine dialogue in which I was 'experiencing the other side' (Buber, cited in Atterton et al., 2004)? Did I live my values as expressed here? I did not think so, after the encounter.

My intention was to listen to Edvin, to have him explain to me what he wanted to express through the music, to learn how he works with it. With an open mind, maybe I would be able to learn to listen in a different way. With an open mind I might broaden my horizons. I felt like a living contradiction (Whitehead & McNiff, 2006)! Or was I actually offering critique that could be valuable? Maybe, but Edvin had not asked for it, and I did not offer it in the way I had planned.

Similar processes can take place in guiding student teachers. I say that I want the students to become aware of who they are and want to be as teachers, and support their development as best I can. Offering critique that might become valuable is challenging. The intended message is not necessarily the one received by the student. This is even more challenging when the guiding is written and given by e-mail, than when it is delivered face-to-face. In order to try to establish a dialogue, we encourage the students to reply to our guiding texts, so that we might learn about the effect our message has on them but they seldom do.

Through the project-period in general, and after the encounter with Edvin in particular, I started thinking more consciously about my intentions in guiding. Important issues to address might be:

- What values are the students living or wanting to live in their practice?
- What is it that they try to achieve through their practice?

- How are they trying to overcome their uncertainties?
- What are the steps towards their particular teacher-role?
- How might I support them on their way?

These questions seem important to tie in with the more detailed didactic or pedagogic issues that we emphasize in guidance. The didactic questions apply to the level of content in guidance, whereas the value-questions are more directed towards the personal level.[47]

The intention is not to impose values but to facilitate the grounds from which the students become aware of their own values. This will enable them to make conscious choices in their practice. One example of how I addressed values in guiding, after these questions surfaced, can be shown in this response from a student when she reflected on her work and the guiding she had received:

> I received a question in the commentary to my finished assignment, which I found interesting to reflect upon. Sigrid... wrote as follows: 'maybe some of your values are being expressed when you say that 'it should be possible to work on a more advanced level with this class as well.' How would you express the values which are the basis for this statement?' I think it is right that this is an expression for an ethical principle, namely that all human beings benefit when faced with demands within limits of their mastering. And that even pupils with special needs are not without intellectual capacity even if they find it hard to deal with theoretic subjects. (H., personal communication, February, 2008[48])

Another question that emerged was quite disturbing. Was I being supportive of a plurality of teacher-roles or was I looking for and supporting only a variety within narrow borders mirroring my own values and experiences, in the same way as I appreciate only a certain variety of music? This is a question I will not try to answer in this paper, but Elliott (1991) says that the improvement of practice consists of realizing those values which constitute its ends, because in

---

[47]    These two dimensions of guidance are discussed for instance by Pettersen and Løkke (2004).
[48]    All student-texts as well as quotations from colleagues are translated by Gjøtterud unless otherwise stated.

that realization the possibility for change is embedded. Thus change of practice was and is embedded in the question.

Before elaborating the notions of love and critique in guiding student-teachers further, I will clarify the research design of the project and outline the background of the chosen focus.

## CO-OPERATIVE ACTION RESEARCH IN OUR GROUP OF TEACHER EDUCATORS

The design of the project is reminiscent of that described by Heron and Reason (2001) in their article *The Practice of Co-operative Inquiry: Research 'with' rather than 'on' people* in which they emphasize four phases of co-operative inquiry cycles. I will describe the design as well as try to give glimpses into the overall process of our project.

In the first phase the group of co-researchers decides to explore an agreed area of human activity. Our teacher-group decided to explore our guiding practice in order to improve it. This decision was built on data from an inquiry following the students' first assignment in their first semester[49] (January 2005). We asked the students to reflect on how they had benefited from the guiding from co-students and from the teachers in writing the assignment. We also asked how they reacted to, and benefited from, the final evaluation of their work. They handed us their written account of these reflections. As we spend quite a bit of time writing texts of guidance and evaluation it seemed important to get to know more about the students' reactions rather than what became evident just from the assignments themselves. The accounts revealed that overall the students expressed satisfaction with the guiding they had received; they said they became confident essay-writers. Here is one example: 'The guiding was concrete and it helped me

---

[49] The teacher programme is organized as a full-time study for one year, or a part-time study for two years.

to proceed. I feel you were professional, but that you see the individual too – that there is room for being different.' This was what we wanted, but many students said they had been too late in asking for guiding. And there was the significant fact that only a few of the students mentioned that the writing had helped them become more confident in their teacher-role, not only as assignment writers. This example is representative: 'I realized how PPE (Practical Pedagogic Education) wants such assignments to be written.' On the background of this inquiry we agreed that we needed to improve our guiding practice.

In phase two the co-researchers also become co-subjects. We were subjects of the inquiry as we engaged in the cycles of action-planning, action and reflection and as we documented the processes and the outcome of our exploration of practice. During the project-period (2005–2008) we had regular meetings in which we shared the focus each of us had chosen for learning and development through the guiding period. Furthermore we agreed on research-tasks for ourselves such as writing and sharing reflecting notes, sharing guiding texts, writing up narratives from guiding visits to students in practice etc. These documented tasks became our data. We met for in-depth discussions concerning all levels of our practice but with a main focus on the guiding of the first assignment the students are given during their first semester.

In phase one the members become immersed in their actions and experiences. This is when we were engaged in the guiding and teaching, observing our own actions and reflecting on them individually, in collaboration with each other and in collaboration with the students. The notions of 'Love and Critique' in guiding were first presented in a reflection-note from my colleague and supervisor Edvin Østergaard (2006). I will get back to this later.

Phases two and three are repeated cycles. Each one addresses the same issue to make improvements, or one chooses a different aspect. We decided to keep a focus on our guiding primarily tied to the students' first assignment over the three-year cycles of our project; but more and more we became aware of different guiding-settings and brought experiences from these into our discussions as well. Guiding during visits to students' teaching in their practice-school, and guiding a pedagogical development project which the students carry out in groups, are examples of other guiding tasks we brought into the project.

In phase four the group gathered to share experiences, and to look at them critically to see what had been learned and what we were learning by discussing the experiences. We came to conclusions about what changes were to be made in the teaching and organizing, as well as within the individual guiding practice. Changes in my guiding practice will be elaborated later. Here I will just give one example of how the project has affected teaching and organizing. As mentioned above it was through analysing the first assignment that we realized that we did not encourage the students to reflect on their practice in the way we intended (journal-entry, September 2004). The didactic[50] assignment is about describing and reflecting upon a teaching situation from the students' practice in school. We want them to reflect on their influence on the pupils' learning, as well as their own learning, from reflecting upon the specific teaching situation. The aim is that they will get used to reflect on their practice, and thus become reflective practitioners as Schön (1995) emphasizes. However, as very few students stated that working on the text had made any positive contribution to their professional competency, we first changed the guidelines in a way that encouraged the reflection we wanted them to be engaged in. Second, we needed to change the content of our teaching. For instance we needed to address questions of pupil involvement at an earlier stage, and more specifically than before.

During the period of writing the students were organized in writing groups on the internet, where they were encouraged to guide each other. Over two days they started this process on-campus in a writing-course. The above-mentioned inquiry revealed that only a few students had actually engaged in the groups prior

---

[50]     Didactics is understood as 'practical-theoretical planning, carrying out, evaluation and critical analyses of teaching and learning (Hiim & Hippe, 1989, revised edition 1998, p. 99).

to the project. So a third change was the time of the third gathering on campus in order to allow the students to cooperate in writing-groups for a longer period of time than before. For years the students had complained that the third week gathering on campus was too late for them to fully achieve the benefit of the writing-course and cooperation in writing-groups. Why did it not cross our mind earlier to change the time? It was so easy to do something about it, yet it did not happen until we systematically documented student feedback and held it together with other data. By  forming writing-groups before they started writing, by improvements of the writing course and by altering the time of the gathering, and also by further encouragement from the teachers, the participation and outcome of the writing-groups has increased during the project (Strangstadstuen, 2007).

The design of the project is a dynamic process of co-operative action research, and individual research concerning the question 'how can I improve my practice?' as elaborated in Whitehead and McNiff (2006). Carr and Kemmis (1986) claim that this dialectic of individuality and society, as well as of theory and practice, 'is at the heart of action research as a participatory and collaborative process of self-reflection' (p. 184). Individual experiences were discussed and analysed in the group. Shared values were being expressed and recognized as well as the individual values and skills which were being laid out. What I learned from each of the others became evident. My own contributions also were made visible. Later I will present a story of how Erling guided a student in a way I had never done, and how I learned from that. I will also present two stories of my own guiding to show examples of how I think my guiding has developed.

The roles of the group-members differed throughout the project. I was conducting the project as it was also my Ph.D. project. Two of my colleagues who were active in the project were at the same time my supervisors (Edvin and Erling). Solveig was my closest co-worker. She developed her own project within the frames of this project. As already mentioned she introduced new methods for student-collaboration and guiding between them on our learning management system. Seven other colleagues were involved in the project, some for the full period and others for parts of the period as they were hired during the project period, or they were on leave and came back.

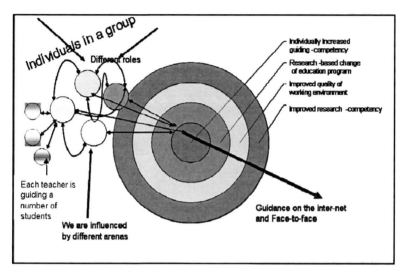

**Figure 1.**    An illustration of co-operative and first-person inquiry in dynamic processes with colleagues and with students, and the four areas of change we experienced during and because of the project

Figure 1 is an illustration of the participants and their different roles as described above. It is not an accurate account of the various relationships, but the intention is to show that some were more engaged in the process than others, everyone had their guiding relationships with their students and we were all influenced by other people and situations that cannot be tied to the project. The layered circle intends to describe how we have experienced change in four different areas of our work. I have briefly mentioned the second area, how the research caused changes in the course-work and this will be elaborated later in the article. How the work affected our working environment will not be discussed in this article, and I just want to say here that our capacity for doing action research has increased. Before this project no-one in our section was doing educational action research, at the end of the project there are at least three other active projects in our section. One of them is a state-funded project called 'Elev-forsk'[51], or 'Pupils' research'. In the following I will focus on the individual level of change, my own development as a student-teacher guide.

When we are doing action research we draw on the Stenhouse (1975) tradition and John Elliott's (1991) pragmatic theory in the sense that we hope, by our research, to contribute useful theory for teacher-education practice and other professional contexts, as the purpose is to improve practice in a wider range than just our own. Hiim (2003, 2007) claims that research and knowledge-development based in the practical work, in the occupational functions, is necessary in order to develop relevant professional concepts. This has encouraged our research.

Living theories (Whitehead, 1989, 2008, March; Whitehead & McNiff, 2006) form a second basis for the work, as we try to make our values as educators explicit and attempt to live and change our practice in accordance with the expressed values by which we want our work to be judged. We create our own living educational theories, in the hope that they may act as contributions to educational epistemologies. By this I mean that I hope that these narratives of my struggle to create my living theory 'may be of value in the generation of your living theories as we combine our voices in enhancing our educational influences in improving our local and global contexts' (Whitehead, 2008, p. 118).

Winter's (1989) six principles for the conduct of an action research inquiry – reflexive critique, dialectic critique, collaborative resource, risk, plural structure and theory-practice transformation – made up a basis for choice and the interpretation of data. I hope I have been able to show this through establishing the context for the inquiry: by questioning my own practice and finding

---

[51]       Information about the project: http://studentresearch.umb-sll.wikispaces.net/

possibilities for change within these questions, by showing how we have contributed to each others growth as teachers and guides, by risking the revelation of my self, by showing a plural structure by revealing my colleagues' and students' own voices, and by choosing diverse cases to show my processes. Lastly I have documented this process in an attempt to theorise my lived experience.


## GUIDING TEACHER STUDENTS WITH LOVE AND CRITIQUE – CHANGED PRACTICE

When the notions of love and critique emerged, the terms reverberated with my intentions and values, and became important tools for analysing and improving my practice. Oestergaard (2006) uses the expression: 'the loving and critical eye' whereas for me it was about the loving and critical encounter (Buber, 2004). With the notion of love and critique present in my mind I suddenly recalled all the discussions we had had during the project-period, as well as before, and it became evident that we had a shared value of love for our work and for our students. We really want the students to achieve to their full potential, within the framework provided by the *Education Act* (Ministry of Education Research, 2005)*, Core Curriculum, subject Curricula* (Ministry of Education Research, 1993) and *National curriculum regulations for teacher-education in Norway* (Ministry of Education Research, 2003). Later I will draw some lines of the framework provided by these documents.

I have made a chart (Figure 2, p. 218) in which I have tried to capture what it is we are doing in order to guide the students towards their potential. The statements are derived from accounts from project-meetings and are also my interpretations of what I have seen in texts of guiding. This chart was made in the middle of our process.

We continue the work of conceptualizing our practice in this sense. I have highlighted a few notions; first 'I want the best for you' which everyone in the group has stated; and attention and awareness I believe is a basis for guiding in general. 'I will show you', 'I seek you out' and 'the goal is for you to have a clearer view of yourself' are highlighted because I want to present three cases, showing where these statements came from. These stories represent some aspects of what has come out of the process of identifying what we are doing that I believe qualify as encounters of love and critique.

**Figure 2.**    Statements drawn from concrete actions in guiding student teachers

### The benefit of working with texts

After showing the chart above to my group of colleagues in a project-meeting, Solveig concluded by saying: 'What it comes down to, is to take the time to go a second round' (personal communication, October 22, 2007). This is possible when working with texts, but not the same when it comes to face-to-face encounters. For me the second round is about going over my feedback-text to see if I have affirmed the work of the student by showing how I have tried fully to understand his or her aims: if I have said what I think is positive about the text and/or the content of the text and if I have asked meaningful questions that have the potential of challenging the student in a desired way. I will get back to what I mean by 'a desired way' later. My first reaction to a text is almost always on the critical side:

- Is the text structured?
- Were the aims of the pupils' learning clear?
- Had the student planned how to evaluate the learning-outcome for the pupils?
- Did the teaching involve the pupils? Was the content of the teaching relevant to the pupils?

These are all important didactical aspects in my opinion. But I have discovered through this inquiry that if I don't go through the text a second time, the critique may become overwhelming, or the praise may not be specific enough; or if the text is positive there may not be challenging enough questions or comments to encourage further work and development. One student entered a statement in the log that many of our students over the years have pointed to:

> It was unbelievably wonderful that we were given such a long and thorough evaluation. One feels happy when the positive aspect is so focused. But a few hints on what one might improve in the next assignment would have been welcome. (Student, personal communication, January 11, 2008)

One of my colleagues (Hans Petter Evensen) claims that: 'It is unbelievable how many compliments a person can take'. However, it has become increasingly evident to me that it is just as important to provide the challenge necessary for growth.

What, then, is the desired direction of development for the student teachers? I will turn to curricula and acts regulating educational policy in Norway to answer that question. *The Core Curriculum* (Ministry of Education Research, 1993) states that:

> The point of departure for schooling is the personal aptitude, social background, and local origin of the pupils themselves. Education must be adapted to the needs of the individual. Greater equality of results can be achieved by differences in the efforts directed towards each individual learner. (p. 5)

Furthermore, the *National curriculum regulations for teacher-education in Norway* (Ministry of Education and Research, 2003) states that:

> If children are to maintain and further develop the desire to learn and believe in their own mastery, the teacher must have the ability to actively include the children, parents/guardians and colleagues in the educational work. (p. 1)

One aim of guiding, then, is to point the students' actions and attitudes in the direction of detecting the individual needs of their pupils and encourage their efforts in planning teaching in order to meet their needs and involve the learners in the learning process.

In the *Act relating to Primary and Secondary Education (Education Act)* (Ministry of Education Research) it is made clear that teachers have an important role in securing for children positive learning-environments:

> The school shall make active and systematic efforts to promote a satisfactory psychosocial environment, where individual pupils can experience security and social ties. If any school employee learns or suspects that a pupil is being subjected to offensive language or acts such as bullying, discrimination, violence or racism, he or she shall investigate the matter as soon as possible and notify the school management and, if necessary and possible, intervene directly. (p. 23)

This, too, is an aim of guiding, to read the students' texts and "listen" to their stories from practice, and to observe them in school-practice, so that we might be able to detect students who do not treat their pupils with respect and 'open their eyes' to what is going on in the learning environment. The hope is that the assignments will set off reflection-processes that will increase the students' ethical awareness and make them realize their important, educational role in society. This is not achieved during the first assignment, which is emphasized in this article, but the intention is for the process to start at the beginning of the course.

These are just a couple of examples of what I mean by the development of competency in a desired direction. I hope this provides a glimpse into the context of the inquiry, and also how the notion of love and critique has pointed my attention towards new aspects for guidance. Further I will present three student-cases; each elaborating specific aspects of the terms love and critique. But first I will account for how I made the choice of particular cases.

**Choice of cases**

All three cases are of students who finished in the second year of the action research project[52]. When I started writing this paper the third year had just started and it was too early to choose a case from that class. I think each narrative represents new aspects of my practice compared to the first year. I wanted one case to show how my learning has been influenced by my colleagues' guiding practice. That is case one. This case is mainly concerned with online guiding. Then I wanted to show my own development. Case two has little to do with online guiding whereas case three was concerned with online guiding as well as face-to-face encounters. The three stories then describe a variety of guiding contexts. Cases one and three are tied to the first assignment I have focused on in the study. Cases two and three are examples of how I felt my awareness of the students seemed to increase as a result of the conscious attention I paid to my practice when constantly asking; 'how can I improve what I do?' and keeping the notions of love and critique living in my mind. As with the challenging encounter and important relationship with Edvin, these three relationships seem significant to me as they represent quite different challenges in my practice. Every student is my

---

[52]    I thank the three students very much for letting me use their names. After having written the cases they have read and commented on the accounts.

concern, but we have delegated the responsibility of primary contact with the student teachers between us, and I have chosen the cases within the group of students for whom I was responsible for guiding throughout the year.

Unfortunately I do not have videos to show the interactions. Whitehead (2007, 2008) is concerned with how visual narratives can communicate living standards of judgment (Laidlaw, 1996). I see that it would have been very powerful and useful indeed. As it is, I will have to trust that the written accounts from the students and myself will be lively enough to create reliable images to show my standards of judgment.

Each case will be presented by an outline of what seemed to be the challenge or problem, then an account of how the challenge was dealt with, and what I learned from each case. For these purposes I have retrieved statements from the students in the following accounts:

- Student journals made official through our Learning Management System;
- the first assignment;
- the final reflection notes[53]

and

- written guiding texts.

### I will show you – case one

Some students have little training in writing. The reasons for the lack of skills vary. Some students have not written much at all or they are out of practice due to years of practical work. Working in the forest does not require much writing. Others come from a scientific tradition in which personal opinions or feelings are not to be expressed. From time to time it has caused me a lot of

---

[53]     For the final, oral examination in pedagogy the students prepare themselves by writing their reflections on their own learning and development during the teacher-education process, expressing their competency as teachers at the end of the education process.

thought and frustration trying to help such students understand how they might write a coherent text. Prior to this project I thought the best way to meet the student was by asking questions and through that facilitating the grounds for the student to discover his or her own way. This practice is based on a reflection model for guiding student teachers (Handal & Lauvås, 1999; Lauvås & Handal, 2000). But I have experienced that sometimes this induces feelings of inferiority, of not being in control, rather than mastering and confidence.

When sharing guiding texts, as we did during the project period, I discovered that my colleague (Erling Krogh) showed a student, Jon, how to write. Jon had a long history of working at a school-farm and had little practice in writing. From what the student had written, which was not lengthy, Erling led him through each part of the assignment from start to finish, referring to the student's text, like this:

> The plan for the teaching, using the six didactic categories, including your reasons for the learning goals of the pupils; why should the pupils learn this? Start by describing the didactic relational model and each of the six categories. Refer to Hiim and Hiippe (Hiim & Hippe, 1989, revised edition 1998) as sources. Then you start by describing the goals for learning.
> Knowledge-based goals: Your four first lines are knowledge-goals;
> Goals for skills: The next two sentences;
> Goals for awareness/ attitude: The two last sentences. (Text of guiding, 2005)[54]

At the end of the finished assignment Jon reflected:

> The first time I heard about this assignment I shivered in fright and started to cold-sweat. Just writing this many pages was a challenge to me. I, who am only used to practical work! First I had to learn how to learn, and that was bad enough. I told myself: This is not going to work!! It was like running into a wall!! - one that I thought I would not be able to break through. But as time has passed and I gained more knowledge, I have slowly managed to break down the barriers ... The guiding worked fine. Erling Krogh has given me valuable knowledge and explained the assignment in an easier way so that I could understand. (Bjerke, 2005)

---

[54] All texts from students and colleagues concerned in the presentation of the three cases are translated by me with the assistance of Linda Jolly.

Jon further explains how the writing course[55] helped him become systematic in his writing, how the process of learning how to use the computer, and how reading and understanding new words and concepts helped him. After two years as a part-time student, in his final reflection-note, Jon wrote:

> First we learned how to write a log. What sort of thing is that? It was absolutely unknown to me. It has been of great value throughout the course, being able to write what you have experienced, felt, reflected on, learned and what the pupils have learned etc.. Particularly the self-reflection and reflecting on the teaching and the pupils' learning was new to me. You were forced to think more and get the thoughts onto paper. This was tricky, especially for me who is not a theorist. It has caused me to become more aware, to ask myself more critical questions both as a person and as a teacher. (Bjerke, 2005)

From having the role as manager for the school's farm, Jon went into teaching. From experiencing writing an assignment as running into a wall, he ended up being able to phrase his reflections as shown above. His starting point was a feeling of frustration and fright. When he was shown how he could write, he was able to write, and he mastered the task. I realized that some students really benefit from being shown. I had not, prior to reading Erling's guiding text, considered showing or instructing like this. I did not want to subjugate my students to my advice in such a manner. But in this situation I experienced it as an act of love to show the student, and by that get him started, without the long and tiring detour of 'a million questions' intending to help him discover for himself. I regard this to be respecting the student and his point of departure.[56]

---

[55] As part of the project Solveig Strangstadstuen has developed a writing-course in which the students learn how to start a writing or thinking process by short intervals of quick writing followed by changing texts in order to give each other feedback. This is the basis for forming writing-groups on our LMS (learning management system).

[56] One condition for guiding via the internet is that we always meet our students face-to-face before starting the on-line guiding, for two weeks of on-campus gatherings. The second gathering is located outside the campus and most of the staff spends two to five days with the students in the mountains. We do this in order to establish relationships between the students as well as between students and teachers. Erling is careful about getting to know the students he is to guide. I consider this to be an important condition for the guiding as we can not observe the students' reactions when working on the computer and might therefore easily cause misunderstandings.

Does the 'showing' also contain constructive critique? My view is that the critique here lies in the student's opportunity to respond (Biesta, 2006, ix). The student may react to Erling's attempt at expressing his thoughts and start his own writing process from there. Erling's attempt may disturb him or actually resonant with his experience. It might be considered to be critique in the sense that it may help the student to see possibilities he did not see before. I think Jon's final reflections show that he was able to benefit from the advice and from that starting-point developed his thinking and learning.

### I seek you out – case two

When students were not making positive progress in their studies, or they met the challenges with indifference or hostility, I used to have problems confronting them in a constructive way. I have felt sorry for them, afraid of making matters worse, or I may even have felt annoyed that they did not appreciate what we offered. During the project-period I realized conversely that these situations are wonderful opportunities for the student to grow, as well as for us to learn more about how the programme is experienced. I no longer fear facing the students, rather the opposite. I am curious. I have experienced that this shift in my attitude and my emotions facilitates open dialogue. As I am neither no longer feeling sorry for the student, nor in a position of defence, I think I am able to face the students in a different way, one that also encourages the student to see possibilities instead of just problems. It was through encounters like the one I will now describe here that caused this shift in my attitude to happen. When challenging my own feelings, the students' reactions showed me I was not making matters worse, but I was rather providing an opportunity for growth, and at the same time I learned something valuable for our teaching and guiding practice.

Guro is a young woman who had just finished her Master of Science degree. I observed Guro during classes. She looked bored and tired to me. She did not participate in discussions and often sat by herself in the classroom. In a mid-term evaluation one question concerned the students' evaluation of their own effort during gatherings, and there were three possible answers: average, below average or above average. Guro crossed out below average. She commented that the teaching was 'boring' because: 'I feel there are many words, that the important points are coming late and that there are few important points'. We asked further what changes they might suggest and she asked for 'more references to course-literature, more examples from everyday-life in school, and more notes... on the most important points made.'

Prior to the project I would have felt bad for not being able to reach the student, and I would have left it at that. Now I realized this was an opportunity to learn something about our practice that we usually do not hear, and I hoped I could help the student develop a more positive attitude so that she could experience something valuable for herself. Therefore I invited her into a dialogue. I listened to her frustrations and asked what we could do to make matters better. She made some suggestions. One was that she needed to be challenged more. She felt the demands of the course were slack. During the year we had a few talks, I tried to challenge her in different ways, for instance by giving her more advanced reading material when she was working on her assignments. At the end of the year she wrote in her reflection-note:

> This school-year I have experienced becoming terribly tired of school. This might give me better understanding of being a pupil and it is an experience I will bring with me. My learning lies in seeing the pupil(s), like I feel I have been seen. I became tired of school even with good teachers (thank you!), it was the system with school year after year that was too much for me, and this year as all other years it was the gatherings with all the sitting still that was too much. (Saurdal, 2007)[57]

She learned something valuable during the year that she might not have unless I had persistently invited her to talk. With this student the loving encounter was about seeking contact, not letting her become invisible, as she might have

---

[57]   It is not evident from this text that it was our encounters that made her feel seen, but she did say that during the oral exam.

been. My responsibility is to be aware of 'the other' and act on the observation. The evaluation mentioned earlier was anonymous, but I guessed it was hers and asked if that was right. This was the opening for the dialogue. Was that an ethically correct act? It was done with the intention of providing an opportunity for improving the situation, for showing her that her views were important, and that we could learn from her experiences. We were reminded how important it is to differentiate teaching and guiding. She was not challenged by the discussions and reflections. To her the points were taken easily, it was all too evident; there was not enough substance to trigger her thoughts and feelings in fruitful ways. So she rightfully critiqued our teaching.

I also think that the persistence in seeking contact with her in the situation may be considered a kind of critique. I believe the encounters, the questions about what we and she might do in order to find meaning in the situation, held the potential for becoming nourishment for development and improvement.

### The goal is for you to have a clearer view of yourself – case three

The third and final aspect of love and critique that I will discuss in this paper has to do with evaluative praise and again persistence. Gitte had her education within ICT. I had guided her and written the final evaluation on her assignment. In my opinion she had delivered a well-written text reflecting a brilliant way of teaching maths to eighth graders. I expressed this. The student in return expressed frustration both in her discussion-group and in a plenary discussion, as well as in the log handed in after having received the evaluation. In it she wrote:

> As long as I agreed, I corrected the text based on the commentaries. That is, I disregarded the commentaries if I did not agree, or thought the comments were irrelevant to what I was trying to express. The final evaluation was so positive I did not believe it – not even now. I might accept a compliment, but I am awfully self-critical. This combined with low self-esteem, made the final evaluation seem totally improbable and I concluded that it was not true. This is not a criticism of the one who wrote

it, but an indication that not everyone regards positive critique equally. (Gitte, personal communication, January 18, 2007)

After she had expressed these thoughts I invited her to a talk. I offered her a second opinion of her text by a colleague who is an expert at writing. A few days later she came to my door with a broad smile. She had started to believe in the praise. She had begun to change her view of herself from being a 'poor writer' to a student who could write interesting and lively texts. In her final reflection-note she wrote:

> I came from one university to another, from a math-professor to an expert in pedagogy. It was indescribable! I thought I had lost my ability to learn, that I had gone both blind and deaf, until the first week at my new university had ended. The joy was enormous; once again I had found a teacher who contributed to my learning! Together with two math-teachers I have had previously; I would characterize these three as my best teachers through all my years as a pupil and student. They are my role models ... Their ability to motivate, their engagement, using the students' contributions, keeping it understandable, building on what is already known and not least their dialogue with the students, are some of the qualities I will bring into my own theory of practice – if I manage. (Mårtensen, 2007)

Prior to this project I would probably just have tried to convince her to believe in the praise, I would not have gone into the ongoing dialogue that was necessary for her in order to benefit from the praise. Engaging in the dialogue, providing a second opinion, providing a number of opportunities for talks are ways in which I believe I 'extended myself for the purpose of another's growth'. One might say that the critique lay in the challenge to revise her self-regard.

I hope I have managed through these examples to show how the notions of love and critique have become tools for improving my practice, tools that have made a significant contribution to the analysis of practice and to action in practice. Through these examples I also hope to have shown how the statements in the chart above have been established through the collaboration within our group. Some of the statements come from my practice and others from my colleagues' practices.

Next I will point to how the action research project has influenced the students' choice of focus in their development project which they have to carry out as part of their coursework.


## STUDENT TEACHERS DEVELOPING THEIR COMPETENCY THROUGH ACTION RESEARCH

The fact that the teacher-educator group put our practice up for inquiry led to another important shift in our education programme. Since we started the course in 1999 one main assignment for the student teachers has been a development project which they carry out in groups and work on through two semesters. They create their project within the frame of the curriculum's aims. One aim of this project is for the students to work on one of six competence described in the *National Curriculum Regulations for Practical and Didactic Education* (Ministry of Education and Research, 2003, p. 16): adaptive and developmental competence. Another aim of the assignment is for them to develop insights in working with this kind of inquiry learning so that they in their turn may become supervisors of their students in their processes of 'researching for learning' (Scardamelia & Bereiter, 1999).

Over the years, as a result of the development project, the students have developed learning games for science, guides on how to conduct meaningful teaching in science outdoors, how to deal with children's sorrow and how schools might improve their strategy for preventing or discovering use of drugs etc. Through the period of our project we have been able to encourage the students to inquire into their practice just as we have inquired into our practice. In the second year of our project there was one group who chose the question, 'how can I improve my practice?' as their project theme. In the third year there were five such groups. Each student in the group focuses on an area they want to improve, and the members seek to support each other's improvement. Learning about guidance becomes an important result of the group-activity.

This approach has helped combine all the elements in the teacher-education in a new way, with closer links between practice and theory. The need for closing the gap between theory and practice in teacher-education in Norway has been emphasized in evaluations, the last one being at the beginning of this century (The National Council of College Education, 2002). Korthagen (2001) has outlined a strategy for what he calls a realistic approach. The main ideas in this approach are that teacher-education should build on concrete, practical problems and that the students need to learn how to reflect on such problems in order to develop professionalism as teachers. He stresses that the education programme needs a strongly integrated form.

The entire education programme is now viewed as a development spiral in which each semester consists of gatherings on campus and online, practices in schools and assignments.[58] Every practice-period the students begin by working out aims for their own learning and development. This document is commented on and approved by a teacher. The topics of the gatherings, as well as the assignments, aim at supporting their work in practice-schools towards their attempts at achieving their goals. Each term ends with reflections that are summed up in an evaluation of the student's development in practice and thus starts a new plan for improvement for the next period in practice. This document is also commented and approved by the staff of the education programme. In this way the entire programme follows the cycle of plan, act and observe, reflect and new plan. This means that the students' plans (learning goals) and reports from practice (what is achieved) are no longer experienced as formal demands, but as dynamic processes they can use in their development. Some students, during classroom-discussions when presenting the idea, said that these tasks now took on

---

[58]    The discussion and decisions are documented in an account from a meeting December 20, 2006.

a whole new dimension. Their learning-outcome from gatherings, their personal journals, and the assignments – all could now be used as data in their development project.

All the students attending the specific groups addressing the question: 'how can I improve my practice?' have, in various ways, documented how the project has helped them develop their own ability as teachers. One student told of the outcome of her first-person inquiry like this:

> The most significant difference for me was that I came to class with more insight into the pupils, the relations between the pupils and between the pupils and me. On the other hand I knew less about what all the books said about the issue in question. (Skjæggestad, 2007, p. 10)

This student was inspired by an article called 'Living Life as Inquiry' by Judi Marshall (1999). She systematically wrote a journal during her work on the development project. She made some significant discoveries about her practice and she expressed how she developed a new confidence as a teacher. All the students in that group accounted for how they made significant changes in their practice or in the way they regarded their teacher-role, in their project reports. When they presented the work for the rest of the class at the end of the year, one student commented by saying she wished she had been courageous enough to go into that group. She realized they had learned something that was valuable for them.

The described change of the development project, and how that altered our view of the entire programme, constitute a major result from the co-operative action research project.


## TRANSFORMATIONS EMERGING FROM THE SEVENTH CORNER OF THE WORLD

*The 7th corner of the world* mirrors the seventh direction. The six commonly used directions are north, south, east, west, upwards and downwards. The seventh is the direction pointing inwards. In this article I have explored and shared with you a few 'pictures' of lived experience, an encounter with my supervisor and three guiding situations with student teachers. These experiences were all informed by the notions of *love and critique*, just as the experiences added new aspects to the notions of *love and critique*. The awareness of the notions helped improve practice and practice added new aspects of meaning to the notions. The inward change of attitudes makes change of practice possible, and change of ones practice may contribute to change inwardly.

The concert situation was not one of guiding, and still I consider it an important aspect of my practice – a situation from which it is possible to draw knowledge valuable for my guiding practice. This encounter shows me in a situation where I felt that my actions contradicted my values. As I reflected on the situation, I came to understand several things that I will form as five crucial elements of any guiding practice:

First it shows how easy it is to act in contradiction with one's intentions and values and how important it is to be conscious of the values one wants the work to be judged by. I want

- the students to succeed in order to become their potential (case one);
- to make an effort to provide a learning environment in which every student may be supported and challenged (case two);
- to provide a mirror for the students in order for them to discover their strengths (case three).

This awareness is what Heron and Reason (2001) describe as meta-intentionality. The awareness has prompted me to facilitate reflections in which students may become aware of their values, and provide opportunities for them to discover when they act in contradiction to their values in teaching situations. Furthermore the awareness points to contradictions in my practice.

Secondly it shows the importance of preparation. Had I read what was written about the music and had I asked for Edvin's intentions before going to the concert, I might have been able to hear something different from what I actually heard and/or delivered the critique in a different manner. This also applies to my work with the students. Finding out what is important to them and exploring their experiences prior to entering the student-teacher role are important tasks belonging to the guiding role. Listening to Guro's experiences of what bored her during campus-gatherings, and why, was crucial in order to provide for a more satisfactory learning environment, one where she at least felt seen. New ways of differentiating teaching and guiding were revealed through that process.

The third point is about paying attention to the emotions in the situation in order to develop one-self. Paying attention to the time I critiqued Edvin's work and the emotions evoked turned out to be a valuable source for learning. I learned (again) that my feelings are strong and that I have to think twice about how I word them. Even though Edvin did not resent my reactions, I would have preferred to deliver them differently. I have gained new insight into how my emotions may become barriers for the learning of others and how they might help me engage in positive encounters even if the situation seems problematic (cases two and three). Kvalsund (2005) points out how important it is to work on personal growth and development to reach greater professionalism as supervisors.

Fourthly, the situation shows how working with and sharing emotions may be transformed to knowledge – knowledge that leads to richer experiences and *fuller relationships*. Buber says: 'Only when I risk and reveal myself as she risks and reveals herself will I grasp her uniqueness and she mine' (cited in Atterton et al., 2004). The relationship with my supervisor was broadened through the experience as we both opened up and revealed ourselves. In the same way the relationships with the students broadened. Learning happened on several levels. Edvin works with the musicians in a more collaborative way after this encounter. I learned more about my values and how I want to address critique, as well as learning about the music. The changed relationship has given way to new areas of collaboration.[59]

The fifth point concerns language. Edvin addressed the issue of balance between support and challenge in guiding when he wrote:

> I began thinking (after the encounter following the concert) of love and critique in musical terms, as harmony/consonance and disharmony/dissonance. These are maybe the two most profound forces in musical composition, - only (or too much) harmony makes the expression dull, whereas only (or too much) disharmony is destroying for the ear and the mind. For the composer, it is crucial to be able to balance these to complementary forces. (E. Østergaard, personal communication, March 11, 2007)

In guidance it is also crucial to find the balance between harmony and disharmony (Laidlaw, 2008), between support and challenge. This is well documented in literature about guidance and supervision (for instance in Handal & Lauvås, 1999). Edvin here adds 'new' ways of thinking about this balance. When developing new ways to describe and understand our practice, at the same time the prospect of enhancing practice is being increased (Gudmundsdottir, 1997).

Lastly, I will summarize the outcome of the project that I have focused on in this paper. At the beginning I defined love as the will to extend one's self for the purpose of nurturing one's own or another's professional and personal growth. The student examples I have chosen, I regard as representing situations when I have extended myself by crossing barriers in the purpose of nurturing both the students' professional growth and my own. What earlier disturbed me and felt like dissonance in student-encounters is now experienced as consonance. There has been change of practice. The examples are further meant to show what I mean when I say I want to see the other in Buber's terms, being in a relation of I-Thou.

---

[59]    On June 2, 2008, there was a gathering of leaders of Norwegian Teacher-education (NRLU) that our section hosted. For this gathering we (Edvin Østergaard, Knut Omholt and myself) created a one-hour performance together with the three musicians playing parts of the concert (some of the pieces linked up earlier in this paper). The performance included the narrative of my experience, as described in this paper.

I have pointed out a variety of challenges students may encounter and shown how they require an awareness to detect the points of challenge in each student, as well as the diverse approaches necessary to see each student's learning needs. This engages the outcome of the project on a personal level. Furthermore, I have shown how the project has influenced the organizing of the postgraduate teacher-education programme, when the development-project took on the form of 'how can I improve what I do as a teacher student?' and by that contributed to narrowing the gap between theory and practice in the programme.

Finally I will now return to the encounter following the concert, in order to close this paper.


## LIVING CONTRADICTION OR LIVING CRITIQUE

Now is the time to return to the question: did I live my values when I imposed my experiences on Edvin and my colleagues after the concert? My first answer was no! I was not following my intentions of an open inquiry where my aim was to understand his expression. On the other hand I was being present and direct, which Buber considers to be qualities of an I-Thou encounter (Atterton et al., 2004). I was exposing my own ignorance as well as my genuine emotions and bodily reactions. What were Edvin's reflections on this encounter? He answered this question in writing:

> ... you chose to give me your response in front of all our colleagues – which to me is a very secure surrounding. It has to do with the fact that you chose to wait several days before giving me your opinions. And it certainly has to do with being able to accept critique from an audience – this should be regarded as a composer's key qualification! (E. Østergaard, personal communication, March 11, 2007)[60]

He also emphasized that this sort of lived critique was a rare experience as his fellow composers listen and give their feedback in a very different manner. In this situation the feedback was sudden and impulsive. The negative criticism was

---

[60]    This letter was written in English.

transformed into what he experienced as constructive critique. Mutual respect was a condition that made this transformation possible. And maybe even more important, we were both engaged in the reflections and awareness of how we live our values of love and critique and therefore were both willing to share the pain of vulnerability. A shared language in which to bring up the situation for reflection was available. It was a shared feeling of importance that made us take the time and effort for exploration. Personal experience was transformed to lived theory.

This was also the case in the three student situations I have described. The students were all willing to do some hard work in order to develop as humans and as teachers, and they were willing to let us partake in that process. There is always the possibility that some students go unnoticed, not being properly challenged. It is an aim to continue striving to see them all.

## CONCLUSION

New ways of thinking about our practice developed as we created new or different concepts to think with. The concept of love and critique informed our practice and brought awareness and consciousness to new areas of our guiding actions. The cycles of action and reflection clarified mine and our lived and contradictory values and pointed out possibilities for new action. I hope I have been able to show how my practice has improved and how I have influenced others' learning by conducting this project with my colleagues and through my encounters with the students. I have not accounted for my colleagues' developed competences, but it is important for me to underline that it was our practice that provided the grounds for, and was crucial for individual growth through the cycles of action and reflection. The project was for me an inspiration to live a life of inquiry (Marshall, 1999), continuing to develop my living theory.

## REFERENCES

Atterton, P., Calarco, M., & Friedman, M. (Eds.). (2004). *Levinas & Buber: Dialogue & difference.* Pittsburgh: Duquesne University Press.

Biesta, G. J. J. (2006). *Beyond learning: Democratic education for a human future.* Boulder: Paradigm Publishers.

Bjerke, J. (2005). *Praktisk undervisning i gulrotopptaking, oppgave i yrkesdidaktikk (Practical teaching in carrot harvesting, vocational didactics assignment).* Aas: University of Life Sciences.

Buber, M. (2004). *I and Thou* (Smith, R. G., Trans.). London & New York: Continuum.

Buber, M. (2007). *Jeg og du (I and thou): Cappelens upopulære skrifter (Cappelen's unpopular writings)* (Wergeland, H., Trans.). Oslo: J.W.Cappelens Vorlag AS.

Carr, W., & Kemmis, S. (1986). *Becoming critical: Education, knowledge, and action research.* London: Falmer Press.

Church, M. (2004). *Creating an uncompromised place to belong: Why do I find myself in networks?* (Doctoral dissertation, University of Bath, 2004). Retrieved from http://www.actionresearch.net/church.shtml

Elliott, J. (1991). *Action research for educational change.* Open University Press: Milton Keynes.

Gudmundsdottir, S. (1997). *Narrativ forskning på pedagogisk praksis (Narrative research of pedagogic practice).* Oslo: Pedagogisk forskningsinstitutt, Universitetet i Oslo.

Handal, G., & Lauvås, P. (1999). *På egne vilkår: En strategi for veiledning med lærere (On your own terms: A strategy for teacher guidance).* Oslo: Cappelen akademisk forl.

Heron, J., & Reason, P. (2001). The practice of co-operative inquiry: Research 'with' rather than 'on' people. In P. R. H. Bradbury (Ed.), *Handbook of action research: Participative inquiry & practice* (pp. 179-188). London: Sage.

Hiim, H. (2003). Læreren som forsker (The teacher as researcher). *Norsk Pedagogisk Tidsskrift, 5*(6), 345-359.

Hiim, H. (2007). A strategy for practice-based education and research. In P. Ponte & B. H. J. Smit (Eds.), *The quality of practitioner research: Reflections on the position of the researcher and the researched* (pp. S. 97-114). Rotterdam: Sense Publishers.

Hiim, H., & Hippe, E. (1989, revised edition 1998). *Undervisningsplanlegging for yrkeslærere (Vocational education and didactics).* Oslo: Universitetsforl.

Korthagen, F. (2001). *Linking practice and theory: The pedagogy of realistic teacher-education.* London: Lawrence Erlbaum Associates.

Kvalsund, R. (2005). Self-insight. A necessary presupposition for professional guidance? In E. Allgood & R. Kvalsund (Eds.), *Learning and discovery for professional educators: Guides, counselors, teachers: An experiential approach to practice and research* (pp. 109-140). Trondheim: Tapir Academic Press.

Laidlaw, M. (1996). *How can I create my own living educational theory as I offer an account of my educational development?* (Doctoral dissertation, University of Bath). Retrieved January 20, 2009, from http://www.actionresearch.net/moira2.shtml

Laidlaw, M. (2004). A Description of my Logic. *China's Experimental Centre for Educational Action Research in Foreign Languages Teaching.* Retrieved September 17, 2008, from http://www.actionresearch.net/living/moira/mllogic.htm

Laidlaw, M. (2008). In pursuit of counterpoint: An educational journey. *Educational Journal of Living Theories, 1*(1), 69-102. Retrieved January 20, 2009, from http://ejolts.net/drupal/node/76

Lauvås, P., & Handal, G. (2000). *Veiledning og praktisk yrkesteori (Guidance and practical professional theory).* Oslo: Cappelen Akademisk.

Levinas, E. (1991). *Otherwise than being, or beyond essence.* Dordrecht: Kluwer.

Lohr, E. (2006). *Love at work: What is my lived experience of love, and how may I become an instrument of love's purpose?* (Doctoral dissertation, University of Bath, 2006), School of Management. University of Bath. Retrieved September 17, 2008, from http://www.actionresearch.net/lohr.shtml

Marshall, J. (1999). Living life as inquiry. *Systemic Practice and Action Research, 12*(2), 155-171.

Ministry of Education Research. (1993). *Core curriculum, for primary, secondary and adult education in Norway.* Retrieved September 17, 2008, from http://www.utdanningsdirektoratet.no/upload/larerplaner/generell_del/Core_Curriculum_English.pdf

Ministry of Education and Research. (2003). *National Curriculum regulations, practical and didactic education.* Retrieved August 28, 2010, from http://www.regjeringen.no/Upload/KD/Vedlegg/UH/Rammeplaner/Lærer/Rammeplan_laerer_eng.pdf

Ministry of Education and Research. (June 17, 2005). *Act relating to primary and secondary education (Education act).* Retrieved August 28, 2010, from http://www.regjeringen.no/upload/kilde/kd/reg/2006/0038/ddd/pdfv/289194-opplaeringsloven_engelsk_oversettelse_sist_endret_2005-06-17.pdf

Moran, D. (2000). *Introduction to phenomenology.* London: Routledge.

Mårtensen, G. (2007). *Pedagogisk refleksjonsnotat, praktisk pedagogisk utdanning, heltid 2006/2007 (Pedagogic reflection note, Practical Pedagogic Education, fulltime 2006/2007).* Aas: University of Life Sciences.

Peck, M. S. (1998). *Further along the road less travelled: The unending Journey Toward Spiritual Growth.* New York: Touchstone.

Peck, M. S. (2008). *The road less travelled: A new psychology of love, traditional values and spiritual growth* (25 ed.). New York: Touchstone.

Pettersen, R. C., & Løkke, J. A. (2004). *Veiledning i praksis: Grunnleggende ferdigheter (Guidance in practice: Fundamental skills).* Oslo: Universitetsforl.

Polanyi, M. (1983). *The tacit dimension.* Glouchester, Mass.: Peter Smith.

Saurdal, G. (2007). *Refleksjonsnotat (Reflection note, preparation for the final exam in pedagogics).* Aas: University of Life Sciences.

Scardamelia, M., & Bereiter, C. (1999). Schools as knowledge-building organizations. In D. Keating & C. Hertzman (Eds.), *Today's children, tomorrow's society: The development of health and wealth of nations* (pp. 274-289). New York: Guilford.

Schön, D. A. (1995). *The reflective practitioner: How professionals think in action.* Aldershot: Arena.

Skjæggestad, M. (2007). Logg og refleksjon som redskap for læring. Eksempel: Undervisning av en liten klasse (Log and reflection as tool for learning. Example: Teaching in a small class). In S. Gjøtterud (Ed.), *Pedagogisk utviklingsprosjekt i praktisk pedagogisk utdanning: Utvikling av egen praksis (Pedagogical development project in post graduate teacher-education: 'How can I improve my practice?')* (Vol. 28/2008). Aas: University of Life Sciences.

Stenhouse, L. (1975). *An introduction to curriculum research and development.* London: Heinemann.

Strangstadstuen, S. (2007). *Skrivegrupper på nettet (Onling writing groups)* Presentation at project meeting. University of Life Sciences.

The National Council of College Education. (2002). *Evaluering av praktisk pedagogisk utdanning ved fem norske institusjoner. (Evaluation of practical pedagogic education by five Norwegian institutions).* Oslo.

Whitehead, J. (1989). Creating a living educational theory from questions of the kind, 'How do I improve my practice?'. *Cambridge Journal of Education, 19*(1), 41-52.

Whitehead, J. (2007). *Generating educational theories that can explain educational influences in learning: Living logics, units of appraisal, standards of judgment.* Paper presented at the British Educational Research Association Annual (BERA) Conference, place, UK. Retrieved October 29, 2008, from http://www.leeds.ac.uk/educol/documents/166811.htm

Whitehead, J. (2008). Using a living theory methodology in improving practice and generating educational knowledge in living theories. *Educational Journal of Living Theories, 1*(1), 103 - 126. Retrieved October 20, 2008, from http://ejolts.net/node/80

Whitehead, J. (2008, March). *How can I~we create living educational theories from research into professional learning?* Paper presented in the Symposium convened by Jean McNiff on Communicating and testing the validity of claims to transformational systemic influence for civic responsibility, at AERA. Retrieved October 20, 2008, from http://www.jackwhitehead.com/jack/jwaera08jmsem.htm

Whitehead, J., & McNiff, J. (2006). *Action research: Living theory.* London: SAGE.

Winter, R., & Burroughs, S. (1989). *Learning from experience: Principles and practice in action-research.* London & New York: Falmer Press.

Østergaard, E. (2006). *Spor av menneskemøter* (Traces of Human encounters). Unpublished. Aas: University of Life Sciences.

# CREATING SPACE: ACCOUNTING FOR WHERE I STAND

Jane Spiro, UK

## INTRODUCTION

This paper explains the values which shape my practice, how I have come to recognise them and the influences from which they derive, and why I continue to stand by them. By *practice*, I am referring to my roles as a *creative writer*, an English language teacher and teacher educator in International Education, and Learning and Teaching Coordinator in a vibrant and successful modern Institute of Education in the UK. In explaining these roles, I am focused in particular on the connecting thread of *creative practice*, and in so doing, am responding to the following questions:

- Why does an understanding of creativity matter?
- What values and beliefs underpin my view of *creativity*?
- Where do I stand amongst current debates about creativity?
- What are the experiences and practices, which have shaped my understanding of the creative process?
- What living theory emerges and why does this matter?

By *living theory* I am working with the definition offered by Whitehead (2008) in the first issue of this journal: 'A living theory is an explanation produced by an individual for their educational influence in their own learning, in the learning of others and in the learning of the social formation in which they live and work' (Whitehead, 2008, p. 104).

I will answer these questions by offering a window into my practice as writer-teacher with its experience of diversity and fragmentation and then explore connecting threads and beliefs and their impact on learning and teaching. The paper ends with a story which acts as a metaphor of the creative learner/teacher partnership, in which participants are both learner and teacher simultaneously, generating new and living understandings in being so.


## WHY DOES AN UNDERSTANDING OF CREATIVITY MATTER?

Three voices in recent "conversation" represent where I stand with regard to the question of why *creativity* is important:

> Creativity develops the capacity to imagine the world differently. We all need an ability not just to cope with change, but also to positively thrive on it and engineer it for ourselves. (Creative Partnerships, 2007)
> It is a pity that the notion of 'creativity' in education has to be fought for or reclaimed, as it should be a central feature of teaching and learning. It is the crucial element in each generation's renewal and enhancement of itself. Without it society would roll backwards. Human imagination and spirit are what drove civilisation forward. (Wragg, 2005, p. 2)
> I ask you to consider the inner life of the student who sits, often reluctantly, before you. Your task is to take that particular person into the living field of your discipline and in some way to change him [sic] by so doing. No transformation, no education! (Abbs, 2003, p. 10)

As an educator over a 25-year career in different educational settings, I have been concerned, because the student-experience in that *freedom to change* has become increasingly constrained by the demands of assessment and prescribed curriculum. The teachers' capacity to *be themselves* as educators and creators of the learning experience, has been minimised by institutional demands:

to meet league tables, which record only what is quantifiable and mainstream, and to match nationally-given objectives and benchmarks. Finally, I celebrate the re-emergence of creativity in the rhetoric of education. The following accounts explore the meaning of creativity for schools and teachers and embed these into the *National Curriculum* (for example Buckingham and Jones, 2001; Qualifications and Curriculum Authority, 2001; Buckingham, 2003; Creative Partnerships in Education, 2004; Department of Education and Science, 2004; Robinson, 2006; Creative Partnerships, 2007). Yet in spite of organisations such as the Department for Education and Skills bringing the notion of creativity into the mainstream, I am concerned that teachers may consider this a further burden to what is expected of them, and even a further category by which to measure and judge them. In 2008 I worked with a group of artists, musicians and storytellers, funded by the Department of Education and Skills, to bring creative projects into schools. Their common experience in schools was that teachers:

- abnegated responsibility for the creative process to the "experts";
- felt their own creative capacities were being undervalued;
- saw the creative project as an "add-on" that detracted from the "real work" of the curriculum (Certificate for Advanced Education Practice, 2008).

The educators I have quoted above echo my own concerns in the following specific ways. They suggest that the capacity to be 'creative' – or in my sense, to generate positive change – is essential to our progress as a community of fellow human beings (Wragg, 2005). Indeed, creativity, 'is essential, not only for science, but for the whole of life. If you get stuck in a mechanical, repetitious order, then you will degenerate. That is one of the problems that has grounded every civilisation' (Bohm, 1998, p. 16). In order, therefore, to limit opportunity in educational contexts becomes a matter of urgent concern. First, Pope (2005) suggests that creativity is a component of the healthy and balanced individual; the capacity to initiate and own change is part of what it is to be *sane* in a community that increasingly appears to forgo emotional health for other values. Secondly, for us to be educators, we need to be aware of our responsibility in this debate, and to consider our role in empowering learners to change, so that learning really makes a difference, both to the learner and to the knowledge-base itself (Abbs, 2003). Thirdly, creative learning goes far beyond specifically educational contexts; it is a capacity to live in the modern world and respond to its challenges and changes (Creative Partnerships, 2007). In my own practice, feedback from students, years after their specific experience of learning with me was over, reveals the impact transformatory learning had on their decisions and aspirations in other aspects of their life. Here is Courtney, formerly an undergraduate student on a Bachelor of Arts course in English Language and Linguistics:

> A few years ago I would have never imagined that I could do a postgraduate degree, and furthermore, I didn't know if there was anything that interested me enough to make it worth my while. But when I was a student in your classes, a "light" finally went on over my head, and now that I am here, I know who I have to thank. (C., personal communication, January 15, 2008)

This paper explores what *being creative* has meant for me in practice, how it has enhanced my own identity as writer, educator and manager, and why and how I have been committed to sharing its transformative potential with students, trainee-teachers, and my teaching team. The contexts I draw on include:

- running undergraduate and postgraduate programmes in English language, linguistics, language teaching and literature in four UK institutions of Further and Higher Education;

- running teacher development programmes for English teachers from one week to two years in length, sponsored by the British Council and Ministries of Education in Mexico, Poland, Hungary, Switzerland, India, China and Japan;

- drawing on recent experience working with creative practitioners working in UK schools and researching their practice;

- experience of leadership-roles as a Head of Applied Linguistics (2004 – 2007) and as Learning and Teaching Leader (from 2007) at Oxford Brookes University.

The following are examples derived from these different teaching-contexts:

- retraining Russian teachers in Hungary to teach English whose lifetime profession has been suddenly discredited by the dismantling of the Berlin wall;

- teaching English to Vietnamese 'Boat People', and finding one of them persistently missing class afraid to confront the English winter;

- developing new literature curriculum drawing on Indian writers, with teachers in India trained to teach Shakespeare, Wordsworth and the traditional English literary canon;

- developing research-vitality in a University Language Centre under threat of privatisation and the loss of academic status.

To be open to change or learning of any kind, the participants in each of these situations had somehow to reclaim a sense of worth, strength and capacity, and it was my role to participate in this process. In order to participate meaningfully, each situation demanded a sensitivity to its specificity and complexity, and a clarity about what was amenable to change and what was not.

While this brief teaching-resumé suggests a single-minded journey, it really tells only half the story. What is hidden is a creative practice as a storyteller, poet and novelist struggling to run alongside, that both emerges and is submerged through these career-moves. 'All through there was a thread I never let go... I wanted [the creative writer role] to be not a parallel life but one that informed all my work' (Spiro, 2007b).[61] As a creative writer I knew there were strategies and skills that had led me towards experiences of excitement and

---

[61]    See www.ukfuturetv.com/janespiro.wmv for a clarification of this idea.

fulfilment, which I could not easily find as an educator. In Further and Higher Education settings, my efforts to bring creative opportunities into classrooms for my learners were marginalised or subversive to the expectations of my role. For example, training primary teachers, I was warned that the daily hour dedicated to literacy did not allow time for *creative ideas*. I was not permitted to share or trial with these teachers any new materials for teaching poetry and story.[62] In 2001, the literature/creative-writing components of the teacher-development programme were deleted and I was made redundant. The combined development of creative-writing and its embedding in teaching were not counted as valid research-output, so it was hard to find a place in a Higher Education setting. On finally finding new employment I was advised through appraisals to redeploy my energies to meet institutionally-recognised criteria. Yet I continue to hold that the writer and the teacher are indeed not parallel lives, but inform one other, and the opportunity to do so is enriching both for myself and my learners. Where it has been possible to bring creative goals and practice into teaching settings, the outcomes for some have been life-changing. Here is Maria, participant in a summer workshop on creative-writing for language teachers: 'Jane's workshop has helped to liberate myself in the way I looked at creative-writing... She has led me to a brand new world where we ourselves can be creative' (M., personal communication, August 8, 2007).

## WHICH VALUES AND BELIEFS UNDERPIN MY VIEW OF CREATIVITY, AND WHERE DO THEY COME FROM?

Through struggling to survive, understand and transform complex challenges such as those described above, certain core values have emerged. I will illustrate this process of emergence and recognition briefly through a critical

---

[62]     These materials (Spiro 2004, 2007a) were later published as two books by Oxford University Press.

incident which relates to the widening sphere of teacher-engagement:  teacher –
student; teacher – class; teacher – school/institution; teacher – community. It
describes a situation, like the account in the section above, capable of only limited
resolution by my intervention alone. However, this incident is one of many that
revealed to me core values and how they might shape actions.

While training a new and first generation of English-language teachers in
southern Hungary, I experienced the hostility and resentment of one of the
students in the class. During sessions he was morose and obstructive, palpably
impacting on the morale of the whole class. During one session, he suddenly ran
out of the class, and it emerged he had accidentally 'stabbed' his neighbour with
the point of his pencil. I found myself not only concerned that this student was
damaging the health of the class as a whole, but also that he may have a similarly
demoralising effect on the children he was being trained to teach. I set up and
carried through a disciplinary process. No other member of staff was prepared to
support me or corroborate my analysis of this student although we had informally
exchanged many examples of how the student behaved in similar ways in their
classes. The disciplinary process returned a verdict in support of the student,
saying 'the teacher from England does not understand the Hungarian way of
teaching' and the student returned to the classroom. The students in his class did
not thank me for trying to "protect" them; in fact, several students appeared to
inherit from this incident the very hostility from which I had tried to shield them.
Various layers of explanation emerged:  his father was a respected member of the
community; colleagues had known this student since childhood; they knew he in
fact had no intention of teaching (and indeed, after graduation, set up a shop
selling leather jackets); combining together to form a collective voice amounted to
"collaboration" – a negative and terror-inducing term in recently ex-Soviet
Hungary. I remember being humbled by my failure to take a nuanced and
culture-sensitive approach. I had assumed the class shared my perceptions of the
situation, and I had not connected with either their position, or those of my

colleagues. My own sense of fairness had overruled theirs, and in doing this I had also overruled their own strategies for repair. There were other ways of dealing with difficulties such as these, without opening the community to public scrutiny or abdicating control to a mistrusted authority. Yet at the same time, I felt some sense of grievance that no one had attempted to understand my position or the motives behind it. They also had not allowed for the possibility that I was amenable to change: I would have changed my view of the situation, had anyone troubled to explain it. At core, I valued the wellbeing of the class over my own safety in the community. I was acting authentically, with integrity on my own terms, even though I was being isolated in doing this. Yet mistakes were made on both sides. I had not really understood the community I was in, asked the right questions, or listened subtly enough to connect with their story. Yet by allowing me to make a mistake of this kind, I felt a lack of empathy shown towards me.

These values were those that emerged for me in many of the situations briefly suggested and illustrated above: wellbeing, authenticity, connection, empathy and empowerment. The section below will briefly define each of these terms.

**Wellbeing**

Wellbeing, for me, involves providing the best possible conditions for learning. These conditions account both for physical wellbeing – warmth, safety, and comfort – as well as spiritual and intellectual wellbeing: the space to explore, experiment, and learn from mistakes. This involves a belief in learners' capacity to achieve at the height of their ability, and a commitment to making the conditions right for this to happen. In this, Maslow's notion of the hierarchy of needs is enshrined; he recognises a chain of dependence from basic physical needs to higher intellectual and spiritual ones, and suggests that one level of need can only be fulfilled in conjunction with others (Maslow 1943).

In this, I am aware of notions of wellbeing emerging explicitly in school curriculum (the Office for Standards in Education[63], 2005; Baylis and Morris, 2007) as well as recent critiques of wellbeing. Ecclestone and Hayes (2009) suggest that explicit focus on wellbeing infantilises the learner, and diverts attention away from content and achievement and towards a therapy-culture in which dysfunctionality and low achievement are the norm. It may be seen from my definition above, that my own meaning of wellbeing is the opposite. It is concerned with creating the space for everyone within it to achieve and be the best they are capable of being. Farren (2008) describes this educational space as 'providing opportunities for participants to accept responsibility for their own learning' (p. 50).

**Connection**

As with the incident in southern Hungary described above, connection is not an "easy" or safe value to hold in the sense I intend it. It includes an honouring of the specificity of a situation. Through care for detail and capacity to listen to the deeper story I recognise not only that every story is uniquely different but also that every story offers insights into the broader human condition. Experiencing a connection with each situation has meant I have disallowed making assumptions that one situation will be like another; that what appears on the surface to be parallel really will be; that what I learnt or the way I behaved in one setting will work for another. Connecting has in fact involved stripping away expectations and stereotypes, and starting again with each situation so that it is possible to continue learning afresh from each. In the examples cited in the section above of teaching challenges, I cited as a common factor the sense of disempowerment experienced by each of the communities: the newly disempowered Russian teachers, the imminently privatised teaching team, the

---

[63]     Usually expressed as an acronym, OfSTED.

colonial reading experience of Indian teachers in a post-colonial world. Yet in order effectively to connect with them, what I learnt was the specificity of each of these circumstances, the non-transferability of experiences from one to the other, and the unique story of each case. Whilst at surface levels there might have been similarities, what was important about each were their differences.

**Empathy**

Whilst connection involves, in my sense of this, learning the story of the other, in the notion of empathy I am bringing myself into the equation. I empathise with others in recognising that their experiences and dreams resonate with mine, and it is through this mutuality that we can better understand one another. Through empathy I am finding and learning what is common in my experience and yours, and acting on this understanding. Mutual empathy, for example, might have repaired the Hungarian example described above: here I would have reached towards an understanding of why colleagues chose non-involvement, and they would have reached towards why I chose the opposite. In this dialogue, we would have understood that both of us in fact held the same ideal of wellbeing. I am engaging here with the notion of inclusionality developed by Rayner and colleagues at the University of Bath. Rayner writes that 'through inclusionality we can soften the hard-line definition of our selves and others as independent subjects and objects isolated by gaps, into interdependent, dynamic relational flow-forms, pooled together in space' (Rayner, 2009). Rayner's wish through the practice of inclusionality is to:

> develop a more empathic, more fulfilling way of thinking/feeling about relationships amongst ourselves, other organisms and our living space, which acknowledges the fact that the boundaries we inhabit are not absolute and fixed but rather inform dynamic, interactive domains that allow a rich variety of patterns to emerge and transform our lives. (Rayner, 2008)

This kind of empathy and inclusion has real and political implications. For example, Mandela's view of the liberation of South Africa included empathy for his oppressors and the desire for their liberation too (Mandela, 1994). His government demonstrated this empathy in the Commission for Truth and Reconciliation, a vehicle for mutual understanding as an alternative to punishment and blame.

**Empowerment**

In the descriptions of different teaching settings described above, I cited the importance of each community to reclaim their power. I regard it as a core responsibility of the teacher: to give power back to the learner and to provide a rich environment that allows this to happen. In precise terms, this has meant energising learners' highest capacities and raising the bar of their aspirations. Here the teacher makes the learner aware of what he/she is capable of doing, and provides him/her with the tools to achieve this. In the story at the end of this paper, Thought Doctor is contrasted with the Fellow Traveller. The Thought Doctor engenders in learners awe for the teacher's knowledge and skills whilst the Fellow Traveller leads the learner towards a discovery of his/her own knowledge.

**Authenticity**

I am only prepared to act through these beliefs, rather than through desire for power, status, recognition, or fashion. I regard my own authenticity as acting with integrity in congruence with these beliefs, and wherever they are compromised or threatened I will seek repair and resolution, however hard-earned these might be.

Living with and by these values has provided a means to navigate the struggle for creative space. It has also provided a way of accommodating setbacks, challenges and failures such as those mentioned in earlier sections.

## WHERE DO I STAND AMONGST CURRENT DEBATES ABOUT CREATIVITY?

I claim, as part of the experience from which I derive understandings, to be a creative writer. Why do I use this term and with what meanings and implications? Writers do not call themselves creative writers, and indeed I have only done so in this paper in order to differentiate two dis-integrated kinds of writing and being. One of these writers writes the paper you read at this moment. Here I struggle to make meaning direct and transparent, and to embed this in a community of shared academic conventions and discourse. The other 'self' wrote the story that concludes this paper. Here I am searching to change my meanings into the symbolic, by making the experiences not-mine and at the same time universal, by inventing places and people that both do and do not exist, by using the tools and conventions of myth and metaphor. In most cases, these two kinds of writer would not appear in one place: they tend to publish, be read, work, and live in different places.

The word family (creative/creativity) derives from the Latin verb *creo* – to make, or do, and its range of synonyms: to generate, to give birth, to produce, to manufacture, to change, to invent, to transform. *To make* is the capacity of the principle of life - to make artefacts which are both life's quest for survival and crafted, as are hand-thrown pots, woven carpets, spiders' webs and birds' nests. Thus creativity in this sense does not privilege the activity to the specially gifted or the unique; on the contrary, it is the essential skill of the survivor. Other synonyms are ethically ambiguous; *to invent* semantically carries the idea of *to lie*, as in *creative accounting*, and indeed, the capacity of the storyteller to fictionalise the truth. *To give birth* suggests the notion of creation from first beginnings; whilst *to transform/change* assumes raw material, a pre-existing starting point (Pope, 2005). Thus the word itself suggests the core debates and dilemmas, which attach to creativity as a phenomenon. In defining some of these core debates in the section below, I am also identifying those which have been part of my own authentic and continuing struggle to create space as a writer-teacher.

- Do creative ideas derive from the stimulus of the outside world, or do they spring from nowhere, *ex nihilo,* the unbidden voice of a muse? Sartre (1964) and Cocteau (1952) claim god-like inspiration which 'comes from beyond and is offered us by the gods' (Cocteau, 1952, p. 82). Yet, these same artists are simultaneously articulate about the influences that shape them – cultural, social, psychological. The novelist Joseph Conrad describes the inspiration that sparked his novel *The Secret Agent* (Conrad, 1920); Isabel Allende (2007) describes the drives that make her a storyteller. By unravelling the sources, influences and shaping forces, do we minimise creative uniqueness, or illuminate it?

- Is creativity part of the 'natural and normal state of anyone healthy in a sane and stimulating community' (Pope, 2005, xvi) or is the creative person specially, mystically gifted? Is there any value or meaning in the notion of 'genius' as part of a-normality, or does this simply serve to offer us elitist and alienating paradigms of the creative process? (Weisberg, 1993; Miller, 2000; Nettle, 2001).

- Does creativity *do* something, or is it merely decorative and luxurious? What is the artist's responsibility to the outside world, and what is the point of his/her work? Most artists have a powerful sense of the worth of their work: the composer Leonard Bernstein, in interview, said 'I believe that man's noblest endowment is his [sic] capacity to change. We must know ourselves better through art' (Bernstein, 2007, p. 21). To share this with the world is an artistic imperative: 'what is the point of having experience, knowledge or talent if I don't give it away? Of having stories if I don't tell them to others?' (Allende, 2007, p. 15). Yet how far does the sense of worth depend on recognition by others? Is it helpful – or misleading and unhelpful - to measure the worth of creative process, by the impact it has on others?

- Can we call all examples of human enterprise creative, or only selected and privileged examples? Carter, for example, develops the idea of a decline of literariness in texts, in which literary/creative language lies at one end and non-literary lies at the other (Carter, 2006). A cluster of categories define this distinction, including the conscious and crafted use of language. An ethnographic approach, alternatively, values all human productivity as windows into the human condition and the culture/context in which it finds itself (Clifford and Marcus, 2004; Morrison, 2007). Yet, to describe everything we do, or make, as creative could empty the word of meaning. Do we need such a label at all, if it is incapable of distinguishing one action, or outcome, or product, from another?

- Can creativity be developed and trained, or does it spring fully formed for those privileged to do so? In other words, is it teachable, and to whom? In placing creativity within the curriculum, educators have made a commitment to its developmental capacity (Buckingham, 2003; Balshaw, 2004, Creative Partnerships in Education, 2004; Creative Partnerships, 2007). Yet, how can creativity be taught and developed, if there is so much disagreement about what it actually is? If creative outcomes lie at each point along the spectrum from everything attainable by the healthy human being, to privileged examples of exceptional talent, how can it possibly be taught – and why should it be?

- In analysing the creative process, a broad agreement emerges that there is a chaotic, free association stage – what traditionally and mythically was described as *inspiration* - and a stage involving detailed crafting, honing, shaping and ordering. These two processes have been described metaphorically: the potter throwing down the clay and then shaping it (Elbow, 1973); 'writing down the bones' and then fleshing them out

(Goldberg, 1986). How do artists themselves perceive and live with this relationship? How do inspiration and discipline work together to generate creative outcomes? What do analysts of the creative process (such as Hayles, 1991; Coveney and Highfield, 1995) tell us and how does this map over what artists actually do?

In exploring my own experience as writer-teacher, it has been possible to understand my own position amongst these several debates and to arrive at my own living theory of what it means to be *creative*. The next section will offer "windows" for the reader into the practice and experience which has enabled me to recognize the theory which I live, and the values which underlie it.


## WHAT ARE THE EXPERIENCES AND PRACTICES WHICH HAVE SHAPED MY UNDERSTANDING OF THE CREATIVE PROCESS?

### Writing a novel

In June 1995, my twice yearly working visits to Poland took me to a new place called Vigry, high up by the north eastern border near Beloruss – or what was once part of Lithuania. I had been walking through the flat bleak fields on the north eastern border, with two colleagues who had each moved to Poland, learnt the language fluently, and dedicated their careers to Polish culture. We were walking in this bleakly remote open landscapes when the heavens opened, and a torrential downfall almost blinded us. We beat our way through this shelterless terrain, the ground turning to swamp underfoot, when the scene below took place.

> They all three felt it together and moved together in a line towards the place of being saved, and the person there in the threshold, another person with eyes and a nose and a face stood there watching stood still as stone but they knew she was real by the moving of the eyes and the falling of the hair under the scarf and the jumping of the hair in her breath.
> As they came nearer, she stayed planted there, without moving. Her eyes and theirs focused, and narrowed. They were all human, she in the threshold newly warm from the fire inside, and they the three of them

drowned into transparent ghosts of themselves, washed in and out and in
by the storm. She watched them and took in the story of them, learnt it by
heart and learnt what to do. She swivelled round, like a doll on a stick.
They saw the strings of her shawl spiking down her neck. She moved
faster than they did, by a footstep. As they moved nearer, she moved into
the door, opened it, slid behind it, and as they came into its shadow, it
closed clack matt against the wall. (J. Spiro, personal communication,
1995)

I remember being aghast that the woman had offered us no shelter – but
had established our humanity before doing so. It was not that I minded being
soaked by the storm: we were not really far from home and our situation was not
serious. What I felt powerfully, was that, had the situation actually been serious,
her rejection would have been the same. It seemed to me a replaying of something
that had happened here before. It was not my own plight I could feel in this: I
could hear others, almost palpably, in this plain between Poland and Lithuania, for
whom 'not offering shelter' was a matter of life and death.

In February 1996, I visited another town in the north eastern corner of
Poland, called Suwalki. While I was there, I was able to befriend an ex-patriot
teacher of whom I could ask the questions I chose to avoid with the Poles
themselves:

- Were there any Jews in this town?

- Do you know if there is any record or memorial to them?

Yes, there was not merely a memorial, but in fact, it was still possible to
visit the whole site of the former Jewish cemetery. My friend led me to this place
on an exceptionally bleak slate-grey February day. Our journey took us through
the back streets of Suwalki, where chickens ran across the wooden porches of
long low houses, and women in black headscarves shooed them away from their
doorways. The experience felt powerfully that I had become my own
grandmother, and was running through the back streets of my Lithuanian shtetl[64]
to find the small Jewish enclave where I could be safe. When we reached the

---

[64]     Shtetl: a Jewish village or small-town community in Eastern Europe.

place which had been the cemetery, what I saw, and later recorded in my notebook, was this:

> In the middle of the field was a wall. It was impossible to ignore because the rest was so flat, a snow desert, and so far from anything standing that man had made. It had wandered in from a town, and stayed there.
> I took to the field. Every footstep piped down into a tube of snow, and I loped towards the wall, the wall loped towards me, my boots picking up giant moulds of snow with each step.
> Nearer to it, the stone sent out a layer of heat. I scraped the frost from the surface, and as it lifted onto my glove, images hoved into view under the cobweb of snow. Each piece was covered with tight stone scribblings, Hebrew words, some Russian, names and pictures. There was half a Rachel with her last letters butted in beside an Avram, and an Eva with a wrist cut at the hand, a Jacob with a lion's paw on his head, and a Rebecca with half a holy book.
> It was a wall of tombs, broken tombs that had been snapped off like teeth and crisscrossed in together. This had been the cemetery, this field: all that was left a single standing jigsaw puzzle of people and their picture descriptions. (J. Spiro, personal communication, 1996)
> I knew this scene was haunting in a way I could not resist.

I knew it was the beginning of a long story: mine, my family's, the unknown people carved on the tombs. I knew that this, and the accumulated images of loneliness and rejection, were primal ones that belonged to my ancestry, and that I had a collective responsibility to speak of it. I knew that it was the beginning of a profoundly compelling creative project, the moment described by Seamus Heaney as a 'marriage between the geographical country and the country of the mind' (Heaney, 1980, p. 131).

As part of the journey towards an artistic or creative account of this experience, I researched the story behind my own family's escape from Poland in 1938. Through a series of interviews with my uncle, Julek, extensive reading and further travel, I accumulated knowledge of details such as: the home-made vodka which was both purple and powerful; the horse and droschka[65] which took the family out into the countryside for holidays; the safe houses that sheltered the

---

[65]  This is a kind of cart.

refugees in the forest; the trains they clung to, the open ditches they hid in, and a great deal of further reading besides that expanded, confirmed, and deepened what I had sensed in northern Poland. But *I* still needed to make the poetic leap into the narrative, the 'metaphorical confrontation' with myself that would turn this cluster of scenes into driven narrative (Cox and Thielgard, 1987, p. 45). In other words, I needed still to 'put (myself) on the line and to take risks. These risks are predicated on a simple proposition: this writer's personal experiences are worth sharing with others. Messy texts make the writer a part of the writing project (Denzin, 1997, p. 225).

The catalyst, or alchemical transformation, came with a *what if?* question. What if I had happened to be born a generation ago, in the same situation as my uncle or his sisters, the ones left behind? How would the *I* have felt, behaved and lived, dropped into this very different world? What if I were to compare that hypothetical girl, with this one? From this evolved the idea of a double narrative and a specific time-lapse between them: one girl living in Poland in 1939 in the wake of the Nazi occupation of Poland, and another girl living in 1989 in north London, the year the Berlin wall came down. How would their two lives compare or run parallel? What if both had potentially the same spirit and yet were shaped by such different worlds, if, in fact, they are blood relations - say, grandmother and grand-daughter? Now, imagine the contemporary girl, as I did, ends her journey by the memorial wall in northern Poland:  and the 1939 girl ends her journey as a refugee in north London, each travelling in opposite directions across Europe. What if they somehow *cross-spiritually*, or meta/physically, on the way?

Here I had everything I needed. As Conrad (1920) said when he found the central idea for his novel *The Secret Agent*: 'There was room enough there to place any story, depth enough there for any passion, variety enough there for any setting, darkness enough to bury five millions of life' (p. 6). The issues, sensibilities, personal mythologies this plot-structure offered were huge: belonging and not belonging, separation and loss, my own family's story of regeneration and starting again, the different meaning of *escape* for the 1939 and the 1989 girls, the different options for *finding themselves* and discovering their personal courage.

With this clear vision of the parallel women, fifty years apart, I set about planning them, being them, hearing them. The 1939 grandmother character, Rosa, adopted composite characteristics of all grandmothers I had known – including my own. Rosa is feisty, brave, clever, strong, and is not prepared to be left behind – like the sisters in my uncle's story, who had encouraged him on his escape without a consideration for their own safety. The 1989 girl, Laura, has had few opportunities to understand her own strengths, having been sheltered and cosseted by an over-loving family, so her slant on the world is freshly naïve. To place Laura psychologically and physically in the story, I developed episodes in her childhood which were significant – even quintessential – moments for me too.

The Laura stories were great opportunities for creative play. I "became" her, speaking in her voice as she grew from child to adolescent to young woman in the course of the novel. Here is an extract from Laura's childhood. She has in error joined the Christian prayers at school, not realising that she belongs to the much smaller group that meets in the classroom down the corridor.

> I had never seen anything like it. There was a picture of a man in a white nightie with brown hair down to his shoulders and strange brown eyes and there was a light bulb round his head. He seemed quite nice, but I didn't know anyone like that at all. Polly and Lisa seemed to know him quite well and even knew his name.

Eventually the mistake is realised by the teachers, and she is led away to Jewish prayers down the corridor. The extract below tells the story in the child's words as they gradually mingle with the words from the scriptures that she recognises.

> The words in English made me tingle all over and made my ears go red.
> *Let these words which I command you this day, be always in your heart, teach them diligently to your children and speak of them in your home*
> Yes and on your doorposts and foreheads I will do what you say and the words will shower down like great walls of thunder
> We are from the desert all of us in the room with the baking sand and men

with rolling white beards and sticks
Inside us we are all wearing white sheets and veils and wash our clothes in
the Dead Sea
Inside our plaits and white socks we are ancient which means very very
very old because Jessie beget David beget Deborah beget Susannah beget
Samson beget Daniel beget Hagar beget Rebecca beget Rachel beget
Sarah beget Peter beget Jonathan beget Jacob beget Laura
Beget means to have a baby
If you were beget you lived in a tent and wore a veil if you were a girl and
collected water in a vase from the well
In the other Sembly[66] room they must have had different sorts of grandmas
or maybe fathers who wore nighties. (Spiro, 2002, pp. 17 – 19)

There are more epiphanies for Laura, struggling to understand her identity
and place herself in the outside world. Here she describes her first experience of
singing with boys in the school choir:

We began the Kyrie Elieson with Miss Doubleday on the piano and the
girls came in with papery voices and floated off into little puffs of ash.
Then the boys' voices rolled in and I was knocked through the back of my
neck into a beanstalk world with giants rolling boulders round the edges of
the world. I could feel them thumping behind me with their giant feet, and
the benches were purring like cats. The sound through the floor grew trees
up through my heels and washed my stomach dark like a plum.
'Now boys, you need to watch the beat, not each other!' Miss Doubleday
shouted. I could feel the dinosaurs snorting behind me, and the giants with
troll-black hair thundering through the mountains like yetis. But when I
turned round to have a quick look, I was shocked to see the row of boys
still there, some of them spotty and with dandruff on their blazers. (Spiro,
2002, p. 97)

Meanwhile Rosa, became a symbol for all those who had left their lives
behind, by train, boat, on foot. Here is Rosa on her last journey out of Poland,
lucky enough to have time to leave by train (as my uncle did), her lover left
behind on the station platform. Like the sisters in Julek's journey, he has chosen
to stay for the sake of family – in this case, his elderly father who would not have
survived the journey.

The train was moving in a tunnel of freezing darkness and there seemed
never to be landscape, only the laughter of the guards in the corridor
drinking vodka and playing cards, the long rattled breathing of the old

---

[66]     Assembly

woman snoring in the corner of the carriage, the chundering of her grown-up sons in their sleep. And Rosa sat upright looking out through the window at her own image, a ghostly negative in the glass.
All through the journey, the rattling, the snoring, the chundering, the vodka-drinking, Jacob repeated through her as if they had turned inside out and it was she left behind and him on the train. The landscape crumbled as they passed it, broke off and hurtled out into the blackness so she wanted to stop the trees and barns flash by, shout, 'Let me keep that,' before they passed and crumbled and were lost. (Spiro, 2002, p. 88)

She also came to symbolise for me all the language learners I had ever known, (including myself living in Hungary and Switzerland), whose flight forced them to function without their mother tongue. I grew up with empathy for the second culture-learner, was fascinated to know how my family and their large circle of resettled compatriots, had come to learn English. None had learnt comfortably, or even tediously, in a school class. One had learnt by reading a dictionary while in hiding between the floorboards of a Warsaw apartment block. My grandmother had learnt by reading everything she could lay hands on in English, whether she understood it or not. My uncle learnt by giving the other boys English lessons, always being three words ahead of his pupils. My father started off with three words of English, 'I bicky par' (*I beg your pardon*) which he was told would take him anywhere: and learnt the rest within a year of arriving in England, by studying and reading so he ruined his sight. There were no kindly teachers to mediate for any of them, no communicative methods to make it palatable: and yet they learnt it anyway, to brilliant effect. Rosa represents, and is in honour, of all of them. In the extract below, she tries to learn English by reading the dictionary in the local library:

In the afternoons for one hour she sat in the public library and read at the no smoking table. Her favourite was the Shorter Oxford English Dictionary. Each day she read ten new words, starting with A. She learnt Aardvark, Aaron's beard (a name), abaca[67] and abaciscus[68] on the first day, but even with the dictionary explanation she couldn't really understand them, and there didn't seem to be any opportunities to use them. So the

[67]    Fibre.
[68]    A tile or square of a tessellated pavement.

next day she started volume 2 and learnt marl, marlite (a variety of marl[69]), marmalade and marmoset. These seemed more useful words, because she knew for a fact that marmalade really existed because Mr. Gobelman had a pot with the word written on it. Anyway, with words written in front of her she had hope again, even if she couldn't understand them; and she could talk quietly into books and they quietly back to her. They were the best conversations of the day. (Spiro, 2002, p. 52)

The Laura/Rosa roles, and the engagement with character at a symbolic level, helped me to 'find myself' in the narrative and drive it forward with 'passionate conviction'.

Hunt (2000) writes: "When a writer says that she has 'found her voice' it seems to me she is saying that she has developed a deep connection in her writing between her inner life and the words she places on the page" (p. 16). It is true, that through Rosa and Laura I was able to explore again the sources of my own identity and the collective memory of my community. The opportunities to slide between inner and outer voices, child and adult, to become Rosa and Laura, was liberating and empowering. Like Heaney, when he found his voice as a young poet, 'I felt that I had let down a shaft into real life' (Heaney, 1980, p. 41).

## Teaching as a writer

In 1987, I progressed from being a teacher of access, General Certificate of Secondary Education examinations[70] and the Advanced Level examination[71] in English in a further education college closeted in the privacy of my own classroom, to course-manager of a Diploma in English Language Teaching in Switzerland. My early English teaching days had been gloriously unsupervised and, as my first experiences in the classroom, filled with trial and error. Yet I was able to resolve my mistakes quietly within the sanctuary of my own classroom

---

[69]    Marl is a calcium-carbonate, mudstone.
[70]    Examinations taken in England and Wales usually taken at 16, referred to normally as GCSEs.
[71]    Examinations taken at 18 as a rule, and referred to as 'A' Levels.

and with the trust of my students. My passion for good practice was in place, but my knowledge of how to arrive at this was still limited and untested.

Through constant exposure now to classes and conference groups of teachers, the components of best practice needed to be explicit and rationalised. Specifically, I came to understand more clearly my own answer to the questions: how can non-English speaking students become excited and empowered by reading and writing in English? The following realisations emerged, based on experiences in my first teaching incarnation:

- appreciation of a text is more meaningful when readers have 'entered into the shoes' of the writer, and experimented, themselves, with the writer's strategies and themes;
- creating personal texts such as a poem or story engages the 'whole' learner in a way that other, merely language-focused, exercises will not;
- it provides them with an incentive to write for an audience, and thus to edit and reformulate their work, with an awareness of both the writer and the reader;
- more importantly, it gives the learner the opportunity to share information, which is unique and not replicable by the teacher or any other learner in the class: and thus alters the balance of informant: informee in a way that gives the learner power and autonomy;
- it provides a context in which new language can be learnt in order to fill a perceived communicative need, rather than to meet the needs of the course-book or syllabus.

As the practice became refined and moulded by these more clearly stated values, new questions arose:

- What are the strategies and processes which have worked (or failed to work) for me as a writer, and are these generalisable or teachable?

- What processes, for me, characterise movement into linguistic adventure and change lived story into created story/text?
- How could these strategies be transformed into learning activities and with what effect on learners and learning?

With these questions, subliminal or otherwise, I began to formulate activities which were more carefully structured, theorised and recorded. Rather than 'scraps' of poems copied from student work at the end of class, I began meticulously to collect notes recording the full process by which these texts were arrived at. Below is an example of such a process, evolved over a number of years, and in a number of guises: with young newly-arrived Bedford refugees, Swiss trainee-teachers, adult language-learners in evening classes, adult pre-university international students in the UK.

Fundamentally, the activity draws on two powerful strategies which are part of my own practice: first, it draws on what is deeply and personally known and thus unique to the writer; secondly, it transforms this knowledge into the symbolic, so that the personal and specific become metaphors for the human condition itself. Thus here I uncover the *transformation of knowledge* as a creative process; the discovery of deep personal knowledge (knowledge as experience, feeling, belief), and the changing of this into something new.

The activity starts by discussing the notion of *praise song*. Much can be unpacked from the two words:

- *praise* – something we love, value, admire, describe in words, an admiration made known, *flung to the heavens*.
- *song* – something chanted out loud, perhaps with musical instruments such as drums, perhaps accompanied by dance and movement.

All of these are the case with traditional praise song from black Africa. Just a few lines capture their quality and impact:

> *You lime of the forest, honey among rocks,*
> *Lemon of the cloister, grape in the savannah.*

(from an Amharic love song, highlands of Ethiopia, Heath, 1993, p. 102)

*My bull is white like the silver fish in the river,*
*White like the shimmering crane bird on the river bank*
*White like fresh milk!*
(from a Dinka praise song, south of Sudan, Heath, 1993, p. 104)
Having introduced the topic of praise song, shared interpretations of what
it might mean, and offered examples, the stages of the activity involve moving
ever nearer to the learners generating songs of their own. The first example above
is praising a lover; the second is praising a bull. But praise songs could be about
anything we admire. Pablo Neruda (1973), for example, writes in praise of
ironing:

*It wrinkles, and it piles up,*
*The skin of the planet must be stretched,*
*The sea of its whiteness must be ironed.*
A moment of visualisation gives time for the group to conjure up
something loved and admired, object, activity, human being, and animal. In my
own experience of this activity, I conjured up my violin, to which I have been
monogamously attached since the age of 14. Other participants have chosen to
praise: the hairdresser, the washing machine, new shoes, although more
frequently, praise is for best friends and family members. Especially is this the
case when the learners are distant from home, and my examples in this section
will be from such a group – a group of adult international learners on a short
course in the UK, away from home for three weeks during a cool English
summer.

Our next stage is to form a collective list of the objects of praise, as in
Column A below. Having done so, and allowed this to illustrate the shared values
in the group, I offer to the class a second list of words describing the natural
world, side by side with the first. The task is simply to choose the word from the
'natural' list that most exactly describes/compares with, the praise object; or to
add a new one that suits better.

**Table 1:**      Blackboard plan for praise poems

| COLUMN A | COLUMN B |
|---|---|
| Husband | Shell |
| Wife | Rock |
| Sister | River |
| Brother | Lake |
| Mother | Stream |
| Father | Mountain |
| Aunt | Flower (rose, violet) |
| Friend | Fruit (lemon, lime, peach, fig) |

With this choice, a simple first sentence is formulated. There are two choices here:

Simile:  My _____ is like a _____ (eg. my mother is like a lake, my father is like a rock).

Metaphor: My _____ is a _____ (eg. my friend is a shell, my wife is a rose).

We have, in one move, leapt into the realm of linguistic adventure. However new the process of writing creatively in English, however great the blocks, few participants have been unable to respond to this process.

From this point, the writers are asked to 'grow' their metaphor (or simile) by explaining in two or three short lines, why mother and lake (or father and rock, or wife and rose) are similar.

**Poems from Oxford International Summer School class**

My sister is a tree
*She is tall and I look up at her*
*She is freshly green and she gives me oxygen.*

*When the wind blows at me, she sings for me through the leaves.*
*When the cloud comes, she cries for me through the rain.*

*She keeps growing and offers me bigger shelter,*
*Oh, how I love my sister!*
*And I hug her round with both my arms*
(Student from China)

*My grandmother is now an orange*
*Her skin is no longer smooth*
*She's seen – not only – sun in her days*
*At 90 she's still full of juice.*
(Student from Peru)

*My brother is a tree.*
*While his roots burrow deep,*
*He grows up into a new world.*
(Student from China)

*My husband is a river*
*He flows quietly along*
*My daughters are flowers*
*Even their skin blooms*
(Student from Switzerland)

In some ways, the poems are their own testimony. They reveal both the universal story -the common experience of life and loves, and the specificity of these stories; the lively 90-year-old grandmother, the brother just leaving home who 'grows up into a new world', the fresh skin of young daughters: 'even their skin blooms'. The poems also illustrate the balance between revealing self: 'Oh how I love my sister!' and establishes a safe distance through metaphor: 'she is a tree'. Most of all, the poems also make clear that capturing feelings creatively and memorably is within the capacity of every language-user and learner, if they choose to make the *poetic leap*.

To be fully congruent with the process, I offer here a poem I wrote alongside my students, in response to this task. I began with the violin as my love object. The violin then became a metaphor for marriage: my violin is my husband/my husband is a violin. As the one became the other, the following poem evolved, and I add this to the mix. It will be apparent to the reader that I broke my own 'rules' – starting with the simple figurative sentence and proceeding to 'unpack' the metaphor. As a writer, I edited out this first opening line, making the poem something of a riddle, making the reader work at interpreting, and making both halves of the metaphor equally strong: is this about a husband, or is it about a violin? The process of editing, selecting, introducing further layers of ambiguity, is something my learners may have progressed to, had there been the purpose and objective to do so.

---

*I knew from the first moment*
*we would find a voice, a way to sing,*
*you just wood and string*
*without me, and I a reaching*
*in space, a breath between notes*
*without you.*

*I knew how the singing*
*would be, like a kite on air,*
*a running like a wild child*
*into sea.*

*I wonder now about the mystery*
*in your wood, if you mourn the forest*
*where you were, if the wine-brown memory*
*in your grain holds all the singing*
*we have done, all the ways we have*
*reached for new notes,*
*all the ways we have found our place.*

---

Other examples of students responding to creative space can be found in the following locations:

- poems generated with teachers at a British Council workshop;
- lessons and student-writing: in a national journal for English teachers.

I have found that being congruent with my own practice and beliefs has made it possible to communicate within increasingly broad parameters: from my own classroom, to communities of fellow teachers on Master of Arts and teacher-development programmes, to large conference audiences, to global publishers such as Oxford University Press (Spiro, 2004; Spiro, 2007). The image (http://ejolts.net/files/images/spiro_figure.jpg) represents a number of developments for me: visually it shows how very small one person is, and potentially invisible, amongst a large sea of people. Yet interestingly, the same image can suggest the opposite, in that it shows how one person can inhabit a space which is commanding and draws attention to itself. The situation itself, of course, offers permission to 'hold the floor' and includes expectation of 'something to say'. In fact, discourse conventions would suggest that the audience will struggle to find meaning and value in the speaker, simply by virtue of these conditions. However I have stepped off the stage which was set up for the speaker; I have also broken the conventional silence between speaker/audience by involving them in the dialogue and walking between the aisles, eliciting responses to my story-cues and openings.

## WHAT LIVING THEORY EMERGES AND WHY DOES THIS MATTER?

It is interesting for me to observe that my expanding terrain of influence has emerged concurrent with my own understanding of what it is I am doing and why. As I have lived the experience of teaching/writing, I have also understood what the values are which guide me, and where I stand within the struggle for creative space. In effect, as I have created this space for myself, I have been able to expand it so more and more are able to share it with me. In so doing, it is possible to return to, and respond to, the debates about creative process identified in the section above (p. 252).

### The creative process as finding a voice

As a novelist, I explored ways of shuttling between timescales, so that narrator-as-child and narrator-as-young-woman 'spoke' to one another using their own contrasting voices. Only through finding *their* voice was I able to fully define their character and the architecture of the novel as a whole. In so doing, in effect I found my own voice and confronted the issues and concerns which had subliminally influenced me. Similarly, these approaches formed a basis for guiding students to find their own voices through hearing and empathising with one another, and speaking to (and sometimes for) influential people in their lives.

### The nature of research/information as the stimulus for creative process

Here I refer to the transformational nature of *information* as a grounding for empathy and connection. Conrad described this sudden transformation of information into creative process, as catalyst: 'what a student of chemistry would best understand from the analogy of the tiniest little drop of the right kind, precipitating the process of crystallisation in a test tube' (Conrad, 1920, p. 6). I too engaged in this 'chain' of learning when writing my novel, by drawing on library research and oral history as catalysts for the story. In effect, the writing process involved an interweaving of system (what there was to learn from life narratives other than my own), and freedom (how I might change and transform these to create story).

### The creative process as connecting the specific and the universal

The process of moving from a single point to an all-embracing one is described by the Turkish Nobel prize-winner Pamuk: 'when a writer shuts himself up in a room for years on end, with this gesture he suggests a single humanity, a world without a centre' (Pamuk, 2006, p. 17). In describing the specific, personal or anecdotal, storytellers invite the 'compassionate leap' of the reader to recognize these stories as part of the larger human story, and deriving from an honest account of this. So, whilst my novel drew on the stories of a specific uncle, it also became symbolic for me of all displaced people. The poems written by students over the years of experimentation and practice, describe both the small and the large: homesickness for Cyprus, Iraq or Chechnya and at the same time, the pain of war, separation, loss and longing.

### The creative process as the embracing of paradox

This is the possibility of holding several truths simultaneously. Several of the creative processes described above, are also parallel truths which are held side by side: as a writer one must balance the specific and the symbolic. As a teacher one must balance the role of empowering the individual, with the role of preparing the individual for public and accountable success; assessment as the bridge between individual learning and external validation.

### The creative process as capable of development, nurturing and 'scaffolding'

Understanding the "machinery" of the creative process can help to drive it more energetically forward. As an educator it has been important for me to anatomise the skills and knowledges I mean by *creative* in order to frame it for others. As a writer it has been important for me to deconstruct what I have practiced intuitively since childhood, in order to understand what it is that continues to drive and shape me as a writer. In this enterprise I have been able to arrive at an understanding of my own values as a writer, and to recognize a commitment to perpetual self-improvement as a driving principle.

### The creative process as doing something in the world

This paper premises that the creative process does something in the world because it makes something happen: growth in self-esteem, in knowledge of self or other, in curiosity and purpose; improved practice in the classroom, a shift amongst learners from readers to reader/writers.

Thus, I arrive at my own meanings of *creative* as I describe myself as a *creative writer:*

- the capacity to transform knowledge (knowledge-as-experience) into something new, unpredictable and unique;
- an inner drive to continue doing this;
- a belief in the value of what I am doing;
- an awareness of audience, and the continued tuning of my message for this purpose;
- a dedication to the discipline of writing as craft, and to a process of perpetual self-improvement.

In my own definition, the creative process involves the discovery of deep knowledge and the changing of it into something specific, shaped and new that communicates to others. By knowledge, I include: what emerges freely from the unconscious; deeply felt experience; the understanding that emanates from empathy and connection; the insights derived from new information. All or one of these are starting points for creative transformation. When I write, in addition, I aim to trigger in the reader a similar leap in understanding, to be perhaps the starting point for another chain of learning and transformation. In unravelling this process educationally, I have aimed to provide the opportunity for learners to discover their own deep knowledge and to transform it into a new shape that communicates powerfully. This new shape may be a story, a poem, a performance, a speech, an image, but it carries the knowledge beyond the self and towards others, extending the collective understanding of what is possible, what can be made, and what can be imagined. In doing this, the writer/learner is him/herself transformed. The experience of writing or 'making' in this way can lead to changes such as an expansion in understanding, in self confidence, in independence, in self discovery, in motivation to do or say something new, in the shape and scope of knowledge itself in the learner's mind and what the learner can then do with this. It is this chain of discovering knowledge, making of it something new, and being transformed by it, that I call *knowledge-transformation*.

Whilst *knowledge-transformation* explains where I stand in relation to the creative process, *creative space* defines the environment needed for this to happen. This is the space created by the teacher/mentor in virtual or actual classrooms that allows the learner to work at the height of his/her capacity. It is no therapeutic, comfortable space. It combines the expectation of best possible achievement, with the opportunity for this. It maximises the possibilities, stretches the boundaries, and raises the bar of expectations. In creative space, the learner/writer strives for the best he/she is able to be, patient with the trial and error, the discipline and the tedium, that this entails. Here the chaos and the order of the creative process are at liberty to come together as they need to, both for the project and its maker.

My story, 'Eye and the Fellow Traveller', enacts the meanings I have discussed above. The story describes my journey towards a doctorate in education, a goal which seemed unachievable without the kind of supervision I was fortunate to experience from my University of Bath tutor, Jack Whitehead. The story emerged as part of my reflection:

- Why was this so successful a learning experience?
- What did it look like, feel like, and lead to?
- What did it teach me about the optimal conditions for learning – about *creative space* itself?

I answer these questions by setting up my own myth – characters that are representative rather than specific and named and a setting which is any-place. The journey is both guided by the teacher – in that he understands the destination- but also by the learner, in that she/I am permitted to find my own route and stepping stones on the way. My story at one level is an example of what it means to transform knowledge-as-experience into something new. On another level, it illustrates what *creative space* might look like, translated into myth: an open landscape with multiple pathways, in which the traveller needs to discover his/her own capacity in order to reach the destination. It contrasts the controlling teacher who creates the learner in his/her own likeness, with the empowering educator whose influence allows the learner to become more truly and fully him/herself. This optimal learning relationship, and my own supervision-experience in particular, seemed to contain these ingredients:

- A mutual sense between learner and teacher of the intrinsic value of the enterprise;
- the time for 'slow' learning to take its natural time and course (including false starts and mistakes on the way);
- the mutual commitment of learner and teacher to work at the highest level of their capacity;
- a mutual belief that learning comes from a deep investigation of one's own resources; a mutual openness to learning from one another.

In representing this experience of optimal learning as story, I am enacting the values I have explored in this paper: discovering the deep knowledge that emerges from a life as a poet/writer and a life as an educator, and transforming this duality into something symbolic and new. In this article, too, I am joining academic and creative selves, allowing the two to live, and write, and publish, side by side.

---

### Story epilogue: Eye and fellow traveller

One day I came to the edge of a cliff. There seemed no way forward, and the way back was blocked by a strange and faceless creature that stood with his huge arms stretched across my path.

'Only members of the Laurel Crown Club may proceed,' he said.

'Which Club is that?' I cried, tired from all my many travels, 'and how can I join it?'

'You join it by following my dance, step by step, and after each step, proving you are as good as I am.'

'But that's ridiculous,' I said. 'Why should I want to do that? Look, here is the garland of the storyteller, woven by myself from a thousand stories.'

'That is nothing,' said the creature.

'And here is the crown of the teacher, made of shells excavated from a thousand shores and threaded together with spun learning.'

The faceless creature laughed a bitter icy laugh.

'None of these will bring you the Laurel Crown, because none of the steps are like mine,' he crowed. 'Without this, how do I know you are good enough to continue the journey?'

'Because of all the journeys I've already travelled!' I shouted. 'The bridge-building journey, the river-crossing, the boat-making, the flower-blooming, the story-making, the wisdom-excavating journeys. Do none of those count?'

'None are mine!' yelled the creature. 'And I, Thought Doctor, am the only one that can lead the way. Take my journey or none at all.'

''OK, if you must, show me the way then. Since I have travelled so far, I might as well do this further journey.'

Thought Doctor pointed with his long bony finger towards the hills. I noticed a long narrow track like a railway that burned an unbending route through the valleys, tunnelled through the hillside, and plunged into the woods the other side.

'That's it,' he said. 'You follow me, along the track, copying my dance, and at the end you win the crown.'

The journey seemed possible, and better than throwing myself over the cliff. But still, it did not seem a very exciting or useful way to travel, with so much landscape to explore on either side of the narrow track, and so many ways to explore apart from following his single step. And how would I carry with me all the garlands, sarongs, shells, and songs of previous journeys, if I was not allowed to offer them and share them on the way?

I threw myself down onto the grassy ground to think about my options. As I did so, I noticed appearing from behind Thought Doctor's cloak, a silent group of people, cloaked, pale and downcast, gathering around me on the cliff.

'We are members of the Laurel Crown Club,' they said.

I looked at them now as they stood nearer me.

'But you all look the same!' I cried.

'When we started we were all different,' one of them said, 'but by the end we have all learnt Thought Doctor's moves so well, we look just like him.'

'If you are Laurel Crown members, where are your crowns?'

'Here!' said one, and threw off his hood to reveal a shiny metallic crown that looked far too heavy for him and made him stoop forward.

'Here!' said another, and revealed the same metallic shiny crown but it was so large it kept dropping over her eyes, and she had to push it up every few minutes.

'Here!' said another, and there was the crown again, but every so often the poor owner picked up a corner and began scratching underneath, shifting it round so it would sit more comfortably.

'None of your crowns fit!' I cried, concerned for them.

They laughed in chorus, like a pond of hippopotami.

'Of course not. There's only one size crown. If it doesn't fit, well that's just too bad. They all need to be the same size, to make sure it's all fair.'

'But being just the same size makes it NOT fair,' I cried.

Thought Doctor rolled his eyes, exasperated, and turned away.

'She clearly doesn't understand,' he snorted. 'Come, Club, let's leave her here to think.'

I sat by the cliff edge, suddenly alone, and looked in both directions. In one direction was a sheer drop down to a fast running river gorge. On the other was the Laurel Crown track, long and straight, with bunches of flowers every so often along the route where travellers had failed to survive. What to do?  Now, with the Thought Doctor gone, there seemed to be many more possibilities. Looking again at the landsCape ahead, it seemed laughable that there should be only one track forwards; on the contrary, there seemed to be an infinite number of paths, and surely nothing would stop me exploring them?

Encouraged by this thought, I stood up and again reviewed my options. In one direction was open hillside scattered with a blue dusting of heather; in the other direction was the path I had come from, winding over the cliff edge and dropping back down to a chain of rocky bays. I chose the new direction, the open hillside. Surely, if I set foot there, Thought Doctor wouldn't stop me?

So I began the new path, into the blue heather and the unmarked terrain. It was welcoming underfoot, and comforting to walk inland away from the cliff edge, wading through the tall grass, not knowing where it would lead me. After a while, as I walked, I suddenly became aware that there was a Fellow Traveller quietly beside me, and like me, quietly tracing the path of the wild flowers. I looked up to take note of him, and to my surprise, saw he was wearing a crown too.

'Oh! Your crown fits!' I cried.

'Of course it does,' said Fellow Traveller. 'I made it myself.'

We carried on walking, quietly for a while.

'But is it a Laurel Crown, like the others?'

'Yes, of course it is.'

'But did you do that long journey, like the others?'

'Yes, yes I did,' said the Traveller patiently.

'But how is it you don't look just like all the others? How is it you have strayed off the track?'

'Well I worked out the route for myself.'

'Is that allowed?'

'Of course it is. That's what I did, and I have a Crown and it fits just fine.'

I could see that all of those things were true. It seemed an exciting and revolutionary way to become a member of the Club.

'Could you show me how I might get a Crown that way too?'

'Sure, of course.'

We carried on walking, and the Fellow Traveller didn't seem to be showing me anything at all, but just following where I went along the hillside.

'But you aren't showing me. Shouldn't you be showing me the way?'

'No, quite the reverse. You choose which way you want to go, and I'll come along with you.'

'Are you sure?' I asked, nervously. It all seemed so different to Thought Doctor.

'Look, the end of the journey is over there.' He pointed beyond the wood where the narrow track disappeared. 'You can get there any way you like.'

I took from my sack a handful of shiny stones gathered from a Mexican beach and threw them down.

'Can I use these as stepping stones?'

'Sure, of course,' and we jumped from one to the other, first me, and Fellow Traveller following.

'Take a stepping stone to put in your crown,' he said, as we reached the end. 'Now, where next?'

'If I scatter the marigold garland we could follow its scent,'

'Sure, try that,' said Fellow Traveller.

It was tiring, running after the scent of the marigold as it blew in the wind, and at the end, I threw myself down on a rock and sighed.

'I don't know where to go next.'

'Yes you do. Look in your bag.'

'I've nothing there. Nothing useful at all.'

'Of course you have. Just have a look.'

'A sari from India, a sarong from Hawaii, a branch from the learning tree.'

'OK, let's start with the first one. Find out where the sari wants us to go next.'

I took the sari out of its bag. It was buttercup yellow with streaks of quiet lavender, and as it unfolded from the bag it began to blow like a sail towards the east.

'There we are then,' said Fellow Traveller, 'that's the direction we have to go in.'

So we followed the sail of the sari, and then the kite of the sarong; and then the branch of the learning tree doused us around the tors and I hardly knew we had travelled so far before I realised the station had appeared at the end of the Thought Doctor's narrow track.

'Do you mean we are nearly there?'

'Sure. You need to get your laurel crown ready for submission to the Club.'

'Oh no, one of those terrible metal ones that fall over your eyes and itch?'

Fellow Traveller laughed

'A made-to-measure one, made with all the mementoes of your journey. It will take two months to craft'

'Are you sure?' I said. 'Will it be as good as the others?'

'Well, I think it might be better, because for one thing it will fit, for another it will be quite unique and for another it will have mementoes of your journey inside it.'

'What do I do when I reach the last station?'

'When you arrive, and put on the crown, look in the mirror. There you will see what you have become and where the journey led.'

In a quiet place at the station gates, I unfolded all the contents of my travels around me and spread them on the ground. How to fit them together? Surely they could never be crafted into one coherent and beautiful piece?

But as I stared at them hour after hour alone now outside the gates of my destination, it all became clear.

The learning branch became the strong anchor that held the crown together. With the golden learning thread I wove in the Mexican stepping stones, securely at the front. Then I rolled the lavender and buttercup sari and the sarong with the silver fish and turtles, into long narrow drapes and plaited them together with the learning thread to hold the branch in place. Between the binds and threads, I planted small clusters of heather from the journey. The crown was fragrant and colourful as a spring garden. Then I lifted it to my head, and tied the plaited fronds behind just tightly enough to be comfortable and secure.

'Will this do?' I asked.

'What does the mirror say?'

I looked in the mirror. I saw myself, like a spring goddess with all the colours of the hillside in her hair. I didn't look a bit like Thought Doctor or even like Fellow Traveller.

'I look like the goddess of my story!' I cried, surprised.

'Exactly that, 'said Fellow Traveller. 'The journey was yourself, so it follows that the journey leads to yourself. And your Crown celebrates yourself.'

'Is that going to be alright, do you think?'

'That's the only way it *would* be alright. I think you are ready to submit your Crown to the Club,' said Fellow Traveller.

And together we walked towards the gates of the station at the end of the mountain path, both of us with heads high, wearing our Laurel Crowns.

## REFERENCES

Abbs, P. (1994). *The educational imperative: A defence of socratic and aesthetic learning.* London and Washington DC: Falmer Press.

Abbs, P. (2003). *Against the flow: Education, the arts and postmodern culture.* London: RoutledgeFalmer.

Allende, I. (2007). In giving I connect. In Allison, J. and Gediman, D. (Eds.), *This I believe* (pp. 13–15). New York: Holt.

Allott, M. (1959). *Novelists on the novel.* London: Routledge.

Balshaw, M. (2004). Risking creativity: Building the creative context. *Support for learning 19*(2), 71–76.

Baylis, N. and Morris, I. (2006). *The skills of well-being.* Wellington College: Personal Health and Social Education Department.

Bernstein, L. (2007). The mountain disappears. In J. Allison and D. Gediman (Eds.), *This I believe* (pp. 19 – 21). New York: Holt.

Bohm, D. (1998). *On creativity.* Routledge: London.

Bourdieu, P. (1984). *Distinction: A social critique of judgment and taste.* Cambridge, MA: Harvard University Press.

Buckingham, D. (2003). Living in a young culture? Youthful creativity and cultural policy in the United Kingdom. In K. Mallan and S. Pearce (Eds.), *Youth cultures: Texts, images and identities* (pp. 92–107). Westport Connecticut, London: Praeger.

Buckingham, D. and Jones, K. (2001). New labour's cultural turn: some tensions in contemporary educational and cultural policy. *Journal of Education Policy, 16*(1), 1–14.

Certificate in Advanced Educational Practice. (2008). *Practitioner reports from Lancashire Creative Partnership projects.* Unpublished manuscript, certificate in Advanced Educational Practice, validated by Oxford Brookes University.

Carter, R. (2006). Is there a literary language? In S. Goodman and K. O'Halloran (Eds.), *The art of English: Literary creativity* (pp. 84–88). Basingstoke, Hampshire: Palgrave Macmillan/Open University.

Clifford, J. and Marcus, G. (Eds.). (1986). *Writing culture: The poetics and politics of ethnography.* Berkeley: University of California Press.

Cocteau, J. (1952). The process of inspiration. In Ghiselin, B. (Ed.), *The creative process: A symposium* (p. 81). New York: New American Library.

Conrad, J. (1920). Author's note. In Conrad, J. (1993, ed.). *The secret agent.* Ware, Hertfordshire: Wordsworth.

Coveney, P. and Highfield, R. (1995) *Frontiers of complexity: The search for order in a chaotic world.* London: Faber and Faber.

Cox, M. and Thielgard, A. (1987). *Mutative metaphors in psychotherapy: The aeolian mode.* London: Tavistock.

Creative Partnerships in Education. (2004). *Young roots, your roots: Creativity, schools and community cohesion - how to give children a voice.* London: Creative Partnerships in Education. Retrieved February 24, 2009, from http://www.creative-partnerships.com/data/files/young20roots20toolkit-36.pdf

Creative Partnerships. (2007). *Preferred learning styles and creativity: Action research programme.* Retrieved February 26, 2009, from http://www.artssmarts.ca/media/preferredlearningstylesandcreativityintro.pdf

Denzin, N. K. (1997). *Interpretative ethnography: Ethnographic practices for the 21$^{st}$ century.* Thousand Oaks: Sage.

Department of Education and Science. (2004). *Excellence and enjoyment and creating conditions for learning.* London: Department for Education and Skills.

Ecclestone, K. (2007). Resisting images of the diminished self: The implications of emotional well-being and emotional engagement in educational policy. *Journal of Education Policy, 22*(4), 445-470.

Ecclestone, K. and Hayes, D. (2009). *The dangerous rise of therapeutic education.* Abingdon, Oxon: Routledge.

Education Guardian. (2005, November 14). *Tedd Wragg retrospective.* p. 2.

Elbow, P. (1973). *Writing without teachers.* Oxford: Oxford University Press.

Elbow, P. (1986). *Embracing contraries: Explorations in learning and teaching.* Oxford: Oxford University Press.

Farren, M. (2008). Co-creating educational space. *Educational Journal of Living Theories, 1*(1), 50–68. Retrieved February 24, 2009, from http://ejolts.net/node/78

Goldberg, N. (1986). *Writing down the bones.* Boston, Massachusetts: Shambhala Publications.

Hayles, N. (1991). *Chaos and order: Complex dynamics in literature and science.* Chicago: University of Chicago Press.

Heaney, S. (1980). *Preoccupations: Selected prose 1968 – 1978.* London: Faber.

Heath, R. B. (ed.). (1993). *Tradewinds* (3$^{rd}$ Impression). Harlow: Longman.

Hunt, C. (2000). *Therapeutic dimensions of autobiography in creative-writing.* London & Philadelphia: Jessica Kingsley Publishers.

Mandela, N. (1994). *Long walk to freedom.* London: Abacus.

Maslow, A. (1943). A theory of human motivation. *Psychological Review, 50*, 370–396.

Miller, A. L. (2000). *Insights of genius: Imagery and creativity in science and art.* Cambridge, MA: MIT Press.

Morrison, M. (2007). What do we mean by educational research? In Coleman, M. & Briggs, A. (Eds.), *Research methods in educational leadership and management* (pp. 13-36). London: Paul Chapman Publishers.

Neruda, P. (1973). La poesia e blanca. In D. D. Walsh (Ed.), *Residence on Earth.* Losada, S. A., Buenos Aires and New York: New Directions.

Nettle, D. (2001). *Strong imagination: Madness, creativity and human nature.* Oxford: Oxford University Press.

OfSTED (2005). *Healthy minds: Promoting emotional health and wellbeing in schools.* Retrieved January 12, 2007, from www.ofsted.gov.uk.

Pamuk, O. (2006) *My father's suitcase: The nobel lecture* (M. Freely, trans.). London: Faber and Faber.

Pope, R., (2005). *Creativity: Theory, practice and history.* London: RoutledgeFalmer.

Pope, R. (2005). The return of creativity: Common, singular and otherwise. *Language and Literature, 14*(4), 376-389.

Qualifications and Curriculum Authority. (2001). *Creativity: Find it, promote it.* Retrieved March 29, 2006, from http://www.ncaction.org.uk/creativity/whatis.htm

Rayner, A. (2008). *Essays and talks about inclusionality.* Retrieved 12 January, 2009, from http://people.bath.ac.uk/bssadmr/inclusionality

Rayner, A. (2009). *Introduction to inclusional research.* Retrieved February 13, 2009, from http://www.inclusional-research.org/introduction.php

Robinson, K. (2006). *All our futures: Creativity, culture and education.* London: National Advisory Committee on Creative and Cultural Education.

Sartre, J. P. (1964). *The words.* Greenwich, USA: Fawcett Crest Books.

Spiro, J. (2002). *Nothing I touch stands still.* Norton St. Phillip: Crucible Press.

Spiro, J. (2004). *Creative poetry writing.* Oxford: Oxford University Press.

Spiro, J. (2007a). *Storybuilding.* Oxford: Oxford University Press.

Spiro, J. (2007b). *Television interview.* English UK. Retrieved from www.ukfuturetv.com/janespiro.wmv.

Weisberg, R.W. (1993). *Creativity: Beyond the myth of genius.* New York: W.H. Freeman.

Whitehead, J. (2008). Using a living theory methodology in improving practice and generating educational knowledge in living theories. *Educational Journal of Living Theories, 1*(1), 103-12. Retrieved February 24, 2009, from http://ejolts.net/node/78

# HOW CAN I ENCOURAGE MY PUPILS TO THINK CRITICALLY THROUGH COLLABORATIVE ONLINE-LEARNING?

Donal O'Mahony, Ireland

## MY CONTEXT

### Portmarnock Community School

I am a teacher in Portmarnock Community School with a particular interest in ICT and education. Portmarnock Community School (http://portmarnockcommunityschool.ie/index.php) is a co-educational secondary school in North County Dublin, Ireland. The History students I worked with were about seventeen years of age.

At the start of my research both the students and I were new to encouraging critical historical thinking through the medium of e-learning. By the end of the research, we were engaging critically with each other in an online-environment.

**Figure 1.**    Gavin Brennan and Denise McKenna with Donal O'Mahony – all
new to encouraging critical thinking in an online-environment.


### ICT in Irish education

Seven rationales are used by governments to justify expenditure on ICT
resources in schools (Hawkridge, Jaworski and McMahon, 1990, pp. 16-26).
The rationales include vocational, catalytic, social, pedagogic, industrial,
cost-effective and special needs. Historically, the Irish government's ICT policy
for education is found in the 1997 document, Schools IT2000: A Policy
Framework for the New Millennium (Department of Education, 1997). Four of
these rationales: the social, catalytic, pedagogic and industrial, are referenced in
this paper. Two rationales are especially relevant to my context. They are the
pedagogical and catalytic, since the purpose of my research is to enhance the
quality of teaching and learning.

In order to achieve the pedagogical and catalytic rationales there is a need
for teachers to change their practice in relation to ICT. This is a challenge
because, as Prensky (2001) outlines, students are digital natives, while teachers

are digital immigrants. Richardson (2006) addresses teachers at high-school level in the United States of America and concludes that they will have to re-define themselves in five ways: as connectors of people, as creators of content, as collaborators with their own students, as coaches in the new literacies and as agents of change.

The National Council for Curriculum and Assessment (NCCA, http://www.ncca.ie/) who advise the Irish Government on curriculum issues, argue that change is a necessary challenge if we are to allow ICT to add 'value to the curriculum' (2004, p. 31).

The NCCA outline that value is added in several ways, summarised as:

- student's active involvement in their own learning and in their own assessment;
- enhancement of student interest and development of higher order thinking skills,

and,

- the possibility of working in an authentic environment in both a differentiated and collaborative manner.

Continued financial support for such developments in teaching practice was promised in the National Development Plan (Department of Finance, Sectoral Policy Division., 2007). In the section entitled *ICT in Schools Sub-Programme* (p. 199-200), the Department of Finance promises two hundred and fifty two million euro in funding to schools, over the period of the plan, 2007–2013. They specifically target teaching and learning, saying that their strategy will deal with, 'developing an e-learning culture in schools that will ensure that ICT usage is embedded in teaching and learning across the curriculum' (p. 200).

This promised funding coincided with the completion of the Schools' Broadband Programme in 2007 (connecting most Irish classrooms to the Internet) and subsequently led to the publication of two documents by the Department of Education and Science (DES) (2008a, 2008b): *ICT in Schools*, a report of the

Inspectorate of the DES and *Investing Effectively in Information and Communications Technology in Schools, 2008-2013*, a report from the Minister's Strategy Group appointed by former Minister, Mary Hannifin. Both documents encourage teachers and students to exploit the potential of ICT.

### My understanding of the nature of ICT

My particular interest in ICT is in its communicative rich characteristics as understood by Farren (2006a) in which she shows how such characteristics can support a dialogic-collaborative approach to learning: 'ICT and emerging media technologies can support a dialogic-collaborative approach to learning and bring us closer to the meanings of our educational values as they emerge in the course of our practice' (p. 22). This is the approach I used with the students in my research into collaborative online-learning with them.

### The Leaving Certificate History examination

The Leaving Certificate is the terminal examination Irish Students take at the end of their second-level education. The Leaving Certificate History syllabus was revised in 2003, with both the content of the course and the terminal examination undergoing considerable change. The syllabus encourages students to develop the ability to think critically. The aims and objectives of the *Department of Education and Science syllabus* (2003) specifically highlight that: 'Through their study of History, students should acquire a unique combination of skill and understanding, which will contribute to their personal growth as individuals and help to prepare them for life and work in society' (p. 4).

It asks that students be able to look at controversial issues from more than one point of view and that students learn that their own judgments 'be subjected to the most searching analysis and criticism' (ibid, p. 2).

### My concern as I research my practice.

My concern is to engage with students in critical thinking as they undertake their Leaving Certificate History studies, not just for the purposes of completing the course, but also to engage with what the syllabus calls issues of life and citizenship. I will use technology for the purpose of teaching and learning, and examine whether technology can encourage critical thinking amongst the students.

### My research question

This concern led to the development of my research question, how can I use Moodle, a collaborative online-learning environment, to improve my practice as a History teacher, as I encourage my pupils to think critically?

A number of terms are used when describing online technology to assist teaching and learning. These include learning-platforms, collaborative-online-learning environments, virtual-learning environments and technology-mediated learning environments.

Moodle is one such online technology. It is built on the principles of constructivism (http://docs.moodle.org/en/Philosophy) and is open-source (http://www.opensource.org/), meaning that there is open access to the source code of the software and a commitment to free redistribution of the software. Thus, the software itself is without charge, and schools and colleges can choose to serve it themselves or use a Moodle partner to do it for them.

Moodle is the online-learning platform for Dublin City University (http://moodle.dcu.ie/), which was where I first came to use it. I also subscribe to the ideas of constructivism, open-source software and the community of practice that has developed around Moodle users.

**LITERATURE**

I examined three themes in the literature in order to inform my understanding of my research question. They are:

- Critical Thinking and Democratic Education;
- Social Software as a Key to Students' Learning with Technology;
- Collaborative Online-learning Environments.


**Critical thinking and democratic education**

In education, much discussion of critical thinking requires students to examine the credibility of evidence, to develop and assess arguments, resolve dilemmas and look at issues of logic, presumption and fallacies. The value of critical thinking is that students develop a range of thinking skills, enhance their meta-cognition and are better able to live in a world in which flawed arguments often hold sway (Larsen and Hodge, 2005; Chapman, 2006).

This approach places the emphasis on the student's ability to live in the world but it does not speak of any vision of what living in that world is actually for. A review of some of the seminal literature written on education and critical thinking provides a framework for this vision. Two authors in particular inform that vision: John Dewey and Paulo Freire.

Dewey (1916) believes that democracy provides us with a better type of human experience. It is a form of life, a way of living together, with opportunity accessible to all, on equitable terms. He argued that progressive education is democratic, as opposed to traditional education which is autocratic. In the autocratic classroom, order was of 'the teachers keeping' (1938, p. 61) while in the democratic classroom order 'resided in the shared work being done' (ibid).

Like Dewey, Freire believed that knowledge emerges through invention and reinvention (Freire, 1970). Freire believed in 'creating pedagogical spaces' (Freire and Macedo, 1999, p. 53) in which students are afforded the opportunity to be critical. This is done in a dialogue between students and teachers who are co-investigators in the process of critical thinking. This approach is very important because it is value-driven. People are empowered. A skills-approach to critical thinking, found in the competency model of education is not enough (Hatton and Smith, 1995; Veugelers, 1996; Bertrand, 2003).

Both Dewey and Freire rebelled about teaching a set of techniques or a boxed piece of knowledge. Dewey rebelked against the 'static, cold-storage idea of knowledge' (1916, p. 129), because it was contrary to the development of thinking. Similarly Freire (1970) rejected what he called the banking concept of education in which knowledge is the property of the teacher, rather than an act of knowing between teacher and student. This act of knowing is what Freire called dialogue, in which teachers and students empower each other and fulfil each other's vocation to be more fully human (Freire, 1970).

### Teaching and evaluating critical thinking

The challenge is to find a way of evaluating the teaching and learning of critical thinking, which is open to the democratic concept of education argued for by Dewey and Freire.

Garrison and Anderson (2003) discuss critical thinking in the context that there must be cognitive outcomes. Drawing on Dewey, they use the concept of cognitive presence which they define as: 'The intellectual environment that supports sustained critical discourse and higher order knowledge acquisition and application' (p. 55).

In order to assess critical thinking, it is necessary to have some criteria to judge students' standards of reflection i.e. the cognitive presence of the students within the online-environment. I settled on the work of Australian educators Hatton and Smith as both are clear in thought and are emancipatory and reflect the values of Dewey and Freire. Hatton and Smith (1995) put forward a five-part framework to examine what constitutes evidence of critical thinking:

1.  Technical Reflection – reports on events or reports on literature;
2.  Descriptive Reflection – provides reasons based on personal judgments or reasons based on reading literature;
3.  Dialogic Reflection – exploring alternatives with oneself or others;
4.  Critical Reflection – giving reasons for decisions, taking into account broader social, historical and political contexts;
5.  Contextualisation of multiple viewpoints – drawing from the previous four and applying them to situations as they actually occur (Adapted from Hatton and Smith, 1995).

Hatton and Smith's work is with trainee teachers, whilst mine is with a Leaving Certificate History class in Portmarnock Community School. I believe that the first four criteria have validity in the secondary school classroom and I will use them to examine critical thinking in the collaborative online-learning environment I create for the purposes of this research.


### Social software

Social software is defined as 'software that supports group-interaction' (Shirky in Owen et al, 2006, p. 12). There are many examples of social software, and all allow people to communicate in a variety of ways e.g. blogs, wikis, social-networking etc. There are a number of reasons why social software is so popular with young people: interaction with friends, the generation of online-identity and reputation, constant feedback in an environment that can be accessed anywhere or anytime (Boyd, 2005; New Media Consortium, 2007; Anchor Youth Centre, 2007).

Through their use of social software, students are becoming creators of knowledge and information: 'Current social software allows users to communicate, collaborate and publish in a number of ways, in a variety of media, and it also helps learners act together to build knowledge bases that fit their specific needs' (Owen et al, 2006, p. 28).

The literature concludes that as students create this knowledge and information they are doing so in a social process. Their learning is thus essentially social in nature, as minds and ideas come into contact with each other (Sefton-Green, 2004; Owen et al, 2006; Rudd, 2006).

### Collaborative online-learning environments

The educator and computer programmer, Martin Dougiamas developed a collaborative online-learning environment using the pedagogical goals of constructivism. Constructivism stresses the active participation of learners in coming to understand the world they live in. It looks less at the teacher, as the traditional provider of content, but as the creator of a social process in which learning takes place (Bertrand, 2003; Oliver and Herrington, 2003). Dougiamas addresses the role of the teacher and argues that constructivism and its associated ideas:

> ...help[s] you to focus on the experiences that would be best for learning from the learner's point of view...Your job as a 'teacher' can change from being 'the source of knowledge' to being an influencer and role model of class culture, connecting with students in a personal way that addresses their own learning needs, and moderating discussions and activities in a way that collectively leads students towards the learning goals of the class. (Moodle, 2006)

Dougiamas called his collaborative online-learning environment, Moodle.

The introduction of an online-learning environment requires hard work and commitment. The learning experience does not just happen. It needs to be organised and well planned. Dougiamas and Taylor (2003) record how an analysis of their teaching using Moodle over two years, resulted in a need to examine moderation practices in the online-environment.

Bonk et al (2004) comment on the lack of pedagogical tools for online education, resulting in the loss of its transformative potential. Salmon (2002) promotes 'e-tivities' as the key to active online-learning, while Richardson (2006) encourages the pedagogical use of the most recent resources of the internet; blogs, wikis and podcasts.

In choosing Moodle as a collaborative online-environment, the teacher is adopting an approach to knowledge and an approach to pedagogy. The effectiveness in teaching and moderating on Moodle will depend on how committed teachers are to the social construction of knowledge that underpins it. Once committed, the teacher/moderator's online personality, technical skills and level of organisation become important. The literature suggests that it is in this way that the moderator in a collaborative online-learning environment will create and support a learner-centred experience, leading to its institutionalisation within the school (Kukulska-Hulme, 2004; Packham *et al*, 2004; Donnelly and O'Rourke, 2007).

I began by examining what I believe is the purpose of education, namely, a democratic activity conducted by students and teachers who think critically together, for the purpose of creating a just society. I then sought to find a framework to achieve the possibility of teaching and assessing critical thinking and found the work of Garrison and Anderson (2003) and Hatton and Smith (1995) particularly instructive for my context.

My interest is to achieve this in an online-environment. I reflected therefore on the students' use of social software and its educational implications for collaborative online-learning environments. I concluded by examining issues of teacher moderation in such an environment, in order to achieve an online cognitive presence in teaching and learning.

During the Masters' programme I practiced many of the activities described above, particularly in the area of Moodle and online-collaboration. Examining the literature affirmed my own developing practice both as a student and as a teacher. It is important to understand that that I did not find the literature review static. I returned to it when I became dissatisfied with my research. I was particularly challenged to examine my understanding of cognitive presence and how critical thinking could be encouraged in discussion forums in Moodle.

### Action research – living educational theory

A seminal definition of action research is, 'a form of self-reflective inquiry undertaken by participants in social situations in order to improve the rationality and justice of their own practices, their understanding of these practices, and the situations in which the practices are carried out' (Carr and Kemmis, 1986, p. 162).

McNiff and Whitehead say that the result of self-reflective inquiry enables practitioners 'to create their own theories of practice' (2005, p. 1). My action research methodology involved asking, researching and answering the question 'how do I improve my practice?' I generated my own living educational theory as I explained my answer to this question through clarifications of my educational influences in learning.

My decision to choose action research is influenced by my democratic values, very much in the Jefferson mould as explained by Chomsky (1994) in which people share power together (as democrats), rather than leaving power in the hands of the few (as aristocrats).

In developing my living educational theory I am engaging with my 'I', and am reflecting on my experiences as they happen. I understand living educational theory as looking at my personal and educational values, and seeing if I can live them through a piece of practical educational research in my own context. As I began to examine my practice, I came to an understanding that my research is personal, value laden, practice-based, rigorous, unique, singular to my context and open to new possibilities.

Developing my own living educational theory is a challenge, because as Whitehead says, we are living contradictions 'holding educational values while at the same time negating them' (1989, p. 4). This understanding is integral to a living methodology, as contradictory experiences become a source of transformation within our educational practice.

**Action plan**

The action plan I used in my research is the one developed by Jack Whitehead. His plan helps researchers ask, research, and answer questions about how they improve practice. The action plan is a cycle of research in which I:

- experience a concern when some of my educational values are denied in my practice;
- imagine a solution to the concern;
- act in the direction of the imagined solution;
- evaluate the outcome of the solution;
- modify my practice, plans and ideas in light of the evaluation. (Whitehead and McNiff, 2006, p. 91)

**Data collection**

McNiff and Whitehead (2006) see data being collected in two distinct areas. On the one hand, data will be collected from episodes of my own practice that show my own learning; whilst on the other hand, data will be collected from episodes of practice that show the practitioner's influence in the learning of others.

In looking for data that shows the influence in my own learning I examined practices that I carried out intentionally and in an informed way. These episodes of practice took place during the course of my research and showed (or perhaps otherwise) that I am turning my research-question into reality.

The data that I collected explained what I learned from these episodes of practice. My learning journals, and in particular my own critical reflection on the online-classroom I set up, are examples of data sources. McNiff and Whitehead (2006) write about this 'You are now looking for data that show how your practice (informed by your learning) is influencing the learning of others (as is manifested in their practice)' (p. 134).

### Turning the data into evidence

McNiff and Whitehead, (2006) describe four steps taken in generating evidence from data:

- The action researcher must make some claim to knowledge;
- There must be a standard of judgment to examine that claim to knowledge;
- The data must now be examined to see if there is evidence of the claim to knowledge using the standard of judgment as set out;
- Evidence is generated to back up the claim to knowledge.

In making a claim to knowledge, I am not only making a claim to have improved my practice, I am also making a claim to have a new theory about that practice. This theory is my claim to knowledge. The standards of judgment I set for that claim to knowledge are ones that emerged during the course of my research.

### Validating the evidence

The action researcher allows their research to be subject to public critique in a validation group and with a critical friend.

A validation group examines the research-conclusions in the light of the researcher's standards of judgment. The group is essentially a community of equals who, whether they are 'participants, practitioners or judges' (Whitehead and McNiff, 2006, p. 102) equally apply 'criteria of social validity' (p. 138), that Habermas (1986) says are necessary to address the truth of a claim to knowledge. These criteria are that the account of the research presented to the validation group is comprehensible, truthful, sincere and appropriate. The group, including the researcher, can be made up of between three and ten people. Validation is a process with the group meeting at regular intervals. McNiff and Whitehead define a critical friend as 'a person who will listen to a researcher's account of practice and critique the thinking behind the account' (2006, p. 256).

## IMPLEMENTATION AND EVALUATION

### Introduction

I engaged in this research because I value education as a democratic activity conducted by students and teachers who think critically together. I also value that I encourage my own students to think critically, but am aware that my didactic approach to teaching sometimes negates this. I examined whether a collaborative online-learning environment might become a space to encourage critical thinking and help me overcome that particular contradiction in my practice. There were three cycles in my research that evolved from my concern:

- creating the pedagogical space for teaching and learning in Moodle;
- consolidation and questioning;
- encouraging deep learning.

These cycles evolved over the course of the research.

**Research cycle one – creating the pedagogical space for teaching and learning in Moodle**

There are two important elements in how I came to understand how best to use Moodle. Both involved its discussion-forum feature. A forum is an online activity where a lecturer or teacher can place a topic for discussion and moderate and direct it as required.

The first element was that, through my own use of Moodle, I found the experience of using online forums pivotal in shaping my own learning in the Master's programme. In her Ph.D. thesis, Margaret Farren (2006a), the Chair of the Masters programme, showed how she developed a web of betweenness through the communications-rich characteristics of Information and Communications Technoloy (ICT). 'ICT and emerging media technologies can support a dialogic-collaborative approach to learning and bring us closer to the meanings of our educational values as they emerge in the course of our practice' (Farren, 2006a, p. 22).

As I started to post contributions to the discussion forums and receive responses from fellow participants and former students in the Master's class, deep personal learning began to occur, as the interconnectivity of the 'web of betweenness' began to emerge. Not alone was I discussing, for example, an educational theory with fellow teachers but also with trainers from the public service, who deal with clients from a variety of social background, or with nurses bringing their particular healthcare perspective to the debate.

The course-philosophy of a web of betweenness was empowering me to begin to identify and understand my own educational values. I then started to clarify the educational value central to this research. The following is a response from Darragh Power, a graduate of the Master's course to a posting I had made on Paulo Freire.

> Donal you said: 'It is a fine balancing act to a degree, but Secondary school education has to be more than 'learning' in a narrow sense – more

than how many points did you get? It has to transform students, so that
they move outside of themselves towards their communities and be active
in them. Difficult in these materialistic times.

This is an educational value that you hold, which to my mind is a very
positive one. I think this transformational value is a nice idea, and the
challenge from a living theory action research perspective, is how can you
integrate this value into your practice? (D. Power, personal
communication, April 24, 2006)

This posting represented an important moment in my understanding of
my own learning.

The second element was an unplanned forum the students created
themselves, within days of their Moodle class going online (October 19, 2006).
Roger Jones posted a video entitled 'Nazi Propaganda Village People' from
YouTube, the video-sharing website, to the online-classroom. This video parodies
Leni Riefenstahl's documentary, *Triumph of the Will*, which records the 1934
Nuremberg Rally in Nazi Germany. This created an online-discussion between
some of the students and myself, initially about who controls the forum, but
subsequently and more importantly, it developed into a discussion about the
appropriateness or otherwise of making fun of historical personalities, when the
consequences of their actions resulted in the deaths of millions of people. This is
an               extract            from            that            discussion
(http://portmarnockcommunityschool.ie/images/appendix%20kejolts.pdf).      The
video was subsequently removed from YouTube for a copyright violation.

These two elements: my own learning on Moodle and the students'
unprompted and enthusiastic online-debate, are fundamental in my decision to use
the forum facility on Moodle as a central part of my research.

As a teacher, I always try to relate the historical topic I am teaching to the
real world. This concern would be no different in the online-classroom. The
democratic value of participation and discussion that I encourage in my real
classroom (but often negate in practice) could now be reflected in my Moodle
classroom. I began to realise that I was creating a new pedagogical space for the
students. Could this space become what Freire and Macedo (1999) spoke of, a

space where students are afforded the opportunity to be critical, in a dialogue between students and teachers as co-investigators in the process of critical thinking?

Cycle one had helped me realise that this was a possibility. It also helped me understand how my own learning on the Master's programme was developing as I gained insights from my own use of Moodle in my study and from its use in school. I realise now that I was becoming responsive to my own learning from my participation in the Master's forums and also from working with the students in my class. I was now prepared to explore this responsiveness and imagine a way forward with the class I teach.

### Research cycle two – consolidation and questioning

In Cycle Two, I set up three online forums for the class (Table 1), worked on moderating them and examined four themes that then emerged.

**Table 1.**     Original online forums

| Moodle Forum: | Were the Americans right to drop the Atomic Bomb? |
|---|---|
| Historical Context: | The technology of warfare |
| Forum Start Date: | November 2006. |
| Moodle Forum: | Was Parnell the Author of His Own Downfall? |
| Historical Context: | Charles Stewarts Parnell's affair with Catherine O'Shea and his subsequent refusal to resign from the Irish Parliamentary Party. |
| Forum Start Date: | January 2007. |
| Moodle Forum | What Does It Mean to be Irish in 2007? |
| Historical Context: | The Irish Ireland movement of the late nineteenth and early twentieth centuries. |
| Forum Start Date | February 2007. |

I examined the student's contributions to these three forums and saw four themes develop in their online discussions (http://portmarnockcommunityschool.ie/images/appendixnejolts.pdf):

1.    argument about historical issues;

2.   expanding the topic for discussion;

3.   moving away from the context of the discussion;

4.   making moral judgments.

The criterion I then used for examining these themes was the Leaving Certificate History Syllabus, particularly the sections on the nature of the history, the nature of the syllabus and the aims and objectives of the History programme. I now asked two important questions that sent me back to the literature review:

- What is going on in the three forums?

- Are the forums encouraging critical thinking?

I could see that I had successfully implemented Moodle and had judged properly that social software ensured students' ease in an online-environment. I was unhappy, however, that I was interpreting the forums in a meaningful way. I could see that they were encouraging critical thinking, but as I isolated the four themes above, I understood I was not adequately expressing my educational values in examining them.

I was taking the Leaving Certificate History Syllabus as my criterion and looking for phrases from it that backed up some of the discourses in the forums. It was not, however, establishing in a meaningful way, that dialogue and critical thinking were taking place.

As I re-engaged with the literature, I came to understand that it was possible to explore different levels of critical thinking, using ideas developed by Hatton and Smith (1995). These were explained in the literature-review. This realisation was developed through discussions with my own supervisor, presentations of work in progress to dissertation supervisors other than my own, and discussions with my fellow students on the Master's programme. There was no one moment of sudden realisation, but a slow understanding that I needed a more rigorous framework to look at the online-discussion forums.

I now revisited the three forums I had examined using the Leaving Certificate History syllabus as a criterion, and looked at them in the light of

Hatton and Smith's (1995) understanding of critical thinking. I concluded that some critical thinking was taking place and that students had engaged in dialogue with each other.

As I reflected on the student online discussions I realised that I could possibly improve the quality of these as the students interacted with each other.

This would involve pre-teaching the students about learning and critical thinking. This realisation became the basis for moving forward into cycle three.

**Cycle three - encouraging deep learning**

I now decided to teach the students about two issues in relation to my research. The first was in regard to learning. The other was in regard to critical thinking. When I returned to the literature, I found that in order to ensure a greater understanding of what they were at, students should be taught about the processes involved. Students needed to make meta-cognitive sense of where they were going, in order to achieve a cognitive presence in the online-environment (Garrison & Anderson, 2003).

I therefore planned and taught the students a lesson about learning and critical    thinking.    This    is    a    copy    of    the    presentation (http://portmarnockcommunityschool.ie/images/critical%20thinkingejolts.pdf). On reflection, this was the first time in twenty five years of practice that I had ever really spoken to students about 'learning'. I recorded the class, as a visual attempt to show the lived expression of my interest in bringing the students forward in learning and critical thinking.

I told the students that I would now organise two further forums (Table 2):

**Table 2.**      Further online forums.

| Moodle Forum: | Using the study of the Church in Nazi Germany, comment on the role of the Christian Churches when faced with Fascism. |
|---|---|
| Historical Context: | Church State relations under Hitler. |
| Forum Start Date: | Tuesday 24 April 2007. |
| **Moodle Forum:** | **Socialism and Capitalism.** |
| Historical Context: | The Dublin Strike and Lockout 1913 |
| Forum Start Date: | Monday 16th April and Wednesday 9th May 2007. |

Cycle Three was significant because I pre-taught my students about learning and critical thinking. This was a new development in my own practice. Pre-teaching reinforced my value of developing critical thinking in the online History class. Pre-teaching was also indicative of my enthusiasm to move my students' school-work to a new level, both in terms of the Leaving Certificate and in terms of their own abilities in critical thinking. This interest was commented on by my critical friend who saw my sense of excitement, as I told him how I developed my research project in this way.

Cycle Three was also significant because it generated some student learning (http://portmarnockcommunityschool.ie/images/appendixgerejolts.pdf) reflecting Hatton and Smith's (1995) fourth criterion of critical thinking: giving reasons for decisions, taking into account broader social, historical and political contexts.

**Reflection on my research**

I believe that through this research I have influenced my own learning and that of the students'. I began this research because I value critical thinking. I also value that I encourage students to think critically. I am aware that my didactic approach to teaching sometimes negates this. In order to engage with this contradiction I explored different ways of using technology, reflecting on my own learning and on the learning of others.

Technology afforded many possibilities e.g. blogs, wikis, podcasts, digital video. Discussion-forums online constituted the route I took with this research.

I now believe that it is possible to create a space to encourage critical thinking in a History class using a collaborative online-learning environment. I enjoy teaching, and engaging with the students in a new and personally exciting way. In reflecting on the reasons for that excitement I came to understand that I am living out my educational values. Technology, in the form of collaborative online-learning environments, afforded me this opportunity.

**The validity of my research inquiry**

During the research process, I formally presented my work on three occasions to participants in the Masters programme. I met twice with my critical friend, Seamus Ó'Braonáin. I engaged with my research supervisor, Margaret Farren and further met with Teresa Hennessy and Yvonne Mulligan (students from the Masters Programme also engaging with action research) as we clarified, in particular, our educational values. Mary O'Mahony, a primary school teacher, read my work for meaning. I increasingly began to use digital video, to try and capture moments of enthusiasm and insight (Farren, 2008), in order to support the validation process.

**CONCLUSION**

I believe that my research shows that I discern and demonstrate how my embodied values have become living standards of judgment (Laidlaw, 1996), as my thinking developed through engaging in a dialogic, collaborative approach to learning. My dialogues with the various partners in the validation-process strengthened the social validity of my research and gave me the confidence to state the source of my enthusiasm, which is my love for teaching. My ontological values have therefore become the living epistemological standards of judgment. My love of teaching moved my research along.

I believe I have shown that I am a reflective researcher demonstrating the rigour necessary in an action research project and that I have made evidence of this available. I have engaged with my living contradiction (Whitehead 1989), of encouraging critical thinking while negating it through a didactic approach to teaching, by engaging with the part of my research question that asks 'how do I improve my practice?' Risk comes from one of my conclusions, my explicit statement of my love of teaching. After twenty-five years of practice, I find it surprising to describe such a conclusion as a risk. But I could not explain my enthusiasm without its articulation.

I worked in collaboration with the students in Portmarnock and acknowledge their influence in my learning. I also acknowledge my work with all the participants in the Masters programme, and my willingness to change as I engaged with them. This was a project revealed in many forms of media, for example, through video, online dialogues, and reflection. It resulted in a genuine interplay between theory and practice. An interplay drawing together critical thinking, collaboration, dialogue and online technologies, resulting in a transformation of my understanding and practice of teaching and learning.

## REFERENCES

Anchor Youth Centre. (2007). *The Anchor WATCH_YOUR_SPACE Survey.* Retrieved March 3, 2007, from http://www.webwise.ie/GenPDF.aspx?id=1744

Bertrand, Y. (2003). *Contemporary Theories and Practice in Education* (2nd ed.). Madison: Atwood Publishing.

Bonk, C. J., Wisher, R.A. and Lee, J. (2004). Moderating Learner-Centered E-Learning: Problems and Solutions, Benefits and Implications In Roberts, T.S. (Ed.), *Online Collaborative Learning: Theory and Practice.* London: Information Science Publishing.

Boyd, S. (2005). *Are You Ready for Social Software?* Retrieved February 4, 2007, from http://www.stoweboyd.com/message/2006/10/are_you_ready_f.html

Carr, W. and Kemmis, S. (1986). *Becoming Critical.* London: RoutledgeFalmer.

Chapman, A. (2006). Asses, Archers and Assumptions: Strategies for Improving Thinking Skills in History in Years 9 to 13. *Teaching History,* 123, 6-13. Retrieved November 15, 2006, from http://www.library.dcu.ie/Eresources/index.htm

Chomsky, N. (2004). Democracy and Education. In Chomsky, N., Macedo, D. P. (Ed.), *Chomsky on miseducation* (pp. 37-55). Lanham, Boulder, New York & Oxford: Rowman & Littlefield. Retrieved February 16, 2009, from http://www.scribd.com/doc/6934739/NoamChomskyDemocracyAndEducation

Department of Education (1997). *Schools IT2000: A Policy Framework for the New Millennium.* Dublin: The Stationery Office.

Department of Education and Science (2003). *Leaving Certificate History Syllabus.* Dublin: The Stationery Office.

Department of Education and Science. (2008a). *ICT in schools.* Dublin: Evaluation Support and Research Unit, Inspectorate, Department of Education and Science. Retrieved December 14, 2008, from http://www.education.ie/servlet/blobservlet/ICT_in_schools_insp_report.pdf

Department of Education and Science. (2008b). *Investing effectively in information and communications technology in schools, 2008-2013.* Retrieved December 14, 2008, from http://www.education.ie/servlet/blobservlet/ministers_strategy_group_report.pdf

Department of Finance, Sectoral Policy Division. (2007). *National Development Plan 2007 – 2013 Transforming Ireland.* Dublin: The Stationery Office. Retrieved December 14, 2008, from http://www.ndp.ie/docs/NDP_2007-2013_-_All_sections_downloadable_by_chapter/1900.htm

Dewey, J. (1916). *Democracy and Education. An Introduction to the Philosophy of Education.* Montana: Kessinger Publishing Reprint.

Dewey, J. (1938). *Experience and Education: The 60th Anniversary Edition.* West Lafayette, Indiana. Kappa Delta Pi.

Donnelly, R. and O'Rourke, K. C. (2007). What now? Evaluating eLearning CPD practice in Irish third level education. *Journal of Further and Higher Education, 31*(1), 31-40.

Dougiamas, M. and Taylor, P. C. (2003). *Moodle: Using Learning Communities to Create an Open Source Course Management System.* Refereed paper presented at EDMEDIA 2003. Retrieved December 16, 2006, from http://dougiamas.com/writing/edmedia2003/

Farren, M. (2006a). *How can I create a pedagogy of the unique through a web of betweenness?* (Doctoral dissertation, University of Bath, UK). Retrieved August 28, 2010, from http://www.actionresearch.net/living/farren.shtml

Farren, M. (2008). Co-creating an Educational Space. *Educational Journal of Living Theories.* 1(1), 50-68. Retrieved 25 August, 2010, from http://ejolts.net/node/78

Freire, P. (1970). *Pedagogy of the Oppressed.* London: Penguin Books.

Freire, P. and Macedo, D. P. (1999). Pedagogy, Culture, Language and Race: a Dialogue. In Leach, J., and Moon, B. (Eds.) *Learners & Pedagogy* (pp. 46-58). London: Paul Chapman Publishing.

Garrison, D. R. & Anderson, T. (2003). *E-Learning in the 21st Century: A Framework for Research and Practice.* Abingdon: RoutledgeFalmer.

Habermas, J. (1986). *Knowledge and Human Interests.* Boston, Oxford: Polity Press.

Hatton, N. and Smith, D. (1995). Reflection in Teacher Education: Towards Definition and Implementation. *Teaching & Teacher Education*, 11 (1), 33-49. Retrieved March 1, 2007, from http://www.library.dcu.ie/Eresources/databases-az.htm

Hawkridge, D., Jaworski, J. and McMahon, H. (1990). *Computers in Third-World schools: examples, experiences and issues.* London: Macmillan.

Joint Information Systems Committee. 2007. VLE Procurement. Retrieved February 16, 2009, from http://www.jisc.ac.uk/uploaded_documents/bp2.pdf

Kukulska-Hulme, A. (2004). Do Online Collaborative Groups Need Leaders? In Roberts, T. S. (Ed.), *Online Collaborative Learning: Theory and Practice* (pp. 262-280). London: Information Science Publishing.

Laidlaw, M. (1996). How can I create my own living educational theory as I offer you an account of my educational development? (Doctoral dissertation, University of Bath, UK). Retrieved February 11, 2009, from http://www.actionresearch.net/moira2.shtml

Larsen, A. and Hodge, J. (2005). *The Art of Argument.* Philadelphia: Classical Academic Press.

McNiff, J. and Whitehead, J. (2005). *Action Research for Teachers - A Practical Guide.* London: David Fulton.

McNiff, J. and Whitehead, J. (2006). *All You Need to Know about Action Research.* London: Sage Publications.

Moodle. (2006). *Philosophy.* Retrieved March 8, 2007, from http://docs.moodle.org/en/Philosophy

National Council for Curriculum and Assessment (2004). *Curriculum Assessment and ICT in the Irish Context: A Discussion Paper.* Retrieved October 10, 2007, from http://www.ncca.ie/index.asp?locID=62&docID=-1

New Media Consortium and Educause Learning Initiative. (2007). *The Horizon Report.* Retrieved February 10, 2007, from http://www.nmc.org/pdf/2007_Horizon_Report.pdf

Oliver, R. and Herrington, J. (2003). Exploring Technology Mediated Learning from a Pedagogical Perspective. *Interactive Learning Environments, 11*(2), 111-126 Retrieved March 7, 2007, from http://www.library.dcu.ie/Eresources/databases-az.htm

Owen, M., Grant, L., Sayers, S. and Facer, K. (2006). *Opening Education - Social Software and Learning.* Retrieved October 10, 2006, from http://www.futurelab.org.uk/resources/documents/opening_education/Social_Software_report.pdf

Packham, G., Watland, P., Pirotte, S. and Verday N. (2004). *Roles and Competencies of the e-Tutor.* Retrieved March 9, 2007, from http://www.networkedlearningconference.org.uk/past/nlc2004/proceedings/individual_papers/packham_et_al.htm

Prensky, M. (2001). Digital Natives, Digital Immigrants. *On the Horizon, 9*(5), 1-6. Retrieved December 8, 2006, from http://www.marcprensky.com/writing/Prensky%20-%20Digital%20Natives,%20Digital%20Immigrants%20-%20Part1.pdf

Richardson, W. (2006). *Blogs, Wikis, Podcasts, and Other Powerful Web Tools for Classrooms.* California: Corwin Press.

Rudd, T. 2006. *Futurelab Seminar Series - Re-thinking Learning Networks: Home, School and Community: A provocation paper.* Retrieved November 15, 2007, from http://www.futurelab.org.uk/resources/documents/project_reports/Learning_Networks_provocation_paper.pdf

Salmon, G. (2002). *E-tivities.* London: Kogan Page.

Sefton-Green, J. (2004). *Literature Review in Informal Learning with Technology Outside School.* Retrieved October 10, 2006, from http://www.futurelab.org.uk/resources/documents/lit_reviews/Informal_Learning_Review.pdf

Veugelers, W. (1996). *Teaching Values and Critical Thinking.* Paper presented at The Annual Meeting of the American Educational Research Association, April 1996. Retrieved February 2, 2007, from http://www.library.dcu.ie/Eresources/databases-az.htm

Whitehead, J. (1989). Creating a Living Educational Theory from Questions of the Kind, 'How do I Improve my Practice?'. *Cambridge Journal of Education*, *19*(1), 41-52. Retrieved December 2, 2005, from http://www.actionresearch.net/writings/livtheory.html

Whitehead, J. and McNiff, J. (2006). *Action Research Living Theory*. London: Sage.

# HOW CAN I ENCOURAGE MULTI-STAKEHOLDER NARRATIVE AND REFLECTION ON THE USE OF ICT IN TEACHER PROFESSIONAL DEVELOPMENT PROGRAMMES IN RWANDA?

**Mary Hooker, Ireland**

## MY RESEARCH CONTEXT

The context of my study is Rwanda and specifically the Information and Communication Technology (ICT) landscape for Teacher Professional Development (TPD) in Rwanda. The Government of Rwanda has set a national goal that the country will achieve middle-income status by 2020 based on an information-rich, knowledge-based society and economy, achieved by modernising its key sectors using ICT (Farrell and Isaacs, 2007). Rwanda *Vision 2020* identifies the strengthening of teacher development in an ICT-rich environment as one of the top government priorities for the achievement of its national socio-economic development goals (Ministry of Finance and Economic Planning, 2001). The target is that each primary and secondary school should have a computer-literacy teacher by 2010 (Mukama & Andersson, 2008). With respect to training structures to support the development of ICT in the educational system, higher educational institutions are required to make computer studies and basic computing an integral and a compulsory subject within their teacher education programmes (Mukama & Andersson, 2008).

The drive to utilize ICT as an integral feature in all professional learning programmes has led to the emergence of a myriad of national and international initiatives and schemes for new technology integration over the last decade (Farrell & Isaacs, 2007). The current development of a Rwanda National ICT in Education policy represents a timely process to create a regulatory and governance framework to shape 'the interventions and initiatives that are taking place and for those needed in this sector' (Ministry of Education, 2008, p. 12).

I am an Education Specialist working for the Global e-Schools and Communities Initiative (GeSCI), an International Non-Government Organization (INGO). GeSCI was set up under the auspices of a United Nations (UN) Information and Communication Technology (ICT) Task Force in 2004 as a designated body to provide demand-driven assistance to developing countries seeking to harness the potential of ICT to improve access to, and the quality and effectiveness of, their education systems.

I am also affiliated to the creative space of the Action Research Collaboratory set up by Dr. Margaret Farren at Dublin City University (DCU), Ireland, 'to enable practitioner-researchers to provide evidence-based accounts of how they are improving work practices within their organisations and generating new knowledge through the use of ICT' (Farren, 2007). This research was carried out as part of an M.Sc. in Education and Training Management (eLearning strand) programme that I undertook as a part-time student in DCU from 2007 to 2009.

In my practice within the framework of GeSCI's organizational mission, we seek to work with Ministries of Education in developing countries to address fundamental causes of poor quality and access to Education provision and to assess how ICT can be used to address these problems at different system levels. Currently over 75 million children worldwide are not in school (UNESCO,

2008a). Countless millions more are dropping out of school systems due to the seeming irrelevance of education to their lives (Ainscow & Miles, 2008). Yates (as cited in Teacher Education Policy Forum for Sub-Saharan Africa, 2007) sees the Education for All (EFA) agenda as a Global Social Justice (GSJ) Project and asserts that the concept of quality is fundamental to its achievement.

A quality education is dependent on the development of high quality teachers (Haddad, as cited in The Teacher Education Policy Forum for Sub-Saharan Africa, 2007). The challenge is momentous in a global context of ever more complex demands on systems for educational provision coupled with acute shortages in the supply of suitably qualified and experienced teachers north and south (Davis, 2000; Leach, 2008). Eighteen million new primary teachers are needed to achieve Education for All (EFA) by 2015 (UNESCO, 2009). Meanwhile regional disparities in quality-provision accelerate as richer countries lure qualified teachers from less favoured regions with incentive-packages (Davis, 2000).

The challenge is in almost all respects greatest in sub-Saharan Africa where a third of existing teachers are untrained. Of the thousands recruited each year, they largely have inadequate subject knowledge and little if any pedagogic training (Evoh, 2007; Bennell, 2005, as cited in Leach, 2008). Many experts in the field of Teacher Professional Development and ICT believe that the evidence makes clear the incapacity of existing institutional structures to cope with the scale and urgency of the issues (Swarts, 2006; Evoh, 2007; Dladla & Moon, 2002; Moon, 2007, as cited in Leach, 2008). In this context Leach (2008) believes that the thoughtful use of new forms of ICT can be exploited to strengthen and enhance TPD programmes and improve the quality of education in general.

One of GeSCI's partner countries of engagement in sub-Saharan Africa is Rwanda. At a meeting in October 2008 between GeSCI and members of the Teacher Education Services (TES) of the Ministry of Education (MinEduc) of

Rwanda, discussion focused on a need for development of a framework for the use of ICT in TPD. The framework would provide a mechanism for coordinating programmes and improving school support towards a more productive integration of new technology. A prelude to developing an ICT for TPD framework would be an analysis of current programmes and initiatives in order to understand the challenges, opportunities and lessons that are being learned from the different levels, perspectives and contexts of programme-implementation.

The process of enabling discourse among teachers, teacher educators, curriculum developers, partners and policy makers to trigger deep reflection on the various possibilities for ICT integration in professional learning in Rwanda constitutes the focus of my research.


## KNOWLEDGE, TECHNOLOGY AND DEVELOPMENT IN A KNOWLEDGE SOCIETY

The Global e-Schools and Communities Initiative (GeSCI) believes that ICT can be a powerful enabler of development goals and that the proper and effective use of ICT can improve the quality of teaching and learning at all levels of the education system. As an organization, we are committed to a vision of a *Knowledge Society for All* 'where every person has equitable access to knowledge, and the ability and capacity to create and share knowledge for society's overall development' (GeSCI, 2008, p. 22).

At the heart of GeSCI's mission is the concept of Knowledge Building and Sharing: working together with our developing country partners to strengthen their knowledge systems and to develop their own visionary thinking, strategic capacity and sustainable solutions effectively to manage, deploy and integrate ICT in their education systems. GeSCI's work can be described in terms of 'Knowledge-based Aid', an emergent concept captured in a recent United Nations Conference on Trade and Development report (UNCTAD, 2007) as a new form of development-assistance to support learning and innovation in Lesser Developed Countries (LDCs).

The foremost challenge to developing countries' successful utilization of ICT in their educational and developmental programmes is 'ownership of the knowledge' and the 'control of the technology' according to Addo (2001, p. 146). In this regard he considers that technologies are not 'neutral instruments' as they 'shape the social choice mechanisms of the communities that use them' (ibid.). It is Unwin's (2004a) view that while most global initiatives have tended to voice the positive benefits of ICT in development, 'some have placed insufficient emphasis on the less desirable effects' (p. 154). In particular he laments the lack of a critical lens for analysing the "implications of transfer of a 'northern' or 'western' technology to an entirely different cultural context" (Unwin, 2004a). He believes that much policy discussion on ICT is top-down led by governments and the private sector. He notes that it is rare for the voices of the poor or marginalized to be listened to and as a result ICT-development issues tend to be 'supply-led' rather than 'demand driven' (Unwin, 2004a).

Taylor and Clarke (2007), referring to Chambers' (1997) oft-cited question 'Whose knowledge counts?' (Chambers in Taylor & Clarke 2007, p. 11), consider that the concept of 'Knowledge' in the 'Knowledge Society' requires an expansion of our understanding of knowledge beyond the intellectual dimension – to include the personal and particular dimensions. Such authors are now stressing increasingly the importance of learning processes 'that are based on co-construction and subjectifying of knowledge, through processes of critical reflection and experience' (Chambers in Taylor & Clarke 2007, p. 11).

My first concern in my research inquiry is that I engage with our partners in teacher professional development institutions and agencies in Rwanda on a basis of an equitable relationship that is developed upon processes of mutual learning. My second concern is to ensure that the research dialogue captures the voices of teachers, teacher educators, managers, lecturers, researchers and policy makers, in a way that reflects a real process of empowering discourse from 'classroots' (O'Sullivan, 2004, p. 559) to policy-level in the constituency of our partner engagement.

My research question is: 'How am I improving my practice and contributing to knowledge as I encourage multi-stakeholder narrative and reflection on the use of ICT in Teacher Professional Development programmes in Rwanda?' I ask this question mindful that I am examining my own learning and that I am taking responsibility for the way I exercise my influence in the learning of partners.

## LITERATURE

In the literature review I examine the emergent field of ICT integration in education systems generally and in Teacher Professional Development (TPD) specifically. I draw on educational mainstream and ICT literature to verify emergent conceptual frameworks for ICT in TPD. I look briefly at the use of Activity Theory as a lens to examine ICT use in TPD activity systems.

### ICT and the knowledge society

There is a commonly-accepted rhetoric that education-systems need to effect changes in the preparation of its citizens for lifelong learning in a 21$^{st}$ Century Knowledge-based or Information Society. The rhetoric can be characterized as follows:

- Systemic economic growth is the key to poverty-reduction and increased prosperity;
- 'New Growth' economic models emphasize the importance of new knowledge, innovation, and the development of human capacity as the sources of sustainable economic growth;

- ICTs are engines for new growth and tools for empowering societies to change into knowledge economies or information societies;
- Citizens in these information societies will need to be prepared in new technology literacy competencies inclusive of higher order thinking and sound reasoning skills - *the ability to learn how to learn* (i.e. to be a life-long learner), *the ability to reflect, to analyse, synthesise, to find solutions and to adapt*;
- Education is a major pillar of a knowledge economy and a human right;

Through access to an inclusive high-quality education by all – regardless of gender, ethnicity, religion, or language – benefits to individual, business, private and public enterprise are multiplied and will lead to growth and development that is more equitably distributed and enjoyed by all (Burkhardt et al., 2003; Swarts 2008; UNESCO, 2008a; Global e-Schools and Communities Initiative, 2008).

The growing demands in knowledge specialization will require a change in the traditional view of the learning process. It will further require an understanding of how new technology can be used to facilitate learning environments in which students are engaged in the kind of team and project work that can enable them to take greater responsibility for their own learning and construction of knowledge (Pelgrum & Law, 2003). This is a view that has influenced a paradigm shift in teacher professional development programmes as the pivotal role of teachers, especially in the effective use of new technologies, is being recognized globally (Davis, 2000).

## Global trends in ICT and teacher professional development

The extremely rapid growth and turn around in new technology and knowledge content mean that this emergent field is changing faster than education personnel can track (Coolahan, 2002). Thus the new models for TPD embrace a concept of '3 I's' – initial, induction and in-service teacher education. These new trends in professional learning represent a paradigm-shift which replaces the prevailing assumption of one-time initial or specialized training with a lifelong learning approach for professional preparedness, development and research (Coolahan, 2002; Haddad, 2002; Dladla & Moon, 2002; Gaido & Carlson, 2003).

New models for technology integration in professional development should represent a 'reconceptualization' of teacher professional learning for a digital age according to Butler (2001). The models should look beyond how teachers engage with technology, to how teachers use technology as they work alongside their students to redefine learning itself and to become co-learners in the process. Hepp et al. (2004) observe that teachers' beliefs and attitudes to ICT influence the rate of adoption of ICT in TPD programmes and classroom-practice. The authors identify three group-adoption processes: (i) the 'innovators' who will recognize the potential of ICT early in TPD programmes and will explore quickly tools in their practice; (ii) the 'resistors' who tend to resist change in all its forms; (iii) the 'mainstreamers' or late adopters of technology, arguably 'the largest group in education systems and therefore the most important' (Hepp et al., 2004, pp. 18-19).

The assimilation of new technologies according to Drenoyanni (2006) cannot be understood in isolation from the broader context of the prevailing and more powerful social, economic and political contexts and dynamics. The incorporation and use of ICT in TPD will 'mirror to a certain degree contemporary socio-economic problems and prevailing educational conditions' (Drenoyanni, 2006, p. 405).

**ICT and teacher professional development in Africa**

Olakulehim (2007) reports that across Africa there is a deluge of challenges confronting the educative process in general and the application of ICT in TPD programmes in particular. While ICT has found its way into the formal curricula in most educational practices, the author considers their existence is still at an embryonic stage due to a lack of computers, connections and staff-expertise.

Research conducted by SchoolNet Africa, the Commonwealth of Learning and the International Institute for Communication and Development (2004) identified an estimated sixty ICT-related TPD programmes underway in Africa. A large proportion of the programmes are small scale, dependent on funding from donors and driven externally by donors as opposed to being Ministry-led programmes. They generally lack a whole-school approach. Such initiatives fail to live up to the ambitious aspirations of their proponents because they speak to the supply-side, have not been demand-led historically as they give insufficient attention to the involvement of stakeholders in defining the needs and purpose of the development-process (Unwin, 2004b; Isaacs, 2006; Ottevanger et al., 2007; Kontiainen, 2007, as cited in Hakkarainen et al., 2008).

In their survey of ICT in Education in Africa, Farrell and Isaacs (2007) suggest that the emergence of multi-country regional initiatives such as UNESCO's Teacher Training Initiative for Sub-Saharan Africa (TTISSA), the African Virtual University (AVU) Teacher Education Project, the New Partnership for Africa's Development (NEPAD) e-Schools Project, the Educator Development Network of SchoolNet South Africa, is indicative of a shift in the prevailing paradigm towards longer term, systemic initiatives in professional development promoting quality-innovation.

### A conceptual framework for ICT-integration

There is a general absence of conceptual clarity on the objectives of ICT for TPD initiatives in the African region according to Isaacs (2006). Mandinach (2005) suggests that the lack of clarity is pervasive in education-systems globally, noting that while educational institutions seem to be aware they should be joining the ICT integration-movement, they are not clear as to the purpose or the gains.

From the mainstream education-literature Kennedy (2005) proposes that defining whether the fundamental purpose of a TPD intervention is to achieve transmission or to facilitate transformative practice can provide a powerful tool for conceptual analysis. Drawing from the literature, she developed a framework for categorizing nine different models of TPD provision along a continuum of delivery inherent in their purposes of provision - moving from *transmission* through *transitional* to *transformative* purposes which develop increasing capacity for teacher-empowerment.

From the ICT domain Olakulehin (2008) identifies four broad approaches from the literature for the adoption of ICT in TPD-programmes. The adoption model depicts a continuum of the four approaches correspondent to the Kennedy trajectory – moving from *emerging* to *applying* to *infusing* to *transforming* purposes which develop increasing teacher and support staff-capability to use ICT as a 'natural part of the everyday life of the system' (ibid., p. 140).

The UNESCO (2008a) Information and Communication Technology – Competency Standards for Teacher's (ICT-CST) project, attempts to bridge both mainstream and ICT specialist domains into a holistic framework for a modular continuum of ICT integration in all TPD programmes - moving from *technology literacy*, through to *knowledge-deepening* to *knowledge-creation* purposes which develop increasing capacity for the empowerment of teachers in the utilization of ICT as a tool to enhance the quality of learning (Figure 1, p. 321).

The consolidated continuum of approaches represents a *conceptual framework* in which practitioners and institutions seek to move from isolated, passive consumers of externally-defined programmes for ICT-knowledge and skills-acquisition towards more open communities of active learners and learning-organizations that generate new knowledge on the use of ICT to enhance educational practice (Kennedy, 2005; Olakulehin, 2008; UNESCO, 2008a).

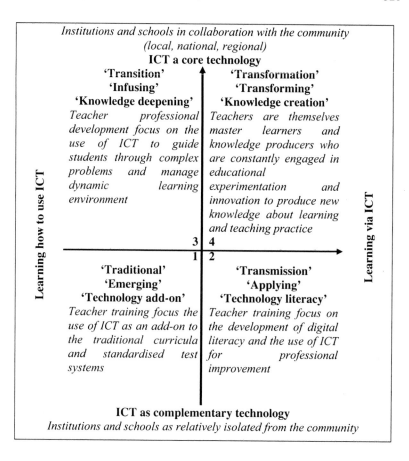

**Figure 1.**    A consolidated continuum of approaches for ICT Integration in TPD (Vygotsky, 1978; Kennedy, 2005; Hakkarainen et al., 2008; Olakulehin, 2008; UNESCO, 2008a)

**Looking at ICT integration through an activity theory lens**

Activity Theory (AT) (Vygotsky, 1978; Engstrom, 2001) is currently widely applied to study technology-based learning and working situations (Issroff and Scanlon, 2001). Three basic principles of AT theory are helpful for understanding and analysing the process of integrating ICT in TPD systems:

- Teachers' professional learning and development are social processes growing out of joint activity;
- People are active cognizing agents (Sen, 1999, as cited in Leach, 2008, p. 785) but they work in sites that are not necessarily of their choosing with tools that constrain and afford their actions;
- Teaching and learning systems are constantly subject to change and these changes are driven by contradictions and tensions which can lead to expansive learning. (Cole & Russel 2002, as cited in Hardman, 2004)

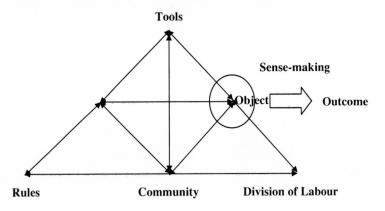

**Figure 2.**   The six elements of an activity-system (Engestrom, 2001)

AT concepts can provide a framework to explore a socio-cultural perspective for analysing ICT practices, which supports the idea that ICT needs to be studied within the learning environment and also within the broader and more powerful social, economic and political contexts in which it is situated (Agalianos, 2001; Lim & Hang, 2003; Drenoyianni, 2006). A key feature of the theory is the extended model of Activity Systems developed by Engestrom (2001) that conceptualizes all human activity as the interaction of six inseparable and mutually-constitutive elements: *subjects, tools, object and outcome, rules, community and division of labour* (Figure 2).

The common language defined by the six elements of the activity-system's structure can provide a useful mechanism to engage institutional reflection on ICT in TPD. If the assumption is that the *object* (purpose) is the use of the ICT *tool* to enhance institutional practice through a continuum of TPD programme development from *technology literacy* to *knowledge deepening* to *knowledge creation*, then the *outcome* progressively changes between past, present and future systems of provision.

Based on the elements of the activity-system's structure, tools can be developed to investigate and 'mirror' historical and current models of institutional practice (Hakkarainen et al., 2008). The exploration of the complex pedagogical, organizational and technological issues inherent in the integration of ICT marks the start of a system's process of reflection (Robertson, 2008).

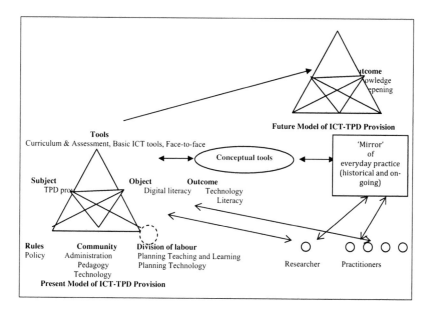

**Figure 3.**    Expansive learning through reflection on past, present and future models (Adapted from Engestrom, 2003)

The conceptual tools for analysing practice can be used to facilitate dialogue about the needs, possibilities and strategies for future models of ICT-TPD provision that are aligned to institutional and national policy and vision for a Knowledge Society (Figure 3, p. 323).

Activity Theory presents a flexible framework for facilitating a space for reflection, debate, discussion, critique, validation and ultimately expansionist learning – that is 'learning beyond what would have been possible if actors from each perspective remained insulated' (Robertson, 2008, p. 819). I sought to use the Activity Theory lens in my inquiry as I endeavoured to facilitate discourse and reflection with stakeholder institutions in Rwanda on their vision for ICT-integration in Teacher Professional Development.

## METHODOLOGY

### Action research living theory

Action research developed from the critical paradigm and takes its emancipatory agenda into a research realm that focuses and impacts on practice (McNiff & Whitehead, 2006; Cohen, Manion & Morrison, 2007). The cyclical, systematic, reflexive, iterative, participatory and democratic dynamic inherent in action research is the source of my affiliation to this research paradigm. While there are many forms and variants of action research, its fundamental purpose is to generate new knowledge (McNiff & Whitehead, 2006), that is useful to people in the everyday conduct of their lives (Reason & Bradbury, 2006) and that involves the participation and contribution of practitioner action researchers (Whitehead & McNiff, 2006).

The practice of transformation of the social order, as in transforming the exclusionary dominance of knowledge elites to a more inclusionary order of knowledge plurality, begins with practitioners as they ask, 'How do I improve what I am doing?' (Whitehead & McNiff, 2006, p. 147). The ontological *I* of the researcher-practitioner is what essentially distinguishes a living theory form of action research from other forms. The focus on *I* is connected to Sen's notion of the development of the capabilities of people (I, we) as a means of removing the "unfreedoms" that prevent them (me, us) from acting for good change (Sen, 2001, as cited in Taylor & Clarke, 2007). Freedom then brings with it responsibility for each one of us to live our values, to make good decisions about our lives, to improve learning, to encourage others to do the same and to recognize ourselves as 'living contradictions' when our values are being denied in practice (McNiff & Whitehead, 2006, p. 47).

As a researcher-practitioner, my real work, according to McNiff and Whitehead, is 'to improve learning, both my own and others, in order to improve practice' (McNiff & Whitehead, 2006, p. 51). Improvement can be brought about through influence as 'you do not set out to impose change on people and their ways' (McNiff & Whitehead, 2006, p. 51). I am conscious of the inequities in relationships in partner-engagements in the developing world that as an organization we have come to recognize. It is a 'living contradiction' that is well documented in the literature with much evidence pointing to development thinking and practice that is still trapped in a paradigm of predictable, linear causality and top-down command and control (Hakkarainen et al., 2008; Ramalingam & Jones, 2008; Taylor & Clarke, 2007).

My ontological values are centred on the belief that there are different ways of coming to know and different forms of knowing. I value the capacity of other people, my colleagues and my partners to come to know in their own way. I value the concept of a new scholarship of practice that is tentatively extending the epistemological boundaries to include and legitimate the voices and contributions of the practitioner communities to the knowledge base.

My *epistemological* stance flows from my ontological view. I do not consider that knowledge represents a packaged commodity that is transferable from one constituency to another. I value my own and other peoples' independent agency to communicate and act on the basis of our own sense-making. I value a new conception of knowledge that is no longer a factor of exclusion particular to the elitist model of knowledge-societies in the past, but that promotes alternative views of knowledge that present new possibilities for inclusive knowledge-societies in the future. I value equal partnership in the building and production of knowledge. I value the development of a participatory worldview involving an inclusive extended epistemology that incorporates diverse forms of knowing.

### Action plan

I believe that collaboration and joint knowledge-building are core activities in assisting our partners to strengthen their own capabilities for knowledge creation and innovation and to develop their strategic capacity to effectively manage, deploy and integrate ICT, in their education systems. My aim was to improve my practice as an education specialist, advisor and facilitator in assisting GeSCI's partners to develop an understanding of and develop their own solutions to address the major challenges of ICT integration in their education systems.

I collected data to demonstrate the story of my learning as it unfolded and to understand my educational influence in my own learning and that of others. I followed the story in a cyclical process incorporating a tentative trajectory described by Whitehead as follows:

- I experience a concern when some of my educational values are denied in my practice;
- I imagine a solution to the concern;
- I act in the direction of the imagined solution;
- I evaluate the outcome of the solution;
- I modify my practice, plans and ideas in the light of the evaluation (Whitehead, 1989; 2003, in McNiff & Whitehead, 2006, p. 91).

**Data collection methods and techniques**

My action research design involved developing a hybrid approach in the first research cycle using dialogical and narrative tools for data collection and analysis. The process involved adapting 'Activity Theory' (AT) and 'Most Significant Change' (MSC) frameworks and tools into an interview-protocol for the collection of data. The hybrid approach combines a dual strategy for sense-making in anticipation of the complexity and volume of information that would be collected from many stakeholders across a range of educational settings from national institutions to classrooms in schools. In discussions with my supervisor, Dr. Margaret Farren, prior to the first cycle, emphasized that traditional theory can be used as a method of analysis and integrated within the generation of a living theory.

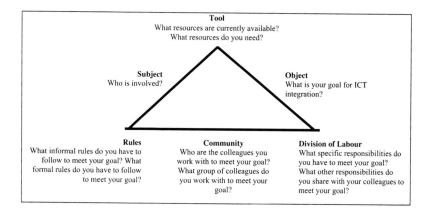

**Figure 4.**   Activity system interview protocol (Mwanza & Engestrom, 2003, as cited in Robertson, 2008; Yamagata-Lynch & Smaldino, 2007)

I modified the element of Activity Theory (AT) in terms of the interview-protocol from an eclectic range of tools and frameworks developed by the AT and ICT research communities (Lim & Hang, 2003; Mwanza &

Engestrom, 2003, as cited in Robertson, 2008; Demiraslan & Usluel, 2008; UNESCO, 2008a; Yamagata-Lynch & Smaldino, 2007). I derived an Activity System (AS) Interview Protocol from the six elements of the AT model (*subject, tool, object, rules, community, division of labour*) (Engestrom, 2001). I used categories drawn from the six components of the model as a basis for thematic analysis of the data collection which ensured to some degree the reliability of the process (Figure 4).

I modified the Most Significant Change (MSC) protocol from formats devised by Davis & Dart (2005) who developed the technique. I used the MSC protocol to collect stories of significant change from stakeholders on the use of technology in their practices. The most significant of stakeholder stories at one system level is reviewed by panels or groups of stakeholders at the next level using change domains and criteria defined by them to select stories most illustrative of change in each domain.

## IMPLEMENTATION AND EVALUATION

> It is not our role to speak to the people about our own view of the world, nor to attempt to impose that view on them, but rather to dialogue with the people about their view and ours. (Freire, 1970, p. 77)

### Introduction

I engaged in this research because I value our organisational vision of a 'Knowledge Society for All' (GeSCI, 2008) incorporating the dual notions of *universal access* and *participation of all* in Knowledge Societies (UNESCO, 2005). In my work as an education specialist in the developing world, I am conscious of the inequities that are sometimes evident in partner relationships, a 'living contradiction' (Whitehead, 1989, as cited in Whitehead & McNiff, 2006) of our espoused values for knowledge building and sharing on the basis of equal partnership. I wished to explore in the research cycles the potential of a hybrid of tools and frameworks to support authentic and participatory processes of knowledge-building and mutual learning within the context of an ICT in Teacher Professional Development discussion agenda.

### Research cycle one - organizing tools and frameworks for knowledge building and sharing

The first cycle of my action research project centred on a survey of the ICT in Teacher Professional Development (TPD) landscape in Rwanda conducted during the week of March 2 to 6, 2009. I travelled to Rwanda to assist the ICT Unit in the Ministry of Education (MinEduc) to carry out the survey. The programme for the survey identified a purposive sample of pre- and in-service, distance, school-based and partnership programmes to be visited. A purposive sample is a feature of qualitative research in which 'researchers handpick the cases to be included in the sample on the basis of their judgment of their typicality or possession of the particular characteristic being sought' (Cohen et al., 2007, pp. 114 – 115).

The sample, albeit restricted and biased in terms of selection, nevertheless served the needs of the survey at two levels. On a consultation-level the purpose of the survey was to access stakeholders (teacher educators, teacher trainers, school heads, teachers and students) affiliated to the various TPD initiatives and programmes with experiences on the use of ICT in their practices. The purpose of the survey on the level of my research was to examine the potential of a toolkit adapted from Activity Theory (AT) (Engestrom, 2001) to support a communicative space for authentic interaction, diverse reflection and thinking on the issues of ICT integration.

**Exploring an 'activity systems' (as) mirror**

I used the Activity System protocol derived from the Activity Theory Framework to conduct four interviews with stakeholders in national institution providers/affiliates of ICT in TPD programmes. All national institutions are identified in a generic way according to their function in deference to research agreement stipulations for confidentiality. Focus group interviews were conducted in:

1. The national institute for pre-service/distance education - four participants representing Management, the Computer Science Division, The Academic Studies Division and the ICT Unit;

2. The national centre for curriculum and development - one participant representing the Technical and Vocational Unit;

3. The national centre for in-service - five participants representing the Management, the Quality Assurance and Research Division and Master Training teams.

4. A regional teacher education college consulate of the national institution for preservice/distance education - three participants representing Management, the Academic Studies Division and the ICT Unit.

The interviews lasted between forty-five minutes and one and a half hours. As the participants indicated their discomfort with tape recording I conducted each interview with the support of the Country Programme Facilitator (CPF) and wrote comprehensive notes from which I prepared a summary report for institutional checking (MinEduc-GeSCI, 2009a).

I initiated each interview with a broad question asking participants to explain the goals of ICT integration in their TPD programmes. I anticipated from reading the literature (Hardman, 2004; Yamagata-Lynch & Smaldino, 2007) that enabling participants to clarify what they perceived to be individual and institutional goals and expectations of technology integration would lead to a deeper analysis of other characteristics of the impact of ICT in their activity-systems. What emerged was a consensus across all institutional discussions that the goal of ICT integration in general was defined by the national socio-economic development-vision and the goal of ICT in professional development programmes centred on the acquisition of skills in the use of technology.

The following extract exemplifies a typical response that dominated the opening stages of all focus-groups' discussions:

> **National Centre in-service discussion:** The overall goal is to help the government to educate the people in the region, to create employment, to achieve the government Vision 20/20 and in the process benchmarking Rwanda education with international standards, making Rwanda an international hub, increasing ICT literacy.
> The overall goal of the (in-service) programme is to enhance the quality of education through ICT and the specific objectives are to give teachers the knowledge to a) equip themselves with ICT tools, b) use the acquired skills for teaching and c) research and administer assessments.

There were however different perceptions as to the specifics on how ICT skills and knowledge might be integrated or used by teacher educators/ teachers and students/ learners in their teaching and learning programmes. The following extracts illustrate the institutions grappling with various interpretations and dilemmas regarding how ICT should be articulated in their programmes:

> **National Centre – Curriculum and Development discussion:** The objectives of the secondary school ordinary level programme are threefold and they are to a) familiarize students with and build their knowledge of computers-architecture, b) familiarize learners with the use of X (IT Partner) ICT tools in daily office activities and 3) familiarize learners with the use the internet for communication and research.
> **National Institute Pre-service/Distance Education discussion:** There is a need for interaction between those who write curriculum-modules, those who teach them and those who apply them
> **Regional Teacher Education College discussion:** Training for teachers to use the computer to deliver their courses is not deliberately articulated. It is not planned in the curriculum with regard to basic subjects – for example there is no help for a history teacher who wishes to deliver their subject with the assistance of ICT tools. The teaching of ICT is directed toward the literacy-basics – how to use the computer, to access databases.

We need to think more broadly about the use of ICT in teacher education programmes.

In these perspectives the emergent thread of institutional reflection is on the complexity of ICT integration processes, as the Head of the Computer Science Division in the National Institute for Pre-service/Distance Education observed 'ICT is a new field and the challenge is to make it a reality.'

As I moved from one group interview to the next and became more confident and at ease with the AS protocol I observed the rich dynamic that the protocol stimulated in the discussions, as participants explicated the challenges and issues that the integration of technology produces within and beyond the boundaries of their institutional activity-system frameworks. The following extracts present group reflections on the disruptive force of technology that affects cultural practices and creates tensions and contradictions in the underpinning elements of tools, community, rules, roles and responsibilities of their institutional activity systems:

### Regional Teacher Education College discussion
*Community-roles tension:* The structure for ICT programmes is absent. There is no administrative structure and it is difficult to clarify who is involved in the delivery of programmes.

### National Centre In-service discussion
*Tools-rules contradiction:* The timing of the training programmes to coincide with the 1:1 deployment during the period of national examinations was not helpful. Teachers were deterred from experimenting with projects in their practice during the critical post-training phase.

### National Institute Pre-service/Distance Education discussion
*Tools-community contradiction:* The programme dynamic for ICT integration under development in the National Institute is not followed in schools. The programme is not the problem – rather it is the teachers who are adhering to educational objectives that have no clearly defined parameters and assessment standards for ICT integration.

### National Centre – Curriculum and Development discussion
*Rules-community tension:* The standards for all curricula are set by the General Inspectorate. At the same time teachers do have a voice in determining policy and standards through their collaboration on curriculum panels.

The discussions illustrate palpable tensions between different layers of the system for policy-formulation and practice-implementation with correspondent contradictions in assumptions about teachers' appropriation of change and the articulation of their voice in the change-process. I felt, however, that the information emerging from the different sites was rich but fragmented. There was a lack of cross-institutional and multi-voiced reflection and interpretation on the issues from different system-levels.

While the survey-process was a factor in the limitations, I was also beginning to question my role of engagement with participants. Part of the problem certainly was the linear singularity in the analytical process. I interpreted the data-sets from the interviews. I prepared the report-summaries for distribution to each institution for checking. I recognized that part of the problem was the AT's theoretical framework I was using that was in essence exclusionary. The framework could not be easily understood by participants unless they had studied the literature.

A colleague in GeSCI had alerted me to this potential conflict in partnership engagement on researching the use of the tools. He wrote in an email dated 9<sup>th</sup> of January 2009:

> On the role of GeSCI – this might need some sharpening and discussion. Should we use these tools ourselves or should we build the capacity of the relevant stakeholders to use these tools or use a hybrid approach?...
> ...It goes back to the question we have begun asking more regularly – what is the role of GeSCI and what is the role of the stakeholders? I think some clarity might be required. (A. Twinomuguisha, personal communication, January 9, 2009)

**Exploring a 'most significant change' (MSC) mirror**

I was determined to rectify the imbalance in the partnership dialogue in the survey process by incorporating a more participatory approach. I was interested in the potential of the MSC technique both as a means of capturing stories of significant change at different levels and for involving stakeholders' analysis in the selection of story about what constitutes the criteria of success or non-success – of significant or insignificant change.

With the support of staff from the ICT Unit I collected 44 stories from rural and urban zones, capturing data of significant change from the perspectives of primary teachers (nine urban and five rural), secondary teachers (two urban), teacher-educators (three rural), a primary school principal (one urban), a primary school ICT coordinator (one urban), a primary school director of studies (one urban), secondary school students (seven urban), tertiary computer science students (twelve urban), college students with visual impairments (three urban).

Each interview lasted between forty-five minutes and one and a half hours depending on the size of the focus-groups. All interviews were recorded with the permission of participants. Like the AS protocol and as suggested in the MSC literature (Davies and Dart 2005) I initiated each interview with a broad opening question as a starting point of the type: 'Since the computers came into your classroom (or since you started using technology in your classroom), what has been the most significant change in your practice?'

My preference was to use the MSC protocol in focus-group interviews to explore the group interaction that sharing stories might trigger. The following extract is from the very first focus-group discussion I conducted with a group of seven urban primary teachers who were introducing 1:1 laptops in their classrooms (Appendix A). All research participants are identified by pseudonyms in deference to research-agreement stipulations for confidentiality. In the extract, the story of Teacher Anastase has triggered a group-reflection as to whether his learners' tendency to play with the computer-software during class should be considered a positive or negative story of change. An audio of the extract can be accessed at http://gesci.org/old/files/docman/Audio1TLICT.wma.

> **Teacher Anastase said:** The children they like all those things which, only girls in the laptops, they like music, I don't know if you have mentioned 'snappy', other things I think can cause... cannot be easy for the teacher to teach another thing as you said...
> **Teacher Jacqueline said:** Another thing he says, (Teacher Anastase) says that the student he likes to play music and he says that he says that it is a negative point and his neighbour says that it is not negative because

actually the student, they want to discover so many things on their laptops…

…it is not negative because it is the beginning, when it is the beginning the laptops, the children need to discover, they need to play, they need to do so many things on the laptops…

The struggle to categorize Teacher Anastase's story is prompting the group to reflect on learning and what the group understands by learning. This reflection constitutes perhaps a tentative 'reconceptualization' of their understandings about learning (Butler, 2001). I transcribed all the interviews into a summary document for participant checking (MinEduc-GeSCI, 2009a). An artefact entitled 'Perspectives from Rwanda' developed by my organization on the basis of the stories can be accessed on GeSCI's website.


**Reflection on cycle one**

As an advisor I have always been aware of the dilemmas in our engagement fields and of the failure to translate into practice the values, principles and concepts we espouse in our strategies. I felt a sense of frustration in the first cycle that I had not managed to encourage a more participatory discourse and analysis throughout the survey process.

Having trialled the dialogical tools and frameworks I was satisfied that the use of the tools enabled a rich dynamic of interaction in the focus-group discussions and established a vibrant communication space for reflection on the issues. I was dissatisfied however that the knowledge sharing established in each communication space was fragmented - dissipated as I progressed from one focus group to the next.

I recognized that the survey had limitations in that the institutional homogeneity of the focus-groups diminished the potential for participants to think differently on the issues, as Butler (2001) says, to reconceptualize ideas about professional learning for a digital age.

I became more acutely aware that the partnership in the dialogue was not an equal one and that I was responsible to a degree for the inequity. The theoretical framework that I was utilizing through the interview-protocol was not understood by participants. I was reinforcing the status-quo of the external expert in my use of this framework. I was essentially inhibiting a more authentic level of participation and empowerment in the analysis of the discussion. I was experiencing myself as a 'living contradiction' (Whitehead, 1989, as cited in Whitehead & McNiff, 2006) denying my values for equal partnership and mutual learning in practice.

In my preparation for the second cycle I would need to modify my approach and utilize the tools to encourage a more participatory analysis of the tensions of ICT, their systemic impact and strategies to overcome them.

### Cycle two – creating a communicative space for collective reflection

The focus of my research project in Cycle Two is the partnership discussion analysis which took place during a three day workshop retreat held in Kigali Rwanda from 27 to 29 April 2009 on the theme of *Teacher Professional Development Tomorrow, Today*. The workshop drew together a multi-stakeholder participation of twenty representatives from national institutions for Teacher Professional Development, Curriculum Development, Research and Development Partners. The workshop was jointly coordinated and facilitated by the Ministry of Education (MinEduc) and the Global eSchools and Communities Initiative (GeSCI). Documentation related to global, regional and national trends for ICT-integration in Teacher Professional Development (Butler, 2001; Olakulehin, 2008; Swarts, 2008; UNESCO, 2008a,b,c; Gasane, 2009; Kumar, 2009; Nduwingoma, 2009; Vuningungo, 2009) was disseminated prior to and throughout the workshop to all participants.

The workshop programme outlines the strategic objective of the workshop 'to examine the parameters for ICT integration in Teacher Professional Development (TPD) in Rwanda through the identification of current challenges and possible futures for provision and ways to prepare for future scenarios now.'

## A programme framework for reflection

The challenge posed by the workshop would be in organizing a reflection across a distributed community of stakeholders and institutions. Working with colleagues in the facilitation-team (MinEduc and GeSCI), I assisted in the design of the workshop-sessions to incorporate an exploration of issues and future scenarios for ICT in TPD-models through a three-stage reflection-process of (i) *diagnosis*, (ii) *scenario building*, and (iii) *synthesis*. We determined that the *diagnosis* session should use data from the baseline survey of prevailing practices, to trigger collective reflection and analysis of tensions in the system as a prelude to the *scenario-building*, and *synthesis* sessions.

In the *diagnosis* session of the workshop I gave an overview of the Most Significant Change (MSC) technique and the Activity Systems (AS) model as a basis for introducing the hybrid approach to the workshop discussion. I proposed that we use the approach to analyse episodes of practice from the baseline survey data. I suggested that the use of the hybrid approach would provide us with two 'mirrors' for looking into the ICT use in educational environments:

> **Mirror 1** – 'Most Significant Change' story: Which story from the base line survey represents the most significant change?
> **Mirror 2** – 'Activity Systems' model: What tensions do the stories reveal about educational practice?

### The 'most significant change' mirror

I prepared a purposive sample from the survey data of four practitioner stories of significant change to 'mirror' change practices in programmes affiliated with national pre-service/in-service/school-based ICT in TPD initiatives. I presented the four stories in a group-task for selecting the most significant story about change from the set (Appendix B):

a. Teacher Anastase's story – a primary teacher in a TPD in-service programme for 1:1 laptop-saturation (access to audio at: http://gesci.org/old/files/docman/Audio2MSC.wma);

b. Teacher Alinne's story - a secondary teacher liaison in a TPD partner whole-school programme for IT literacy (access to audio at: http://gesci.org/old/files/docman/Audio-3MSC.wma);

c. Teacher Jacque's story - a secondary teacher newly graduated from a tertiary pre-service programme in Computer Science (access to audio at: http://gesci.org/old/files/docman/Audio4MSC.wma);

d. Student Ronah's story - a secondary student attending an innovative ICT school of excellence (access to audio at: http://gesci.org/old/files/docman/Audio5MSC.wma).

Significantly all groups selected the stories of Teacher Anastase and Student Ronah as the most significant. The change-domains they identified in these stories focus on shifts in the power-relations between the teacher and learner with indicators of the 'teacher emerging as co-learner' and the student 'more confident in using technology than the teacher.' Revealingly the stories of Teachers Alinne and Jacque were not selected by any group.

In the plenary session I questioned participants on whether there was anything to learn from the stories of Teachers Alinne and Jacque. It was at this point that participants suggested that the story of Teacher Alinne in particular represented a narrative of 'most *insignificant* change'. I wondered why her story was deemed insignificant by all of us. I wondered whether Teacher Alinne presented the profile of a 'mainstreamer' or 'late adopter' of technology – a profile representing 'arguably the largest group in education systems and therefore the most important' (Hepp et al., 2004, p. 19). We suggested as a facilitation team that unpacking Teacher Alinne's story – looking more closely at her school-setting using our 'activity-systems' mirror – may reveal something 'significant' about late adopters and their environments.

### The 'activity systems' mirror

As a follow up to her story on Most Significant Change, Teacher Alinne was interviewed using the Activity System protocol (access to audio at: http://gesci.org/old/files/docman/Audio6Interview.wma) (Appendix C). During the interview she was asked about her role and responsibilities as the school-liaison for the IT partner programme. She responded: 'My role in this programme I think is to... to help students and teachers to be in contact with X (IT Partner) – they have to learn something' (Teacher Alinne, personal communication).

I wondered why Teacher Alinne was so hesitant. What are the opportunities and constraints that affect her work? More specifically what is it in her environment that is affecting her capability or her 'cognizant agency' (Sen, 1999, as cited in Leach, 2008, p. 785) to carry out her work? The following extract from the interview suggests a communication tension between staff, school management and the IT partner which prevents Teacher Alinne from introducing the programme in the school:

> **Interviewer:** Do you intend to go on using ICT?
> **Teacher Alinne:** Yes...ah, yes, I can use it if I have an opportunity, ah...
> **Interviewer:** Why do you say if you have an opportunity?

**Teacher Alinne:** Because as I started to say, this is a Centre of X (IT Partner), maybe if they gave us the opportunity to, to teach the programme here, we can go through ICT and use some computers and that...

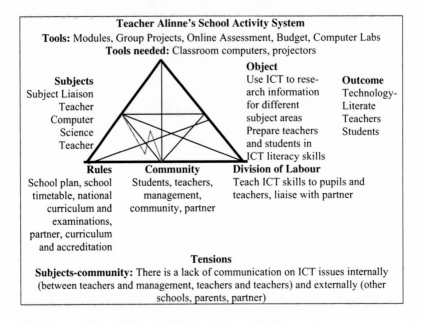

**Teacher Alinne's School Activity System**

**Tools:** Modules, Group Projects, Online Assessment, Budget, Computer Labs
**Tools needed:** Classroom computers, projectors

**Subjects**
Subject Liaison
Teacher
Computer
Science
Teacher

**Object**
Use ICT to rese-
arch information
for different
subject areas
Prepare teachers
and students in
ICT literacy skills

**Outcome**
Technology-
Literate
Teachers
Students

**Rules**
School plan, school
timetable, national
curriculum and
examinations,
partner, curriculum
and accreditation

**Community**
Students, teachers,
management,
community, partner

**Division of Labour**
Teach ICT skills to pupils and
teachers, liaise with partner

**Tensions**
**Subjects-community:** There is a lack of communication on ICT issues internally
(between teachers and management, teachers and teachers) and externally (other
schools, parents, partner)

**Figure 5.**      Activity system tensions in Teacher Alinne's School

We invited participants to participate in a group-discussion analysis of Teacher Alinne's school setting using the Activity Systems mirror. To accommodate the discussions I prepared a group task orientation to provide participants with a general overview of Teacher Alinne's school activity-system that was based on the interview data. Prior to the group discussions I worked through an analysis of a sample of the tension in communication that was emerging in the school community with the introduction of technology (Figure 5).

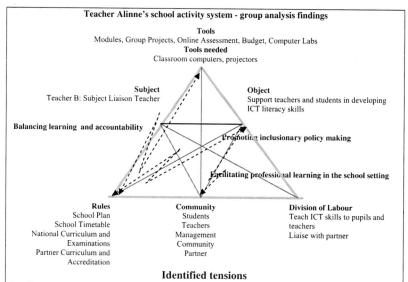

**Teacher Alinne's school activity system - group analysis findings**

**Tools**
Modules, Group Projects, Online Assessment, Budget, Computer Labs
**Tools needed**
Classroom computers, projectors

**Subject**
Teacher B: Subject Liaison Teacher

**Object**
Support teachers and students in developing ICT literacy skills

Balancing learning and accountability

Promoting inclusionary policy making

Facilitating professional learning in the school setting

**Rules**
School Plan
School Timetable
National Curriculum and Examinations
Partner Curriculum and Accreditation

**Community**
Students
Teachers
Management
Community
Partner

**Division of Labour**
Teach ICT skills to pupils and teachers
Liaise with partner

## Identified tensions

*Facilitating professional learning in the school setting*
There is a lack of clarity as to the role of the liaison teacher between the school community and the technology partner to promote school based ICT-TPD programmes. The teachers are not involved in defining the objectives for their training needs. The lack of communication between the liaison teacher and other teachers in the school community inhibits collective participation and inter-disciplinary collaboration within the school and between schools. These tensions were brought about by a lack of established procedures to support partnership activities for facilitating school based capacity building.

*Balancing learning and accountability*
The teacher is anxious over her inability to achieve the ICT literacy objective for all staff within the constraints of the school regulatory environment. Tight time-tables and bureaucratic planning inhibit opportunities for the teachers to research, to direct self-learning to communicate with other teachers on ICT use. The overemphasis on examinations in the school system results in teacher unwillingness to use ICT. The requirement of accountability in the top-down school system creates tension and contradictions that are counterproductive to the development of staff capability. There is little scope for promoting practitioner experimentation to explore the affordances of ICT tools to improve practice and develop more learner centred approaches. Regulations to integrate ICT into the curriculum in the field of assessment would be required to create a more conducive environment for technology oriented change across all curriculum areas.

*Promoting inclusionary policy formulation*
The emerging community of ICT teacher practitioners are not involved in planning policy or contributing to curriculum for ICT use. Teachers tend to be excluded from planning on ICT use in the school environment. The lack of adequate communication between teachers and parents in the community brings about tensions in understanding as to the purpose of ICT integration and teachers encounter a lack of support from the community for experimentation. The extended school community is not consulted or involved in the formulation of objectives.

**Figure 6.**     Activity System representation of results

During the group discussion analysis, participants worked with activity-system models of Teacher Alinne's school-setting on flip-charts. Observing the discussions I was impressed by the manner in which the participants explored tensions across all elements of the activity system expanding the issues in Teacher Alinne's story into a forensic analysis of the education system. The activity-system analysis that the participants presented in plenary represented a rich reflection on the issues from the local to the broader educational perspectives. From the group-discussion analysis I was able to prepare a composite activity-system representing the common themes and tensions which emerged. The significant tensions that the groups identified from Teacher Alinne's school environment included:

- facilitating professional learning in the school setting;
- balancing professional learning with accountability;
- promoting inclusionary policy formulation;

The significant tensions in Teacher Alinne's school activity system are explored more fully in Figure 6. The tensions and contradictions illustrate the complexity of the change process in educational settings. They further demonstrate the 'insignificance' of introducing technology if there is insufficient capacity and knowledge within the system 'to develop new processes, to alter institutional settings and to effectively utilize the given technology' (Pulkkinen, 2009).

### Reflection on cycle two

Cycle two was significant because I focused on encouraging arrangements for a communicative space in which to engage partners in a more collaborative approach for joint knowledge building. In adapting the narrative and dialogical tools into a hybrid approach my aim was to encourage a more equitable communication process for dialogue, knowledge building and mutual learning. I could see in the diagnostic stage of the workshop process that participants who had limited knowledge of the theories behind the hybrid approach were able (i) to appreciate its structure and (ii) to access and use tools for discussion-analysis on complex issues of the integration of technology in systems.

Throughout the workshop I took photographs and video-taped snatches of group discussions and plenary sessions. My tutor Yvonne Crotty had worked with us in Dublin City University on using photography, audio taping and video-taping tools to document, to capture and to store conversations and recordings of reality of our practice for retrieval and evaluation later.

The workshop photo gallery and video-artefact document the quality of participant engagement in the workshop process. The photographs seem to show participants' ease in using the 'Most Significant Change' and 'Activity System' theoretical tools and frameworks to reflect deeply and interactively on the issues and to envision scenarios and development paths for ICT in TPD.

The video montage is somewhat jerky. It is a product of my circulation from group to group with my mini camcorder attempting to 'capture' the group discussion dynamic as the deeper reflection on the issues took hold. This was perhaps a contradictory endeavour as the roving eye of the camcorder may have been perceived by some as somewhat intrusive.

There is one episode in the video however that in my view presents a 'most significant moment' or a 'critical episode' that shows a nuanced improvement in our work of engagement with partners. It is the moment where my colleague and co-facilitator Dr. Patti Swarts spontaneously asks participants for their opinion on the manner of our facilitation of the workshop. She then explains:

> **Dr. Patti Swarts**: I'm sure you've also noticed that we (GeSCI facilitators) didn't really participate in the group-work and that was intentional... The issue was... we didn't want to interfere in that dynamic because both Mary and I... we are... you know we provide certain perspectives but we don't want to influence the discussion in the group,

we wanted you to discuss with each other and not try and explain things to Mary and myself... but to discuss with each other...

It is precisely in this moment that my colleague describes my values, our team values, our organizational values to the group. She articulates our commitment to a dialogue with our partners that is 'about their view and ours' (Freire, 1970, p. 77) – in which each can make their own unique contribution to the dialogue and each can come to know in their own way. These are the ontological values and standards I believe that we have embodied in our tacit being and understanding and which we have turned into our epistemological values and standards for our work, standards by which we assess our practice and with which we invite others to assess our work.

### Reflection on my research

I began this research because of my commitment to the social purpose inherent in my organization's strategic vision for building a *Knowledge Society for All* (GeSCI, 2008). I value the capacity of other people, my colleagues and my partners to come to know in their own way. This is evident in the way I became aware in the first cycle of this research that I can negate my values in practice and bring inequities into the partner-dialogue in the fragile environments of our engagements. In order to address this contradiction I have been continuously engaging with the literature, participating in DCU Collaboratory forums, researching theoretical frameworks, reflecting on my own learning in order to improve my practice in assisting knowledge-building and sharing partnerships in our engagements.

I now believe that it is possible to create a space for communication to encourage inclusionary multi-layered and multi-voiced dialogue in our partner engagements. I have experienced the rich potential of the dynamic of communication in that space to push the boundaries of our thinking jointly, and I am both excited by its possibilities and wary of its tentative nature. I have come to understand that I must continue to reflect on my practice, to value mutual learning, to sense the contradiction in the actions of my engagement with partners, in order to live my values.

I believe that I have influenced the learning of colleagues and partners. The workshop process, using the hybrid model, provided opportunities for participants properly to understand the issues, their significance or insignificance and their impact on educational activity-systems. In this approach, partners were able to clarify and take ownership of the issues from individual, institutional and systemic perspectives and to design their own development paths for the way forward.

### The validity of my research inquiry

During the process of undertaking this research, I formally presented my work on two occasions on the 4th and 25th May within a peer validation group setting – on the former occasion in the presence of Dr. Jack Whitehead. The peer validation meeting is a requirement of the Masters in Education and Training Management programme (eLearning strand). The purpose of a validation meeting is to provide practitioner-researchers with the opportunity to present their research to others.

Validation also enables participants to gain new insights into the research process (Farren, 2008). Following the validation session on the 4th May, Dr. Jack Whitehead shared the following reflection in an email on my use of Activity Theory in the generation of my own living educational theory:

> I've been thinking about your engagement with cultural-historical activity theory in relation to the creation of your own living educational theory... There is a way of thinking about your living educational theory as a 'potentially shared object' of 'activity theory...' I make my living theory available through the web as a 'potentially shared object' for understanding dialogue, multiple perspectives and voices, and networks of interacting activity systems. I also make it available with the intention of helping others in responding to their questions 'How do I improve what I

am doing?' in their community and workplace contexts and in making their own unique contributions to public knowledge (J. Whitehead, personal communication, May 12, 2009).

In this way I engaged in critical reflection throughout the research inquiry with colleagues and peers in general and with my supervisor, Dr. Margaret Farren in particular. In our meetings before and after my visits to Rwanda we discussed issues such as using Activity Theory as a method of analysis and integrating this into Living Theory. We had several discussions on my use of the Activity System and Most Significant Change tools and frameworks in the first cycle and the need to adapt these tools in the second cycle to encourage a more equitable communication space for dialogue and knowledge-building.

From these processes of feedback, critical reflection and learning I believe that I have adhered to Habermas' (1998, as cited in McNiff & Whitehead, 2006) criteria of social validity, in presenting an account of my work that is comprehensible, truthful, sincere and appropriate to the context of my engagement with partners.

I believe my research-account is comprehensible in that the process of inquiry documents an emerging *conscientization* (Freire, 1970) on how I actually lived my values in practice. As I worked through each cycle of engagement I came to a realization through self and peer reflection of the contradictions and inequities that I was promoting in partner-dialogue. These inequities were occurring as I denied my values and the values of our organization by using tools in a manner that was exclusionary.

I believe my explanation is truthful, sincere and appropriate in the way it illustrates the emergence of my embodied consciousness of my values as I came to recognize the contradictions in my practice and focused on adapting the tools and frameworks to promote a more inclusionary process for authentic dialogue and mutual learning.

My explanation documents the potential in the 'shared object' of Living Educational Theory and Activity Theory to effect a deeper understanding of the multiple perspectives and voices that emerged through the cycles of the research process – voices that engaged in debate, discussion, analysis, validation and ultimately in expansive learning.

## FUTURE ACTION

### A hybrid approach for knowledge-building and sharing

I have shown that improvement in practice was achieved through action research cycles exploring the use of a hybrid 'Most Significant Change' and 'Activity Theory' approach for fostering authentic cross-institutional dialogue on ICT in Teacher Professional Development (TPD).

The first cycle of the research revealed the disconnections and tensions that exist within and across institutional activity systems on policy, planning and practice in ICT-TPD programmes and initiatives. The use of the hybrid approach in the second cycle of the research enabled key stakeholders from professional development, curriculum development and research institutions to jointly engage in constructive discussion on the issues emerging from the 'thick description' (Geertz, 1973, as cited in Davis & Dart, 2005) of the *practitioner narrative* and from the tensions and contradictions of the *activity system analysis* components of the approach.

The research was limited however to investigating the dynamic interactions that emerged during one multi-stakeholder workshop process. As the research findings lack an in-depth historical perspective, I recommend that we engage our partners in multiple action research iterations of narrative and activity system-analysis of the ICT-TPD landscape in national and regional programmes. A comparative study of national and regional experiences and solutions over time could help us build a better picture on sources of tension in the integration of technology within the broader professional development-landscape and promote mutual learning on strategies to overcome these.

I conclude that I have gone some way towards creating a communication space that is not simply confined to the building and sharing of knowledge but that is inclusionary and promotes each stakeholder's *active participation* in the process of the creation of knowledge.

## APPENDIX A

### Stories of 'positive' and 'negative' change

*All research participants are identified by pseudonyms in deference to research agreement stipulations for confidentiality. Stories were presented for the most part in English – a second or third language for most participants. In Rwanda the official languages are Kinyarwanda, English and French.*

The following is an extract from a focus group discussion I conducted with a group of seven urban primary teachers who were introducing 1:1 laptops in their classrooms. In the extract they ponder on what constitutes 'positive' or 'negative' change (http://gesci.org/old/files/docman/Audio1TLICT.wma).

> **Anastase:** Another point we have forgotten and which is important to remember, ah the children, the discipline of the children, have you seen the discipline how the children are disciplined if you tell them I will not give you the computer, they will keep quiet in the classroom, anything you ask them, you make the condition of not giving them the laptops, the work is done very well, the condition of not giving them the computer, the work is done very well? That is another thing I mentioned. But a negative thing I have mentioned, the children they like all those things which, only girls in the laptops, they like music, I don't know if you have mentioned 'snappy', other things which I think can cause cannot be easy for the teacher to teach another thing as you said.

> **James (librarian/ ICT technician):** There is also another positive effect he mentioned earlier, saying that there is no more to come late at school, because for him in his class, the students in his class, whoever comes late he never gives them a laptop, for now all the students arrive at school on time, they are punctual now because of that.

> **Jacqueline:** Another thing that he says, he says that the student he likes to play music and he says that he says that it is a negative point and his neighbour says that it is not negative because actually the student, they want to discover so many things on their laptops, because there is another programme that the X (IT Partner) will import in our laptops, which will give, which will permit us to connect my activity to my children's, it means that the menu is called sharing, sharing activities, but that kind of programme is not available now, because that programme is not available, when you teach the laptops, the children do everything they want on the laptops (yes... ok...) because we don't have some work on our laptops (yes...) that is not negative because it is the beginning, when it is the

beginning... the laptops... the children need to discover, they need to play, they need to do so many things on the laptops, I think that they if they play music, it is not negative, because they don't have something to do.

**Anastase:** I can support that because I think that if we accept that the children to have computers, these laptops during the holidays, so that they be familiar to the computer, so that when we start the New Year, ah the children will have already become familiar to the computer. The reason why it is disturbing now is because the time goes the children will think about other things...

## APPENDIX B

### Four stories of significant change

*All research participants are identified by pseudonyms in deference to research agreement stipulations for confidentiality.*

*Stories were presented for the most part in English – a second or third language for most participants. In Rwanda the official languages are Kinyarwanda, English and French.*

**Teacher Anastase:** Primary teacher attending school-based in-service programme for use of 1:1 laptop technology.
*Interviewer (addressing a focus group of primary teachers): Since the laptops came into your school and into your classroom, what has been the most significant change for you in your practice?*
**Teacher Anastase's Story**
(http://gesci.org/old/files/docman/Audio2MSC.wma)
Ok in my classroom I think I am now holding a very heavy task to avail the children to use the laptops – they like laptops very much - they want to survey what is being done in computers - the laptops – they discover so many things which I myself did not know them for – they also to teach me – I gain from them – although it is my secret that I did not know before – but sometimes I meet something they have written somewhere which I did not know – something like that (inaudible)... yeah, they want to use laptops, to be with laptops fluently for hours...that it was not easy to prepare them for the terminal examination this year ...yeah we were very strict too – but they were annoyed always – they wanted to remain with laptops in their hands.. and they want to be with them even at home, sometimes, eh, first there is very great pressure eh... with the children – but I can say on my behalf I wanted to learn about the computer before this time, but ah, as soon as the programme has come on at my school, I gained a lot from the laptop, I can now write and punctuate my data, and keep into in the computer... (inaudible)... I can keep my reports, I have already reached the internet and I can communicate with the world outside the country, I'm very happy with it...
**Teacher Alinne:** Secondary teacher liaison attending joint university/technology partner in-service ICT literacy programme for whole school integration of ICT.
*Interviewer: From your point of view, can you tell a story ah...which describes the most significant change in your practice as a teacher that ICT has brought, or that computers have brought in your practice as a teacher?*

**Teacher Alinne's Story** (http://gesci.org/old/files/docman/Audio-3MSC.wma)
Emmm...Ah, ok... I don't know what to do, ah, to say, but, for me, emm...
it was a good occasion to learn about computers because, I did at
University only language, so it was my first time to... to be in contact with
computers, ah... to open it, you know, practice and we learn about all
programmes, excel, word, windows, and whatever, as you see, I don't
know...em...
*Interviewer: The question is, has these... this access to computer skills
brought about a significant change in your practice as a teacher?*
**Teacher Alinne:** As a teacher now I can use computer ah... maybe in
making into certificates, I can do it myself, yeah... that's all... emmm...
*Interviewer: No other significant change... where you use computers...*
**Teacher Alinne:** I don't think so.
*Interviewer: Do you have access to a computer yourself?*
**Teacher Alinne:** Yes, I have my own laptop at home.
*Interviewer: Do you use the laptop for any aspect of your professional
practice, your work as a teacher of English?*
**Teacher Alinne:** Yeah, I can use it ah... when I want to mark ah... notes,
marks for students...em... the certificate, when they want to leave the
school and I can go Internet, because I have a modem, MTN modem...
yes... that's it...
*Interviewer: Why is it important to..., ah...you mentioned quite a bit the
certificates and the students' marks, why is this significant, why is this
important?*
**Teacher Alinne:** Maybe for the internet, you can say that when you have
it, you have your own work in your hand, you can get news...ah... and
many things... and be informed with many things with the internet...
*Interviewer: And, but you also mentioned the student marking and the
certificates – why is that important... the use of the computer important for
that in your practice? Why does that make a difference?*
**Teacher Alinne:** The difference is that maybe when we are working with
your pen and paper, it can be... it can take more time, but with the
computer it's ok... and even the paper it's very clear, instead of writing by
the pen...
**Teacher Jacque:** Secondary teacher newly qualified graduate in
Computer Science.
*Interviewer: You are the computer science teacher in the school. What
significant change do you think computers are bringing to teaching and
learning in this secondary school?*
**Teacher Jacque's Story** (http://gesci.org/old/files/docman/Audio4MSC.wma)
Ah, well, the use of computer is of great importance, because if students
are taught nicely how to use them, the computer can help them in their
activities. For example, when I can say, according to what I'm teaching, to
what I'm telling the students right now, because now if I'm introducing,

they are studying the introduction to computers, the introduction VITE, where they come from and what is the history of it, and how can they use the computer, how can they use ICT to develop their country, to develop the individual, all they know, and if everybody, if a student knows how to manipulate, how to use computer, writing a text, writing a document and so on, or how a student can be, can know how to search, he or she goes to the computer, goes to a certain website, she can put a word like maybe biology, and she'll be able to get more detail about something, so the student get that information on how computers are used and how they can use that information, playing games, chatting, and if they can know beyond that, beyond playing games, beyond chatting and so on, but if they can know computer, how they can do some research concerning the other subjects, for example, if it is mathematics, physics, we know there are some sites, that they have detail, that they have information that are detailed, also some books here, because we tell them to go to the library to read, but also another way round if the computer or internet is used, they will do his own, his work, that's one, if they understand how they can used, oh, something else, they can communicate with one another, writing messages, they can communicate, so if a student or student here understand that, how a computer is used, I think it will make a great significant eh... today...

**Student Ronah (G12)** - Girls' Secondary School.

*Interviewer (addressing a focus group of secondary students): ...Now you use computers, so what difference has it made to your studies? Can you tell a story which describes the most significant change, the most important difference? Anyone?*

**Student Ronah's Story** (http://gesci.org/old/files/docman/Audio5MSC.wma)
Ok, thank you. As my friends also say that it was a change to us, and once we started doing our researches on the computer, it was like we used to think that maybe you are the only person taking that course, maybe this chemistry is kind of like too tough or something, but when you go there you get the opportunity to do your research, make research and you meet other students, other children from all over the world, who tell you that you know, they're doing the same thing, and you interchange ideas, you get their programme, you get... that's how you get the more explanations.. I think that, that's what kind of, that's the most thing that's the most thing that's emphasizing, that's impressed me in the computer thing, cos you meet new people and you know that if other people are doing it why can't I, I can also do this computers has made has brought this (inaudible) between us.

*Interviewer: Why is it different? Why is it significant to you to actually meet other students who are studying in these areas? Why is that important?*

The important thing is that, when you're studying a course and, as mostly people say, two heads are better than one, when you get someone you know that there is a student somewhere in Miami, there is a student in London who is taking the same course, we are doing the same things, so, it's like, you develop that spirit of togetherness, now we are doing the things together and of course when you go for research, she is helping you, he is helping you, you are also doing the same, and...

## GROUP CRITERIA FOR STORY SELECTION

### Teacher Anastase's Story

Shift in teacher role:

- teacher is no longer the gatekeeper of knowledge;
- teacher is emerging as co-learner - learning with and from students about the technology;

Shift in pedagogy:

- student-centred approach;
- discovering learning through exploring.

ICT as catalyst for change:

- ICTs can change pedagogy;
- student can become 'addicted' and distracted from learning;
- 'war' inside teacher leading to anxiety.

### Student Ronah's Story

Shift in learner role:

- from passive to active engagement;
- student more confident in using technology than teacher.

Shift in pedagogy:

- Learning becomes real - changes worldview;

- Student can learn from research, team work, communication (self-learning).

ICT as catalyst for change:

- ICT breaking down geographic barriers - world accessible through the internet;
- 3d multi-media dynamic learning instead of 2d static learning;
- interactivity for student;
- Education For All Relationship.

ICT tool focus:

- Focus of student – use of ICT as a tool for learning;
- Focus of teacher – use ICT to teach technology literacy.

## APPENDIX C

### Activity system interview transcript

*All research participants are identified by pseudonyms in deference to research agreement stipulations for confidentiality.*

*Interviews were conducted in English – a second or third language for most participants. In Rwanda the official languages are Kinyarwanda, English and French.*

### INTERVIEW TRANSCRIPT - TEACHERS ALINNE & JACQUE

(http://gesci.org/old/files/docman/Audio6Interview.wma)

#### Programme goals

*Interviewer: What are the most important factors that encourage you to use ICT in your personal or your professional practice?*
**Teacher Alinne:** I say that ICT make life easy, emm... it's easy and simple with ICT.
*Interviewer: And when you say make life easy, ah, what, how, what is it in your professional life that you want made easy?*
**Teacher Alinne:** Ok, I mean when you want to look for information, instead of coming here through books and library, you can go through Google and you can find something and write it down, you can find something to say, to teach your students.
*Interviewer: Do you plan to go on using ICT?*
**Teacher Alinne:** Yes...ah, yes, I can use it if I have an opportunity, ah...
*Interviewer: And why do you say if you have an opportunity?*
**Teacher Alinne:** Because as I started to say, this is a Centre of X (IT Partner), maybe if they gave us the opportunity to, to teach the programme here, we can go through ICT and use some computers and that...
*Interviewer: Why do you think there hasn't been that opportunity?*
**Teacher Alinne:** Because we have to have an extra time. Yeah. The fact it may be during the weekend and it's not easy.
*Interviewer: Who would you be working with during the weekend?*
**Teacher Alinne:** Maybe some teachers and students, if possible, because they are here, they live here, for students no problem, maybe teachers I don't know...ah...

**Tools**

*Interviewer: What are the ICT tools that you would be using in this programme?*
**Teacher Alinne:** We need computer, em...projector, I think...
*Interviewer: Do you have any manuals?*
**Teacher Alinne:** Yeah, we have her school properties. Yeah we have to use school properties, and they have it here. We have to... to use what we have here at school.
*Interviewer: What methods, what approaches would you be using in this course?*
**Teacher Alinne:** Normally they gave us notes, we have to read notes and we have some projects and then we can ah… do tests...that's what we have in the programme... and everything is online.
*Interviewer: The course is online? So the projects that you do… are they for individuals or for groups?*
**Teacher Alinne:** For groups
*Interviewer: Can you describe the projects?*
**Teacher Alinne:** How?
*Interviewer: What is that you do in groups?*
**Teacher Alinne:** The projects are for groups – in groups you normally give notes, after reading notes we can do quiz, after doing the quiz, now you can do a test, the quiz is in notes, but the test, you have to do it online and there are specific hours that you have to, only one hour.. and they can, they can give you maybe 40 questions, and you have to do them in only one hour.
*Interviewer: What is the actual goal in this programme, what is the objective?*
**Teacher Alinne:** The objective is emm... ah....
*Interviewer: What do you... When you carry out the programme with other teachers and students, what is the purpose, what will they have by the end of the programme?*
**Teacher Alinne:** I think that all (inaudible) is about ICT, about computer and programme, different programmes.
*Interviewer: So the evaluation online is carried out externally...*
**Teacher Alinne:** Emm...


**Roles and responsibilities**

*Interviewer: So what is your role in this programme?*

**Teacher Alinne:** My role in this programme I think is to... to help students or teachers to be in contact with X (IT Partner) – they have to learn something.
*Interviewer: So it's to facilitate contact...*
**Teacher Alinne:** Yes...
*Interviewer: Do you have any responsibilities?*
**Teacher Alinne:** For now, no. I didn't start yet.
*Interviewer: Do you have any information on the responsibilities you will have?*
**Teacher Alinne:** Yes, we have everything – after we completed, they gave us everything, about X (IT Partner), about what you can do at school.
*Interviewer: Do you find that the school administration is supportive for this programme?*
**Teacher Alinne:** Yes. The problem is time, the problem is time, but they know.
*Interviewer: Time in the school calendar...*
**Teacher Alinne:** The availability of teachers, I don't know...They have to think about it.

**Community**

*Interviewer: Is there collaboration among teachers in the school on ICT? Do you collaborate with each other on ICT in your programmes, inside the school?*
**Teacher Alinne:** Inside, inside?
*Interviewer: Yes here in the school... about the use of ICT in teaching and learning, do you collaborate, do you meet, do you discuss how it can be used in teaching and learning?*
**Teacher Jacque:** Well for now, for now no, because well, this is the beginning of the year whereby the teacher has a lot of, many periods, 27, 28, like that, so you find that eh, eh, we are not yet permitted to get time to discuss about it, how they can use ICT in general, in their respective subjects, for now not yet, but maybe we can put in the plan for few months to come, maybe, and maybe we can see if it is possible to administration, and maybe other teachers we can talk, and we can discuss during our holidays we can see if there is time, during our holidays, because some of them they don't know ICT, they find if now they are poor, some of them actually they don't know, but if we can discuss with the teachers, during our time, our free time, and we can say, we can help each other...
*Interviewer: Em... you have pointed out also school planning... emm... bringing it into ah... the school plan. Is there any other reason why teachers would not collaborate on ICT?*

**Teacher Jacque:** Well the first point was that about time, if I am not mistaken, there is a low priority behind, they value time, but also priority, low priority should be there. Eh, two, maybe we could talk about them, maybe other responsibilities that they have, maybe to, because if time collapses, that is four thirty, everyone has to go to family, to see how we can plan to show him, and he has family, so maybe you find that they have a lot of responsibility to learn... I don't know if I am clear...

*Interviewer: You're very clear... Is there any other reason you think that teachers don't collaborate on ICT... one is obviously time... if ICT is a low priority what are the high priorities?*

**Teacher Alinne:** The high priorities eh... for teachers to prepare notes for what they have to teach their students in their subjects... and marking... that is what I think...

## Rules and regulations

*Interviewer: And... what about for example... other rules and regulations that might influence teachers... for example assessment and examinations... you talked about marking quite a bit... Is this a high priority for teachers?*

**Teacher Alinne:** Yes.

*Interviewer: Why?*

**Teacher Alinne:** Because you have to evaluate students in your subjects... em...

*Interviewer: And why is this important?*

**Teacher Alinne:** Maybe, they, what they, in marking they have to use the computer, then maybe you can have time to explain something, when they are marking, the use of excel, you can get time to, the opportunity...

*Interviewer: If the computer is used for marking and for examinations, this will be useful to teachers, but otherwise it is not useful.*

**Teacher Alinne:** Emm... yes...

*Interviewer: Why not?*

**Teacher Alinne:** I don't know... Emm...

*Interviewer: Why is it a low priority?*

**Teacher Alinne:** Emm...

**Teacher Jacque:** Emmm... maybe you can say that it's a new, a new innovation, it's still new, so if a teacher has been spending twenty years teaching mathematics and physics for example, ten with experiences, telling him to go to a computer to use what and what, that's why I say it's a low priority...

*Interviewer: Thank you very much. We talked about teachers in the school looking at ICT. Do you ever communicate with other teachers in other schools about ICT?*

**Teacher Jacque:** But maybe… Actually that's what I am, I want to, for the few months to come, maybe to start. But, for now, I have been meeting other teachers at different schools, how they are going on, like that, but not so much actually, not so much, because for the last two months, we are starting…

*Interviewer: And I would like to thank you very much.*

**Teachers Alinne and Jacque:** You're welcome.

## REFERENCES

Addo, H. (2001). Utilizing information and communication technology for education and development: Issues and challenges for developing countries. *IFLA Journal, 27*(3), 143-151

Agalianos, A., Noss, R., & Whitty, G. (2001). Logo in mainstream schools: The struggle over the soul of an educational innovation. *British Journal of Sociology of Education, 22*(4), 479 – 500.

Ainscow, M., & Miles, S. (2008). Making education for all inclusive: Where next?. *Prospects, 38*(1), 15-24.

Burkhardt, G., Monsour, M., Valdez, G., Gunn, C., Dawson, M., Lemke, C., et al. (2003). *enGgauge 21$^{st}$ century skills: Literacy in the digital age.* Naperville: NCREL and METIRI.

Butler, D. (2001). *Reconceptualising teacher learning in a digital context.* Retrieved October 3, 2008, from http://empoweringminds.spd.dcu.ie/documents/doc-index?category=temporary

Butler, D., & Leahy, M. (2003). *The TeachNet Ireland Project as a model for professional development for teachers.* Dublin: St, Patrick's College of Education, Dublin City University.

Center for Activity Theory and Development Work Research (2003). *The Activity System.* Retrieved April 19, 2009, from http://www.edu.helsinki.fi/activity/pages/chatanddwr/activitysystem

Cohen, L., Manion, L., & Morrison, K. (2007). *Research methods in education* (6$^{th}$ ed.). London: Routledge.

Coolahan, J. (2002). Teacher education and the teaching career in an era of lifelong learning. *OECD Education Working Papers, 2*, OECD Publishing. doi:10.1787/226408628504.

Davis, N. (2000). International contrast of information technology in teacher education: Multiple perspectives of change. Editorial. *Journal of Technology for Teacher Education, 9*(2), 139-147.

Davis, R., & Dart, J. (2005). *The 'Most Significant Change' (MSC) technique: A Guide to its use.* Retrieved July 7, 2009 from http://www.mande.co.uk/docs/MSCGuide.pdf

Demirsalem, Y., & Usluel, Y. K. (2008). ICT integration processes in Turkish schools: Using activity theory to study issues and contradictions. *Australasian Journal of Educational Technology, 24*(4), 458-474.

Dladla, N., & Moon, B. (2002, August). *Challenging the assumptions about teacher education and training in Sub-Saharan Africa: A new role for open learning and ICT.* Paper presented to the Pan-Commonwealth Forum on Open Learning International Convention Centre, Durban, South Africa. Retrieved        April        4,        2009,        from http://www.open.ac.uk/deep/Public/web/publications/pdfs/NDladlaBMoon 2002-PCF.pdf

Drenoyianni, H. (2006). Reconsidering change and ICT: Perspectives of a human and democratic education. *Education and Information Technologies, 11*(3), 401-413.

Engestrom, Y. (2001). Expansive learning at work: Toward and activity theoretical reconceptualization. *Journal of Education and Work, 14*(1), 133-156.

Engestrom, R. (2003). *Change lab – a new perspective to teachers' professional development.*        Retrieved        April        19,        2009,        from www.witfor.org.bw/doc/dr_ritva_education.ppt

Evoh, C. J. (2007). Collaborative partnerships and the transformation of secondary education through ICTs in South Africa. *Educational Media International, 44*(2), 81-98.

Farrell, G., Isaacs, S., & Trucano, M. (Eds.). (2007). *Survey of ICT in education in Africa (Vol. 2): 53 country reports.* Retrieved June 4, 2009, from http://www.infodev.org/en/Publication.354.html

Farren, M. (2007). How am I creating a pedagogy of the unique through a web of betweenness with a new epistemology for educational knowledge? *Action Research Expeditions, December, 2007.* Retrieved October 21, 2008, from http://doras.dcu.ie/669/

Farren, M. (2008). Co-creating an educational space. *Educational Journal of Living Theories, 1*(1), 50-68.

Freire, P. (1970). *Pedagogy of the Oppressed.* London: Penguin.

Gasane, J. (2009). *ICT training and research center.* Retrieved May 18, 2009, from http://www.gesci.org/old/files/docman/Presentation_RITC.ppt

Global eSchools and Communities Initiative. (2008). *Strategic plan 2009 – 2011: Building a knowledge society for all.* Retrieved April 19, 2009, from http://www.gesci.org/index.php?option=com_content&task=view&id=197 &Itemid=64

Global eSchools and Communities Initiative. (2009a). Perspectives from Rwanda [Video file]. Video posted to http://vimeo.com/4884345

Global eSchools and Communities Initiative. (2009b). ICT in teacher professional development        –        Rwanda        [Video        file].        Video        posted        to http://www.vimeo.com/6030825

Government of Rwanda (2005). *Integrated ICT-led socio-economic development (NICI 2006 - 2010) plan.* Retrieved July 28, 2009, from http://www.uneca.org/aisi/NICI/country_profiles/rwanda/rwanpap3.htm

Hakkarainen, K., Engestrom, R., Miettinen, R., Sinko, M., Virkkunen, J., Aston, M., Hardman, J., Nleya, P., & Senteni, A. (2008). *A research plan for the academy of Finland.* Helsinki: University of Helsinki.

Hardman, J. (2004). Activity theory as a framework for understanding teachers' perceptions of computer usage at a primary school level in South Africa. *South African Journal of Education, 25*(4), 258–265.

Hepp, P. K., Hinostroza, S., Laval, M. E., & Rehbein, L. F. (2004). *Technology in schools – sducation, ICT and the knowledge society.* Retrieved June 6, 2009, from http://siteresources.worldbank.org/EDUCATION/Resources/278200-1099079877269/547664-1099079947580/ICT_report_oct04a.pdf

Isaacs, S. (2006). *Towards a GeSCI initiative on teacher professional development in Africa.* Dublin: GeSCI.

Isroff, K., & Scanlon, E. (2001). *Case studies revisited: What can activity theory offer?.* Retrieved December 21, 2008, from http://209.85.229.132/search?q=cache:MEopeQrNdW4J:www.ll.unimaas.nl/euro-cscl/Papers/73.doc+Case+Studies+Revisted:+What+can+Activity+Theory+offer%3F&hl=en&ct=clnk&cd=1&gl=ie&client=firefox-a

Kennedy, A. (2005). Models for continuing professional development: A framework for Analysis. *Journal of In-Service Education, 31*(2), 235-250.

Kumar, S. (2009). *Problem definition: Teacher professional development in the area of ICT in education.* Kigali: MinEduc.

Leach, J. (2008). Do new information and communications technologies have a role to play in the achievement of education for all? *British Educational Research Journal, 34*(6), 783 – 805.

Lim, C. P., & Hang, D. (2003). An activity theory approach to research of ICT integration in Singapore schools. *Computers and Education, 41*(1), 49-63.

Mandinach, E. B. (2005). The development of effective evaluation methods for e-learning: A concept paper and action plan. *Teachers College Record, 107*(8), 1814-1835.

McNiff, J., & Whitehead, J. (2006). *All you need to know about Action Research.* London: Sage Publications.

Ministry of Education. (2008). *Rwanda ICT in Education Policy* (Draft). Kigali: MinEduc.

Ministry of Education (MinEduc) & Global eSchools and Communities Initiative (GeSCI). (2009a). *Survey summary of the information and communication technology in teacher professional development landscape* (internal document). Kigali: MinEduc-GeSCI.

Ministry of Education (MinEduc) & Global eSchools and Communities Initiative (GeSCI). (2009b). Teacher professional development for today, tomorrow [Slide show file]. Slide show posted to http://www.flickr.com/photos/38180567@N05/show/

Ministry of Education (MinEduc) and Global eSchools and Communities Initiative (GeSCI). (2009c). *Workshop report and evaluation: Teacher professional development for today, tomorrow*. Kigali: MinEduc-GeSCI.

Ministry of Education (MinEduc) and Global eSchools and Communities Initiative (GeSCI). (2009d). Teacher professional development for today, tomorrow: Workshop evaluation [Online Survey]. Retrieved from http://www.surveymonkey.com/sr.aspx?sm=j4S3QJgs_2b3UiIA2D1CYX 4BVr2HxOsztdV7JJAXqKCTA_3d

Ministry of Finance and Economic Planning (MinEcoFin). (2001). *Vision 2020*. Retrieved August 17, 2009, from http://www.minecofin.gov.rw/en/inno-read_article.php?articleId=52

Mukama, E. and Andersson, S. B. (2008). Coping with change in ICT-based learning environments: newly qualified Rwandan teachers' reflections. *Journal of Computer Assisted Learning, 24*(2), 156 – 166.

Nduwingoma, M. (2009). *Overview of Rwanda: Teacher professional development in ICT programmes Pre-service and In-service*. Retrieved May 14, 2009, from http://www.gesci.org/old/files/docman/Presentation_Head_Computer_Scie nce_KIE.ppt

O'Sullivan, M. (2004). The reconceptualisation of learner-centred approaches: a Namibian case study. *International Journal of Educational Development, 24*(6), 585-602.

Olakulehin, F. K. (2007). Information and communication technologies in teacher training and professional development in Nigeria. *Turkish Online Journal of Distance Education, 8*(1), 133-142.

Ottevanger, W., van den Akker, J., & de Feiter, L. (2007). *Developing science, mathematics, and ICT education in sub-Saharan Africa: Patterns and promising practices*. Washington, D. C.: World Bank Africa Region Human Development Department.

Pelgrum, W. J., & Law, N. (2003). *ICT in education around the world: trends, problems and prospects*. Paris: UNESCO.

Pulkkinen, J. (2009, March 11). Preliminary conclusions and the way froward. Message posted to http://un-gaid.ning.com/forum/topics/preliminary-conclusions-and-1

Ramalingam, B., & Jones, H. (2008). *Exploring the science of complexity: Ideas and implications for development and humanitarian efforts*. Retrieved June 16, 2009, from http://www.odi.org.uk/resources/download/583.pdf

Robertson, I. (2008). Sustainable e-learning, activity theory and professional development. In R. Atkinson & C. McBeath (Eds.), *Hello! Where are you in the landscape of educational technology? Proceedings ascilite Melbourne 2008*. Retrieved January 6, 2009, from http://www.ascilite.org.au/conferences/melbourne08/procs/robertson.pdf

Swarts, P. (2006). *Teacher professional development workshop report*. Dublin: GeSCI.

Swarts, P. (2008). *Perspectives on ICT4D in the developing world.* Retrieved April 11, 2009, from http://www.gesci.org/files/docman/Perspectives-developing-world.pdf

Taylor, P., & Clarke, P. (2007). *Capacity for a change: From the capacity collective workshop.* Retrieved June 2, 2009, from: http://www.impactalliance.org/ev02.php?ID=45676_201&ID2=DO_TOPIC

Teacher Education Policy Forum for Sub-Saharan Africa. (2007). Report of the Teacher education policy for Sub-Saharan Africa. Paris: UNESCO. Retrieved April 8, 2009, from http://unesdoc.unesco.org/images/0016/001627/162798e.pdf

United Nations Conference on Trade and Development Secretariat (UNCTAD). (2007). *The least developed countries report 2007.* Retrieved May 24, 2009, from http://www.unctad.org/Templates/webflyer.asp?docid=8674&intItemID=4314&lang=1&mode=downloads

UNESCO. (2005). *Towards knowledge societies.* Retrieved June 10, 2009, from http://unesdoc.unesco.org/images/0014/001418/141843e.pdf

UNESCO. (2008a). *ICT competency standards for teachers: Policy framework.* Retrieved April 11, 2009, from http://unesdoc.unesco.org/images/0015/001562/156210E.pdf

UNESCO. (2008b). *ICT competency standards for teachers: Competency standard modules.* Retrieved April 11, 2009, from http://unesdoc.unesco.org/images/0015/001562/156207e.pdf

UNESCO. (2008c). *ICT competency standards for teachers: Implementation guidelines.* Retrieved April 11, 2009, from http://unesdoc.unesco.org/images/0015/001562/156209E.pdf

UNESCO. (2009). EFA *Global monitoring report: Overcoming inequality: Why governance matters.* Retrieved April 11, 2009, from http://unesdoc.unesco.org/images/0017/001776/177609e.pdf

Unwin, T. (2004a). ICT and education in Africa: Partnership, practice and knowledge sharing. *Review of African Political Economy. 31*(99), 150-160. Retrieved June 2, 2009, from http://pdfserve.informaworld.com.remote.library.dcu.ie/234534_750429245_713946970.pdf

Unwin, T. (2004b). Towards a framework for the use of ICT in teacher training in Africa. *Open Learning: The Journal of Open and Distance Education, 20*(2), 113-129.

Vuningungo, V. (2009). *Teacher professional development for tomorrow, today.* Retrieved May 14, 2009, from http://www.gesci.org/old/files/docman/Presentation_Vice_Rector_KIE.ppt

Vygotsky, L. S. (1978). *Mind in society: The development of higher psychological processes.* Cambridge: Harvard University Press.

Whitehead, J., & McNiff, J. (2006). *Action research living theory.* London: Sage Publications.

Yamagata-Lynch, L. C., & Smaldino, S. (2007). Using activity theory to evaluate and improve K-12 school and university partnership. *Evaluation and Program Planning, 30*(4), 364-380.

# HOW CAN I HELP MY STUDENTS PROMOTE LEARNER-AUTONOMY IN ENGLISH LANGUAGE LEARNING?

**Li Yahong, People's Republic of China**

## INTRODUCTION

Traditionally in China, learning is widely accepted as a long process of knowledge accumulation which takes great diligence and prolonged effort, and students are encouraged to gain knowledge primarily by reading printed work or listening to their teachers (Zhang & Wu, 2004, p. 73, Qu, 2003, p. 196). As a Confucian slogan for young men goes, 'He who excels in study can follow an official career', young students are expected to perform well in their school lessons, usually to attend a prominent university so as to give glory to their family (Zhang & Wu, 2004, p. 74). Thus, children and young people are persuaded to give up playing in the yard by their parents or teachers to work hard on their school lessons so as to achieve high scores or grades. Those who are doing well in textbook-reading or examinations will be admired by neighbours and then set as models to their own children by saying, 'Look, Xiaoming has gained the highest score of his class in the examination once again. You should learn from him and work hard on your lessons. How I wish you could do as well as he often does!'

In the classroom, learning is completely controlled by teachers. Many teachers believe that their duty is mainly to transmit knowledge to younger generations (Zhang, 2006, p. 385). Therefore, they lecture and speak during most of the class time whilst students are expected to listen and busy themselves with taking notes and then memorizing what they have taken down after class (Zhang, 2006, p. 385). This is in contrast with developing thoughts by talking to their fellow students or asking questions, although now and then they are nominated to answer a few questions (Qi, 2005, p. 89). Generally, teachers are 'higher on the platform', and they tell their students what is right and wrong. For the students' part, it is quite natural to be obedient and accept what is true from their teachers (Qi, 2005, p. 88). After class, they are given lots of homework and examination-exercise paper which occupy nearly all of their spare time. They have to squeeze themselves by giving up outdoor or social activities to cope with piles of homework or exercise-papers (Xi, 2008). From the first day they attend school, they will have to pass a series of examinations and try to get high grades so as to enrol in the university and then get a satisfactory job. I lived such a life in my school-days

I was born and raised in a farmer-family in the 1970s. When I was young, farmers sweated and toiled in the fields all year round while suffering great hunger and poverty. My parents were always saying to me, 'Work hard with your lessons, and you can live a better life.' In their eyes – in fact, in the eyes of most people in my village – only if someone does well in school and goes to college, can s/he have the opportunity to leave the village and become a "townie." At that time, about 80% of China's population consisted of farmers. They admired those who had a job in a factory, in a government office, in a hospital, or in a school. I believed they were right. Only in that way could I fulfill the promise of my own future as well as my parents' secure life in their old age[72] because I love them.

---

[72]    In China parents bring up their children and in return expect to be supported and looked after by their children when they are old.

Therefore, I always tried hard in my schoolwork. When I was young, I often got up very early, sometimes with stars or the moon shining in the sky, and went to school and waited at the school-gate for the school to open because I was not sure of the time as we didn't have a clock. Then I started my school-days with the morning reading[73] – reading textbooks, reviewing notes and memorizing Chinese characters. I listened carefully and answered questions actively in class and finished my homework on time. With the heavier burden in high school, together with my fellow students, I had to give up relaxation at the weekends and devote myself to my lessons and continue my reading for about an hour after the usual evening reading[74] by candlelight. At that time the earnest goal of my life was to go to college. Hence, I managed to seize each opportunity to prepare for the College Entrance Examination. At last, I succeeded.

In 1994, I was admitted by Baoji College of Arts and Science, a teacher-training college in Baoji, which is in Shaanxi Province in the northwest of China. I was trained to be an English-language teacher. Once there, life went on as usual: attending classes, reading books and preparing for a series of examinations. I hadn't doubted anything about such a life until the day I graduated from college. When I was packing my luggage, I felt a little disappointed and I couldn't help asking myself, 'Does my school-learning end in this way?' I couldn't find much to impress me because most of my teachers were far removed from me, and what I managed to memorize for my examinations had swept far away with the wind as well. I had been trained as a prospective English-language teacher, but it seemed that I didn't have much confidence.

---

[73]  Generally speaking, there is a tradition of doing morning reading, reading the texts and vocabulary aloud, for Chinese students to pursue their language-acquisition. The morning reading often occurs before the first morning class starts (8:00 o'clock) and lasts for about half an hour. There is a requirement for elementary school students to do the morning reading but not for college students. They can take charge of it on their own.

[74]  The evening reading usually lasts from 7:30 p.m. to 9: 30 p.m. for secondary school students to review what they have learned that day or preview what they are going to learning the next day. School authorities arrange teachers to offer help to students if necessary.

Directly after graduation, I worked as an English-language teacher in a high school in Baoji. I happened to share a corner of the office room with Ms. Zhang Fengxian, a very skillful teacher. As a novice, I went to observe her classroom. When I entered her classroom for the first time, her teaching impressed me a lot. I observed that she had the power to attract her students by using gestures and various visual aids: blackboard drawings, pictures, cards. She used very little Chinese in the classroom though it was a beginner-class. She moved around the classroom rather than standing on the platform, which is the traditional way. She made a lot of eye-contact with the class in order to encourage a shy student to speak or to divert the attention of an absent-minded one back to language learning. As for the students, they seemed highly-motivated to learn: they would actively respond to questions or move around to find their partners and participate in activities (usually making a dialogue) energetically when tasks were assigned. I could feel their enjoyment of their learning from their cheerful and bright smiles. It was the first time for me to sense what happiness there could be in learning and teaching.

Thus I decided to improve my teaching as I valued positive emotions like happiness and motivation in learning. I opened my teaching to her and invited her to my classroom and asked for her feedback and suggestions. From her, I learned how to motivate and interest my students by using visual aids or gestures. I managed to get them engaged in their learning with some group-work such as making a dialogue or role playing. In addition, I loved them and tried my best to help them with their troubles. In the classroom, when I observed they were frowning, I knew I needed to repeat what I said or put it in an easier way; when some of them averted their eyes from the blackboard now and then, I knew they had lost interest and I needed to revise my teaching ways; when they were engaging themselves in the language learning, I would feel more confident in my teaching. I usually talked to them in a friendly way, so they became used to having pleasant chats with me after class. They talked to me about issues ranging from their troubles in learning English to their favourite movie stars and pop singers. In short, I enjoyed my work and I gained more confidence day by day.

In 2003, I furthered my studies by doing a Master's Degree in Shaanxi Normal University. There I met Professor Zhang Lichang, my supervisor. He loved his students. He often showed his care for us. With his help, I read a lot on pedagogy – about Comenius, Rousseau, Herbart, and about John Dewey. It was Professor Zhang who opened up the whole notion of critical thinking to me by encouraging me to challenge his opinions or ideas in the books. He introduced me to *China's New Curriculum* (http://www.actionresearch.net/writings/china/mlhand105.htm) and invited me to visit some experimental schools with him for times. There, I learnt that the New Curriculum values something more than knowledge such as students' critical thinking, individual learning potentials, learner-autonomy, attitude, confidence and interest as all these were absent from China's schooling for a long time. Moreover, I discovered that it was rather difficult for teachers to adopt new methods to change their teaching styles and improve their teaching practice, although there were some good ways such as doing school-based educational research, keeping a teaching journal and reflecting on their teaching, and also doing action research on their practice.

Three years later (still continuing), I started working at the Department of Foreign Languages in Shangluo University. Shangluo, lying in the southeast of Shaanxi province, is a highly mountainous area. Most of the local people are engaged in farming. For several decades after China's Liberation[75], there was only one highway passing here and connecting it with the outside world. As Jia Pingwa (2006), one of the most famous Chinese writers, who was born and raised in a

---

75  Since the first Opium War (1839-1842), China had been a semi-feudal and semi-colonial country for about 100 years, but it has been changed since the People's Republic of China was founded on October 1st, 1949. This was after the Chinese people's 28-year-struggle for liberation under the leadership of the Chinese Communist Party since it was founded in 1921.

village in Shangluo, described in his work *Shangzhou,* his hometown was so rocky that his village was surrounded by rolls of mountains and hills. When he was young, his great pleasure and desire was to travel around and learn about different traditions and customs in the villages. Yet he couldn't fulfill his dream for he found when he arrived at a new village he saw another mountain standing in front of him. However, he felt lucky that the highway near his house brought him great pleasure. There he could see all kinds of passengers, whom he thought were probably well-travelled, passing by on the bus. He admired them so much that he wanted to chat with them when the bus stopped. When the bus left, he dreamed of being on it with them, leaving for the capital city. For the villagers, mountain-ranges and rivers were their world at that time. Their lifelong dream was to go to the city beyond the mountains. And now things have changed a lot as China has carried out the policy of developing the Western part. A railway has been built which introduced more products, information and new things. In 2008, the government constructed an express-way to help the local people travel in and out.

The college is the only one in this region. It was established as a teacher-training college in 1976, when China's Cultural Revolution[76] came to an end. According to Mr. Liu, a retired teacher who worked here since it was founded, there were, at its inception, only two departments, four classes, about 150 students and 20 staff in total, with simple, crude classrooms and office-rooms

---

[76]     The Cultural Revolution, also the Great Proletarian Cultural Revolution, was a period of widespread social and political upheaval in China between 1966 and 1976, resulting in nation-wide chaos and economic disarray. It was launched by Mao Zedong, the chairman of the Communist Party of China, on May 16, 1966, who alleged that 'liberal bourgeois' elements were permeating the party and society at large and that they wanted to restore Capitalism (Wikipedia, 2009). During this period, those knowledgeable or well-educated, who were believed to have thoughts denoted as 'liberal bourgeois', were treated badly by being suspended from their position and sent to do some rough work, such as farm-work or cleaning the streets, so as to refine their thoughts. Thus, schools were closed while students were encouraged to work on farmland to strengthen their sense of socialism and class-struggle by experiencing hardship (Tian, 1996, p. 1155). Since 1977, schools began to re-open and young people were recalled to school to continue their learning (Zhao, 1998, p. 222). (See more in http://en.wikipedia.org/wiki/Cultural_Revolution)

and the barest necessities for teaching. After that a three-storied building was set up for classrooms in 1984. At that time, its tenet, as well as the National Education Policy, was to train socialist constructors and successors with firm beliefs in Marxism and Socialism to serve China's socialist construction and the Chinese people. For more than ten years, graduates were sent back to where they came from to work for the local people (Li, personal communication, Sept. 25th). However, with China's policy of reform and development of the Western provinces it has developed very fast during this time. Since 2006, the organisation has been designated as moving towards university-status. Several new buildings have been set up for classrooms, library and students' accommodation and lodging. Now there are more than 6,000 students from a massive area – about nineteen provinces across China – studying here. About 1,500 students graduate every year. Of course they can now go wherever they wish and do whatever they like after graduation. More and more employees with a Master's Degree, some even with a Ph.D. are working as teachers here. A new library has been built to supply more books for students and teachers. Professors and scholars are invited to give lectures regularly. For English learners, there is an English Film Club, an English Library and an English Corner[77] (Figure 1, p. 374) organized at the respective time once a week. These activities expose the learners to authentic English language and culture. Furthermore, a new linguistic laboratory has been opened since November 2008, which offers the students more opportunities to learn English language autonomously.

---

[77]    English Corner is a very popular activity on college and university campuses across China. These events are organized for English language learners or amateurs to get together to talk to one another freely in English and thus develop their proficiency in speaking. It tends to be held once a week at a fixed place and time. In our college, English Corner takes place at 7.30 p.m. – 9.00 p.m. every Monday evening in the Teaching Building.

**Figure 1.**    An English Corner

Once again, I work as an English language teacher here, but it is all rather new to me. The students are not teenagers but young adults. In their college years, students are struggling to become independent (Hartman, 1998). In academic learning, they develop new ways, which are quite different from those they learnt in high school, 'to organize and use knowledge', that is, they are faced with 'the challenges of academic life which not only introduce them to new knowledge but force them to evaluate how they gather, process and apply knowledge in their lives' (Hartman, 1998, p. 23). This may be a painful experience but will benefit them in the future (Hartman, 1998). For language learners, 'Learning a language effectively is a long process and one that includes hypothesis-formation, hypothesis-revision, and many errors along the way' (Rubin & Thompson, 2004, p. 11). Some learners will 'feel so frustrated that they may want to give up' because 'they are impatient with the length of time it takes to learn how to do this' (Rubin & Thompson, ibid, p. 10). Thus they will inevitably encounter lots of difficulties in handling their learning during this process. Indeed my students were not exceptional. They had encountered troubles and failures in their language learning and sometimes they turned to me for help.

When Dr. Vadna Murrell-Abery[78] presented it to me again, I found action research appealing for I knew it to be, 'a systematic approach to investigation that enables people to find effective solutions to problems they confront in their everyday lives' (Stringer, 2007, p. 1). Different from empirical research in which researchers study others, action research is 'an inquiry conducted by the self into the self' through self-reflection to pursue development with an open end (McNiff, 2002). It is a living educational theory by inquiring into questions of the kind, 'How can I help you to improve your learning' (Whitehead, 1989). The living theory methodology is distinguished at least in the following aspects: first, it relates to methodological inventiveness, action-reflection cycles, narrative inquiry and personal and social validation in propositional perspectives; secondly it involves a dialectical perspective. The *I* exists as a living contradiction that holds together values and their denial together in *my* practice which generates challenges to improve practice and then development into action-reflection cycles; thirdly, it is living, from an inclusive perspective, in life-affirming energy and values in explanation of educational influence (Whitehead, 2008).

With Vadna's encouragement and support, I took up my own action research project. I chose a Grade-Two-English-major class. It was a big class with 55 students. I taught them Contemporary College English, an intensive reading-course but designed as a combination to strengthen the training of English listening, speaking, reading and writing. We often had classes in Room 406. It was a typical Chinese classroom, with desks and chairs fixed on the floor in rows, and some great scientists and philosophers and their wise sayings on learning on the walls which were designed to inspire the students. On the front wall, just above the blackboard were pictures of the Chinese and international Marxist

---

[78]    Dr. Vadna Murrell-Abery, a VSO volunteer from England, worked as a teacher-training advisor in Shangluo University for two years.

leaders to intensify a sense of patriotism from education.

My action research project lasted about two months, from late September to the end of November in 2008. During the process, I made attempts to live my values in my practice by assisting my students in becoming autonomous and happy in their language-learning; I made use of my action research cycle to develop my thoughts and skills in improving my teaching; and in this report I present to you how I have improved my teaching by narration and explanation, by using my teaching journals as personal validation and my students' journals and my colleagues' comments as social validation.

## WHAT DID I WANT TO IMPROVE?

I value what the New Curriculum values rather than the transmission of knowledge in teaching: to teach students how to learn; to build their learning skills and strategies; and to encourage them to discover something meaningful in their learning (Ministry of Education as cited in Zhong, 2001, p. 3). Meanwhile, I have a strong belief that learning is a student's responsibility because 'students ultimately become independent of teachers and teaching and become able to pursue learning projects autonomously' (Dickinson, 1994, p. 2). As a teacher, I value freedom, democracy, critical thinking, individual potential ability, and it is vital for teachers to 'bring them about, to discover the most effective means' (Dickinson, 1994, p. 3).

On the evening before the new school day[79], I received messages on the internet sent by one of my students, Zheng, a 22-year-old man. He was depressed because of failing his examination again the previous term. He raised the question:

Zheng: How should I handle my language learning?
Li:  Have you tried hard?

---

[79]    It was on 31 Aug. 2008. In China, the autumn semester starts around September 1st.

Zheng: Yes.

Li: How hard?

Zheng: I listened carefully in the classroom.

Li: What else?

Zheng: I am sorry I did little for I couldn't persevere in my learning because there are so many new words to memorize and so lots of exercises to do. When I managed to keep those words in my mind, I would forget even most of them the next day. I don't know what I can do. (Li, personal communication, August 31, 2008)

Obviously, he was accustomed to listening to teachers in classroom and waiting to be told what to do with his learning as they used to do in high school. In fact, I have been asked such painful questions on many other occasions when many of my students suffered from their failure to learn to a sufficiently high level. I felt it necessary at that time to make them aware that the learning-process was their own responsibility. They needed to learn to take charge of their own learning, to make all necessary decisions concerning all aspects of the learning – in other words, to develop learner-autonomy (Holec, 1981, as cited in Little, 2006; see Farren, 2008). As for me, I would like to challenge myself to be a facilitator rather than a knowledge-distributor. I would like to offer a helping hand to them. I developed my role in this way because I believed developing learner-autonomy 'is likely to be directed by the teacher initially' (Dickinson, 1994, p. 3) and 'learner-training' seems to 'be the key to autonomy' (Dickinson, 1994, p. 5).

## WHY WAS I CONCERNED?

### Learner-autonomy plays an important role in language learning

As I mentioned above, students will ultimately become independent from teachers and teaching and thus in education, 'the development of autonomy and self-sufficiency may be desirable ends' (Dickinson, 1994, p. 3). The communicative language teaching methodology tends to develop learner-autonomy. In communicative language teaching, language learners are expected to 'take on a greater degree of responsibility for their own learning' (Richards, 2006, p. 5). while teachers work as facilitators helping learners to develop their own purposes in learning and giving them greater choice over their own learning, which involves the content and processes of learning, self-assessment and their use and awareness of learning-strategies (Richards, 2006, pp. 24-25). The idea is that if learners have developed their own autonomy, they will then take the necessary responsibility for their own learning and become intrinsically motivated and engage themselves in their learning initiatively and actively (Little, 2006). In addition, autonomous learners can apply the knowledge and skills acquired in the classroom to situations outside the classroom (Little, 2006).

### Learner-autonomy is advocated by the New Curriculum of China

If a state is to develop and flourish as a democracy, it must take educational measures to develop the capacity of its citizens 'to think and act as free and self-determining individuals' (Holec, 1981, as cited in Little, 1994, p. 81). To meet the challenges of this rapidly changing world, Jacques Delors (1996) expressed his idea of Life Throughout Education in his report to UNESCO of the International Commission on Education for the Twenty-first Century which, 'is based upon four pillars: learning to know, learning to do, learning to live together and learning to be.' The Chinese government has taken action – implementing the New Curriculum - as a response to reform its educational system since 2001. One target of the New Curriculum is to develop learner-autonomy. In *The new English curriculum standards* (Ministry of Education, 2003), it stated that changes of students are expected in many ways – their interest, motivation, attitudes and learning strategies in English language learning to promote autonomous learning (p. 2).

Specifically in *The new curriculum* there is a great shift in school teaching and learning – the shift from *teacher-centred* to *student-centred* methods in the classroom teaching and learning. '[The new curriculum] advocates process-oriented teaching and learning' (Laidlaw, 2005) and aims to help the students 'move from competence to performance', that is from 'what the students know in their minds, their theoretical knowledge' to 'what it is that the students can do with that theoretical knowledge' (Chen, 2002, as cited in Laidlaw, 2005, p. 5). It suggests 'a task-based approach to language teaching and learning' (Zhou, 2006) in which more opportunities will be provided for students to take much of their initiative 'to use the knowledge they gain' in the situation which can resemble real life rather than just 'remaining as knowledge in their mind' (Chen, 2002, as cited in Laidlaw, 2005, p. 5). Students are encouraged to experience and learn the language by self-discovery and participate actively and positively in discussion and negotiation activities rather than just receive the information passively from teachers (Laidlaw, 2005, p. 5). During the process of English language learning, students are expected to develop their interest, motivation, confidence as well as learning strategies and cultural awareness along together with their language knowledge and skills (Laidlaw, 2005, p. 5). Thus in such a creative learning atmosphere, it is quite necessary for the students to develop learner-autonomy.

## HOW DID I IMPROVE IT? WHAT CLAIMS AM I MAKING IN THIS PAPER?

Last term I aimed to build the students' confidence in their English language learning for I knew attitude and motivation would affect the results of their learning. It also works the other way. I believed if students have achieved academically in their learning, they will be more motivated and desire to achieve more goals.

**I claim that I helped the students make decisions to achieve more in their learning**

I felt my first job was to get them to know what they'd gained and what they lost during the past year by reflection and then learned to make decisions on their own.

Two weeks after the first school-day, I had a discussion with them about what and how they learned in the past. Then I discovered they focused mostly on the reading of their textbooks whilst ignoring any listening and speaking components except for some unavoidable activities in class. They were able to recognize these aspects but it was difficult for them to carry out these aspects because Chinese students do seem to be shy and afraid of making mistakes in their speaking. Before they spoke in English, some of the students tended to seek a less vulnerable way by writing it down on paper first. When they recognized a mistake, they would blush and correct the mistake immediately. In addition when reading, they would read out what they had written word by painful word rather than using more effective strategies. Furthermore, they didn't tend to spend much time in their academic studies after class – about 8-10 hours a week, which approximated to 35-40% of their spare time, because they seemed to lack the ability to handle their own learning-agenda as they were used to having their learning controlled by their teachers in high school.

Next, I asked them why they were here to study English to help them realize the purpose of their language learning. Most of them responded that they wanted to make a career in it. Although it was not intrinsic, I nodded to them to show my understanding of having such a motivation for learning English in China. Then I stressed the significance of listening and speaking in language learning and their later professional development and the necessity of broadening their reading to read English literary works, magazines and newspapers.

As I knew clearly that Chinese students were likely to listen to their teachers, I gave them some suggestions on what they could do next. I proposed they reflect on their learning in the past college-year again after class and try to set a realistic goal for learning in a comparatively short period. I also encouraged them to work out a feasible plan for it in which I advised them to practice listening and speaking regularly (Appendix A). The classroom was quiet and no one said anything. I knew they accept it as an assignment as usual, but I was not sure how much they were willingly to accept it.

### I asked the students to keep their learning journals once a week

A week later, after they had drawn up their plans, they began to carry them out. I advised them to keep a journal every week to check how they got along with them. As far as I am aware my students did as I suggested and I kept records of this in my data archive. I felt a little excited when I read about their reflection on what they had done and also what they hadn't in their journals. They did the work better than I had expected. They could fulfil their plan actually. Take the following as an example:

> Everything went on well this week. I carried out my plan strictly — I previewed my lessons, and completed assignments independently. I did the morning reading and listening practice for half an hour every day. I went to English corner on Monday evening... (Meng, personal communication, Week 7)

Of course, I could read, now and then, something they'd lost and their disappointment and then their reflections on what to be improved: 'I felt very disappointed this week for I acquired little. I simply memorized some words. I need to work harder on something else next week' (Yang, personal communication, Week 9). What excited me more was that I could read something new in her next week journal: 'I did much better than last week. Apart from doing with my course-lessons, I talked to some new friends in the English Corner happily and went to the English Library and did one hour reading there on Wednesday afternoon. I was feeling pleasant this week.' It seemed that sometimes they had the initiative to improve their learning practice. This was beyond my imagination.

Sometimes, they wrote down what they were still puzzled by and hoped that I could help solve the problems. I discovered the following in a student's journal-book: 'Dear Ms. Li, I feel confused with pronunciation of some sounds in words. For example, *thousand* and *thought*; *wind* and *wing*; *said* and *sad*. Could you show me how to pronounce these words?' (Zhang, personal communication, October 17, 2008)

When I got to know their puzzles, I would help them solve their problems as soon as possible. Take the above for example, I spoke to her about her concern the next day after class, I pronounced her chosen words very slowly and asked her to observe and notice differences between the sounds. I also added some necessary explanation about pronunciation so that she would be clearer. After that, she did the pronunciation until I was satisfied with it. Then I suggested she borrow a book on phonetics and asked someone who is good at pronunciation and that would be able to help her. She said she would and left, apparently cheerfully. In other words, I responded to the learning-need of my student, rather than assuming I knew what their learning needs were, which is often the case in a Chinese classroom in my experience.

### I acknowledged their achievement and thus encouraged them to move on

As the students started putting their plans into practice, I began to collect and read their journals regularly. I could only read and respond to each journal about once every three weeks. After reading carefully, I would record my thoughts about their learning in the past few weeks. The first time I read their journals through, I found most of my students were not content with their performance even though I could see they had done lots of work. I believed this was because Chinese students are often too humble to admit that they have done well in their work. Trying to change that cultural behaviour was, of course, very difficult, but necessary if I was going to help them to achieve their potentials.

Yang, an industrious (female) student, wrote down as her journal entry from the 9th week, 'I spent a lot of my time and energy in my learning but acquired little.' I could see she was working as hard in the classroom as she described. She listened carefully, took notes, asked and answered questions and finished assignments independently. How much did she acquire? Did she acquire very little in spite of her hard work? I was not sure. However, what she did the next day impressed me. With five other girls, instead of giving a usual speech for her duty report, she acted out a short play, an adaptation of an episode of the movie *The Titanic*. The class reacted very enthusiastically. After class, she told me that although she enjoyed the process when she began to put this fantastic idea into practice –adapting the story, selecting the actors, rehearsing the play and acting it out, she wasn't satisfied with the language-constructions because she said she had only used very simple words and structures. I told her: 'It is excellent! You've done something no one else has done.' It was important to praise what she had achieved.

As a result of what I learned from Yang's creativity, I decided to express my appreciation even if they had made only slight progress. Everyone has the need for recognition to hear themselves being praised at what they have achieved (Li, 1995, p. 578). In this way students could become highly-motivated and encouraged and then gain self-confidence in accomplishing their goals.

Gong, 21 years old, liked sports and social activities very much. He told me that he enjoyed spending several hours in the basketball field, but admitted to a lack of motivation when he concentrated on language learning. However, this seemed to be changing a little when he began to engage himself in his learning plan to accomplish his goal. The following comes from his journal:

> I went to English corner every Monday evening and I found talking in English with foreign teachers was not as difficult as I had thought. I was more interested in speaking English. However, I feel it a little difficult to

complete other tasks on my list. Next week, I will do my best. (Gong, personal communication, Week 9)

As for my feedback, I underlined the part 'talking in English with foreign teachers was not as difficult as I had thought' and 'was more interested in speaking English' with my comments 'Excellent' in the margin showing my appreciation at his progress which was designed to promote his self-confidence in language-learning. I also wrote down 'I believe you' to emphasize my respect for him and what he had accomplished. Again, this kind of relationship with a student in China is still relatively unusual, at least from my experience and what I have read. Teachers are seen as the distributors of knowledge, rather than having anything to learn from students about their learning-needs.

Then in the next few days, I discovered he engaged more in the classroom activities. He moved his seat from the back row to the front and listened more carefully. When I asked 'Do you have any questions for this part', sometimes he would raise questions like, 'Sorry, Ms. Li. I cannot understand the first sentence. It is too long and has a complicated structure.' It seemed that he was at least beginning to become curious about something he didn't know and then try to find solutions. It was a different approach to his learning.

**I did something in the classroom to promote the students' autonomous learning**

Autonomous learning is not isolated from teachers and classrooms (Little, 1994, p. 81; Dickinson, 1994, p. 3). On the contrary, teachers have to take great responsibility for developing learner-autonomy in the classroom. I had been a 'helping hand' in their autonomous learning. I did the following things to further help my students develop their learning autonomy.

*I tried to find chances in the classroom to monitor and promote their independent learning*

A few days after the first school day, as texts and exercises in *Book 3 of Contemporary College English* were much more difficult, I noticed that many of my students, even some of the more proficient ones, were depending too much on their reference books. When they had difficulties in understanding the text, they would turn to translation. Some may even have been copying the answers because they were not able to respond to my further inquiries. However, I thought more challenging lessons and exercises would be necessary for them as they were developing in their language-knowledge and skills. Then I had the idea to let them know that learning didn't mean finding a predetermined answer but giving them strategies to solve their own problems. Thus I tried to find ways of asking them to give further explanations about the idioms, paraphrase the sentences they were studying, and even give reasons for why they chose those particular words as the answer.

The following is an extract from my journal:

> Today I found some of the students hadn't completed the assignment carefully and independently. Take one of the Gap-filling exercises for example, *When I look at the _____ face of the children, I said to myself, 'I can't leave them to their own devices. They need me.'* When we tried to cope with it, one of the students answered 'eager' as the reference provided. I didn't let it go at that for I knew *'can't leave them to their own devices'* is critical to understand the whole sentence. So I questioned him on it. He remained silent, with his head lowered. Then I invited suggestions in class, but no one responded to me. I asked them, 'What do you think of your learning in such a way—just get the direct answer?' The class was completely in silence. I realized they had understood my question, and then I continued, 'I am sure you're clearer about what has happened than me. I hope you can do more exploitation in your learning. If you can do so, I think it will benefit you.' (Li, personal communication, September 10, 2008)
> To my delight, what happened in the classroom in the next week seemed

to show that they had a positive attitude to their learning. The following is an extract from my journal:

Today I found surprisingly that the students changed a lot. They performed very well in class when they did the language exercises. For example, they created some meaningful sentences:

Wang:  He credited his success to the fact that *he was given a good education in that country.*

Yan:  He credited his success to the fact that *his friend helped him a lot.*

Hu:  He credited his success to the fact that *he worked hard.*

I knew this could, to some extent, prove they had changed their attitude more positively toward language learning. They might have completed the task independently ahead of the class time. At least, it could show that they had drawn their attention to the language learning and thought about it actively and carefully in class. (Li, personal communication, September 16, 2008)

*I dictated the new words and short paragraphs regularly in the classroom*

The development of vocabulary is one of the critical areas of second language learning. A gradual and close study of vocabulary can provide consistent development and growth to increasing knowledge of words (Anderson, 2004, p. 21). However, my students often expected to remember all of the words even if they'd only met them once. Of course the result was often just the opposite. Many of them told me they had trouble in developing their vocabulary-range. Thus I decided to use very prominently myself in the words they were learning as I considered this one way to help them check how they were getting on with their retention of the vocabulary, as well as calling on their persistent efforts in vocabulary-learning when I, for example, dictated some short paragraphs. I believed these might promote their skills of listening and taking notes. With these, my students valued vocabulary learning much more than before. In the morning when I went into the classroom, I noticed many of them were reading aloud the glossary for texts. I also found some of them borrowed books on the lexicon from the library. They extended their learning-time to more than two and a half hours a day and 15 -18 hours outside the classroom a week. They spent about one hour on average in previewing and reviewing the texts, and studying new words. To my surprise, Zheng, the student who talked to me about his trouble with language-learning on the evening before the new school day, made much progress in his dictation on October 28. He only missed two words out of the ten and two phrases in the paragraph-dictation[80]. I gave him a big 'A' with my congratulations.

*I was constantly persuading them to take risks in developing their language skills*

Chinese people are 'characteristically timid and docile', 'but while deficient in active courage and daring' compared with Europeans they 'have great powers of physical endurance, as well as great persistency and obstinacy' (Nevius, 1882, p. 278). My students seemed diligent, studious and hard working but less brave or adventurous in their language learning. They listened carefully and painstakingly took down notes but were likely to keep silent in the classroom. When I asked a question, very few students were ready to respond to me verbally. Let me offer the following as an example.

One day just before we were to read the story *Discovery of a Father,* I prepared some questions related to the topic *Father* to warm up the atmosphere and arouse their interest in the story: *What is your father like? Does your father have any expectations for you? What about you?* I believed they would have a lot to say as I believe the concept of father is a very significant one to us all. However, most of them kept silent when I asked them to talk with their friends and classmates. I had no alternative but to repeat my instructions to them. Then they began to talk to each other a little. Whilst they were talking, I noticed that some students still weren't opening their mouths. Instead they were writing down

---

[80]  I often selected ten of the newly-learnt words at random and a short paragraph from the text which often consisted of five or six sentences for dictation. When the students missed fewer than two words and two parts of paragraph sentences, they would get an 'A' while if missed about three or four words and three or four parts, they would get a 'B'. If more than four words and four parts, they would get a 'C'.

the words. I reminded them of the speaking-time again. They said they were preparing for the speech. Later I discovered some of the students just read what they wrote down to their group members instead of speaking. My job then was to let them see the difference between speaking and reading something aloud and the significance of speaking. I encouraged them to speak by telling them that errors are quite a natural part in language-learning (Rubin & Thompson, 2004, p. 10). So, when some of them made progress in speaking, I would praise them and give them encouragement.

To my delight, it seemed much improved the next week. When I assigned the task of discussing the topic *Happiness* to them, they, particularly the ones who had been quiet before, moved around and, talked more actively and contributed their ideas to the group. For example, as I walked round I happened to hear Wang, a very quiet student whom I'd never heard speak English publicly in class, say to his group that he thought *happiness was to share what he has and offer help to those in trouble*. Although he didn't speak fluently, he was trying hard to express and share his thoughts with his group members. This, to me, seemed a great breakthrough. He was learning, I believe, the courage to take risks with his learning.

## WHO HELPED ME AND HOW?

### Dr. Vadna Murrell-Abery

Vadna is a skillful and experienced professional trainer. She has worked as a Management and Leadership trainer at the Police Staff College at Bramshill in Hampshire (UK), a Government funded institution which offers residential training courses to senior and middle ranking police officers in leadership and management. She has also been the Academic Course Director of the International Faculty, which provided a similar form of training to senior police officers coming from different countries all over the world.

As a professional action researcher, she won our admiration by her sophisticated skills and sharp insights. During her stay in Shangluo University, she did lots of work to facilitate action research. First, she got us to know about action research by presenting a series of papers. Then she helped us define the problems in our teaching by talking to us individually. Next she placed us in groups to form action learning sets based on our interests. Later she guided us to carry out our action research plans with the five typical questions (McNiff, 1992). She organized the action research meetings every Wednesday afternoon and encouraged us to share what we had done and observed and also to discuss and reflect on what were our areas of concern within the classroom.

During my action research project I talked to her a lot. Once, I invited her to observe my teaching and she gave me constructive feedback that, I believe, helped me to improve my teaching. Here are some extracts from her feedback:

> 1. It was an inquisitive lesson in which students were questioned a lot and it is quite reasonable to give students some time to think before they answer the question. The students seemed engaged in their reading and responded to you actively.
> 2. You moved around the classroom instead of only standing in front of the classroom...
> 6. Maybe the result of discussion would be better if you had grouped the students in four or five rather than through the whole class. The reason was that for such a big question to describe the characters in the story, the students would feel more comfortable to negotiate their ideas in small groups. (Murrel-Abery, personal communication, March 19, 2008)

No matter when I turned to her for help, she would always give help. When I had difficulty in understanding how to develop a case study, and she spent two hours one evening explaining how to choose cases and collect the data. With her help and encouragement, I completed my first spiral of action research. Later she instructed me in how to draft the report, particularly in drafting the introduction. She told me, 'Please visualize the readers first by describing your background, the background of the community, the learning environment as well as the students whom you chose for the case study.' The main points here she noted was that the readers would want to have a whole picture of what the researcher had done in order to understand fully the context of the research-process. She also helped me to improve my report by defining the problem of claims and finding the evidence to justify them. For instance, in my case study I once described the student Yang thus: He was not confident in his writing as his scores were not satisfying, and she challenged me, 'Are you sure he was not confident? How do you know? You said his scores were not satisfying? What were his scores?' After I answered her questions, I found I started to become more critical in thinking and more sensitive in observation. I am very grateful that she was constantly showing her great concern to my action research project. In fact, she had contributed a great deal to my professional development. She was doing with me what it was I learned to do with my own students.

### My students

I was lucky to have such friendly, warm-hearted, and empathetic students to work with. They were my best partners in my action research. They seemed to be enthusiastic with their learning in the classroom. They were willing to listen carefully, take notes and ready to answer questions. Most of the time, they responded to me actively and gave me feedback in time so that I could re-plan my lessons or change my methods. They often made full use of the questioning time. Now and then they asked for more than what was expected from them. They were inclined to engage themselves in language learning after class. Sometimes when I happened to stay in the classroom during the 10-minute-breaks, I discovered some of my students were discussing what they learnt in small groups. They made painstaking efforts to keep their journals once a week for two months and handed them in at the time when I required. They appeared to concentrate themselves on their own goals. They were inclined to invite new learning strategies to improve their learning. With their kind cooperation, the action research project was conducted smoothly. I believe they co-operated so fully because they were gaining educational benefit from my learning about their learning.


## My colleagues

Ever since Vadna had been addressing the importance of collaboration with colleagues and helped us form the action learning sets, I had been including some of my colleagues in my action research. We had our action research meetings on Wednesday afternoons. At the meetings, I was developing my thoughts by sharing what I had achieved with other members and discussed any problems that troubled us together such as my troubles — *how can I start my case study* and *how can I motivate my student to speak actively in class*. When I reported to them what had happened recently in the classroom and what troubled me. My group members gave me some suggestions and proposals such as 'Give the students some smaller topics for discussion', and 'Don't impose much pressure on them. Encourage them to speak anything they like.' Some of those suggestions were feasible. For example, once I was troubled for quite a long time with the whispered conversations among the students in the classroom when I did some writing on the blackboard. Then one of my group members advised me to shorten the time of writing and talk more with them, and another one agreed that students might feel a little boring during this period, so they would like to find something to do. I thought they might be right. I should make them fulfill this period of time. I re-planned my lesson. The next day I did as they suggested, extending my talking while just writing down some key words or the parts they were puzzled about. Furthermore, I assigned them some tasks such as reading when the long writing on the blackboard could not be avoided. I discovered things changed a lot when I noticed that their whispering talks reduced a lot. They seemed to pay more attention to what I talked about as I could see they nodded which seemed to show their agreement.

Moreover, I once invited five of my colleagues to observe my teaching. Later they gave me a formal feedback after discussion about it. The following is an excerpt from their feedback:

> This was a nice lesson. The students concentrated on their learning. They performed actively in answering questions. You looked very kind as you were smiling throughout the lesson which promoted your interaction between you and your students... however, we kindly suggest that you should introduce the students to more cultural background of English language because in the classroom we heard some students whisper to each other what was a 'highland fling.' (Critical friend, personal communication, October 22, 2008)

I thought they were right, for I believe that language conveys thoughts and its culture, so I took their comments seriously. From then on, I focused on introducing cultural background relating to their reading in my lesson planning. I often went on websites[81] to find as many sources as we needed.

In addition, I sometimes looked for ways of helping myself to develop my methodological skills in the 10-minute breaks between lessons, by discussing my problems with some of my colleagues who were familiar with my students. I would ask them for suggestions. For example, on one occasion I felt a little annoyed with some of my students because they were late handing in their assignments. One of my colleagues suggested that I talk to them kindly and ask what excuses they had for being unreliable. I thought she might mean that I should get the students to know my close attention to their learning so as to urge their further reaction to it. Then I followed her suggestion and talked to them privately to avoid their feeling of disgrace and asked what the trouble was with their assignments. Then I got to know that it was mainly because the assignment was a little difficult for them. They asked for permission to do some easier work, and I allowed them to choose something they could do or they were interested in.

---

[81]     Here are some websites urls on English Culture for readers who might be interested:
http://www.britainexpress.com/History/english-culture.htm
http://www.woodlands-junior.kent.sch.uk/customs/questions/
http://en.wikipedia.org/wiki/Main_Page
http://www.usa.gov/Citizen/Topics/History_Culture.shtml

Later I found their work in the pile of assignment work. What I learnt from them was that students are individual and are in proficiency of learning and thus they had different needs to develop themselves. Therefore, I gave them more chances to have choices in performing tasks by giving them more topics as the assignments.

With my thoughts developed by all those of my colleagues' aids, I felt more confident in employing new methods to promote my students' awareness, attitude and confidence in language learning.

## HOW DO I KNOW IT HAS IMPROVED?

After nearly two months' hard work, I could sense the changes that my students had made although these changes were in varying degrees of course.

### What I observed in the classroom

*I found they were working more diligently in the classroom*

Most of my students listened carefully, answered questions willingly and took down notes carefully, which I could read in their exercise books. What impressed me most was that since the fifth week (in the middle of October) I found they were coming to the classroom at least half an hour earlier than their 8 o'clock start to do morning reading. This was new.

*They became more active in the classroom activities*

Compared with before, they seemed to be thinking more actively in the classroom. They interrupted when they wanted to add something to what I was saying. Even the 'quiet' ones sometimes whispered something amongst themselves. When I noticed, I would give them chances to express their ideas. Take the following for example:

> Today we read an article about *Time*. In class I expressed my ideas of time such as 'Time waits for no man. We need to arrange our time very carefully, or it will slip through our fingers very easily...' Suddenly I heard one of my students, who sat in the third row near the window, uttering something in a low voice. Then I invited her to make a speech. She said that *time looked like something you'd lost. It could be yesterday, the happiest childhood, or the enjoyable moment you stayed with your old friends, while sometimes time looked like what you'd gained. It may be your high marks in your school lessons, or (your) parents' satisfactory smiles at you.* What she said surprised me. Her performance helped me discovered a student in deep thought. It seems quite reasonable for me to give chance to them in class. (Li, personal communication, October 18, 2008)

Additionally, they were more likely to raise questions. Look at another extract from my journal:

> These days I have kept promoting students' awareness of asking questions. I would like to ask, 'Do you have any questions about this part?' and I would be ready to help them solve any problems. Gradually, I found more and more students are willing to question, either in the class time or after class. They would stop you anywhere at any time. Today I was very delighted that Jin asked me a question on grammar and Hu asked one on phonetics. I explained their questions in details until they nodded with smiles. (Li, personal communication, October 9, 2008)

*They were able to complete their assignments independently*

As I mentioned above, my students depended too much on their reference books at the beginning of the new semester. Later I found it changed for I saw them using the dictionary a lot in the classroom. As it was an intensive reading course, using the dictionary was necessary for a thorough understanding. Sometimes they were able to explain the new words by themselves. The following episode is from my teaching journal:

> The usage of synonyms is quite difficult for students for sometimes the difference among these words are quite slight or subtle. Traditionally, they relied on me to distinguish these words first and show examples to them and then they could learn to use the words properly. But I thought they

needed to become independent from me and do the work autonomously if they could look up the words and try to distinguish them by themselves. So the other day I told them to try this part on their own. How had they done the work? I moved around the classroom with my wondering. Then I found some of them had done the work. They wrote down what they found in the dictionary on a piece of paper. I gave them a chance individually to do the exercises and asked them to give the reasons. The result was that they used the words quite properly and correctly. I praised them highly. It was the very moment to set them as models for other students to encourage learner-autonomy. (Li, personal communication, October 15, 2008)

### What I read in their journals

I appreciated that my students kept their learning journals in which I could discover more about their learning after class. From them I was able to read how my students took charge of their learning outside the classroom, in ways that were difficult to observe in the classroom. From their notes I could also detect whether my students had taken another step in their own independent learning.

*They recorded and evaluated their learning based on their initial plan*

As I mentioned above, my students focused on their learning in their journals. Apart from recording what they had and hadn't done according to their plan, they reflected on what needed to be improved the next weeks. They could recognize what they acquired and what they missed. For example, Gong wrote down in his journal:

This article is about my study during last week. Firstly, I listened to some English songs, but I seldom did listening practice for 20 minutes. I will work hard on it next week. Secondly, I feel a little satisfied with me at speaking. I talked a lot with Vadna. Thirdly, I got up early and did morning reading every day, but I read little in the evening. Fourthly, I didn't write something. It seems that I need to work harder next week. Yes, I need to and I will. (Gong, personal communication, October 6, 2008)

Although he had reflective thought on his learning and could recognize his deficiency, changes seemed a little hard to occur to him. For the next several weeks, I didn't read anything encouraging but something like *I do my best next week* until four weeks later.

> I did best last week since my plan started. I kept listening to English every evening although I couldn't understand fully. I visited Film Club on Wednesday afternoon. I find it is really helpful to improve my listening. What's more I visited library for several times and read *the 21ˢᵗ century* and *the weekend*... when you've gained something from your hard work, you may have some pleasant feelings. At this moment I had a kind of such feeling. (Gong, personal communication, November 2, 2008)

Nevertheless, I could feel that they were making efforts to improve their learning by achieving what they had missed and what they wanted to although changes seemed a bit difficult for them.

*They made use of some resources and facilities to expand their language-learning*

Over time it became possible for me to read something more than mere prevision and revision of the texts, memorizing vocabulary and completing the assignments. Many of my students extended their language-learning by using the available resources or facilities on campus. As I stated previously, it was not easy for my students to carry out their listening and speaking programmes after class. However, later they were constantly visiting English Corner, English Library, or the newly-opened linguistic laboratory to fulfill their learning plans. Some students even created opportunities by themselves to promote their language-learning. An was a newcomer in May, 2008. She had originally studied Political Science and later changed her major to English language. She seemed to have some trouble in pronunciation and speaking. I had encouraged her to speak by telling her not to pay too much attention to mistakes she'd made. She nodded to me and was seemingly determined to improve it. Once she attended the English

Speaking Contest to challenge herself. Besides, she was developing some other new ways. Here is an excerpt from her journals:

> These days I kept visiting English corner on Monday evenings and English library on Thursday afternoon to find chances to express myself in English. Furthermore I kept the habit to talk to my friend Zhu in English on the way back to my dormitory after Evening Reading. I feel I am not as nervous as before when I speak. (An, personal communication, Week 12)

*They tried to use some effective learning strategies*

As their learning was progressing, my students reacted actively to difficulties in their learning. They didn't wait to see as before but began to employ some strategies to improve their learning.

Wang had been greatly troubled with his writing. I had tried to correct some structure-problems of his sentence writing in his homework and helped him to develop his writing skills. At one time, he seemed to give up by telling me that he didn't know what to do. However, one day I was pleased to read something encouraging in his journals:

> Writing is very difficult for me. Sometimes I even didn't know how to start. I had no choice but to read some model essays and then I follow the writing patterns. To my surprise, it was a rather efficient way to improve my writing... (Wang, personal communication, Week 13)

**Feedback from my colleagues**

During my action research, I had asked one of my colleagues, Ms. Zhang, an advanced teacher with 16 years' experience in teaching, to come to my classroom for observation in the 16th week. She was very skillful in teaching reading and often sent to inspect and observe teaching in our department. After class, she gave me a formal feedback, which read as follows:

> Generally speaking, it was quite a pleasant class. You had done much to interact with the students. The students engaged themselves completely in the classroom activities both in the reading and discussion. What impressed me most was that they were so interested in the learning. I was

moved by their sympathy and understanding for others who were stunned with what to say next… In short, I like the classroom atmosphere. (Zhang, personal communication, December 20, 2008)

I felt more confident with her encouraging comments for I felt that she was engaged as much in the teaching as the students in the learning.


## CASE STUDIES

Now you may have got some idea about what I did and how my students were developing their learning autonomy in my action research project. In order to help you to get a clearer picture of how they were developing, I've chosen three of my students to write about in more detail.

Yang, at 22, seemed determined and highly-motivated in his learning. He listened carefully, asked and answered questions voluntarily in the classroom. He was trying to look for possible ways and opportunities to develop his language-proficiency, especially in listening and speaking. For example, he liked to spend time with foreign teachers and attend English activities like visiting English Corner and the English Library. Thus he looked very confident in speaking by his long speeches in class.

Jin was 21 from Henan Province, which lies on the east of Shangluo. Like most of my students, she appeared to work hard by listening carefully and taking notes in class. She looked quiet but thoughtful in class. She could understand what was expected to and she often raised some questions on grammar and vocabulary like *How can I use "chance" and "opportunity" properly.*

Fang, at 22, was such a shy and taciturn girl that she needed courage to say hello to a teacher. When she talked to you, she would lower her eyes for the most time and blushed slightly. What's worse, she suffered greater pains from too much examination when in high school and hence developed a feeling of hatred of language learning.

Individuals are characteristically different from each other. As you can read above, these three students were quite different in character, background, learning style, attitude and motivation in language learning. Of course they had different difficulties in their learning. Their development, as I will show you, may give you something of a picture of how individual students gained greater learner-autonomy in this action research project.

**Yang**

Yang[82] didn't seem confident in his writing. Once he said that he felt little confidence in his English language learning because his examination score[83] was not high due to his not very good writing. He had expressed hopes to achieve more in his writing. Thus, during this action research project, he was one of the very few students who managed to keep his journals in English. He cherished my feedback so much that he stuck them on the margins of his journal book. I would like to take some excerpts from his journals to show how he managed his learning outside the classroom.

> I have done most of things I wrote in my plan. I did some dictation about one hour everyday ... I went to English Corner on Monday evening ... I went to the English Library and discussed the topics about the next Monday evening with Vadna. I also did reading (here he referred to 'reading aloud') in my spare time because it is good for me to pronounce every word properly ...
> I have not done the writing much. Maybe the reason is that I prefer listening and speaking; ... on the whole, I think I did my best to do it according to my learning plan. (Yang, personal communication, week 5)
> Like many students he recorded what he had done and what he had failed

to do in accordance with his learning plan during the first few weeks. From his

---

[82]    It is customary to refer to someone by their surname in China, and this in no way represents a lack of respect as it might in some English-speaking countries.

[83]    In China ninety marks out of a hundred is considered excellent; above 80 is considered good; between 60-70 is reasonable; while below 60 is a failure. Yang often scored in the 60-70 region in the course I taught him.

account, we can see he was a little reluctant to do writing. Maybe he didn't have much confidence in it.

> How times flies! It is the 8$^{th}$ week. ... Suddenly, I found life is too short to waste. Looking back what I did this week, I feel proud of myself ... first, I did dictation and reading every evening as usual. The more I listen, the more progress I make. Second, I went to English corner... I developed my confidence greatly... Finally, I tried to keep a balance among the four skills in learning English and I began to focus on improving my writing skill. I borrowed a book named 'College English Writing'. It is very useful and thoughtful for me to learn something from it. On the whole, I still have a long way to go in learning English... but I won't give up until I get it ... I want to create a bright future by myself. I believe in myself. (Yang, personal communication, Week 8)

After several weeks' effort, it seemed that his self-confidence was, to some degree, improved as he was willing to take up writing. In addition, I found his writing was not as bad as he thought. As I mentioned above, it was mainly because Chinese students were humble to admit themselves. In fact, his narration went quite smoothly and clearly although he used many simple sentence structures. Then I gave him my following feedback:

> To be honest, it is a pleasure for me to read your learning journal. Firstly, your narration goes so smoothly that no one in the class can compete with you; secondly, I can read your confidence, your attitude to your learning. You're very determined to learn English well. I would like to say the same word again, 'excellent!' (Li, personal communication, October 28, 2008)

It seemed that he was greatly encouraged by my comment in the next few weeks as on a cold but pleasant Monday morning, he handed me his journal book surprisingly (without being nominated to). Then I read something special. Here I would like to present it to you:

> It was an interesting and unforgettable week for me because I discovered something about myself and the place where I live. ... Looking back what I did last week, I think I have a lot to say. Firstly, I did dictation and reading as much as I could. I could sense my listening and reading skills are improving every day. Secondly I know exactly my writing is poorer than other skills, so I spent much more time in writing last week. Hopefully, I can improve as quickly as I expect.
> Finally, I want to say something to my dear teacher (Ms. Li). In the first place, you are a wonderful teacher. You are responsible and professional to your job and students. I admire you. At the same time, I like you very

much. I hope you can be my teacher until I graduate. In the second place, thank you very much for your encouragement last time. It gave me more confidence about English learning and I will keep doing it... (Yang, personal communication, Week 11)

From his journal, we can read that he stepped further to meet his difficulties, spending much time in doing his writing. I felt more pleased that he was so highly motivated by my encouragement that he was really making constant efforts on his writing. More important, what I did in the class won his recognition which increased my confidence in improving my teaching. Then I wrote back to show my determination to help him with his language learning: 'I am really happy to read that you're making progress in your learning these days. I hope you can achieve more. And I will try my best to offer a hand in your learning if you need' (Li, personal communication, November 20, 2008).

When the College English Test-Band 4(CET-4), was approaching, he was busy traveling between the classroom and the library to work as hard as his fellow students. The following comprised part of his journal in Week 13:

It was a special week for me personally. I gained something that I never expected this week. To my surprise, I found that I am more useful in some aspects. Life is getting better and better for me... looking back what I did this week, I suppose that I spent most time in doing CET-4. I am preparing for it. I really want to pass it because it is a good way for me to test my English. At present, nothing is more important than to pass that exam... I will try my best to do it. Once I pass it, it will give me more confidence. (Yang, personal communication, Week 13)

As we can read, he showed he valued the examination very much for if he could succeed in it, it would give him more confidence in language-learning.

### Jin

Jin had admitted truthfully that she had wasted a lot of time in Grade One, so she was determined to make full use of her time to achieve something that was to pass the College English Test-Band 4 in this semester. Then she worked out a full and busy schedule which involved her in listening, speaking, reading and writing. She worked diligently towards it during those two months. Here is an excerpt from her journal:

> Generally speaking, I am satisfied with what I did this week. I went to library to read some books about English language. What I need to improve is that I should last my learning and improving the effect of learning. I will work harder. (Jin, personal communication, October 7, 2008)

At the beginning, she recorded simply what she had done in a particular week. She also reflected on her ideas and discovered what it was she wanted to improve for next week. I read her journal for the first time on Oct. 9th with the encouragement of the word *work hard* as my feedback.

> I have kept a book on CET-4 exercises for a long time. Now it is the time that I should return it but I haven't read it at all. I find there was no time to memorize the words in it because every morning when I finished reading the glossary in the textbook, it was time for class. I did carry out my plan for CET-4. What bothered me most was listening. It was too difficult for me to understand. What should I do to improve my listening? (Jin, personal communication, Week 7)

Judging from her journal, she had some difficulty in handling her learning affairs and was troubled with listening. Thinking she might need my help and encouragement, I suggested some listening strategies:

> Listening is a skill rather than knowledge. Thus you must be patient as it is rather difficult to improve. What you need to do is that you must practice it regularly and massively. So first putting on your earphones whenever possible may be useful to you. Next you could browse the title, vocabulary and even the content of exercise work and predicted what the text was mainly about before listening and then try to verify what you predict in the listening. And then you can predict the sequence of the information that will be presented. For example, in a news story, it may be in such sequence: who- what- when- where while in an airport announcement, it may be: who- flight number-arriving/ departure time-gate number. (Li, personal communication, October 29, 2008)

It seemed she was likely to employ learning strategies in her learning as I found something new about her learning in her journal of the next week:

> This week, I did a lot of listening practice. I felt very pleased that your suggested strategies worked very well, especially browsing the content of the tasks and predicting what it was mainly about. In this way, I found it easier for me to comprehend the listening text and complete the task. Now

> I feel more enjoyable in listening. Thank you, my dear teacher. (Jin, personal communication, Week 8)

Moreover, she was quickly encouraged in her learning in the classroom. The day after the first short play was presented in class she demonstrated a short dialogue with one of her roommates, which was in fact a combination of narration, conversation, singing and acting. Once again, the class was enthusiastic and called out their appreciation. They enjoyed it very much, it seemed, and so did I.

With the opening of the new linguistic laboratory, Jin became a frequent visitor as she said she enjoyed those pleasant learning programmes. Here are some excerpts from her journal:

> I kept the habit to get up early in the morning and go to the classroom to do morning reading. I like to visit room 408 (the new language lab) very much for I can practice and improve my listening. What's more, I've seen some wonderful movies in it which can broaden my vision and enlarge the knowledge of English culture and language. In my spare time, I went to library to read something I am interested. I felt I did the work fine. (Jin, personal communication, Week 9)

Sometimes I could sense she was not content to be bound to a textbook. She desired to know about other fields beyond grammar and vocabulary and she tried to broaden her vision. If she failed in doing so, she felt a little disappointed. Take the following for example:

> How time flies! These days I felt I achieved little. I would like to read the books in other field but I found little time because it took me a lot of time to read the textbook and to do the grammatical exercises. I was disappointed with myself.... (Jin, personal communication, Week 10)

When the College Test was approaching, she concentrated her attention completely on it as most of her fellow students did although sometimes she was able to recognize the imbalances in her learning as she recounted in her journal:

> I was loyal to my schedule. I felt content with myself for I persisted in everything on the list. However, I was worried about my speaking as it had not improved much. I lost my interest in English Corner because it didn't help much developing my speaking. I have never had real communication with others in English these days. I know it was not good to my language learning. I need to mend my ways... (Jin, personal communication, Week 12)

At last, here came the College English Test- Band 4, and she wrote down her thoughts and feeling, seemingly a little painful, after the examination in her journals:

> We took the CET-4 exam yesterday. I don't want to think of the result. What I needed most was to have a good rest to relax myself psychologically. So I went on an outing with my roommates to enjoy the sunshine. It was the first time for us to experience the tense since the college Entrance Examination. We felt very nervous for fear that we could not finish the exam paper. Some of my fellow students even said that their hands were shaking for there was very little time left. How I want a good rest and a long holiday! However, we could do nothing because we have to prepare for the coming final examination. How tired we are! (Jin, personal communication, Week 16)

As most Chinese college students, she valued the examination-grades and gaining certification. This would vindicate her proficiency in English language learning although she felt sick of it because this, it seemed was all the school authority, the employers, even the whole society seemed to valued. This was one of the reasons, I believe, why China has taken action to reform its education system.

### Fang

Fang was so shy and quiet that it was easy not to pay much attention to her for a long time. It was last September when she gave her duty report that I began to get to know her properly. When she stood in front of the class, she asked me for permission to speak Chinese. I refused because I was simply sticking to the principle that everyone should speak English in an English classroom. With tears in her eyes she started to tell her story in Chinese anyway.

From her story I learned something of her background, her family and her growing-up. She was such an obedient child that she had never said *no* to her parents for fear that they would be unhappy. She was sensitive to the fact of her parents' hard work for many years and that they had paid a lot for bringing her up and for her education. She knew that she should work hard and get high grades in her school lessons to please her family. However, she had suffered a lot from so many years' stress of preparing for examinations, in particular for the College Entrance Examination. She had had so many sleepless nights and suffered heavy headaches while she had to pretend to be able to attend classes, read books and do the examination exercises. She had to keep everything to herself for she didn't know who she could turn for help because everyone else was busy with their futures as well. Gradually, she became silent, timid, and ineffective in her daily life. On a later occasion she told me she didn't in fact like English and it was her brother who made the decision for her, because these days there were more opportunities for English majors to look for a job. She was a little isolated from her fellow students because she didn't know how to communicate with them although they were friendly and kind to her.

I felt sympathy for what she had suffered whilst a little ashamed of my arbitrary denial to her which may add something to her depression. It was her who reminded me that individuals have more needs rather than developing language skills in learning. It was obvious that she was suffering psychological depressions and was too eager to get herself to be known and understood by others. With such thoughts, I decided to make attempts to help her out of her trouble.

As for her language-learning, she said she had made a plan and kept her learning journals every week, but she said little about them. Mostly, she expressed much of what she longed for: understanding, compassion, tolerance and considerateness. She also expressed her wish to handle her life in her own way and to do what she liked. Meanwhile, she betrayed a little of her antipathy to school lessons. Even so, she had still performed her obligations as a student. When she had learned something, she would be happy and confident, though and here is an excerpt from her journal:

> I found my plan was infeasible, so I changed some parts of it. Every day I tried to do something. When I succeeded, I would be steady and sure and often have a sound sleep at night. (Fang, personal communication, Week 8)

Sometimes she showed her interest in learning, especially through those programmes that she enjoyed. For example:

> I don't think I did the work well this week mainly because I was a little idle and lazy, but I managed to see English movies. I enjoyed myself in those humorous episodes. Meanwhile I exposed myself in the language and its culture. I like this way of learning. (Fang, personal communication, Week 9)

I didn't impose any pressure on her for I knew she needed time to recover. What she needed most was others' understanding and consideration. Therefore, I encouraged her to become independent from her family. For instance, she could make her own decisions such as choosing the clothes she liked or make suggestions to her friends, etc. She nodded quietly to me. I told her I would like to be her friend and to listen to her if she was willing to speak to me.

On November 17th, she handed me a journal with her thoughts in it and told me that it had taken her five hours that weekend to compose. She wrote a very long story (eight pages in Chinese, about 120 lines) about her childhood, her parents' love and expectation for her and her terrible suffering from the examinations. She also expressed her philosophy of life, her dreams of an ideal life and desire for friendship.

I read it very carefully in order to experience what she experienced, and then pondered on what I could do for her. On November 23rd, I wrote a letter to express my empathy and concern for her, my views on life and the nature of learning, hoping that she could read something special which is different from the traditional idea of learning and my recognition of what she had done which can encourage a cheerful feeling in her life. Here is an extract from the letter:

> I can feel what you were suffering from being your parents' 'obedient' child. Then one day when you couldn't stand it any more, you began to betray them and search for the meaning and value of the existence of life to support your own position. And then you were absorbed in philosophy, psychology, religion and ethics. It seemed that you were lucky that you had found what you wanted. However, when you looked backward in your real life, you felt as frustrated as you discovered that sometimes kindness, beauty, and truth were so far away from you. Here I need to remind you

that kindness, beauty and truth are things that cost us to pursue all life long. Thus we need to work hard to go ahead of ourselves constantly.
I can understand your dislike of 'learning.' However, what do you mean by learning? Does it simply involve textbook reading or getting a high grade in the examination? If so, you had a misunderstanding of learning. In my opinion, you were doing the real learning when you were thinking about the meaning and the value of life and trying to read some literatures. You were doing the work better than others. I admire you... (Li, personal communication, November 23, 2008)

As time went on, Fang continued to struggle against those negative thoughts of learning and managed her learning normally. These two completely opposed thoughts came across in her learning journals. However, on December 2nd I got up early to get ready for the morning class and happened to see her pass by my window hurriedly to the classroom. The next day I mentioned the event to her. She smiled at me shyly and said that with the College English Test - Band 4 examination drawing near, she would like to cope with it as her classmates did. When I asked about her dislike of English language learning, she replied that she didn't hate learning so much after all. She could concentrate on it sometimes in fact.

What she said surprised me a little. Had she changed her attitude to learning? I wondered. A week before the final examination, all of the students had come to the Christmas party and enjoyed their play *Cinderella* very much – except her. One of her room mates told me that she had gone to the library as she was not accustomed to noisy and social occasions. The girl added that she had changed a lot during that time, that she appeared happier and more cheerful than before and that she even went surfing on the internet with friends.

In my opinion, happiness, understanding, empathy and consideration are more important than the course-learning and its score. What pleased me was that she had become happier and more cheerful than before. What's more, she had changed her attitude a little to learning. She had a tendency to engage herself more fully in language learning.

## CONCLUSION

After two months' work, I can draw the conclusion that those three students as described in the short case studies have progressed a lot in their own ways. They took the responsibility for making decisions to set their goals, draw up plans and worked hard toward them by thinking critically and exploring new learning strategies. More importantly they've developed something of self-confidence, a positive attitude and even an enjoyment of learning. Yang could recognize he was poor in writing, but then gain a positive attitude to working hard on it. As he progressed, he gained some self-confidence in accomplishing his goal. Jin knew quite clearly that she had not devoted herself sufficiently in her learning. She then was able to work on a plan and carry it out to achieve her goal. She developed some learning strategies in coping with problems in language learning. Most important of all, she was more creative than before. As for Fang, she made efforts to fight against her negative thoughts about learning, and gradually she developed a cheerful attitude and seemed to enjoy her learning and life a little more than before.

For learners, self-confidence, positive attitude, learning strategies, thinking critically and enjoyment in learning can drive and enable them achieve more in the future. Everyone likes to do what they enjoy. I believe when one enjoys something, s/he will make every attempt to learn more about it. I have found through this project how important it is to help students learn to help themselves, an insight fully in keeping with the New Curriculum. However, all of these ideas and values have been missing, I believe, in teaching and learning in China. That is why the New Curriculum values them very much and seeks to encourage them in our education system.

Regarding the whole class, although I have not been able to assess each student's level of learning, I have felt a more positive classroom atmosphere and a readiness to learn. I regard this change as helpful and important as I am now able to present my lessons in an atmosphere that I believe is conducive to learning. I am delighted with this small but significant step.

However, I should confess to the fact that the students continued to concentrate on a range of examinations that constitute the requirement to obtain their degrees as school authorities, parents and the society value these very much although sometimes the students are sick and tired of them.

This action research project has enabled me to describe a journey in which my professional development as a teacher has been an enabling experience. I have been challenging myself to facilitate my students to learn to take charge of learning affairs by employing new methods which might be developed either in my reflection on what happened in the classroom or in the contribution of my action research set. During the whole process, I've been keeping a more critical eye on my teaching which helped me become more sensitive to the teaching environment. With such a critical eye, I've discovered something new and different from the traditional perspective, that is, students could be more creative in learning than you expect them to if they have a chance to show and manage themselves. What's more, each student has individual interests, needs, learning styles and skills in learning and they will work in their own way to learn. They cannot acquire the same thing on the same level at the same time. Thus it is more important to offer them opportunities and help to facilitate them to develop at an individual pace than to require them a standard knowledge acquisition by testing which may bring greater mental pressure. All these new discoveries enabled me think, re-plan and act again in my teaching. Apart from this aspect, the small changes I've made in this project helped me build my confidence in continuing to improve my practice.

Now, it is very important to develop another action research project over a longer period. In addition, I want to be able to collaborate with my colleagues and help them commence their action research projects in the near future. This will give me the opportunity to share my learning, offer advice and support and learn from them too. Such interaction would be a very powerful way for us teachers, within our rapidly expanding department to continue to look at our practice for change, development and growth.

## APPENDIX A

### Gong's learning plan

I've made up my mind to work hard on my lessons at the beginning of the new semester. I will do my best to win the scholarship. To achieve this, I will do my English language learning as follows:

| Reading | <ul><li>I will get up earlier in the morning and do morning reading for at least 20 minutes.</li><li>In the evening I will read a piece of English writing.</li></ul> |
|---|---|
| Listening | <ul><li>Every evening I will listening to English about half an hour before I go to bed.</li><li>I will listen to English songs as I enjoy them very much.</li></ul> |
| Speaking | <ul><li>I will try my best to answer questions voluntarily in the classroom.</li><li>I will visit English Corner every Monday evening.</li><li>I will try to speak to my friends and classmates in English as often as possible.</li></ul> |
| Writing | <ul><li>I will finish teachers' assignments in time independently.</li><li>I will keep my learning journal once a week.</li></ul> |

## REFERENCES

Anderson, N. J. (2004). *Exploring second language reading: Issues and strategies*. Beijing: Foreign Language Teaching and Research Press.

Delors, J. et al (1996). *Learning: The treasure within: Report to UNESCO of the International Commission on Education for the twenty-first century*. Paris: UNESCO. Retrieved March 16, 2009, from http://www.unesco.org/delors/

Dickinson, L. (1994). Learner-autonomy: What, why and how? In V. J. Leffa (Ed.), *Autonomy in language learning* (pp. 2-12*)*. Porto Alegre: Universidade/UFRGS. Retrieved November 5, 2008, from http://coralx.ufsm.br/desireemroth/publi/autonomy.pdf#page=15

Farren, P. (2008). The European language portfolio in pre-service teacher education in Ireland: Reflection, interaction and autonomy. (Doctoral dissertation, Trinity College Dublin, Ireland).

Hartman, B. (1998). Your college years. In L. Yang (Eds.), *Contemporary college English* (pp. 1-4). Beijing: Foreign Language Teaching and Research Press. 4. The article was first appeared *The Glasgow Herald* in February 1998.

Jia, P. (2006). *Shangzhou*. Shenyang: Chunfeng Literature Press.

Laidlaw, M. (2005). *Handbook one 'From competence to performance': English-teaching methodology for 'The new curriculum' in China*. Retrieved June 26, 2009, from http://www.jackwhitehead.com/china/mlhand105.htm

Li, D. (Eds). (1995). *Dictionary of axiology*. Beijing: Press of Renmin University of China.

Little, D. (1994). Autonomy in language learning: Some theoretical and practical considerations. In A. Swarbrick. (Ed.), *Teaching modern languages* (pp. 81-87). New York: Routledge.

Little, D. (2006). *Learner-autonomy: Drawing together the threads of self-assessment, goal-setting and reflection*. Retrieved March 4, 2009, from http://www.ecml.at/mtp2/ELP_TT/ELP_TT_CDROM/DM_layout/00_10/06/06%20Supplementary%20text.pdf

McNiff, J. (1992). *Action research: Principles and practice*. London: Routledge.

McNiff, J. (2002). *Action research for professional development: Concise advice for new action researchers* (3rd ed.). Retrieved September 24, 2009, from http://www.jeanmcniff.com/booklet1.html

Ministry of Education. (2003). *The new English curriculum standard for high schools*. Beijing: The People's Education Press.

Nevius, J. L. (1882). *China and Chinese* (Rev. ed.). Philadelphia: Presbyterian Board of Publication.

Qi, Y. (2005). *Classroom management and communication*. Beijing: Beijing Normal University Press.

Qu, B. (Ed.). (2003). *The new development of China's education research in 2001*. Shanghai: East China Normal University Press.

Richards, J. C. (2006). *Communicative language teaching today.* New York: Cambridge University Press.

Rubin, J. & Thompson, I. (2004). *How to be a more successful language learner.* Beijing: Foreign Language Teaching and Research Press.

Stringer, E. T. (2007). *Action research* (3$^{rd}$ ed.). Thousand Oaks, CA: Sage.

Tian, B. (Ed.). (1996). *An encyclopedia for Chinese college students.* Shanghai: Tongji University Press.

Whitehead, J. (1989). Creating a living educational theory from questions of the kind, 'how do I improve my practice?' *Cambridge Journal of Education, 19*(1), 41-52. Retrieved September 16, 2009 from http://www.actionresearch.net/writings/livtheory.html

Whitehead, J. (2008). *How do I influence the generation of living educational theories for personal and social accountability in improving practice? Using a living theory methodology in improving educational practice.* Retrieved September 12, 2009, from http://www.jackwhitehead.com/jack/jwLTM080508.pdf

Wikipedia. (2009). *Cultural revolution.* Retrieved October 15, 2009, from http://en.wikipedia.org/wiki/Cultural_Revolution

Xi, M. (2008). On the Morbidness of High School Students' Mental Development. *Education exploration.* 3, 2008). 总第201期 (Serial No. 201). 117-118.

Zhang, X., & Wu, X. (Eds.). (2004). *Monitoring classroom teaching and learning.* Beijing: The People's Education Press.

Zhang, J. (2006). *On interaction of English dormitory and classroom-teaching.* Hangzhou: Zhejiang Education Press.

Zhao, T. (Eds.). (1998). *Knowledge about China.* Nanchang: Jiangxi Education Press.

Zhong, Q. (Ed.). (2001). *An interpretation of outline for China's elementary education reform.* Shanghai: East China Normal University Press.

Zhou, Y. (2006). Task-based Approach and Its Application in Classroom English Teaching & Learning. *Sino-US English Teaching, 3*(12), 32-36. Retrieved September 12, 2009, from http://www.linguist.org.cn/doc/su200612/su20061206.pdf

# INDEX

## A

Abbs, P. .........................242, 244, 281
Abdul-Rahman S. A. ................23, 28
academic freedom ..........................20
academic learning ...............188, 374
academic responsibility..................20
action learning.7, 125, 135, 162, 163, 389
action plan.12, 40, 67–75, 71, 78, 81, 86, 87, 90, 91, 105, 212, 296, 326, 363
action reflection cycles .6, 11, 12, 14, 375
action reflection method ..................7
action research xiii, 7, 23, 28, 29, 30, 32, 40, 47, 51, 52, 53, 54, 55, 56, 59, 60, 62, 63, 64, 66, 67, 68, 69, 70, 71, 72, 73, 74, 75, 76, 77, 78, 79, 80, 81, 82, 83, 84, 85, 86, 87, 88, 89, 90, 91, 92, 93, 94, 95, 96, 98, 99, 100, 101, 102, 103, 104, 105, 106, 107, 108, 109, 110, 111, 112, 113, 114, 135, 145, 146, 149, 150, 151, 152, 153, 158, 159, 161, 163, 164, 187, 201, 202, 216, 221, 229, 237, 240, 282, 295, 305, 306, 324, 325, 327, 329, 347, 365, 371, 375, 376, 389, 390, 391, 397, 398, 399, 409, 412, 413
action research as an educational strategy.....................................109
action research cycles .....44, 63, 124, 347, 376
action research reports ......70, 75, 94, 104, 107
action research with Chinese characteristics ...24, 115, 152, 158, 159
action researchers xiii, 23, 24, 28, 31, 51, 63, 64, 65, 67, 68, 70, 71, 72, 73, 74, 75, 82, 84, 85, 86, 88, 89, 94, 95, 96, 98, 102, 104, 105, 106, 107, 108, 110, 111, 152, 161, 180, 193, 202, 297, 389, 412
active learning........................67, 153
activity system ....316, 322, 323, 327, 328, 330, 331, 332, 337, 339, 340, 341, 342, 343, 345, 346, 347, 356, 361
activity theory .....316, 321, 324, 327, 329, 330, 345, 346, 347, 361
Addo, H..............................315, 361
Adler-Collins, Je Kan xiv, 22, 26, 28, 94, 165–202, 165, 168, 169, 172, 177, 191, 192, 195, 201

Agalianos, A. .......................322, 361
Ainscow, M...........................313, 361
Alderson, P...........................70, 111
Allende, I. ...........................253, 281
Allender, J. & Allender, D. S.3, 4, 28
Allott, M. ......................................281
Altrichter, H. ..........................73, 111
Amaeru................................187, 188
American Educational Research
    Association...................31, 39, 309
Anderson, N. J. .....................386, 412
Anderson, T. ........................291, 294
Andersson, S. B. ..........311, 312, 364
anger...........................17, 20, 21, 181
Apollinaire, G. .....................175, 183
Argyris, C..............................65, 111
Aristotle .........................................58
assessment.. xii, 86, 94, 97, 107, 146,
    242, 271, 287, 309, 323, 332, 340,
    341, 359, 412
Atterton, P.....................................237
Atweh, B. ..........................69, 70, 111
audiovisual glossary......................74
authentic truth ...........*see living truth*
authenticity...8, 17, 21, 143, 248, 251
autocratic classroom ...................290

**B**

Babbie, E...............................57, 111
Bach, J. S. ............117, 118, 128, 142
Balshaw, M. .........................254, 281
banking education.......................168
banking educator.........................168
Barnett, R. .........................34, 40, 51
Bateson, G.....................................74
Baylis, N. ............................249, 281
Beatty, A. ............................74, 114
Bereiter, C....................................239
Bernstein, B.171, 182, 183, 187, 189,
    201
Bernstein, L.........................253, 281
Bertrand, Y.......34, 51, 291, 293, 307
Biesta, G. J. J. ..............205, 225, 237

Bjerke, J. .....................................237
Blake, W. .............................133, 140
blogs............................292, 294, 305
Bloom, B. S.................................188
body-language.............................191
Bognar, B.ix, xiii, 22, 28, 40, 51, 54–
    114, 55, 57, 58, 62, 63, 64, 65, 66,
    72, 73, 80, 82, 85, 86, 87, 88, 89,
    90, 91, 92, 93, 94, 98, 104, 106,
    107, 108, 110, 111, 112, 127, 139,
    161, 206
Bohm, D..............125, 161, 243, 281
Bonk, C. J. ...........................294, 307
Bourdieu, P. ................9, 10, 28, 281
Bowers, C. ...........................126, 161
Boyd, S. ...............................292, 307
Bradbury, H. ..........56, 113, 237, 324
British Educational Research
    Association ............22, 29, 54, 239
Bruce Ferguson, P.....4, 6, 22, 28, 29,
    31, 41, 51
Buber, M. ....203, 204, 209, 217, 233,
    234, 235, 237
Buckingham, D. ...........243, 254, 281
Buddhist teaching ...............178, 183
Burke, A.......................................201
Burkhardt, G. .......................317, 361
Butler, D. .............318, 335, 336, 361

**C**

Cahill, M. .......................................25
Calarco, M. ..................................237
Carr, W. ..............214, 237, 295, 307
Carter, R...............................254, 281
case-studies...124, 146, 147, 221–29,
    398–407
Celtic Spirituality.......41, 42, 49, 124
change of practice.......211, 232, 234,
    349–50
Chapman, A. ........................290, 307
Charles, E............................5, 18, 28
child-centred action research .........98
child-centred school.................97, 98

child-oriented classroom........96, 112
China's Cultural Revolution........372
China's Experimental Centre for
    Educational Action Research in
    Foreign Languages Teaching.....24
Chomsky, N. .......................295, 307
Christensen, C.................69, 70, 111
Church, M. ...........................206, 237
Civille, J. R. ..........................121, 161
Clandinin, J. ............................43, 51
Clarke, P.....................315, 325, 365
Clifford, J. ...........................254, 281
Cloke, C. ........................................51
Cocteau, J...........................253, 281
cognitive presence291, 294, 295, 303
Cohen, L......................324, 329, 361
Coleridge, S. T. ...........................161
collaboration ....44, 48, 151, 326, 391
collaborative online-learning ...... xiv,
    288, 289, 290, 292, 293, 294, 298,
    305
collaborative online-learning
    environment .......293–95, 293, 294
Collier, J...............................55, 112
Collingwood, R. G. ..................11, 28
communication space..335, 344, 346,
    348
communicative power..............5, 103
community of practice .........110, 289
compassion..x, 7, 116, 159, 168, 173,
    177, 178, 180, 190, 193, 197, 405
comprehensibility.......................8, 87
computer-literacy.........................311
concept-mapping...........................52
confidence...xv, 7, 63, 71, 78, 79, 96,
    117, 223, 231, 272, 305, 369, 371,
    379, 393, 399, 400, 401, 408, 409
Confucius....................................367
congruence............................99, 251
connection.....248, 249–50, 250, 270,
    272
Connelly, M. ...........................43, 51
Conrad, J.............253, 258, 270, 281
constructivism.....................289, 293

Cooke, B. ..............................56, 112
Coolahan, J. .................317, 318, 361
co-operative action research 214, 231
co-operative inquiry.............211, 237
cooperative learning.....................43
counterpoint xiii, 115, 116, 117, 118,
    119, 120, 121, 123, 125, 126, 128,
    129, 131, 132, 133, 138, 141, 145,
    148, 151, 155, 156, 159, 161, 238
Coveney, P..........................255, 281
Cox, M. ..............................258, 281
creative action .........................40, 59
creative approach to science .........60
creative approaches to action
    research ..............................55–61
creative learner...........................242
creative learning.............34, 244, 379
Creative Partnerships in Education
    .............................................243
creative person ...........................253
creative potentials ..........60, 100, 109
creative practice ...................241, 245
creative practitioners....................244
creative processxiv, 59, 60, 108, 241,
    243, 253, 254, 264, 269, 270, 271,
    272, 273, 281
creative space..5, 251, 268, 269, 273,
    312
creative writer ..23, 30, 245, 252, 271
creative-writing............246, 266, 282
creativity . xiv, 16, 23, 43, 57, 58, 59,
    63, 66, 78, 96, 99, 101, 105, 106,
    108, 111, 114, 118, 119, 127, 133,
    241, 242, 243, 244, 252–55, 252,
    253, 254, 281, 282, 283, 383
crisis.............................................78
critical analyses....77, 81, 82, 93, 213
critical friends .72, 73, 75, 80, 81, 82,
    85, 86, 88, 91, 92, 93, 107, 297,
    298, 304, 305
critical inquiry...............48, 188, 198
critical paradigm ........................324
critical thinking... xiv, xv, 52, 63, 67,
    78, 85, 96, 98, 125, 141, 146, 147,

153, 286, 289, 290–92, 290, 291,
292, 294, 295, 298, 301, 302, 303,
304, 305, 306, 309, 371, 376
critique .. xiv, 35, 112, 183, 203, 205,
206, 209, 211, 216, 217, 218, 219,
221, 225, 227, 228, 232, 233, 234,
235, 236, 281, 297, 298, 324
Crotty, Y. .......24, 46, 47, 51, 52, 343
cultural contexts.........................5, 74
culture ...58, 59, 60, 61, 97, 126, 127,
138, 153, 177, 178, 185, 186, 187,
189, 199, 247, 254, 255, 261, 281,
283, 287, 293, 373, 392, 403, 406
curriculumxii, xiv, 26, 28, 34, 65, 67,
79, 81, 91, 95, 97, 103, 106, 114,
146, 169, 170, 172, 175, 178, 180,
182, 185, 187, 189, 190, 197, 198,
199, 200, 201, 217, 220, 229, 238,
239, 242, 243, 245, 249, 254, 287,
314, 330, 331, 332, 340, 341, 347,
412

**Č**

Čular, G..................................66, 112

**D**

Dart, J...................................347, 361
Davis, N. ......................313, 317, 361
Davis, R. ............................347, 361
Dawson, M................................361
Delong, J. ...........................17, 18, 32
Delors, J. ............................378, 412
Demirsalem, Y. ..........................361
democracy.....7, 23, 55, 66, 112, 113,
119, 120, 121, 137, 150, 158, 290,
376, 378
democratic education ....68, 101, 126,
290, 291, 362
democratic evaluation .....x, 116, 159,
160
democratic practices ............119, 137
democratic processes ...116, 126, 133
democratisation..........................151

Denzin, N. K. .......112, 113, 258, 282
Dewey, J. 68, 69, 101, 112, 122, 161,
188, 290, 291, 292, 307, 308, 371
diagnosis ...................................337
dialectic.....3, 95, 127, 131, 133, 143,
152, 214, 216
dialogic-collaborative approach to
learning ...........................288, 299
dialogue.....19, 35, 42, 43, 44, 45, 46,
117, 157, 209, 225, 226, 227, 228,
250, 269, 291, 301, 302, 303, 306,
315, 324, 328, 333, 336, 342, 344,
345, 346, 347, 370, 403
Dickinson, L. .......376, 377, 384, 412
digital age....................318, 335, 361
digital technologiesxi, xiii, 46, 47, 49
discussion analysis......336, 340, 342,
343
disharmony .................156, 158, 234
Dladla, N.....................313, 318, 362
Doi, T....................................187, 201
Donmoyer, R........................184, 201
Donnelly, R.........................294, 308
Dornan, L. .......................69, 70, 111
Dougiamas, M.....................293, 308
Drenoyianni, H. ..................322, 362
Dublin City University24, 36, 37, 38,
40, 45, 47, 51, 52, 53, 54, 289,
312, 343, 344, 361

**E**

Ecclestone, K. .....................249, 282
economic context.............................5
economic security ...........................5
Education for All ...............313, 365
education for human rights............67
education research ...........................4
education system......xv, 67, 199, 311,
312, 314, 316, 318, 319, 326, 339,
342, 378, 404, 408
educational development xiii, 14, 29,
30, 35, 41, 116, 120, 123, 124,
132, 133, 138, 143, 145, 146, 150,

152, 153, 155, 156, 157, 158, 159, 162, 164, 202, 238, 308

educational influences... ix, x, xi, xiii, 1, 2, 3, 4, 8, 9, 10, 11, 12, 13, 15, 16, 18, 19, 21, 22, 28, 36, 41, 46, 49, 54, 115, 122, 132, 162, 201, 216, 239, 242, 295, 375

Educational Journal of Living Theories x, xi, 4, 22, 51, 110, 115, 116, 124, 127, 129, 132, 136, 141, 148, 159, 160, 161, 164, 174, 238, 239, 282, 283, 362

educational knowledge ...4, 6, 14, 21, 23, 29, 31, 54, 164, 239, 283, 362

educational living theory ....see living theory

educational practice .. xiii, 26, 29, 37, 40, 41, 43, 44, 65, 85, 114, 116, 121, 145, 162, 296, 320, 337, 413

educational processes......97, 99, 100, 118, 119, 120, 126, 145, 155

educational relationships...10, 15, 19, 22, 123, 126, 139, 154

educational research3, 4, 5, 8, 28, 29, 31, 43, 44, 48, 51, 74, 144, 282, 295, 371

    distinction between education research ...............................4–6

educational researcher..........2, 23, 30

educational space xiii, 42, 44, 45, 49, 52, 161, 249, 282, 362

educational theory ix, x, xi, 1, 2, 3, 4, 6, 14, 15, 16, 24, 27, 29, 30, 32, 47, 50, 53, 54, 114, 115, 143, 161, 162, 164, 166, 176, 181, 183, 184, 194, 202, 216, 238, 239, 295, 296, 299, 308, 345, 375, 413

    the disciplines approach.1, 2, 3, 15

educational valuesxiii, xv, 14, 35, 41, 43, 46, 65–67, 67, 75, 118–21, 153, 288, 295, 296, 299, 302, 305, 326

educative relationships.........139, 158

educator xiii, xiv, 23, 30, 35, 46, 168, 191, 197, 229, 241, 242, 244, 246, 271, 274, 293

Eisner, E..................43, 51, 175, 201

Elbow, P..............................254, 282

e-learning ......25, 37, 45, 46, 47, 285, 287, 363, 364

Eliot, T. S.............................159, 161

Elliot, J.................................210, 216

Elliott, J......................................237

email 37, 44, 143, 147, 154, 333, 345

embodied knowledges .....................5

empathy.136, 139, 156, 248, 250–51, 250, 261, 270, 272, 406, 407

empowerment76, 82, 90, 95, 99, 145, 155, 175, 244, 248, 251, 262, 263, 271, 274, 291, 299, 316, 317, 320, 336

Engestrom, R. ..............323, 362, 363

Engestrom, Y. .......322, 328, 329, 362

English Corner ....373, 374, 381, 383, 396, 397, 398, 399, 400, 403, 411

English language learning.....xv, 378, 379, 399, 404, 407, 411

English language teacher ......xv, 241, 247, 374

epistemology.....6, 14, 29, 40, 50, 53, 58, 115, 150, 151, 163, 167, 168, 174, 176, 182, 197, 202, 326, 362

espoused theories ..........................65

essential changes............97, 103, 106

ethnography .....................74, 98, 254

evaluation8, 26, 29, 46, 97, 106, 107, 121, 145, 146, 167, 205, 208, 211, 213, 219, 226, 227, 230, 296, 326, 343, 357, 363, 364

Evoh, C. J............................313, 362

experimental research .................2, 5

experimentation ....96, 101, 270, 321, 341

exquisite connectivity ...................19

**F**

Facer, K. ...........................................309
facilitator........99, 140, 326, 343, 377
Farrell, G. .............311, 312, 319, 362
Farren, M. ix, xiii, 24, 25, 28, 33, 38,
   39, 42, 43, 44, 45, 46, 47, 48, 51, 52,
   74, 112, 124, 130, 161, 249, 282,
   288, 299, 305, 308, 312, 327, 345,
   346, 362
Fink, D. ...................................79, 114
Finnegan, J. ...................................161
first-person inquiry ..............215, 231
Flanagan, F. ..............................43, 52
focus group discussions .......331, 335
focus group interview ..........330, 334
Forrest, M. .......................................13
Foshay, A. W. .........................56, 112
Foucault, M. .................122, 125, 161
four Noble Truths..................176–82
four pillars of education...............378
fragmentation......120, 124, 125, 126,
   131, 242
Frank, A. ..............................171, 201
freedom .7, 12, 18, 20, 31, 55, 56, 58,
   61, 65, 66, 67, 71, 75, 76, 85, 89,
   94, 95, 99, 105, 106, 109, 116,
   119, 120, 121, 124, 127, 134, 137,
   141, 150, 158, 159, 242, 270, 282,
   376
Freire, P.....35, 45, 53, 168, 201, 290,
   291, 292, 299, 300, 308, 328, 344,
   346, 362
Friedman, M...............................237
Friendship Award ........147, 152, 158
Fromm, E. .....................113, 127, 161
Frost, R. ..........................98, 99, 112

**G**

Gage, N. ...............................184, 201
Gallimore R......................................53
Garrison, D. R......291, 294, 303, 308
Garvey, C. ...........................43, 44, 52
Gasane, J. .............................336, 362

gathering data..12, 40, 60, 69, 71, 73,
   75, 76, 77, 79, 83, 85, 86, 89, 93,
   95, 98, 110, 157, 194, 296–97
generation of knowledge.... x, xii, 10,
   12, 13, 14, 24, 37, 47
genuineness.....................................99
Gjøtterud, S. .......... xiv, 203, 210, 239
Glenn, M. ................................25, 28
global contexts ......................22, 216
Global e-Schools and Communities
   Initiative..312, 313, 314, 317, 326,
   328, 330, 333, 335, 336, 337, 343,
   344, 363, 364
Global Social Justice Project .......313
God ..................18, 98, 127, 129, 177
Goldberg, N. ........................255, 282
Goldstein, J. ........................179, 202
Grant, L. ......................................309
group-interview.............................75
Guba, E. ................................68, 113
Gudmundsdottir, S. ..............234, 237
Gunn, C. .......................................361

**H**

Habermas, J.......8, 28, 103, 112, 298,
   308, 346
Hakkarainen, K. ...319, 321, 323, 325,
   363
Hamilton, M. L. .................40, 53, 54
Handal, G. ............223, 234, 237, 238
Hang, D......................322, 327, 363
Hardman, J. .................322, 330, 363
harmony ......120, 125, 127, 129, 133,
   148, 156, 234
Hartman, B..........................374, 412
Hattie, J. ................................46, 52
Hatton, N.....291, 292, 294, 302, 303,
   304, 308
Hawkridge, D..............................308
Hayes, D. ............................249, 282
Hayles, N. ...........................255, 282
healing curriculum xiv, 192, 199, 200

healing space.......168, 169, 189, 190,
    191, 192, 194, 195
Heaney, H. ...................257, 262, 282
Heath, R. B................................282
Hegel, G. W. .............17, 56, 57, 112
Hepp, P. K...................318, 339, 363
Heron, J..........68, 112, 211, 232, 237
Herrington, J. .......................293, 309
Hiebert, J.......................................53
Higher Education Authority of
    Ireland.................................48, 53
Highfield, R. .......................255, 281
Hiim, H. ...............213, 216, 223, 237
Hinostroza, S...............................363
Hippe, E. ......................213, 223, 237
Hirst, P. ....................................3, 28
historical contexts ...........................5
Hobson, R. ....................................46
Hodge, J. .............................290, 308
Hodgkinson, H. L. .................56, 112
Holec, H. .............................377, 378
holistic learning ...................105, 106
holographic universe............171, 202
Hooker, M...............xv, 311–66, 311
How do I improve my practice? ...40,
    48, 135, 214, 229, 231, 239, 295,
    306
How do I improve what I am doing?
    ............. ix, xii, 6, 11, 41, 325, 346
human right..........................120, 317
humanistic theories of learning....99–
    107
humour....................................18, 19
Hunt, C..........................................282
Husain, L................................121, 161
Huxtable, M. ..........................21, 29

I

I-it...............................................204
Ilyenkov, E.................................6, 29
improving practice .. x, xi, xii, 1, 6, 7,
    11, 13, 14, 21, 23, 24, 32, 47, 122,
        143, 158, 164, 216, 232, 239, 271,
        283, 296, 325, 341, 375, 413
inclusionality...6, 16, 30, 44, 53, 108,
    115, 125, 130, 250, 283
independence .......61, 76, 78, 96, 272
indigenous ways of knowing ...........6
information and communications
    technologies xv, 36, 38, 39, 45, 48,
    227, 285, 286, 287, 288, 299, 307,
    309, 311, 312, 313, 314, 315, 316,
    317, 318, 319, 320, 321, 322, 323,
    324, 326, 327, 329, 330, 331, 332,
    334, 336, 337, 338, 339, 340, 341,
    343, 347, 349, 351, 353, 354, 355,
    356, 357, 358, 359, 360, 361, 362,
    363, 364, 365
information society ......................316
in-service programme ..........338, 351
inspiration .....59, 121, 236, 253, 254,
    281
international collaborations .....23, 24
internet ..5, 22, 24, 37, 39, 65, 71, 73,
    87, 94, 104, 117, 213, 224, 287,
    294, 331, 351, 352, 353, 355, 376,
    407
internet forum73, 110, 299, 301, 304,
    305
interview ...71, 76, 77, 79, 92, 95, 96,
    111, 123, 161, 253, 257, 283, 327,
    330, 332, 333, 334, 335, 336, 339,
    340, 356
Isaacs, S. .......311, 312, 319, 362, 363
Isenberg, J. P.........................63, 112
Issroff, K. .....................................321
I-Thou .................204, 209, 234, 235

J

Jalongo, M. R........................63, 112
James, H......................................325
Jaworski, J...................................308
Jia, P....................................371, 412
Jones, K.............................243, 281

justice......7, 18, 26, 30, 69, 111, 116,
    121, 159, 161, 295

## K

Kangrga, M. .....................58, 60, 112
Kemmis, S.56, 98, 99, 103, 111, 112,
    214, 237, 295, 307
Kennedy, A. ..................320, 321, 363
Kilpatrick, W. H...37, 53, 68, 69, 112
Kincheloe, J. L. ..............70, 109, 114
knowledge creation 50, 320, 323, 326
knowledge deepening ..........320, 323
knowledge society.......314, 315, 316,
    324, 344, 362, 363
Knowledge Society for All .314, 328,
    344
knowledge-transformation ....23, 272,
    273
Kornfield, J. .........................179, 202
Korthagen, F. ...........................237
Kukulska-Hulme, A. ............294, 308
Kumar, S. ............................336, 363
Kvalsund, R. .......................233, 238

## L

LaBoskey, V. K. ...............40, 53, 54
Laidlaw, M.... xiii, 22, 24, 29, 30, 45,
    53, 94, 95, 102, 103, 105, 106,
    112, 115–64, 115, 116, 118, 119,
    124, 125, 133, 136, 140, 141, 142,
    143, 144, 147, 149, 151, 152, 157,
    159, 161, 162, 163, 164, 197, 202,
    206, 222, 234, 238, 305, 308, 379,
    412
Lalović, D. ............................66, 113
Lao-zi..................................130, 163
Larsen, A............................290, 308
Lauvås, P.............223, 234, 237, 238
Laval, M. E. ...............................363
Law, N. ..............................317, 364
Leach, J. ......308, 313, 322, 339, 363
leadership....4, 45, 88, 122, 123, 148,
    199, 245, 282, 371, 388

Leahy, M. ....................................361
learner autonomy ....xv, 371, 377–79,
    377, 378, 379, 384–88, 384, 395,
    399
learning journals .....46, 297, 381–84,
    381, 395–97, 395, 405, 407
learning management system......215,
    224
learning process ..34, 40, 43, 44, 105,
    146, 220, 317
learning resources .................47, 105
learning-community....62, 64, 65, 67,
    111, 116
Leitch, R. ..............................98, 113
Lemke, C....................................361
Lennon, J.....................................200
Levinas, E. ...........204, 209, 237, 238
Lewin, K. .........................55, 56, 113
Lewis, C. S...........................129, 163
Li Peidong............146, 151, 152, 153
Li Yahong ..............xv, 367–413, 367
Li, D.............................................383
Li, P..............................................163
life-affirming energy...10, 11, 15, 16,
    17, 18, 22, 27, 116, 154, 159, 375
life-affirming values ........17, 22, 106
lifelong learning.....49, 316, 318, 361
Lim, C. P......................322, 327, 363
Lincoln, Y. ....................68, 112, 113
Lippitt, R. ......................56, 112, 113
literacy competencies...................317
Little, D...............377, 378, 384, 412
Liu, H............................................163
Liu, X............................................163
living contradiction.......66, 136, 139,
    144, 149, 153, 206, 209, 296, 306,
    325, 328, 336, 375
living logic .................115, 116, 129
living standards of judgment . xii, xv,
    4, 5, 14, 18, 22, 115, 197, 222
living theory. ix, xi, xii, 1–32, 1, 5, 6,
    7, 13, 14, 15, 22, 24, 25, 28, 29,
    30, 32, 39–41, 60, 61, 143, 164,
    190, 216, 236, 239, 241, 242, 255,

283, 295, 325, 327, 345, 365, 375, 413

living theory action research...24, 25, 41, 145, 171, 175, 189, 295–96, 295, 300, 324–26

living truth....................................174

Logue, C.......................................175

Lohr, E. .................................206, 238

Løkke, J. A............................210, 239

Lomax, P........73, 113, 136, 162, 163

Loughran, J. .....................40, 53, 54

love x, xiv, 7, 18, 34, 41, 76, 95, 116, 120, 121, 129, 138, 152, 158, 159, 162, 168, 170, 173, 178, 179, 180, 190, 193, 196, 197, 203, 204, 205, 206, 209, 211, 217, 218, 221, 224, 227, 228, 232, 234, 236, 238, 239, 264, 266, 267, 305, 306, 368, 406

love and critique..206, 217, 221, 232, 203–40

loving dynamic energy.......18, 19, 21

Lumley, T.................................17, 29

**M**

Ma, X. ...................................153, 163

Ma, Y. ..........................................163

MacDonald, B..........................8, 29

Macedo, D. P. ......290, 300, 307, 308

MacIntyre, A.........................125, 163

Maclure, M...........................180, 202

Mandela, N.............18, 250, 251, 282

Mandinach, E. B. .................319, 363

Manion, L.............................324, 361

manipulation ...........................70, 99

Marcus, G.............................254, 281

Marcuse, H................................8, 29

Marshall, J....................231, 236, 238

Mårtensen, G.............................238

Marx, K. ..................................97, 113

Maslow, A............129, 188, 248, 282

Matthews, B.................................163

McDonagh, C...........................25, 29

McMahon, H..............................308

McNiff, J...25, 29, 32, 53, 56, 59, 60, 73, 74, 89, 99, 104, 113, 114, 146, 164, 206, 209, 214, 216, 240, 295, 296, 297, 298, 308, 309, 310, 324, 325, 326, 328, 336, 346, 363, 365, 375, 389, 412

McTaggart, R. ....56, 98, 99, 103, 112

Mead, M.......................................74

Mellett, P.......................................18

meta-intentionality......................232

methodology ............7, 13, 55, 59, 70

Miettinen, R. ..............................363

Miles, S. ...............................313, 361

Miller, A. L. .........................253, 282

Mills, G. E............................73, 113

mobile phones.............................37

monitoring.......................60, 89, 365

Monsour, M. ..............................361

Moodle..... xi, xiv, 65, 289, 293, 294, 298, 299, 300, 301, 302, 304, 308, 309

Moon, B. ............308, 313, 318, 362

Moran, D............................204, 238

Morar, R...................................32

Morris, I. ...........................249, 281

Morrison, K..........................324, 361

Morrison, M. .......................254, 282

Most Significant Change protocol 327, 328, 334, 337, 339, 343, 346, 347, 361

Mostert, L. ..................................32

Moules, T. .......................95, 96, 113

Moustakas, C. ............................202

Mr. Richards ........122, 123, 134, 143

Mukama, E..................311, 312, 364

Mulligan, Y. .........................47, 305

multi-media...x, xv, 5, 15, 16, 18, 36, 43, 46, 47, 52, 74, 114, 124, 129, 172, 196, 355

Munn-Giddings, C. ...............99, 114

Murray, Y. P. ...........................5, 29

Murrell-Abery, V...............375, 388

mystical experience ............130, 159

# N

narrative . xiii, xiv, xv, 13, 17, 19, 24,
    169, 171, 201, 221, 234, 258, 262,
    316, 327, 339, 342, 347, 375
Nduwingoma, M. .................336, 364
needs ...34, 35, 46, 48, 49, 66, 67, 89,
    97, 106, 109, 145, 156, 159, 180,
    181, 210, 220, 235, 263, 286, 293,
    319, 324, 341, 382, 384, 393, 405,
    409
Neill, A. S. .............................122, 163
Neruda, P. .............................265, 282
Nettle, D..................................253, 283
networking .............................47, 292
Nevius, J. L. .........................387, 412
New Curriculum ...24, 106, 146, 147,
    152, 153, 164, 371, 376, 378, 379,
    408
Ningxia Teacher's University........24
Ningxia Teachers University .24, 142
Nleya, P.......................................363
Noss, R........................................361

# O

O'Donohue, J. ............................42, 53
O'Mahony, D. xiv, 48, 285–310, 285,
    305
O'Rourke, K. C. ....................294, 308
O'Sullivan, M. .....................316, 364
O'Brien, N. ........................95, 96, 113
OECD.........................67, 113, 361
Olakulehin, F. K. .320, 321, 336, 364
Oliver, R...............................293, 309
online discussion............46, 301, 303
online learning .........................38, 52
online-classroom..................297, 300
online-discussion ................300, 302
online-environment.....285, 286, 291,
    293, 294, 302, 303
ontological 'I' .............................325
ontological values ........306, 325, 344
ontology ......168, 172, 174, 182, 197,
    198

open peer review...................xii, 141
open-source....................................289

# Ø

Østergaard, E. ..............................240

# O

Ottevanger, W.....................319, 364
Owen, M. .....................292, 293, 309

# P

Packham, G..........................294, 309
Palmer, P............................168, 202
Pamuk, O. ..........................270, 283
paradigm wars......184, 187, 189, 201
passion6, 7, 19, 20, 21, 135, 258, 263
Peck, M. S...121, 163, 203, 204, 205,
    239
pedagogue......................................63
pedagogy.28, 34, 39, 49, 51, 53, 174,
    180, 181, 182, 189, 197, 201, 222,
    228, 237, 294, 308, 354, 362, 371
Pelgrum, W. J. .....................317, 364
Perrement, M. ......147, 152, 153, 163
personal growth ..204, 233, 234, 236,
    288
personal knowledge .................7, 264
Pettersen, R. C. ...................210, 239
phases of action research .............75
photographs........xv, 25, 74, 191, 343
Pirotte, S......................................309
play33, 34, 35, 63, 66, 67, 76, 79, 83,
    86, 87, 95, 96, 112, 259, 334, 335
pleasure ...18, 19, 22, 27, 41, 89, 372,
    400
Pogson, B. ....................................123
Polanyi, M..................7, 30, 206, 239
Polić, M............................58, 113
Pope, R.................243, 252, 253, 283
Popper, K. ..............................12, 30
Porter, S. ....................................199
portfolios..............192, 193, 194, 195

Posch, P..................................73, 111
positivism..............................5, 56, 68
post-doctoral research programme.49
postgraduate programme................40
power relations...................5, 15, 338
Power, D. .............................299, 300
practitioner-researchers.x, xv, 17, 24,
   37, 40, 41, 42, 43, 45, 47, 49, 312,
   345
pragmatic theory .........................216
Prensky, M............................286, 309
primacy of practice ........................13
primordial gap......................182, 183
process of inquiry.............38, 68, 346
process-oriented learning.............379
production of knowledge .......35, 326
productive life .................... ix, 19, 21
professional contexts..................x, 61
professional development .xv, 13, 29,
   35, 39, 62, 64, 65, 119, 315, 317,
   318, 319, 321, 331, 347, 348, 361,
   362, 363, 364, 365, 380, 390, 409,
   412
professional learning.....32, 240, 312,
   314, 318, 322, 335, 341, 342
professional practice ix, 37, 118, 131,
   132, 137, 169, 352, 356
progressive education .................290
propositional knowledge.............5, 62
propositional statements .................5
public communication..................7, 9
public networks...........................102
public spheres .............................103
Pulkkinen, J................................364
pupil-action researchers ..54–114, 70,
   75, 94, 95, 104, 107
purposive sample .................329, 338

Q

Qi, Y....................................368, 412
Qu, B............................................412
qualitative research 51, 112, 113, 329
quality of action research...............74

questionnaires ..............71, 76, 77, 96

R

Ramalingam, B. ...................325, 364
rating-scales ............................71, 76
Rawal, S...............................139, 163
Rayner, A..6, 16, 30, 44, 45, 53, 115,
   125, 130, 163, 166, 171, 172, 173,
   174, 182, 202, 250, 283
realness ..........................................99
Reason, P. .56, 68, 71, 112, 113, 211,
   237, 324
reconnaissance ..............................89
Redfield-Jamieson, K. .........125, 163
reflection.....xv, 6, 11, 12, 14, 40, 42,
   43, 44, 68, 89, 106, 145, 167, 168,
   170, 173, 174, 176, 179, 185, 197,
   212, 213, 220, 222, 223, 224, 226,
   228, 236, 238, 239, 273, 291, 297,
   303, 306, 314, 315, 316, 323, 324,
   329, 332, 333, 334, 335, 336, 337,
   342, 343, 345, 346, 375, 380, 381,
   409, 412
reflective journals ........................195
reflective practice..................64, 166
reflective practitioner63, 64, 74, 166,
   213, 239
Rehbein, L. F. ..............................363
research process..xii, xiii, 42, 60, 70,
   86, 305, 345, 347
research programme5, 11, 19, 23, 25,
   26, 36, 40, 45, 49, 143, 282
research question ....6, 289, 290, 306,
   316
research-diary .71, 73, 76, 77, 78, 79,
   80, 83, 93, 110
respect...7, 55, 79, 95, 103, 136, 156,
   163, 209, 220, 236, 311, 384, 399
Richards, J. C. .............................413
Richardson, W. .............287, 294, 309
rightness.........................................8
Robertson, I..........323, 327, 328, 364
Robinson, K. .......................243, 283

Roche, M.............................................25
Rogers, C. .....99, 103, 104, 105, 106,
    107, 109, 113, 122
Roper, J. .............................119, 163
Rowland, S........................34, 35, 53
Rubin, J. .......................374, 388, 413
Rudd, T. ...........................................309
Russell, T. L......................40, 53, 54
Ryan, M. ...........................43, 44, 53
Ryle, G.............................................6, 30

## S

Salmon, G. ...........................294, 309
Sartre, J. P. ..........................253, 283
Saurdal, G. ....................................239
Sayers, S........................................309
Scanlon, E. ..........................322, 363
Scardamelia, M. ...........................239
Scholes-Rhodes, J. ...................19, 30
Schön, D......35, 50, 53, 65, 111, 115,
    163, 167, 184, 188, 202, 213, 239
Schutz, A...............................9, 10, 30
Sefton-Green, J. ...................293, 309
self-assessment............................378
self-confidence82, 85, 163, 383, 384,
    400, 408
self-directed learning ...................107
self-evaluation..40, 97, 106, 107, 146
*self-initiated learning*...................105
self-reflection ...............................214
self-reflective enquiry.................295
self-study.. xii, 31, 32, 39, 40, 43, 53,
    54
Senteni, A......................................363
Shor, I...............................35, 45, 53
significant changes.........231, 351–55
significant learning .....104, 105, 109,
    132
Sinko, M. ......................................363
Skilbeck, M........................36, 48, 53
Skjæggestad, M..............................239
Skolimowski, H. .................176, 202
Smaldino, S..........327, 328, 330, 366

Smith, D.......291, 292, 294, 302, 303
Snyder, W. ..........................110, 114
social action ................................8, 9
social behaviour..........................8, 9
social competences .................78, 96
social contexts.9, 122, 127, 143, 368,
    371
social formations.. x, xi, xiii, xv, 1, 4,
    8, 9, 10, 23, 34, 36, 41, 183, 187,
    242
social laws......................................55
social relations .............................10
social research...................55, 111
social sciences..........8, 10, 56, 57, 68
social software .............292, 294, 302
Socrates.............................42, 117
Somekh, B........................73, 111
Spender, D. ....................................164
Spindler, G........................74, 113
Spindler, L........................74, 113
spirit .............16, 42, 56, 57, 203, 242
spiritual values ...........................165
Spiro, J. ... xiv, 21, 23, 24, 26, 27, 30,
    241–84, 241, 245, 246, 256, 257,
    260, 261, 262, 268, 283
standards of judgment.... xii, 49, 121,
    135, 140, 155, 158, 222, 297, 298
standards of practice ....114, 165, 194
Steinberg, S....................70, 109, 114
Stenhouse, L. .........56, 114, 216, 239
Stigler, J. ......................................53
Stoll, L. ...........................79, 114
Strangstadstuen, S........214, 224, 239
Stringer, E. T..........56, 114, 375, 413
student-action researcher .... *see pupil
    action researcher*
student-centered learning............379
students' inquiries...................68, 69
subject-oriented curriculum..........67
Sullivan, B. .............................25, 30
Sun, W. ...........................................164
survey..182, 319, 329, 333, 335, 337,
    338, 351

Swarts, P. ....313, 317, 336, 343, 364, 365
syllabus ..........38, 263, 288, 289, 302

**T**

tacit knowledge .............................131
Talbot, M. ....................168, 171, 202
talent.....................................253, 254
Tarnas, R..............................168, 202
Taylor, P.......................315, 325, 365
Taylor, P. C................................293
teacher education ... xii, 1, 40, 53, 54, 312, 318, 330, 332, 361, 362
teacher professional development.xv, 311, 313, 314, 316, 317, 318, 319, 320, 321, 322, 323, 324, 329, 330, 336, 337, 338, 341, 343, 347
teacher-centered learning.............379
teacher-craftswoman.......................65
teaching methodology..................145
teaching practices.....................74, 96
teaching profession ................3, 4, 53
technology...5, 25, 36, 38, 43, 46, 48, 51, 74, 110, 114, 124, 155, 289, 301, 304, 307, 312, 314, 315, 317, 318, 321, 323, 328, 330, 332, 334, 338, 339, 340, 341, 342, 348, 351, 354, 355, 361, 363, 364
technology literacy.......................320
Ten Good Schools.........................122
text-based media ............................16
theories..2, 5, 8, 9, 11, 14, 15, 16, 17, 21, 22, 24, 25, 26, 28, 31, 32, 40, 41, 45, 51, 59, 61, 114, 115, 133, 145, 164, 216, 239, 240, 283, 295, 343, 413
theories-in-use...............................65
therapy-culture.............................249
Thielgard, A. .........................258, 281
Thompson, J.................374, 388, 413
Tian F......24, 30, 146, 147, 148, 149, 150, 152, 153, 155, 156, 157, 158, 164, 206, 372, 413

Tillich, P. .................................18, 30
Timperley, H............................46, 52
Tobin, B. .................................43, 54
traditional school ..65, 70, 71, 88, 91, 97, 109, 199, 367–68
transient certainty.................166, 174
Trucano, M. ................................362
truth.......57, 58, 71, 87, 95, 107, 129, 135, 161, 169, 174, 177, 179, 182, 184, 205, 252, 298, 406
truthfulness .......................................8

**U**

Ubuntu .....................................18, 28
Ulewicz, M. ...........................74, 114
UNESCO ....312, 313, 317, 319, 320, 321, 328, 336, 364, 365, 378, 412
United Nations .............312, 314, 365
University of Bath.2, 5, 9, 18, 25, 26, 28, 29, 30, 38, 40, 47, 51, 74, 94, 162, 170, 188, 201, 202, 237, 238, 308
University of Limerick25, 28, 29, 30, 37
Unwin, T. ....................315, 319, 365
Usluel, Y. K. ................................361

**V**

Valdez, G. ....................................361
validation 7, 8, 12, 13, 28, 42, 43, 44, 49, 72, 75, 93, 94, 103, 104, 107, 111, 147, 153, 271, 297, 298, 305, 324, 345, 347, 375, 376
validation group ...............13, 94, 298
validation meeting13, 42, 43, 44, 345
validation meetings........................44
validity ....7, 8, 13, 32, 144, 240, 292, 298, 305, 345, 346
valuesix, x, xi, xii, 5, 7, 8, 11, 12, 15, 16, 18, 22, 23, 25, 34, 36, 41, 42, 43, 44, 49, 55, 56, 58, 60, 65, 66, 67, 76, 77, 82, 85, 86, 87, 88, 89, 91, 95, 97, 99, 101, 102, 103, 106,

109, 112, 113, 114, 116, 118, 120,
121, 122, 124, 127, 131, 132, 134,
137, 138, 141, 147, 149, 151, 152,
153, 155, 158, 159, 162, 165, 166,
167, 168, 171, 172, 173, 174, 175,
176, 181, 182, 183, 185, 188, 189,
196, 197, 199, 200, 201, 205, 206,
209, 210, 214, 216, 217, 232, 233,
235, 236, 239, 241, 244, 246–51,
246, 248, 251, 254, 255, 263, 265,
269, 271, 274, 292, 295, 305, 325,
328, 335, 336, 344, 345, 346, 371,
375, 376, 408
van den Akker, J. .........................364
Van Doren, C. .......................168, 202
variables................................2, 5
Verday N. ...................................309
Veugelers, W. .......................291, 309
video clips............41, 42, 43, 47, 193
videoconferencing.........................39
video-data................................7, 13
video-tape.................................13, 73
visual narrative....................7, 46, 51
Voluntary Services Overseas 94, 142,
146, 147, 164, 375
Vuningungo, V.....................336, 365
Vygotsky..............100, 114, 321, 365

**W**

Walker, M. .......................34, 54, 139
Walton, J. ...............................18, 30
Wang, S........................................164
Wann, K. D. ...........................56, 112
Watland, P....................................309
web of betweenness ..42, 45, 51, 299,
308, 362
Webb, G. ...............................34, 54
web-based technologies .........48, 110
web-forum............ *see internet forum*
web-space....................................24
Weisberg, R. W...................253, 283
wellbeing248–49, 248, 249, 250, 283
Wen, J. .......................................164

Wenger, E. ...........................110, 114
Whitehead, J. .. ix, xii, 1–32, 1, 4, 12,
14, 17, 18, 19, 20, 21, 22, 23, 26,
28, 29, 30, 31, 32, 34, 35, 40, 41,
46, 47, 52, 53, 54, 56, 59, 60, 66,
73, 74, 82, 89, 94, 99, 102, 104,
112, 113, 114, 123, 124, 130, 135,
136, 144, 147, 153, 154, 162, 163,
164, 171, 184, 202, 206, 209, 214,
216, 222, 239, 240, 242, 273, 283,
295, 296, 297, 298, 306, 308, 309,
310, 324, 325, 326, 328, 336, 345,
346, 363, 365, 375, 413
Whitty, G. ...................................361
wholeness....120, 121, 124, 126, 127,
128, 129, 141, 142, 158, 166, 173,
181, 197, 203
whole-school programme ............338
wikis.............................292, 294, 305
Wilber, K. ............................166, 202
Winter, R.30, 99, 114, 176, 180, 193,
202, 216, 240
Winter's six principles for
conducting action research ......216
Wood, L. A. ..................................32
Wragg, T......................242, 243, 282
written reports.......................94, 222
Wu, X.................................367, 413

**X**

Xi, M............................................413

**Y**

Yamagata-Lynch, L. C. ......327, 328,
330, 366
YouTube .............................125, 300

**Z**

Zhang, J...............................368, 413
Zhang, X. .............................367, 413
Zhao, T.......................................413
Zhong, Q. .............................376, 413

Zhou, Y. ...............................379, 413
Zohar, D. ...............................151, 164
zone of proximal development ....100

Zovko, M. ... xiii, 40, 51, 54–114, 55,
    65, 76, 77, 79, 80, 81, 82, 83, 84,
    85, 86, 87, 88, 89, 90, 91, 111,
    127, 161